TURNING THE TIDES OF EXCLUSION

A GUIDE FOR EDUCATORS AND ADVOCATES FOR IMMIGRANT STUDENTS

I

BY
LAURIE OLSEN
ANN JARAMILLO

EDITORS LAURA WOODLIEF AND CAROL DOWELL

THE CALIFORNIA TOMORROW
EQUITY-CENTERED SCHOOL REFORM SERIES

Turning the Tides of Exclusion
A Guide for Educators and Advocates for Immigrant Students
The California Tomorrow Equity-Centered School Reform Series

By Laurie Olsen and Ann Jaramillo
Editors Laura Woodlief and Carol Dowell
Proofreader/Production Assistant Julie Wong
Contributing Editors Amy Muckelroy and Katherine Kam
Designer Elaine Joe
Printed by Coast Litho, Oakland, CA
Copyright © 1999 California Tomorrow

This book is a product of the California Tomorrow Demonstration Project on the Education of Immigrant Students at the Secondary Level, one of four sites supported through a national initiative of the Andrew W. Mellon Foundation. It is also a product of the Mobilization for Equity, an initiative funded by the Ford Foundation to organizations within the National Coalition of Advocates for Students. The opinions expressed in this volume do not necessarily reflect the positions or policies of the Andrew W. Mellon Foundation or the Ford Foundation.

PROJECT STAFF
Laurie Olsen, Project Director
Ann Jaramillo, Salinas Project Coordinator
Zaida McCall-Perez, Project Associate
Catherine Minicucci, Minicucci Associates, Evaluator
Judy White, Hayward Project Coordinator
Amy Muckelroy, Project Associate
Laura Woodlief, Project Associate
Gilberto Arriaza, Project Associate
Kendra Jones, Project Associate
Mamie Chow-Wang, Project Assistant

Front and back cover photos by Kathy Sloane. Special thanks to teachers and students at the Hayward English Language Center pictured.

Photo credits: Brian Fessenden, pp. 22, 70, 91, 114, 131, 171, 193, 209, 234, 301, 362, 381; Tony Saucedo, pp. 62, 144, 312; Paul Mueller, pp. 17, 29, 33, 80, 105, 179, 201, 222, 287, 329, 343, 384, 401; Kendra Jones, pp. 13, 45, 61, 123, 350, 371, 390, 405.

NOW THE MOMENT
OF GREAT POSSIBILITY
OPENS BEFORE US

**MOBILIZATION
FOR EQUITY**

Grateful acknowledgment is made for permission to reprint excerpts from the following copyrighted works:

Always Running: La Vida Loca. Gang Days in L.A. by Luis Rodriguez. © 1993. Used by permission of Curbstone Press, Willimantic, CT.

Hunger of Memory: The Education of Richard Rodriguez by Richard Rodriguez. © 1982. Used by permission of D.R. Godine Publishers, Boston, MA.

"Joy Luck Club," "Double Face," from *The Joy Luck Club* by Amy Tan. © 1989 by Amy Tan. Used by permission of Putnam Berkley, a division of Penguin Putnam Inc., New York, NY.

Made in America: Immigrant Students in Our Public Schools by Laurie Olsen. © 1997. Reproduced by permission of the New Press, New York, NY.

Nobody Could See That I Was a Finn by Antti Jalava. Published in *Bilingualism or Not: The Education of Minorities* by Tove Skutnabb-Kangas. © 1981. Used by permission of Multilingual Matters Ltd., Clevedon, England.

MISSION

California Tomorrow is a nonprofit organization working to help build a strong and fair multiracial, multicultural, multilingual society that is equitable for everyone. We believe creating such a society involves promoting equal opportunity and participation—social, economic and educational—and embracing our diversity as our greatest strength.

California Tomorrow's primary focus is on people, organizations and communities in California. Since our work is connected to national trends, we also share lessons learned from the California experience, draw upon the knowledge of colleagues working on similar issues across the United States, and join with others to influence national policies or practices which impact our respective work.

CALIFORNIA TOMORROW
436 14th Street, Suite 820
Oakland, CA 94612
telephone (510) 496-0220 / fax (510) 496-0225
website www.californiatomorrow.org

TABLE OF CONTENTS

Table of Contents

ACKNOWLEDGMENTS

This book is based upon fifty-six years combined between us working as teachers and advocates to create schools that make good on their promises to educate *all* children. The strategies and learning we share in this book were especially informed and inspired by our work with several groups and school-change efforts over the past ten years. California Tomorrow's Demonstration Project in Immigrant Secondary Education (also known as "the Mellon Project") brought together a team to work with schools in the Hayward Unified School District and Alisal High School in Salinas, California. We were lucky enough to work in that team with two remarkable women—Zaida McCall-Perez and Judy White—whose wisdom, energy and perspectives on what it takes to support advocacy and change schools have greatly enriched both of us. Our project evaluator, Catherine Minicucci of Minicucci Associates, helped shape our understanding of effective, responsive data systems and produced detailed, valuable reports profiling the types of immigrant students in the project schools that are featured in Chapter Four. Thanks also to the teachers, counselors and administrators in the Alisal High School Literacy Project, the Alisal Working Group on Race, Language and Culture and Hayward Tomorrow, by whose sides we spent the better portion of four years learning how to be a supportive outside partner to their change efforts.

For the past two years, we've had the opportunity to take the data and inquiry strategies developed in the Mellon Project and adapt them to the specific challenges of a systemwide professional development effort in all 22 schools in the Glendale Unified School District. Thanks to the vision and hard work of Glendale's Project SUCCESS team, Judy Sanchez, Kelly King and Suzanne Risse, we've learned an enormous amount about how to tailor strategies to different contexts and how to "take them to scale."

In the Spring of 1998, with encouragement from Shelly Spiegel Coleman, we designed and conducted a series of four-day training institutes for school teams and their outside partners on how to use our strategies to build schools that are more responsive to their English Language Learners. Two people joined us as faculty for those institutes, adding their considerable experience and inspiration to our understanding of how to help schools learn and use the strategies. Thanks to Candy McCarthy and Kristin Geiser for this partnership.

Putting together this book took many hands and the involvement of several people on the California Tomorrow staff. Mellon Project team member Amy Muckelroy interviewed many immigrant students and wrote the case studies that appear in Chapter Four. Her work with student information system staff greatly informed our understanding of what an immigrant-responsive data system would look like. Gilberto Arriaza conducted interviews with students. The references and annotated bibliographies are largely thanks to Kendra

Jones' many hours in the library and thoughtful reading and collection of materials. Mamie Chow-Wang contributed extraordinary competence in multiple roles. She researched and put together resource lists, copy-edited sections, and was essential in keeping the whole thing together through the long year it took us to pilot the activities and turn them into print. We thank all our California Tomorrow colleagues, especially our founder and chairman Lew Butler, for standing by our sides as allies and advisors throughout the five years of the demonstration and writing.

As our editors, miracle-workers Laura Woodlief and Carol Dowell somehow kept this book moving despite impossible time-frames and many competing priorities. Convinced of its importance, they kept us writing, provoked more depth through thoughtful and informed critiques, offered good ideas for clarifying the content, made sure our writing was as readable and useful as possible, and shepherded the book through production. Their tremendous hard work and sheer force of will made sure this book was completed. This is their book as surely as it is ours.

Completing the editing and production team, Elaine Joe somehow met impossible deadlines and still managed to design and produce a beautiful book, Julie Wong "moved in" in order to serve as our amazing proofreader, and Katherine Kam lent her clean writing and editing skills to several sections. We thank our manuscript reviewers, Donna Christian of the Center for Applied Linguistics, and Beatriz Chu Clewell and Jorge Ruiz de Velasco of the Urban Institute, for their invaluable advice. Special thanks to Tennyson High School art instructor Ariella Seidenberg and her students, whose art appears in the pages of this book. Tennyson High School in Hayward was one of our demonstration project schools.

The book was funded through two foundations. The Andrew W. Mellon Foundation supported the California Tomorrow Demonstration Project in Immigrant Secondary Education. That school-change effort was the source of many of the strategies and activities in this book, which is one product of the project's effort to disseminate effective strategies for responsive immigrant education. We thank program officer Stephanie Bell-Rose for supporting this effort. The Ford Foundation, through Mobilization for Equity funding to organizations in the National Coalition of Advocates for Students (NCAS), enabled us to develop many of the advocacy strategies and to publish this book as a resource for our ongoing work with school-based advocates for equity. Thanks to Janice Petrovich of the Ford Foundation for her vision of the role of advocacy in creating equity in public education.

Each of us holds in our hearts several people to whom we are deeply indebted for the inspiration they provide as advocates for a more just and equitable society and as models of what it means to try to create schools that do justice to all of our children.

From Laurie: I would like to thank Joan First, Executive Director of NCAS, for her companionship and the inspiring model she always provides of what it means to hang in over the long haul as an advocate for equity in schools. I acknowledge with love and thanks three people who stood with me in the No on Proposition 227 battle: Shelly Spiegel Coleman, Rosalia Salinas and Martha Arevalo. It was in the course of our work together on the campaign that I became convinced that this book needed to shift from what had been planned as a manual for administrators to become a resource for all educators seeking to turn back the tides of exclusion, survive as advocates and build a movement for our children. I give appreciation and love to Joyce Germaine Watts for her friendship, strength and brilliance in forging the path, and to Carol Dowell for her friendship, vision and the model of integrity.

From Ann: I would like to say thank you to my rock-solid Salinas friends, Candy, Alma and Jennifer, constant sources of inspiration for what it looks like to work on a daily basis to create inclusive schools. To my sister, Petrea, who means it when she says, "all children means *all* children." And most especially, to my husband, Luis, the best example there ever could be of advocacy as a way of life.

It is rare in the course of work to find the kind of soul mates and companions we have found in each other. We consider ourselves amazingly lucky. The bonds we have developed of deep respect, real friendship and delight in each other have been forged not only through the shared work but through the shared passions and values that form the core of our work. We look forward to continuing our partnership together over the years that stretch ahead on this long journey.

And finally, we dedicate this book to the remarkable people everywhere, in every school and community, who can and will bring about a new day in education by holding to a vision of inclusiveness, never giving up hope, using creativity and unleashing our collective determination and power.

Ann Jaramillo
Laurie Olsen

Chapter One:

INTRODUCTION

What is an advocate? In this book, advocates are people who work together to create schools that exclude no group of children from the very best education, people who envision wonderful, high-achieving classrooms that are equitable for all students. This book is a resource for such advocates and focuses specifically on the challenges of creating programs and schools appropriate for the millions of children in our nation's public schools whose home languages are not English.

❧ Are you a teacher struggling to teach across the barriers of language and culture to students newly arrived in these United States—and looking for ways to find those other teachers in the school who might share your challenges?

❧ Are you an administrator, searching for approaches to involve staff in assessing and strengthening the programs in your school for English Language Learners?

❧ Are you a member of a district or county office of education who is committed to supporting the hard work of school change at the sites? Are you trying to balance being an "outside eye" and a support to those who advocate at the school site level for access and achievement for excluded groups of students?

🕊 Are you a professor in a teacher credential program, trying to find new ways to help your students prepare for the realities they will face and the roles they will need to play upon entering schools with Limited English Proficient students?

🕊 Are you a "support provider" or school-change "coach" seeking ways to help a school focus on the problems of access and exclusion of their language minority students?

🕊 Are you just entering the profession of teaching, trying to imagine how you could contribute towards building schools that are just and inclusive for all students?

If you care about equity in education, the strategies in this book can be adapted to meet your needs.

Whatever your position in a school community, if you care about changing the ways schools go about their business so that they truly provide an education to all students, then this book is for you.

Turning the Tides of Exclusion was designed to be a toolkit of ideas, activities, strategies and resources to create schools that, once and for all, erase the gaps in access and achievement between children who are fluent in English and those who are not, between those with darker skin colors and those with lighter, between those whose families have the benefit of greater resources and those who do not.

While this book focuses on creating effective programs and inclusive schools for English Language Learners[1], our strategies can be adapted and used to advocate on behalf of other historically excluded groups of students. The inquiry processes, the approaches to creating a strong group of advocates, the examination of data on student achievement and participation, the ways to invite and honor student voice—all support advocating for equity in schools. In addition, while our examples primarily illustrate situations in secondary schools, the strategies can work equally well in elementary schools. If you care about equity in education, the strategies in this book can be adapted to meet your needs.

---

[1] It may be helpful to review a set of terms we use throughout the book, somewhat interchangeably, to refer to students whose first language is not English. "Limited English Proficient" is the official state-designated label and the more commonly recognized term in California. We also use the term "English Language Learners" because it focuses on what students are learning and not on what they cannot yet do. At times we speak of "language minority" students, especially when discussing language status and language relations issues. We also use the term "immigrant" in a broad way, particularly when speaking about adjusting to a new culture and nation.

How to Use This Book

We have designed this book around five major strategies that can help schools become more responsive to the needs of language minority and immigrant students:

🌱 Creating a core of advocates to drive the school change process

🌱 Using data and inquiry to focus and monitor your work

🌱 Understanding more about immigrant students' experiences

🌱 Inviting and supporting student voice

🌱 Changing practice inside the classroom

Each chapter includes a description of how and why each strategy can spark and facilitate school change. To apply each strategy, we include many activities and tools for reflection. Throughout each chapter, we include brief stories that allow you to see what it looks like when people in real schools implement these strategies. For those working at the district or community level, in universities or nonprofit support organizations, we also discuss the kinds of supports, policies and preparation that facilitate the skillful and ongoing use of these strategies. At the end of each chapter, we've included a list of resources and an annotated bibliography.

The five chapters of this book offer different ways into what is, in fact, a set of interrelated strategies for changing a school. Using data-based inquiry is a form of professional development—and it almost always leads to needing to hear from students about their experiences. Trying to understand and change practice in a classroom requires using data and looking deeper at the needs and experiences of students. Using data, listening to students, making efforts to understand students' lives, and working to change classroom practices—all are strategies advocates use to focus on what's actually happening, and what should be happening, for students in schools.

The activities in this book can be used by an individual or a group of people seeking to expand their own thinking and repertoire of strategies for making changes in a school. Some of the activities work best in workshops and group settings where perspectives can be shared—others are designed more as private reflections. Endless adaptations are possible; there is no single path to developing skills in these strategies. We encourage you to mix and match, adapt and embellish. We have found, again and again, that regardless of which way you "enter" this work, each strategy opens the doors for the other strategies.

You can use this book in a variety of ways. For some schools and communities, data use is the most appropriate way to begin—and for others, even the suggestion of looking at data sends shudders up and down the school. One school may be interested in working together to focus on changing classroom practices, another may prefer beginning with inviting student voice. Follow your instincts about where to begin, where the opportunities are in your particular school.

To give you an idea of some pathways through this book, we offer the following suggestions. No matter what your role, begin with the advocacy chapter (Chapter Two). The concept of advocacy, and what it means to be an advocate, is the foundation for moving schools effectively using the strategies in the other chapters. After going through this chapter, you may have a better idea about where it makes sense for you to go next in the book, depending on your role and your situation.

If you are a teacher or a small group of teachers:

You might find the following activities in the advocacy chapter useful in getting your group together and building strong relationships among advocates:

- Activity 2.4 Identifying a Core Group of Advocates
- Activity 2.5 An Advocate's Journey Map
- Activity 2.8 Getting in Touch With and Sharing the Reasons You Are an Advocate
- Activity 2.10 Inventorying Our Collective Strengths

Once you've built a strong group of advocates, you can decide together which of the other strategies (data, student voice, understanding students' experiences, focusing on the classroom) would be the best direction to move in for your school.

If you are a site-level administrator:

You're probably already responsible for reviewing and disseminating site-level data; thus, one place to begin would be the data chapter (Chapter Three). Sections and activities of particular interest are:

- A Process for Analyzing Data Together
- Activity 3.3 Constructing Your Data Group
- Activity 3.4 Setting Guidelines for Dialogue
- Activity 3.7 Assessing the Conditions for Data Use at Your School

If you are a support provider or a coach:

If you've been called in to help a school because of achievement issues, then the data chapter (Chapter Three) might be a good place to start:

- ☛ A Process for Analyzing Data Together
- ☛ Activity 3.3 Constructing Your Data Group
- ☛ Activity 3.4 Setting Guidelines for Dialogue

Or, if you need to find a way to really motivate or focus school staff around the needs of immigrant students, you could start with the student voice chapter (Chapter Five):

- ☛ Activity 5.1 Our School's History with Student Voice
- ☛ Activity 5.2 Our School's Climate for Student Voice
- ☛ Conditions for Speaking and Listening
- ☛ Giving the Findings Legitimacy as Data
- ☛ Student Focus Groups

If you are a professor in a teacher education program:

You might want to begin by giving your students insight into the complexity of the population they will be teaching by looking at Chapter Four:

- ☛ Activity 4.2 Language History Map
- ☛ Activity 4.3 Reading About Four Immigrant Experiences
- ☛ Activity 4.7 Examining Student Profiles: Long-Term LEP Students
- ☛ Knowing Your Students: Dimensions Beyond Language

You might also consider having student teachers work with teachers in their schools to map the school, to help these aspiring teachers get a better sense of the complexities of real schools. Chapter Two offers:

- ☛ Activity 2.14 Mapping Our School's History
- ☛ Activity 2.15 Our School's Social/Political Map of Reform
- ☛ Activity 2.16 Our School's Struggle Maps

If you are a staff developer:

The ways into this content are numerous—you could work with a staff on using data and inquiry (Chapter Three), understanding your immigrant students (Chapter Four) or using student voice strategies (Chapter Five). If you're working with teachers on improving classroom practice, here are some ways into Chapter Six:

- ☞ Activity 6.1A Ranking the Obstacles/Ranking What Works
- ☞ Activity 6.1D Envisioning Classrooms
- ☞ Activity 6.1E Using Before/After Scenarios: Making It Concrete

These are only suggestions; feel free to navigate this book in whatever way seems the most effective for you and your school.

We deliberately designed the activities in this book so that they use and model classroom instructional strategies that are effective with English Language Learners and other students. For example, the jigsaw activity described for involving educators in reading literature together can be equally effective in a classroom. Budget tours, Quick-Writes, mapping activities, ranking approaches, and many other instructional devices are used liberally (we explain several of these instructional strategies below). As you work your way through the activities in this book, we hope you discover instructional approaches you want to adapt and use in your own classrooms.

INSTRUCTIONAL STRATEGIES WE USE AND THEIR CLASSROOM APPLICATIONS

QUICK-WRITES

Quick-Writes are often used at the beginning of a lesson or activity to assess or activate prior knowledge about the content or connect the content to students' experiences. The point is to write quickly what first comes to mind about the topic and think about what the topic means to you. The focus is on generating ideas in writing, not editing or perfecting your writing.

THINK-PAIR-SHARE

Like Quick-Writes, you can use a "think-pair-share" to get students or participants into a topic. The participants work in pairs through a short series of questions or prompts, using the following sequence: 1) Each individual considers the question and thinks about their own answers. 2) In pairs, participants share with each other the ideas they came up with individually. 3) To share their thinking, the teacher then calls on individuals to report on what they discussed with their partners.

FISHBOWLS

Fishbowls are effective tools for listening and reflection. In a fishbowl activity, a teacher-selected or self-selected small group (5-7) place their chairs in a circle. The rest of the class or group place their chairs on the outside of the inner circle so each person is within good listening distance for the conversation. The fishbowl participants then engage in a conversation about a given topic or in response to a series of prompts. The conversation is usually limited in time—somewhere around 10 minutes—and there might be a moderator in the fishbowl to keep the conversation going. It is the job of the outside circle to listen carefully. When the first inside group finishes, they get up and people from the outside circle take their places inside. The second group then describes what they heard the first group say. They also might expand on the first conversation. The goal is to gain an appreciation of different points of view or to arrive at new understandings about a topic.

BUDGET TOURS

After reading a piece of text (a chapter, important pages, etc.), students or participants can use a budget tour format to represent the text in a new way. The budget tour asks respondents to think up their own title for the text, to pick the most important lines or quotes from the selection (and justify their choice), to summarize the text in their own words, and to create a visual representation for the piece. Budget tours have been used extensively in language arts classrooms as one way to reread or review text. As such, they are usually used in the "beyond" part of a "into-through-beyond" sequence.

JIGSAWS

Teachers skilled in cooperative learning have been using the jigsaw format for reading text for many years. It is often used like this: 1) Students or participants are arranged in "home teams." 2) Within each home team, people number off or are assigned to various "expert groups." Each person from the home team becomes part of a different expert group. 3) The expert groups read a portion of text together; expert groups often have a set of teacher-prepared questions, prompts or a graphic organizer to assist them in gathering important information from the reading. 4) After the expert groups finish, the students return to their home teams to share what they have learned. The point is that each participant becomes an expert on some aspect of a larger topic or brings a different perspective to build common understandings within the home team. Teachers who use jigsaws effectively select the text carefully and thoroughly model each step of the jigsaw process for students.

Why is a Book like This Necessary?

IMMIGRANT STUDENTS JOIN AN INCREASINGLY DIVERSE STUDENT POPULATION

With the advent of an unprecedented immigrant wave, bringing immigrants from every continent to join an already very diverse population, our schools are filled with the most ethnically, linguistically and culturally diverse population ever. Our students represent hundreds of different language and cultural groups. Meanwhile, recognition of the high level of skills and knowledge needed for success in the 21st century has driven us to raise our educational standards. Our achievement goals have never been higher—and the diversity of students we are committed to educate to those goals has never been greater.

For California, magnet for many emigrants from the Pacific Rim, Mexico or Central America, the past decade has been a time of astounding growth. We have grown twice as fast as the rest of the nation. Eighty-five percent of that growth has been among Hispanics and Asians, mostly due to immigration. The public schools have been deeply impacted by this immigration wave.

- Children who speak a language other than English at home are the fastest growing segment of our school-age population, now comprising one-third of all students. The number of LEP students has increased threefold in ten years in California.

- Almost 1.4 million students—one fourth of public school children—are Limited English Proficient (LEP) or non-English-speaking.

- Close to one in five students are immigrants, with lives shaped in another culture and nation, and deeply imprinted with the experiences of immigration and dislocation. While more than half of these newcomers arrive in the elementary school years, these changes are also impacting secondary schools, especially in California.

- In 1997, almost one-third of California's LEP students were enrolled in grades 7 through 12, representing 17% of the total secondary school enrollment and almost one quarter of a million students (California Department of Education).

- There has been a 44% increase in the number of LEP students in secondary schools in just the past three years, a proportionately greater growth rate than that at the elementary level.

These changes can have a powerful impact on individual schools and districts, as the words of one teacher in Southern California illustrate:

"We went from the '60s, where it was 'immigrants need not apply,' to the '70s, which were complacent, to the '80s, which were chaos, then the '90s, which we thought was kinda managing chaos as our school population went from 1,700 to 3,600. We also went from approximately 18% LEP students and 82% English Only to just the opposite. Where we really got stuck was in the late '80s, when we basically had a 300% rise in the immigrant population and had no infrastructure at all in the district to accommodate that."

LIMITED ENGLISH PROFICIENT STUDENTS: A NATIONAL PICTURE

- In 1994-95, there were over 3 million Limited English Proficient students in the U.S., accounting for 7% of all public school students (Fleischman and Hopstock, 1993; Macias and Kelly, 1996).

- Between 1990 and 1995, the number of LEP students nationwide increased almost 45% in five years (Macias and Kelly, 1996).

- Forty-two percent of all public school teachers in the U.S. have at least one LEP student in their classrooms (Han and Baker, 1997).

- Many LEP students attend secondary schools: 18% are in grades 7 to 9 and 14% are in grades 10 to 12 (Fleischman and Hopstock, 1993).

- Twenty percent of all LEP students are not receiving educational services targeted to their language needs (Macias and Kelly, 1996).

- Nationwide, there is a shortage of teachers trained to work with LEP students: 32% of U.S. secondary schools had bilingual or ESL positions which were difficult or impossible to fill in 1993-94 (Smith, 1997).

This immigration wave is remarkable not just for its magnitude and the swiftness of the changes, but for its diversity as well. More than 100 different languages are spoken by the school children in California. These students come from rural, isolated villages, as well as major urban industrialized centers. Some come fleeing wars or political oppression; others are joining family members or come with parents seeking work. They arrive at the schoolhouse door with a multitude of specific needs: to learn English quickly and fluently, to access and learn their academic subjects in a language they can understand and to adjust to a new culture and schooling system.

Colored pencil by Iris Arrieta, a high school student from Peru

THE CHALLENGES TEACHERS FACE

Today's teachers face unprecedented challenges in their chosen profession: students with whom they often do not share the same language, culture, ethnicity or even the same zip code; teacher training that is long on theory and short on practice—with many teachers arriving at their schools with university degree in hand, but little pedagogical training and absolutely no preparation for the task of reshaping schools; structures and traditions in secondary schools that mitigate against meaningful collaboration and joint planning; and mounting political pressure for "accountability" and "one-size-fits-all" approaches that further isolate, divide and disempower the very teachers who have the ability to fix the problem that the public perceives.

Layered on to these issues are the other challenges unique to teaching traditionally disenfranchised groups of students: responding to a variety of sociocultural and political factors that affect student motivation and engagement in school; breaking through decades of underachievement endemic in some communities—and breaking through the cycle of lowered expectations of some teachers who believe nothing will really work for "those students" anyway. Those who teach English Language Learners face the additional challenges of teaching grade-level content to students with a variety of English proficiency levels and working with students who may have come to this country with no schooling or with significant gaps in prior schooling (Olsen and Chen, 1988; Minicucci and Olsen, 1993).

To make it possible for teachers to embrace and serve our newcomers well, we need major shifts in how we teach, how we structure our schools, and how we think about our students. Yet the goal of crafting schools and instruction sufficient for all students to reach high standards has remained elusive—and significantly so for secondary schools. A vigorous school reform movement in the past fifteen years has largely bypassed issues of equity, as well-meaning and hardworking reformers simply did not see the ways in which their schools continued to provide different educations to children of different backgrounds (Olsen et al., 1994). The remnants of a long history of providing unequal education remain in many of our schools: a lack of commitment to serving all children; fewer resources devoted to children in poorer and darker-skinned communities; teacher preparation programs that don't enable new teachers to reach across cultures and languages. The challenges facing teachers and schools are enormous.

To address these challenges, many schools and districts turn to professional development. But often staff development programs are like a sower, spreading seeds: some fall on infertile ground and others land on rich soil. There is always the hope that if you do enough high-quality training for everyone, something will grow. To a certain extent, this approach works for certification, when the expectation is that everyone participates. After all, sometimes even rocks have cracks with enough soil to nourish a small but hearty plant. Teachers can make surprising leaps after an epiphany in training. But there is also the small but voracious cluster of burned-out negativists in a staff who choke and smother anything new. And, of course, there is usually one core of staff for whom one seed has the potential to flower endlessly.

But the relatively haphazard nature of much staff development, the broadcasting of seeds of theory, pedagogy and new curriculum, means that districts and schools are never sure what will take root where or if it will survive—not to mention if it will grow and thrive. The complexity of the situation demands a wider, more expansive view of what it means to address the challenges of immigration and diversity. Teachers need opportunities to grapple with the issues facing them in real, productive, ongoing ways. Schools need to be reshaped to become more responsive to the needs of *all* the students they serve.

Teachers need opportunities to grapple with the issues facing them in real, productive, ongoing ways.

A QUESTION OF WILL POWER

To create the changes needed, however, is not only a matter of professional development—it is also a matter of whether or not our schools, state and nation have the *will* to provide what's needed, and the *courage* and *commitment* to reckon with the deep-seated patterns of excluding certain groups of children—especially children of color, poor children and language minority children.

Now, as at the turn of the last century, when the last massive immigration wave came to this country, people have turned to the schools as the battleground to play out our struggles over how inclusive and democratic our nation will be. Schools are trying to meet the needs of a diverse population in the midst of deep political divisions over the role of schools in addressing issues of Americanization, immigration, and language unity. This struggle is occurring in the political arena, and within almost every school site, where there is likely to be a combination of excitement, innovation, confusion, upheaval—and tension from those who are hostile to doing anything they consider "extra" for "those children."

In communities and schools with divided sentiments and beliefs about bilingual education and the education of immigrants, there are multiple tasks facing a school community:

✦ To build the capacity to deliver programs that address the needs of this new population.

✦ To build understanding about the needs of newcomers and about the impacts of language and culture on education.

✦ To provide the leadership, build the will, and create the attitudes so that educators welcome and embrace English Language Learners.

✦ To create the structures that support learning for English Language Learners.

✦ To build accountability and ownership for serving English Language Learners into the life of the schools and district.

Each school community has to forge its own path on the journey towards equitable schools. The shape of that path depends upon the energy and direction of the people within that community who care about making it happen. We wrote this book for those people, whom we call advocates, because in order to be effective as an advocate for change, we need tools, resources, approaches and proven strategies.

DEVELOPING AND DEMONSTRATING THE STRATEGIES

This book draws upon a set of strategies developed and demonstrated through California Tomorrow's work with schools and communities over the past decade. Challenged by the task of how people in schools and communities might accelerate the pace of change in their schools, we set out to define and demonstrate a set of school change strategies. We had been developing the thinking behind these strategies for years when we had a specific opportunity to put that thinking to the test in a four-year demonstration project with two school districts.

In 1993, with support from the Andrew W. Mellon Foundation in New York, an initiative involving a consortium of four demonstration projects and the Center for Applied Linguistics was funded to develop new models and programs which would specifically result in the improvement of secondary school structures and practice for immigrant students. The goals of the program were to:

✦ increase English language literacy,

🌿 improve access to and mastery of core academic content, and

🌿 improve transitions through high school and to post-secondary options.

California Tomorrow was awarded one of these demonstration grants, and we decided to use this opportunity to define and test an equity-centered school change process model. We began by assuming that no single delivery model or program approach can work across the diverse schools and districts that serve immigrant students. Changing demographics affect regions differently. Schools have different capabilities and expertise to deliver programs. And the needs of particular configurations of immigrant students create very specific program demands. Furthermore, there is no single package of steps to take that will change all schools. We began, therefore, with this basic assertion:

"The real challenge is not to reproduce static models or to seek to meet the letter of the law for basic compliance designed for the school population currently enrolled, but to create schools which are continually responsive to the mixes of cultures and languages that present themselves—and which bring accountability inside the school for producing high achievement."

It was not a static model we sought, but an approach that would result in responsive and accountable schools. Based on our knowledge of the challenges and our analysis of what worked and didn't work in whole-school reform efforts in the past, we articulated a set of five basic strategies that would drive our approach. This is the chain of logic behind our approach:

IDENTIFY THE SPARKS AND ESTABLISH
AN INSIDE-OUTSIDE PARTNERSHIP. THEN:

Use flexible strategies, such as:	*In order to build:*	*To produce:*
☛ Data	☛ Capacity	☛ Responsive programs that result in full access and high achievement for English Language Learners
☛ Student voice	☛ Visibility and awareness of English Language Learners' needs	
☛ Professional development		
☛ Immersion in research	☛ Positive attitudes, will, and ownership	
☛ Advocacy and reflective, strategic thinking about school change	☛ More responsive structures	
	☛ Accountability	

The five strategies described in this book formed the basis of a school change process that we implemented and evaluated in this four-year project, which was a partnership between California Tomorrow and two school districts in California between the years of 1994-1998. These strategies rest on the following understandings:

☙ Responsive schools need to have people who take responsibility and ownership for being sure that English Language Learners have access and are achieving. This requires strong advocates and **mechanisms of advocacy** to provide individual student advocacy, close one-to-one monitoring and placement and advising. It also requires legitimizing and creating the spaces and forums in which people concerned about changing schools to meet the needs of immigrants can come together and engage in systemic advocacy.

☙ To build accountability for inclusion and access for immigrant students, and deepened understandings of the needs of immigrant populations, schools need to develop **inquiry-based data systems and the habits and processes of analyzing data** about student achievement, participation and progress through school.

☙ To respond effectively to the needs of immigrant students, educators need to **understand the complexities of English Language Learners' lives.** They need to be able to see that they may be serving different groups of immigrant students with very different needs and to spend time understanding the linguistic, political, social and cultural factors that shape English Language Learners' lives and achievement patterns.

☙ Responsive schools need ways to learn about, learn from and listen to their English Language Learners and parents. Educators need strategies for **inviting and responding to the voices and concerns of immigrant students,** parents and communities—and strategies for developing the skills to build upon those voices to enhance the understanding of educators, to motivate educators to make change and to strengthen relationships within the school community.

☙ The challenges of teaching and schooling in this era of complex cultural and linguistic relations require immersion in inquiry and reflection, as educators seek to work with students across cultural, language and national experiences. In order to build that capacity, schools need to make an investment in **ongoing, sustained professional development** in collaborative and individual formats.

During the four years of the demonstration project, this school change approach was tested in two very different district and community contexts in California—Hayward and Salinas. Hayward is an urban school district with multiple language groups, representing every continent in the world, spread across the district's schools. In Hayward, we worked primarily with two high schools across the district. In Salinas, a rural, agricultural community with a growing urban center, we partnered with one high school which serves over 90% Latino students who mostly come from the same region of Mexico.

Despite these differences in context, California Tomorrow's partnerships with Hayward Unified School District and Salinas Union High School District were able to demonstrate that, by developing habits related to our change principles, each school created programs focused on responding better to immigrant students. In both cases, there was evidence of improvement toward all three project goals related to student achievement: stronger and more rapid English language development, smoother and better transitions through school, and greater preparation for higher education. There were significant improvements in access to the curriculum at all schools, with the addition of many more courses offered by teachers prepared to instruct LEP students.

In the two years since the demonstration project ended, there has been clear evidence that institutionalized habits and roles are being carried on by educators in these schools without outside funding or support. In short, this approach worked to produce real changes in student achievement and in the school program for exactly the populations most often short-changed or overlooked in school reform efforts. (For the full story of the demonstration project, see the companion book in this Equity-Centered Reform Publication Series, *Igniting School Change for Immigrant Students: Portraits of Three High Schools*, 1999.)

When word of the impact of this equity-centered school change model began to get out, California Tomorrow was inundated with requests to work with other schools, in other districts, all over California. Over the past several years, we have taken our change strategies to other schools, communities and contexts—and applied them not only to the challenges of immigrant- and LEP-impacted schools, but also to other populations for whom access and equity have been a problem. The combination of our original demonstration project in Hayward and Salinas, along with our adaptation of strategies to work with schools throughout California, have led to this book. Throughout, we weave stories from our work in Hayward, Salinas and other schools we have worked with since to illustrate how our strategies play out in the context of real schools.

FINDING THE TIME TO CHANGE

Right now many educators who care about equity work long, hard hours trying to bring about changes in their teaching, their school programs and structure. To a large extent, this book is not about adding work to their load, but about offering suggestions for working smarter. The activities in this book help focus planning efforts and deepen understanding so programs and instruction can have more impact. Some of this can be done in the course of the faculty meetings, staff development days, planning meetings, accreditation self-studies, credential program courses, etc., that are already taking place.

But there is one crucial resource that people seeking to bring about significant changes in their school eventually have to garner—time together. As one teacher commented:

> *"We're expected to do so much and they keep throwing new strategies at us, send us to new conferences, new workshops, but we never have time to think about even how you are gonna implement it into your own classroom. We don't even have time to get together as teachers, not only in our own departments, but across departments."*

It takes people working together to bring about change—and working together means time together.

It takes people working together to bring about change—and working together means time together. It may be as small and informal in the beginning as a short meeting after work for a few hours—or require a support as large and significant as restructuring the school day to allow for joint collaboration time among educators. Schools we have worked with have run the gamut: some have used their professional development funds to pay for substitutes to allow teachers to meet together; others have sought special Title VII grants to fund an entire data- or student voice-based strategy for program improvement. Some have sought approval to use collaboration planning time for advocates to meet regularly; others have met after school for a potluck "study group" once a month.

For some schools, finding the time together is a crucial first step. Two sections in this book—Chapter Two's Finding the Time and Activity 6.2A, Plotting the Use of Time at Your School in Chapter Six—are designed to help you figure out how to find or reallocate time together. It's also vital to make sure that, at some point, the work becomes an official part of the school plan. Most schools with significant numbers of immigrant and LEP students receive additional funds that can be targeted toward an inquiry process aimed at increasing achievement and equity for those students. This requires some rethinking of how these funds should be spent. Sources that can be tapped include Title I, EIA-LEP, SB 1882 Staff Development, and

Migrant Education funds. Some schools choose to apply for a Title VII grant to supplement their efforts, while others go to grants from foundations. In California, middle schools can apply for demonstration grants from the state. Funds are available, or can be made available, for the work of changing schools.

A FINAL NOTE AS YOU EMBARK ON THIS JOURNEY

This is not the easiest time to focus schools on including and serving their LEP students. In California, where California Tomorrow has forged these strategies, the political winds have become a hurricane as the public struggles with how to educate children whose first language is not English. Home language or English Only instruction? Are undocumented immigrants allowed a public education or not? The passage of Proposition 227[2] in 1998, aimed at dismantling bilingual education, has tied the hands of many educators and denied many parents the ability to shape the educational programs of their children. This is a time that requires courage and perseverance for those who advocate for immigrant students.

The strategies in this book are designed to help you hold steady in the face of this political whirlwind—to develop and articulate your vision, to examine, pursue and act upon data about what works and what doesn't and to make sure your students get what they need. We also assume that you'll need support along the way, which is why we offer strategies for assembling a core of people who share your concerns and will work together toward a vision.

With this book, we hope to offer the concrete strategies that will help you steer your way against the tide of exclusion. We hope to help you sort out what you hear in the midst of the heat of political battles and face down the denial that pervades much of this society about the degree to which

---

[2] Proposition 227 sought to eliminate bilingual education in California by mandating that: 1) all English Language Learners be placed in "sheltered English immersion" classes for a maximum of one year and then be placed in mainstream classes; 2) English Language Learners be taught "overwhelmingly" in English; 3) waivers allowing students to participate in a different kind of program, including bilingual programs, would only be granted on a limited basis; and 4) teachers, school board members and administrators who "willfully" do not implement 227 can be held personally liable and are vulnerable to lawsuits.

children are excluded from the schooling they need. We hope to help you stand up to those who spread misinformation about language programs in our public schools and support you in becoming an agent of change.

As you work, remember that while you are trying to bring about changes in your school, someone down the road and many people across the state are also working to build a world in which all children are welcomed, nurtured and provided with the skills and knowledge they need to participate fully, proudly and equally in our society. Together, we will turn the tides of exclusion.

REFERENCES

Fleischman, H.L. and Hopstock, P. J. (1993). *Descriptive Study of Services to Limited English Proficient Students.* Arlington, VA: Development Associates, Inc.

Han, M. and Baker, D. (1997). *SASS 1993-94: A Profile of Policies and Practices for Limited English Proficient Students: Screening Methods, Program Support and Teacher Training.* (NCES 97-472). Washington, D.C.: National Center for Educational Statistics, U.S. Department of Education.

Macias, R. F. and Kelly, C. (1996). *Summary Report of the Survey of the States' Limited English Proficient Students and Available Educational Programs and Services, 1994-95.* Santa Barbara, CA: University of California Language Minority Research Institute.

Minicucci, C. and Olsen, L. (1993). Caught Unawares: California Secondary Schools Confront the Immigrant Student Challenge. *Multicultural Education, 1*(2), 16-19.

Olsen, L., Chang, H., De La Roza Salazar, D., Dowell, C. (Ed.), Leong, C., McCall-Perez, Z., McClain, G., and Raffel, L. (1994). *The Unfinished Journey: Restructuring Schools in a Diverse Society.* San Francisco, CA: California Tomorrow.

Olsen, L. and Chen, M. (1988). *Crossing the Schoolhouse Border: Immigrant Students and the California Public Schools.* San Francisco, CA: California Tomorrow.

Olsen, L., Jaramillo, A., McCall-Perez, Z., White, J., and Minicucci, C. (1999). *Igniting Change for Immigrant Students: Portraits of Three High Schools.* Oakland, CA: California Tomorrow.

Smith, T. M. (1997). *The Condition of Education, 1997.* (NCES 97-388) Washington, D.C.: National Center for Educational Statistics.

Chapter Two:

WORKING FROM THE "SPARKS": EDUCATORS AS ADVOCATES FOR IMMIGRANT STUDENTS

In reading the journals of her students, Ms. Anderson discovers that Guadalupe, a bright and hardworking young woman in her ESL 4 class, wants to become a nurse. She pulls Guadalupe aside after class one day and asks what she is studying now in the fall of her junior year of high school. Guadalupe says she is taking Art, two study halls, a Basic Math class and ESL. Aware that entrance to college requires higher-level coursework, and that the nursing profession requires a college education, Ms. Anderson sits down with Guadalupe and explains that she should be taking a Science class and that she should get out of Basic Math and into Algebra as soon as possible. She also suggests that Guadalupe may be ready to take a "regular" English class that counts for college preparation credit and promises to hook her up with a tutoring program. Together, they plot out the program Guadalupe needs this semester, next semester

and through her senior year. Over the next two years, Ms. Anderson meets regularly with Guadalupe—to find out how she is doing in her more intensive academic program, to update her with information about college requirements and nursing programs, and to help her fill out college and financial aid applications. She makes sure Guadalupe signs up to take the SAT test and helps her prepare with practice tests. At one point she meets with Guadalupe's father, using her own halting Spanish to explain the entire process for applying to college and for financial aid.

The faculty at Washington High is excited about instituting a new program, Career Academies, which they will pilot in the fall with a Health Professions Academy. The teachers who have led this reform effort will staff the first academy, and then spend the summer designing the curriculum and preparing everything to open on the first day of school. When Mr. Glover, an ESL teacher, hears about the plans, he, too, is excited, until he receives information about how to help students apply for the academy—no ESL students are to be considered. The faculty who are on the Academy Team don't have the training or credentials to offer ESL, nor is their curriculum designed with a sheltered approach. They propose that ESL students can enter an academy after they become proficient enough in English to participate in the curriculum. Concerned about this exclusion of ESL students, and aware of how greatly ESL students would benefit from an academy approach, Mr. Glover approaches the Academy Team. He says he believes the academy should be open to ESL students and suggests they add an ESL teacher to their team, shelter the curriculum, and get training themselves in how to provide sheltered instruction. It's too much to take on, the team members say. They are stretched enough just designing the program for "regular" kids. So, Mr. Glover gets on the phone and calls colleagues from the California Association for Bilingual Education, professors at a nearby Bilingual Cross-Cultural, Language and Academic Development (BCLAD) credential program and two bilingual teachers he knows at schools that have academy programs. He takes it upon himself to track down bilingual dictionaries with health-related terms, and the names of two schools that include ESL students in their health academies that the team might visit. Armed with these resources, he again approaches the Academy Team— this time including the principal in the meeting and using the words "discrimination" and "legal rights of access."

A new school board member in the Tampa Unified School District is going to introduce a resolution to end bilingual programs in the district. When this news breaks, Eva Sandoval, the Bilingual Resource Teacher at Emerson Middle School, immediately gets on the phone and calls her counterparts in other schools. They hurriedly arrange a meeting after school where they sit down to strategize. Who knows anything about this new school board member? What are his concerns? Has anyone actually seen the resolution? Piecing together what they know, they divide up tasks. Eva will call the school board member and ask him if he has any questions or would like to see data about the effectiveness of their bilingual programs. Perhaps she can convince him not to proceed with the resolution at tonight's meeting; at least she can put him on notice that there are data about the program effectiveness and that there are people on to the fact that he is presenting his resolution that evening. Another teacher begins calling the principals she knows to be most supportive in schools that have strong bilingual programs and asks them to come to the meeting, and also alerts them that parents need to be mobilized to defend the program. A third teacher calls the Chairs of the district's Bilingual Advisory Committees, who in turn activate their phone trees to inform parents of the resolution. By the time the school board begins meeting at 7:30 that evening, there are 200 parents seated and prepared to speak— with signs announcing their support for the bilingual program. Large data displays show the achievement of students who have "graduated" from the bilingual program.

All three of these educators are advocates for their immigrant students. Some would call them "change agents," and indeed much of the literature on school reform speaks of the importance of people with vision and purpose who can prompt and facilitate school change (Carrow-Moffett, 1993; Fullan, 1993; McAloon, 1995; Shachar, 1996). The model for change featured in this book centers on the need to identify, develop and support people like these— advocates who can bring about the changes that lead to access and high achievement for the groups of students often left behind. After all, change occurs in schools because people make change.

This book is about advocates working together to create schools where access and support for immigrant students are institutionalized. We examine how people like Ms. Anderson work individually to impact the lives of particular students, but we also explore the limits of what can be accomplished by only reaching certain students, who, after all, leave our classrooms and head down the hall to the rooms of other teachers who may not share our vision of access. To borrow the African proverb, "It takes a village" to make schools responsive to those students most often served poorly.

In this chapter, we begin by exploring definitions of advocacy and encourage you to examine your own views. Next, we discuss forms of advocacy on the part of individual educators that help particular students make it through the system. The bulk of the chapter, then, focuses on how to develop and work within a group of other advocates to make change in your school. The chapters that follow will go deeper into the many specific strategies and tools that advocates, such as yourself, can use to move schools toward equity-centered reforms.

What Do We Mean by Advocacy?

The central concept at the heart of the California Tomorrow change model is advocacy: the need to identify advocates, create structures to support advocacy, to develop skills of advocacy and, then, to advocate for those students who need it most. But what do we mean by advocacy?

The word "advocacy" sometimes conjures up images of lawyers—and there are some legal aspects that we do wish to invoke. The law has been a crucial tool in defining and protecting the rights of language minority students to attend school and gain full access to an education. Advocates working in a tradition of civil rights continue to need to invoke the law to carry out their commitment to the education of students who have been consistently left out or left behind. But legal advocacy is only one part of what we mean by advocacy.

Another kind of advocacy takes place in a social service context, where advocates help a client make it through a bureaucracy, speak or argue on a client's behalf, and use their knowledge to help others be served. Advocates step up to the plate when a client's needs are not being addressed by an institution. Most educators committed to ensuring access to schooling for their students do some of this kind of advocacy as well.

Advocacy also takes place in political realms, as lobbyists and organizers push for policies in the interest of the groups they represent, or rally people around a cause. In schools, there are certainly times when a political push for policies that directly support the students we advocate for becomes necessary.

In the work of those people committed to creating a real education for excluded students, given that the system is often still unprepared or unwilling to flex to their needs, there is a bit of all of these forms of advocacy. There is a bit of the lawyer in a courtroom appealing to the law, the social worker negotiating an inflexible bureaucracy, the organizer mobilizing support or lobbying for new policies.

In schools, there is something else as well to being an advocate, something specific to being a teacher and educator who takes to heart the responsibility for opening up the world of academic knowledge and skills to our students. There is something specific about standing up for a group of students, with particular needs and historic challenges in schools. The kind of advocacy for immigrant students that we seek to nurture encompasses all of these meanings.

"ADDING VOICE TO A CRY"

In a California Tomorrow institute focused on improving schools for immigrant students, we asked a group of teachers to think about the word "advocate" in the context of their work and tell us what it meant. Some of the definitions discussed above were offered. But then one woman spoke out:

"When I look at the word 'advocacy,' I visually see it come apart: 'ad-vo-ca-cy.' This makes me think of 'Adding Voice to a Cry.'"

That is what advocacy meant to this teacher, because, she said, so much of what she does is see and hear the cries of her students who are pushed aside, can't understand what is being said to them, and find school so overwhelming. She is compelled to speak what she hears. And, she adds her own voice of indignation, of anger, of determination that things will change.

A reflective silence followed her words. Then a young teacher said, "Yes, and I believe that the Latin base is *advocare* — meaning, speaking justice. I would have to add, we don't just speak justice, we act for justice."

And so we use the term "advocacy" because it invokes those twin anchors—of speaking out for and acting on behalf of others. It invokes a history of civil rights law with its passion for justice. Speaking is itself a part of action—speaking for and with our immigrant students. All this is made more imperative because the students themselves do not yet have the language and position to bring about the kinds of changes that will allow them full access and participation in our English-dominant system.

In this advocacy task for immigrant students, we include the daily business of both individual and personal advocacy: helping students get into classes that are most appropriate for them, helping students fill out complicated applications for college, advising students and being their adult friends as they negotiate a new school system and a new homeland. We also see advocacy as the task of changing the system of schooling, designing the new programs and supports that must be institutionalized before schools truly address the needs of immigrant students, of fighting to end exclusionary policies and pushing to put in place inclusive ones. Individual and systemic advocacy require skills, passion and time—and structures wherein advocates can come together, knowing they are not alone, to forge strategy and multiply their voices.

Being an effective advocate for disenfranchised students is not easy. Effective advocates must be able to challenge the status quo. They must be able to raise questions of equity in participation and achievement, diversity and access, without alienating their fellow staff members to the point that they will never join in the struggle. They must be able to push past the silence and blindness about exclusion of some students and engage in a dialogue with others about what access means and looks like. They must be willing to teach and educate others about what they know. They must have a vision for expanding advocacy to include an increasing number of staff so that the burden is understood and shared. They need a sense for how and when to pass the torch, for when to go forward, for when to stop and reflect. Most of all, they must be willing to dig in and do the hard, daily work of opening the doors of educational opportunity for students who find those doors closed.

DOING WHAT YOU CAN ON YOUR OWN— INDIVIDUAL ADVOCACY

Schools in our nation—particularly secondary schools—are not designed to meet the needs of students who are not yet fluent in English or whose home nations and cultures are from beyond the borders of the United States. These students are often unable to take courses in the language they understand best and, so, struggle through the barrier of language to learn Science, Math and Social Studies. They seldom have support in bridging the curriculum they studied in their home nation and the curriculum that is simply assumed as prior background in secondary schools. Information needed to find one's way through the maze of requirements and logistics in secondary schools is, in too many schools, unavailable in a language they can understand. Still too few teachers have the skills to teach across language barriers and help students comprehend a curriculum for which they don't yet have words in English. And there is a severe shortage of counselors and administrators with the training to support students in the process of adjusting to a new nation and culture.

The shifting landscape of a large secondary school often pits the needs of immigrant students against the forces of inertia, overwhelm and ignorance about the role of language and culture in education, incompetence

Effective advocates must be able to challenge the status quo. They must be able to raise questions of equity in participation and achievement, diversity and access, without alienating their fellow staff members to the point that they will never join in the struggle.

ACTIVITY 2.1
REFLECTING ON WHAT THE WORD
"ADVOCACY" MEANS TO YOU

Since advocacy has so many meanings, and it is such a central concept in this book, we invite you to reflect on what it means to you. If you are planning to work with several other advocates at your school, you can share your reflections with each other.

1. Begin by writing the word "advocacy" in the center of a piece of paper. Then draw lines out from that word, like spokes on a wheel, and write on each spoke whatever word associations you have with advocacy or components that give meaning to the word "advocacy." This is a brainstorming tool; all associations are valid and you can create as many spokes as you like. Here is an example:

2. You may also want to reflect on whether you feel the word "advocate" fits you and your role in schools. What aspects of advocacy do you feel reflect what you do or hope to do? Are there any aspects of what we've described above, or the word itself, that don't fit for you? Take a little time to write out your thoughts. If you're working with others, share your reflections and learn about the ways your colleagues would or would not define their work as advocacy.

and inflexibility. Their needs are often pitted against the more insidious forces of racism, xenophobia and discrimination. As the number of language minority students grows in our schools, we crucially need advocates who can represent them through the system. As schools increase graduation requirements, institute career academies and pathways, and experiment with structural and curricular reforms, students who have traditionally been left behind are the most at risk of being lost in this shuffle.

Systemic barriers and the chronic invisibility of immigrant students' needs mean that advocates often take on providing them services and information themselves. Motivated by the needs of the students we advocate for, knowing the system ourselves, we often work on our own to help students make it through secondary school. Such individual advocacy takes several forms:

☛ *Trying to ensure that students receive the instruction they need.*

Many advocates take on monitoring program placement for immigrant students, though this is often not part of their job. Here a teacher reviews the program a student is given and tries to figure out if it is appropriate—for their level of English fluency, for their academic level, for the student to get through high school in a timely manner, and for access to preparation for higher education.

Almost every school has at least one staff person who has come to be recognized as the one who "watches out for" immigrant students. He may be a teacher who takes an interest in these students' lives outside of his classroom, who advocates for the students on many different levels. She may be a counselor, an advisor, activities director or instructional aide.

> *"I knew I had the wrong classes because they put me in a Math class I already had. I tried to talk to a counselor, but I couldn't get in to see him. So I showed my schedule to my ESL teacher, and he helped me change my schedule. He's helped a lot of my friends get the right classes."*
>
> —16-YEAR-OLD ESL 1 STUDENT

Educators like this student's teacher most often act as unofficial advocates for student needs, ranging from assisting with course placement to helping solve personal problems that get in the way of schooling. The work tends to be *ad hoc*, with the advocates doing what they can, but often feeling frustrated as they butt up against institutional walls.

> *"My U.S. History teacher has helped us with our college applications. He even gave us advice about where we might go. I don't have him anymore this year, but he's one person that will always help the students (who*

don't speak English well). I have a counselor, but she's always so busy and I feel like I can trust my teacher. If it weren't for him, I don't know what I would do."

☛ ***Being sure students get the information they need.***

In most secondary schools, counselors have huge student loads. It is difficult enough for a counselor to provide information and advising to large numbers of students. It becomes even harder when the counselor doesn't share a language or cultural background with many of the students, or when students need information explained in a depth that takes more time. In these cases, individual advocacy can be found in those counselors who devote extra time to one-on-one sessions with students, or create small-group forums where information can be provided to students in their primary language. This requires that the counselor get to know enough about the cultures and ways of the students to understand their information gaps and what kinds of supports might help.

Here, individual advocacy on behalf of English Language Learners includes translating materials to be sure that basic sources of information, such as student handbooks, letters home about the grading system, etc., are accessible to immigrant students.

ACTIVITY 2.2
WHAT MATERIALS DO WE HAVE
AVAILABLE IN THE LANGUAGES OF OUR STUDENTS?

This activity can be a useful way of getting a picture of the extent to which your school provides materials in the primary languages of your immigrant and language minority students. Select the key student information materials produced by your school (school orientation pamphlets, student handbooks, etc.). Then answer the following questions for each item:

Key student information materials for our school:	Available in English only	Available in a sheltered form of English	Some languages other than English	All languages spoken in the homes of students
Student handbook				
Student orientation materials				
Information on college planning				
Course planning materials				
Other:				

☛ *Supplying support services: working in the "gray areas"*

Individual tutoring, help with scheduling and advice about school or college are student supports expected of schools. However, there are some supportive and mentoring roles educators play on behalf of immigrant students that fall into a gray area.

Students caught between two worlds — their home culture and language versus the very different world they find in their new land at large — struggle to find their way. Immigrant students often need a caring teacher friend to talk to about conflicts and decisions they face concerning, for example, dating, religious beliefs, following home traditions and parental expectations. Educators can find themselves in difficult and sensitive terrain when a young person comes to them wishing to talk about their struggle to adapt new ways and discard certain family cultural traditions. Whether and how an adult who is not from the student's family or culture can or should play a role in supporting the student is a tough question. There is no escaping the fact that advocates often find themselves in murky waters.

ACTIVITY 2.3
THINKING ABOUT THE "GRAY AREAS" OF ADVOCACY

One way to reflect on the "gray areas" of advocacy is to read cases where others have faced such situations. The following case comes from *Made in America: Immigrant Students in Our Public Schools* by Laurie Olsen (1997). Read it and then reflect on your reactions. What are the guidelines, limits, concerns, dangers and urgencies of entering into a supportive role to a young person trying to break from home traditions? If you can, share your thoughts with a partner or group of advocates also facing "gray areas"—or discuss the situations you've encountered that brought you into similar dilemmas.

It's a Wednesday in June, and the school year is winding down. Linda O'Malley has lessened the pace of activities in her ESL 4 class, and has given students five to ten minutes at the end of the period to just sit and talk with friends. It is in that context that Armina, a Hindu Fijian/Indian student, told O'Malley of her suddenly arranged marriage, and that the next day (Thursday) she wouldn't be in school because she was going to be engaged. She would meet her husband-to-be and his family, and they would exchange rings and matrimonial clothing. Several other girls overheard the conversation. "Aren't you scared?" "What happens on your wedding night?"

Armina was extremely scared and nervous. She told them that if she doesn't bleed on her wedding night, he can divorce her and she would be shamed. O'Malley decided the time for sex information was now, and said outright, "Do you know that there are other ways that hymens break? Has anyone talked to you about sex or about getting pregnant?" The look on Armina's face was enough for O'Malley. She called Lisa Stern on the phone, whose class Armina would be going to next, and arranged to excuse her. Second, O'Malley cancelled a meeting she was supposed to have during her prep period. "Stay next period," she suggested to Armina, "and we'll talk." Armina said, "Yes, please." Her good friend, who O'Malley had suspected from previous conversations might be sleeping with her boyfriend, said, "Me, too." And a third said, "I get married next year," which O'Malley took to mean that she wanted to stay also.

Armina and the two good friends stayed. "I'm afraid that if I get pregnant I won't get to go to college because we have to rent an apartment and support him and his father. I don't want to have children yet. Please help me." So, O'Malley first asked them what they knew. One knew about condoms, another said her boyfriend had reassured her that pulling out keeps you from getting pregnant. O'Malley decided to "tell them everything." She explained about condoms, how they work, what they look like in a package, where you buy them and what you do with them. She explained birth control pills and how hormones work. And, having been raised herself as a Catholic, O'Malley also explained the rhythm method. The girls liked the thought of the rhythm method because they agreed that it wouldn't be right for Armina to trick her husband with pills, and didn't think she could ask him to use a condom. But then the idea of sewing a little pocket into her jacket was developed so she could hide pills in there and just take one every morning in the bathroom. She was worried that she couldn't keep them in her purse in case he needs something and looks there. O'Malley left the issue of ethics regarding honesty with a husband alone, and tried to focus back on the issue of birth control. She explained that to get birth control pills Armina would need to see a doctor. O'Malley offered to make an appointment for Armina at Planned Parenthood and to take her there, even though she knew that she could get into trouble if Armina's parents or the school found out. She felt her presence might be important to help with English and to provide moral support. Her friend then piped up. "Ms. O'Malley, I've already slept with my boyfriend and we are not using a condom." As O'Malley said later:

"I tried to sympathize with her, to say I know that it's hard when you're in the back of his car and your emotions are going wild and you want to be loved, but you either need to make the decision before you get into the position or find a boyfriend who will be more supportive of you and help you use birth control. At that point, I realized my mission was not just about giving information, but giving advice. I didn't want the girls to just happen to get pregnant."

In the end, O'Malley took the girls to Planned Parenthood. She called and told their parents that she needed their daughters' help to prepare some materials at school and that she would drive them home later. On the drive to Planned Parenthood, Armina started to cry. "I don't want to have children." O'Malley asked if she knew whether

her husband-to-be wanted children soon, and Armina reminded her that they had never met before, much less discussed this kind of intimate issue. "Perhaps he will be very modern, and we can decide it together. But it isn't my place to bring it up."

It was at the end of this day that O'Malley talked to me, exhausted and worried.

"Am I crazy? All this was such a risk! I could be fired if the principal found out, or if the parents found out and complained. In a way I don't care. It's worth the risk. It's sad I have to take this risk. But Armina is so bright and intelligent and she deserves to go places and she wants to go places, and so much is out of her control. She deserves to be able to make a choice about having a baby. And so I just kept thinking that and thinking that, and knowing I had to do it. I had to help her have that choice. And for me, I'm not sure what I'm doing. Was it right to help her when clearly birth control is not something her parents were about to help her with? Was I mucking with her culture?"

And yet, from O'Malley's cultural perspective, to get pregnant while young had dire consequences. And her belief that early pregnancy would limit Armina was so strong, she overrode her worries.

"Teaching is secondary to this kind of dilemma for me. There is no real sex education in the school. Here is this young woman who is going to marry and is culturally expected to have children soon, and she personally wants to have a life before she has kids. I need to help her have that opportunity to control that. Nowhere in my teacher training did anyone tell me how to deal with things like this. And if it means taking risks, well, if I can help her make her own choices and not get pregnant, it's worth it to me. But I feel such overwhelming sorrow and pain that this has to be so secretive. That she can't go to her family. That she can't come to anyone at the school openly, and that I have to take a risk to help her. It's so sad, and I'm so drained. I don't want to lose her. I want to see her dreams come true, and I would risk anything to make that happen. And it feels crazy that out in the world, we all know about teenagers having sex with boyfriends and teenage pregnancy and going to Planned Parenthood and buying condoms. But inside school, it's not a talked-about part of life. And do I participate in the big secret? Or do I just refuse to give in to it and go ahead and help kids when they need it?"

O'Malley kept saying, "Maybe this isn't my line of work!"

MOVING FROM INDIVIDUAL TO SYSTEMIC ADVOCACY

Many advocates work with immigrant students in the ways we've described—taking it upon themselves to stay after school, open their classrooms during lunch hour, and do what they can for the students who find their way to them. It simply becomes part of these educators' individual commitment as a teacher, counselor or administrator. But there are limits to how many students any advocate can help in this way, and because these roles are based on interpersonal relationships, there are many students who don't get the help they need.

Inevitably, the limits of what one person can do are reached and advocates must try to elicit support from others as well as push the system to become more responsive. You may see that a student needs to take a more advanced math class, but then find yourself faced with the fact that there aren't any teachers with the training to offer it using a sheltered approach. So, you talk to the counselor about creating a class, try to convince the Math Department Chair that someone should get the training, or talk a colleague into letting the student into her class. People who care about providing access and achievement usually end up recognizing that the school itself has to make some changes.

Working with a group of advocates can also help you feel less alone. At a California Tomorrow institute to increase access and achievement for English Language Learners, one teacher noted with relief:

> *"When we're all here and we can all get together, we have a certain commonality. It's nice to listen and say, 'Yeah, I feel the same way.' We're all on the same page in more ways than I thought."*

An individual cannot change a school alone or begin to meet the needs of all the immigrant students. Simply put, you need more than yourself to pull off the task of creating responsive schools. One of the first major tasks is to find your group of advocates.

ACTIVITY 2.4
IDENTIFYING A CORE GROUP OF ADVOCATES

Whether you are an administrator assembling a team of advocates or an individual seeking colleagues and soulmates in this endeavor, the process is the same. Your aim is to find the "sparks" in your school, the folks who, like you, realize that more needs to be done for immigrant students.

Pull out a piece of paper and brainstorm a list of who in your school community would really care about and contribute toward an effort to focus attention on LEP student needs and figure out how to move the school forward toward responding to those needs. This is not a regular list of stakeholders with power and position. Who in the school has real expertise? Who has deep connections to the immigrant communities in your school? Who really cares about LEP student access and achievement? You need all these qualities, and they don't have to all be found in the same people. You can use the following matrix to help in your brainstorm:

List of names	People with training and expertise in serving LEP students	People with close connections to LEP students and to immigrant communities	People who really care about LEP student access and achievement
1. Al Camarillo		X	X
2. Sandra Jones	X		
3.			
4.			
5.			
6.			

It would be great to have a working group of 10 to 12 folks, but even a few can begin the process. These are your "sparks"—the people whose energy, commitment, passion and knowledge can help move your school around the needs of LEP students. Sparks can be student leaders, instructional assistants, parents or counselors. Every school has its own constellation. The specific role of each person doesn't matter.

INSTITUTIONALIZED ADVOCACY FOR LEP STUDENTS: ONE DISTRICT'S MODEL

A comprehensive educational system that truly responds to English Language Learners formally assigns responsibility to someone to examine and monitor the schedules of all LEP students to be sure they are in classes designed to meet their needs. When there is evidence of failing grades or problems, this person alerts the teachers and counselors to the problem and the need for either support or reassignment. In most schools, this role still falls to those individual advocates who see the need and take it on on behalf of one student at a time. The ability of such "informal advocates" to adjust a program or reassign a student depends on the strength of their relationships to others in the school.

But the Salinas Union High School District has instituted an alternative to individual and *ad hoc* advocacy for many years. This version of "institutionalized" advocacy arose out of a lawsuit and resulting consent decree, part of which required the assignment of at least one bilingual counselor to each school site. Faced with a shortage of the number of bilingual counselors needed, a creative solution was proposed to hire Bilingual Site Facilitators at each school. This approach to advocacy has continued to work effectively for more than fifteen years, in addition to the fact that many of the schools now have bilingual counselors on site.

Bilingual Site Facilitators (BSFs) are teachers, often recognized leaders and advocates, who come from school sites in the district. In fact, one of the qualifications for being a BSF is a "demonstrated commitment to advocacy for the instructional needs of LEP students." The district clearly recognizes the potential this position has to positively affect the education of language minority students. Administrative support does not just come as lip service—facilitators are paid a stipend to oversee the bilingual program at each site.

ELEMENTS OF THE BILINGUAL SITE FACILITATOR MODEL

1. Work collaboratively to ensure that LEP students receive a coordinated set of services.

- Oversee the nuts-and-bolts of assessment and placement.

- Some BSFs review the schedules for each LEP student annually or bi-annually to prevent misplacement.

2. Assist and consult with the site administrator in charge of the bilingual program around program evaluation, the master schedule and staff placement.

🌱 "Anchor" the bilingual program in the sea of shuffling administrators and shifting administrative duties.

🌱 Ensure that program philosophy and continuity are maintained.

🌱 Provide a crucial historical perspective on shifting demographics and master scheduling on a regular basis.

3. Assist the site administrator in charge of the bilingual program in establishing and conducting monthly Parent Bilingual Advisory Committee meetings.

🌱 Often, the BSF job is split between two people: one handles the student and staff side of the job, and the other takes over the parent responsibilities.

4. Attend monthly facilitator meetings, maintain monthly activity logs, provide a year-end summary of major accomplishments and make recommendations for the following year.

🌱 BSFs attend monthly meetings held by the Director of Bilingual Education, to discuss issues, such as new testing procedures, redesignation, funding, budgets and staffing in a safe atmosphere.

🌱 BSFs maintain monthly activity logs which provide accountability.

🌱 BSFs also write a year-end report, with major accomplishments and recommendations for the following year, which forces them to think about the "big picture" at their schools.

Comments from a Bilingual Site Facilitator—Alma Saucedo

Candy McCarthy (the Director of Bilingual and Migrant Education at the time) has made the Bilingual Site Facilitator a position of value, and the administrators know it. If it weren't, they wouldn't pay attention to us. There is some amount of prestige and status attached to the job, and that helps when you're advocating for students.

Having a specific job description helps—what I have to do is spelled out and also what I am responsible for, in terms of assisting the administrator in charge of the program. The district has done a good job of giving the position to people that the administrators respect, and there's power attached to the respect. The teachers hired for the BSF job have a good handle on the type of classes that are needed, for example. The screening process for the newer site facilitators has been there, so even if someone may not have years and years of experience, he or she still is willing to learn and advocate. It is important for people like us to pass our knowledge on—and we need to pass it on to people that are teachable and don't carry hidden agendas.

Time spent upfront in this job is real important. You have to constantly be on top of these things. It's checking and checking and checking again—and even though it seems like we shouldn't have to do that, in a big system there is just a lot of potential for things to get overlooked or glossed over or somehow messed up.

To be effective in a position like this, you just have to have a strong knowledge base, both theoretically and practically. You really have to understand why you are advocating a certain position. I am constantly restating our philosophy of bilingual education. I have to say it over and over, in different ways, and to different people. We also hold the memory, the history of our efforts, in our heads—reminding staff of where we are and how far we have come, and how valuable it is, and what we would be giving up if we let some of it go.

One thing that has made a real difference is that some of us BSFs became trainers in the district, so we were always going back and talking to teachers about the practical implications of the training, and it gave us some credibility. It's an issue of the professionalism of the staff (BSFs) involved and, again, the administrators know that.

There have been several occasions when our advocacy has created some problems. It became "our" program, and not a district program. Of course, the animosity was based on the common misunderstanding that providing content for our students in Spanish is somehow "holding the kids back." The victories that I've had have been because I have put in the time doing a history of enrollment trends, for example, so we could institute Spanish Basic Skills or add ESL sections that we didn't have before. Having the numbers and the facts can help.

WORKING WITH YOUR CORE GROUP OF ADVOCATES

Once we know who the "sparks" are in our schools, it takes some retraining of ourselves and some new structures to bridge our work as individual advocates with the work of a group seeking to make the school more responsive. Schools tend to function in ways that relegate teachers to their own classrooms, working only with their own students—and teachers get very used to this. To learn to work together in a more schoolwide realm, it's helpful to deliberately set up some forums to reflect together on the paths that have led you to become advocates, to assess your school and to build a vision and "theory of action" together. This section provides several activities that will help your group of advocates come together as a supportive, focused, reflective team. Some of these activities are also helpful if you are an individual who does not (yet) have a team of others with which to work, but want to reflect and build a sense of your own vision for access and inclusion. Hopefully soon along the way, you will find others willing to travel that road with you. This goes for people in schools as well as teachers in training.

ACTIVITY 2.5
AN ADVOCATE'S JOURNEY MAP—
WHAT HELPS PEOPLE LEARN TO CARE ABOUT THE ACCESS AND INCLUSION OF OTHERS?

Reflect on the journey that has brought you, as an individual or collection of individuals, to where you are now. What has led you to become an advocate or to consider becoming one? Knowing what has shaped your path, and the paths of others you work with, is a powerful way to begin or reaffirm your direction.

Individually: Draw a map (some kind of visual portrayal) of your personal history as an educator who has become committed to and advocates for immigrant and language minority students. Include past generations if these are the people and experiences that have influenced you. Use words, phrases, colors, symbols and pictures to depict the history. As you draw the map, consider including the following:

🌱 Key events that have impacted you or your family in terms of deepened understandings of your own culture. These might include exposure to other cultures, adopting new cultures, letting go or holding onto original cultures and languages.

❧ How and when important events affected your attitudes and beliefs about the schooling of immigrant students.

❧ Key moments in your unfolding understanding of the kinds of barriers immigrant students face in school.

❧ Positive and negative influences in terms of people you have known and the work you do now to advocate for immigrant students.

❧ Key events, elements or relationships that opened your eyes, developed your commitment to another language or cultural group or to equity/access issues in education in general.

❧

In a group: Find one or two other people with whom to share your journey map. Show your maps to each other and explain the history that you drew. Consider the following questions as you share:

❧ What role do your own languages, cultures and backgrounds play in where you are now in terms of your work with immigrant students?

❧ What are some events that changed you? What moved or propelled you towards today?

❧ Can you identify what started you on your path to advocacy? A particular event, series of events or an important person?

❧ How are your journeys similar or different? What are the commonalities in terms of your work with immigrant students now and your past journeys?

❧ What keeps you going? What sustains you as an advocate?

❧

Here is an example of what one group of advocates for language minority students discovered through doing their journey maps together. They shaped their maps around the prompt: What are the encounters, external circumstances, experiences that help shape people to care, act and keep acting to improve the access and achievement of ELLs? The following represents some of their responses:

❧ Experience being out of your country, culture—travel

❧ Being part of a group with the same vision

❧ Having to take a class as part of a credential program — but it was a great teacher who really opened my eyes

❧ Reading books about immigrants

❧ Experiences of discrimination in my own life

❧ Parental values that always supported learning and valuing cultures and languages

❧ The light that goes on in my students' eyes when I try really hard and find ways to communicate even without language—it made me want to keep finding ways to reach them.

❧ Experiences as an outsider!

❧ Went to a "newcomer" conference, just seeing all those ideas; I was "sent" somewhat unwillingly, but it turned out great!

Use this list to think about what might "spark" more educators in your school or district to join in your mission to make improvements for immigrant students. Perhaps you can create some experiences that lead colleagues to more closely connect their own background and interests to the education of immigrants through, for example, summer study tours, book clubs, focused discussions, etc.

ACTIVITY 2.6
WORKING WITH CASES TO DEVELOP
A SYSTEMIC WAY OF THINKING

Using cases is one way to reflect on schooling through the lens of an advocate. Everyday, things take place in classrooms that raise questions about culture clash, inclusion and exclusion, language and racism, posing dilemmas for educators about how to respond. These are often the moments teachers take it upon themselves to try to offer the support and advocacy students need to make it through school. These moments are rich material for discussions about what a responsive school system could be. The use of cases has the potential to inform a reform effort, build stronger relationships among teachers, and increase your capacity and expertise on issues connected to racism, language and culture. The following structure is one way to begin. You can reflect on cases individually or with a group, depending on your situation.

Group discussions, if you are able to have them, offer the opportunity for faculty to share expertise and hunches. They offer the impetus for examining the comprehensiveness of your programs. And best of all, teachers come to look forward to the chance to talk to each other about their "practice" and dilemmas.

First, read through the following three cases which describe moments in the life of individual teachers in a school. Then, for each case, discuss:

❧ What is going on here for the student(s)? What are their needs? What are the conflicts/issues they are grappling with?

❦ What kind of supportive responses might be possible by an individual teacher or counselor or administrator? What feels appropriate?

❦ Now imagine what would need to be in place in a school (programs, supports, policies, etc.) to respond really comprehensively? To lessen the conflict or meet the need?

Case #1:

One of your favorite students is a very bright young woman named Iris. She emigrated from Mexico just four years ago and is already fluent in English and near the top of her class academically. Iris loves Math and dreams of being a teacher someday. Last year, she missed almost three months of school when her family returned to their village in Mexico upon the death of her grandmother. She worked very hard to make up the work and has managed to catch up sufficiently over the summer to be placed in your Calculus class. Now, just three months into her senior year, you have noticed that she is, again, missing a great deal of school. You talk to her after class one day and ask what's happening. Iris breaks into tears and tells you that her mother has remained in Mexico to take care of her grandfather, and that Iris is largely in charge of her two younger siblings who returned with her to the U.S. to continue their schooling. The younger sister has been ill and Iris has had to stay home to take care of her. Iris' father is living with them but works double shifts and relies on Iris to care for the younger children. She informs you that she will be dropping out of school. She further begs you not to let anyone know, because her father is undocumented and she is fearful that they will call him in and he will be discovered, detained and deported.

Case #2:

You are a World Literature teacher, popular with many students of color because you have taken care to include literature from their own cultures and nations in your class, you hold high expectations for your students and they view you as someone who recognizes and respects who they are. You have been concerned over the past few years by increasing ethnic separation and hostilities among students on the school campus, including fights, taunts and increased gang affiliation. After school one day, a group of four Korean immigrant students approach you in your room. They ask if you are willing to sponsor them in starting a new Korean Club on campus. You are hesitant, wondering if this will just exacerbate problems. The students hand you a carefully worked-over statement in support of their proposal for the club. It begins with the following preamble:

"We left our native homeland and came to this mighty land with great ambitions and hopes that we might better our futures. What we expected and hoped for seems far distant. All are now being slowly tormented by the frustrations and hostility which this new land has to offer. Yes, discrimination, racism and insult, our most fierce enemy,

whom we battle every day in our lives. Our unexplainable and unexpressable thoughts and feelings are slowly building up until they are ready to explode any minute. If others only could, only would, understand us. Together we can support each other in building towards our dreams."

They look to you for support. What do you do?

Case #3:

You are a high-school American History teacher. You love your subject and have a packed, fast-paced curriculum. In the past few years, increasing numbers of immigrants have entered the school district. It seems to you that more and more students are being placed in your class without the English skills to really participate. Last year, you tried pairing the two Spanish-speaking girls who seemed to have trouble with English with another student who was fluent in both languages. This didn't work as well as you had hoped because the bilingual student seemed either reluctant to help or simply did not have the teaching skills to really explain and work with the two students with less English ability. You felt it was important to maintain the pace and standard of the class, but felt badly as the two girls fell further and further behind. You ended up giving one a D and the other an F. This has been weighing on you ever since.

At the beginning of this semester, you assessed the situation and with relief noted that only one student seemed to lack the English skills to keep up. This student, a Cambodian girl named Pao, sits quietly in class. Often you can't tell whether she understands what you're saying or even if she's listening. You have checked with her counselor who tells you that the student is correctly placed in your class, that she has finished the ESL sequence of courses. No one else in the class speaks her language and you have tried several times to converse with her informally but you have trouble understanding her and she seems very shy. You haven't wanted to put her on the spot so you haven't called on her in class. By the fourth week of class, it is apparent that she is not keeping up. You don't want to repeat what happened last semester when the class just left the LEP students behind, but you also don't want to slow things down. And frankly, you're not sure what to do to communicate with Pao.

After you have discussed several cases using the introductory questions as a guide, you might want to start allocating some portion of your regular meetings to presenting and discussing cases from your own lives in the school. Notice cases that lead you to feel called upon to try to respond personally to some student beyond the instructional needs in your classroom. Notice when you feel torn, conflicted or unsure about what kind of response you can or should make. Use these moments as cases to share with your colleagues or to reflect upon on your own.

Based upon a set of cases, you can begin to assess whether your school has the comprehensive program you need. Below is a sample assessment around English Language Learners' needs.

SAMPLE ASSESSMENT OF PROGRAMS

Student Need	*Programs We'd Ideally Have in Place*	*Do We Have This at Our School? (yes/no)*
Trauma from war experiences	• Staff training in recognizing trauma • Referral sources for bilingual counseling • Curriculum to help students understand the wars	
Much movement back and forth between Mexico and U.S.—gaps in schooling as a result	• Independent study • Flexible and partial credit systems • Accelerated and catch-up options for missed curriculum • School-year calendar where semester ends prior to the holidays	
Culture shock	• Orientation materials in primary language • Buddy systems • Staff who can speak the languages of our students and families • A newcomer program	
Hostility from peers	• Bottom-line policies about non-harassment • Anti-prejudice curriculum for all students • Emphasis on the positives of bilingualism • Policies to facilitate involvement of immigrants in extracurricular and sports activities at school	
Underschooled students	• Mechanisms to accelerate and catch up • Assessment that focuses on prior schooling and primary language literacy • Special curriculum for underschooled students	

(Developed by Laurie Olsen in collaboration with Catherine Minicucci of Minicucci Associates, 1992.)

ACTIVITY 2.7
ASSESSING OUR SCHOOL—
HOW SUPPORTIVE AND PREPARED IS OUR SCHOOL TO ADVOCATE FOR ACCESS AND INCLUSION?

One thing advocates can do together is assess their school in light of the needs of immigrant students. The assessment below is one tool for examining how prepared and supportive your school structure and climate is for the kind of advocacy that needs to occur to bring about the inclusion and achievement of English Language Learners.

Consider each of these elements in terms of how close or far your school is from having the conditions that support systems of advocacy. Use the center column to describe what you actually see in your school and to note your assessment. Each person should do his or her own rating first—and then compare notes in a general discussion with the group. Based on this, consider what might be your highest priorities for building a more supportive climate and structure of advocacy.

RESPONSIVE SCHOOLS CREATE AND EMBRACE SYSTEMS OF ADVOCACY

Not Supportive/Not Prepared	Comments/Evidence	Supportive and Prepared
• There is no written or articulated mission statement or policy that explicitly states the school's goal and commitment to access and achievement of LEP students.		• The school has a formal mission or goal statement articulating its commitment to providing access to LEP students and programs leading to high standards, and articulating its program philosophy.
• There is little recognition or acknowledgment throughout the school that access for LEP students is an issue to be addressed and monitored, or that special services might be needed in order to ensure that language is not a barrier to reaching high standards.		• There is overall recognition and acknowledgment in the school that access must be provided and that LEP students require special services to ensure they receive access and attain to high standards.

Not Supportive/Not Prepared	Comments/Evidence	Supportive and Prepared
• Leadership is silent on the issues of LEP student access and achievement; or leadership is openly resistant or hostile to building a program of services that explicitly addresses the needs of LEP students.		• The leadership of our school makes it known that addressing the needs of LEP students is a responsibility of the whole school, is important, and is key to our overall mission.
• There are no forums in which people who share a concern about LEP students come together regularly to share concerns, identify policy issues, etc.		• There are regular forums in which LEP advocates come together for purposes of sharing concerns, identifying policy issues, or reviewing data.
• No one takes primary responsibility for monitoring individual assessment and placement of LEP students, or for reviewing structural features that might impede access.		• The site has a designated person with responsibility for monitoring individual assessment and placement of all LEP students and for reviewing course assignments, class rosters, and master scheduling to ensure access to content.
• There are no designated, knowledgeable counselors or advisors who are available to advocate for students or monitor their progress.		• There are designated LEP counselors/advisors who follow LEP students through school, who have knowledge of LEP student issues and barriers to access, work to ensure smooth transitions through school, and monitor progress.
• Issues of LEP students are never or seldom mentioned, and the program is seldom discussed in the school.		• There is open dialogue and discussion about our school's program for and responses to improving the access and achievement of LEP students.

Not Supportive/Not Prepared	Comments/Evidence	Supportive and Prepared
• I feel very isolated and alone at my school as a person who cares about building a culture and society that is inclusive and welcoming of LEP and immigrant students.		• When there are hard times in the effort to build programs or ensure a welcoming and inclusive culture for LEP and immigrant students, there is a core of people at our school that I can turn to who I know share my concerns.
• It is totally haphazard whether and how LEP students get information about requirements, how the school works, and who to go to for what.		• Our school prints information about how the school works, requirements, who to go to for what, etc. in the home languages of our students, and we have bilingual staff with designated responsibility for providing this information to LEP students.
• It's just happenstance whether we find out about conferences or research about LEP student issues.		• There is a designated bulletin board and we receive regular announcements in our boxes about conferences and professional development opportunities related to addressing the needs of LEP students; there is a professional development library, including articles and materials on bilingual programs and LEP student issues at our school.

BUILDING A VISION

What keeps people going? Often, it is our deeply held values, the things we care about and believe in strongly. It is important to be in touch with this passion—to give us energy in hard moments and to keep us focused. For advocates, the presence, support and partnership of others who share those values play an enormous role in keeping us going.

It is the last afternoon of California Tomorrow's training institute "Creating Access: Building Immigrant Responsive Schools" for school teams and their outside change partners. Everyone is feeling the weight of the responsibility of returning to their schools to try to make their ambitious change plans real. We ask everyone to form one large circle around the room, and, in the final moments of our week together, to hold in their hearts the image of a student or young person for whom they yearn to change schools. We then ask each to simply speak the names out loud, one by one. It is a powerful recitation. "Pedro," "Angie," "Indira," "Jose," "Joshua," "Sundance," "Maria"...In the end, our eyes filled with tears and our minds firmly fixed on the young people who are the reason we do this work, we return to our schools.

ACTIVITY 2.8
GETTING IN TOUCH WITH AND
SHARING THE REASONS YOU ARE AN ADVOCATE

You can do this activity on your own, but it is more powerful as part of a group experience. Each person in the group should think about one student for whom the school experience was painful, exclusionary or inadequate. This young person should be someone you care about. If your group has more than five people, form trios to share your stories. If there are less than five people, take turns sharing the stories with the whole group. After this sharing, go around in a circle and speak the names of the young people out loud.

You may also wish to complete the following sentences, speaking out loud to each other.

❧ The value I care most about that pushes me to be an advocate for immigrant students is...

❧ The core reason I put my time and my heart into trying to change our school is that I care about...

Caring about making a change is not the same thing as understanding what it is you are trying to create. A shared vision develops over time—through working together and developing a concrete set of programs and approaches that speak to the concerns and values you hold. But reflections on vision also need to be part of the initial steps you take together. You need to try to articulate as best you can the vision of what it is you are striving to create. A group of people can all care about making a school a better place—but may hold very different values and visions of what that would ultimately look like.

ACTIVITY 2.9
WHAT IS OUR VISION?

Consider the following five statements:

1. Language is a vehicle for access to an education. Not being able to speak the language used in schools for instruction is, therefore, a barrier to an education, and children in this country have a right to an education.

2. A child's mother tongue is part of who they are. The right to learn to speak and write in one's mother tongue, to have that language incorporated into one's schooling, to make the choice about how and when one uses it, is a basic human right.

3. A common language is a necessary thing for national unity. Language diversity is a problem that poses an internal threat to a nation, a people and a culture.

4. Languages are resources. A child's home language is a resource to be developed, protected and conserved. All children should be able to become fully bilingual and biliterate—as a personal resource in their lives, and as a societal resource.

5. Language is an essential aspect of identity—a symbol and marker of membership in a culture. To ask children to not use their home language or to adopt a new language is the same as asking them to deny their identity or to take on a new one.

Each person in your group should try to choose one statement or orientation that most closely relates to his or her vision and understanding about why schools need to address language issues for LEP students. Share with each other why you chose the one you did.

Then, together, think about what each statement implies in terms of what a school unified around that understanding would need to be like: If you really believe this goal statement is what you are about, what would it look like in a school designed to reach that goal?

If you all agree on a goal statement, the work becomes easier. If you have some disagreement, spend time inviting each other to say more about why you selected the statement you did, and give yourselves the task of answering: What aspects of that goal statement could I get behind?

This activity is one way to begin substantive discussions of vision. However your group goes about it, and whatever direction you discover, remember that vision work is what gives you the big picture that shapes what you actually seek to put in place. The job of actually defining what those programs, supports and practices are that will operationalize your vision takes more work. And it's important to keep revisiting your vision, discussing and reshaping it together over time.

GETTING BRAVE AND SUPPORTING EACH OTHER

If a school is to change, a strong core of advocates must stay connected to each other and work together. This is crucial because the more eyes, hearts and minds focused on the task, the more comprehensive and powerful the plan can be. The more connected and committed people you have, the greater your reach across the school and the fuller your capacity to actually implement changes.

Let's face it—being an advocate for immigrant students ain't easy. And that's why you need a group of advocates to share your experiences with, to find support in a world where you're often seen as too radical, too political, too outspoken, or just "too much" for those who don't see the problems you see. It helps to have others to talk with about the kind of reactions you get when you try speaking out, what it feels like to speak out and what keeps you going.

As you face the courageous task of talking to your colleagues who may not agree with you about the need to respond to LEP students, as you begin to tackle schoolwide forums and speak out more publicly, you need to construct for yourselves the kind of support that you need. Is it someone to check in with right afterwards? Someone to practice with beforehand? Is it someone to be there with you as a partner or as a back-up in case you need help? Is it someone who can help you strategize what to do when that person who always seems to keep everything from going forward starts his routine? Is it a list of people to call when a need arises?

Each of us needs and fears different things. We have better or worse relationships with key people throughout the school and have different speaking, persuasive and writing skills. As a group, do an inventory and develop some shared understanding of what it will take to provide a strong supportive "home base" for your work using Activity 2.10.

ACTIVITY 2.10
INVENTORYING OUR COLLECTIVE STRENGTHS

Begin with each person jotting down some notes on a piece of paper about what they consider their own weaknesses and strengths for being an advocate and for bringing about change in school. You should also note what you need from the others in order to keep going and be effective. Each person should place their name on the top of their sheet of paper and then place them face up on the table.

Example: Ann Marie

What are the strengths I bring to our advocacy work?
—Passion
—I don't give up
—I am a good writer
—I know how to use data
—I'm a fast typist and can do PowerPoint if we ever need to do presentations

What are my weaknesses?
—Find it hard to talk to people who are angry and hostile
—Have a hard time speaking in public

What do I need?
—Someone to practice with if I have to speak in public
—Help me strategize before I have to talk to someone who is scary to me

Everyone is invited to walk around and add "strengths" to one another's lists, filling out the profiles of the members of the group. They should note what others need and think about how they might be able to provide it. Write a little note next to a "need" that you think you can help with. As a group, read all of the "strengths" aloud. This list should later be typed up as a resource for each person to keep reminding them who has what skills, strengths and things to bring to the change effort. Each person should also keep their own sheet.

ACTIVITY 2.11
SHARING THE FEELINGS OF BEING AN ADVOCATE

This tool is for sharing your feelings about being an advocate. First, in a group, brainstorm a web or a list of the hard parts of being an advocate in your school. Add to the list everything you can think of that generates resistance, hostility or silence from others—and what it feels like when that happens. Then generate a list of what makes you feel stronger, more able to move forward—and what that feels like to you.

Use these lists as the foundation for a discussion about the nature of the struggle in your school over responding to the needs of immigrant students. And use it to talk about the kinds of support you may need from each other now and in the future.

One teacher we've worked with commented on dealing with what it's like to try and change a school and include others in your efforts:

"We spend too much time worrying about those people who are not doing the work, who are not on track. You do have to be aware of the people who are out to bring you down, but you need to build by offering something to the rest of the staff. Give them something— money, resources. We have to characterize the people who are holding us back in the way they need to be characterized, then move on and support the people who are very positive. And remember that the fence-sitters will move if things are more interesting on our side of the fence."

STRUCTURING TIME TOGETHER

All of the activities proposed in this book take time to plan and carry out. Changing a school takes time. One of the crucial elements of a successful change process is that advocates find ways to create the space and time to be together.

When your task is legitimated by the principal of the school, finding time can be easier to arrange. Some schools structure in some form of collaborative planning time for staff, some of which could possibly be devoted to focusing on immigrant and LEP student issues. It may be, for example, the second Wednesday of each month during "banking time." Release time, afterschool or Saturday stipends may be provided out of special funding to cover planning time; in California, for example, advocates for LEP students might be able to use EIA-LEP or Title VII funds to cover this.

Here are three examples of how schools have managed to find the time and space to work together to focus on LEP students:

Glendale Unified School District: The district used the opportunity of a Title VII systemwide "professional development" grant to bring together teams from each school site to examine the data about their LEP students, discuss the needs of their LEP students, and design what kind of professional activities would respond to those needs. This formed the basis of a three-year professional development emphasis in the district. Yearly, school teams are brought back together to reflect upon and assess the activities and their impacts—looking again at student data, and exploring deeper levels of whether and how professional development is impacting practice. These special Title VII project resources pay for substitutes to enable the team to take a day together now and then. The grant also provides release time and stipends for teacher inquiry groups, key policy dialogues about program change, and other related efforts to plan and develop the capacity-building efforts.

Salinas Union High School District: At Alisal High School, the teachers who formed a Working Group on Race, Language and Culture were not formally convened by the school and did not have access to school or district resources to buy the time needed to engage together in their work. The teachers also didn't want to take time out of their classrooms unless absolutely necessary. To carve the time they needed together, the group opted for weekly lunchtime meetings for check-ins and connection, once-a-semester weekend retreats for more intensive planning, bimonthly longer meetings after school, and occasional days out of their own classrooms to observe the classrooms of their peers or to "shadow" students (please see Chapter Five on shadowing techniques). While the time was voluntary, it was planned in a way that seemed workable to their needs.

Hayward Unified School District: Hayward high schools have weekly "collaboration time" during an extended Wednesday schedule. Three times a month, these are devoted to department-related meetings—but once a month, special task forces, etc., can meet. During this once-a-month collaboration time, teachers concerned about the program for English Language Learners instituted regular meetings bringing together all teachers of bilingual and sheltered classes and ESL teachers. These became the "on-site" mechanisms for planning and advocacy. But there is more. In an effort to build more of a district-wide movement, and in response to the relative isolation advocates felt within each comprehensive high school, they created a "cross-site" structure. By subject area, sheltered content teachers, ESL teachers and bilingual teachers meet across schools to discuss policies in the district that impact LEP students, to share lesson plans and instructional strategies, and to look together at data and research. These bimonthly meetings are covered by staff development funds.

FINDING THE TIME

Instead of simply giving up or assuming that no time can be found for advocates to work together, take a moment to think about what might work. There may be time, or ways of paying for time, that you have not realized. Sit down with your group of advocates and talk about:

- Is there collaboration time available that is formally built into the schedule? Can we use this time for our group to get together?

- Can a portion of department meetings be used for advocacy?

- Is there professional development money at the discretion of the sites, some of which could be used for the time it takes to assess, reflect and plan activities for immigrant students?

- How possible is it to get substitutes in our school to enable teachers release time?

- How willing are we as a group to use release time as the format?

- How willing are we as a group to use afterschool hours?

- How willing are we as a group to use Saturdays?

- How essential is a stipend for our group if we need to use afterschool or Saturday hours?

- Might we be able to access any federal funds or other specially targeted funding for this purpose?

Chapter Six offers an activity, "Plotting the Use of Time at Your School," on page 364.

DEVELOPING A THEORY OF ACTION

Once you have a sense of your vision and the support you can count on in your school, it helps to take the time to understand your theory of action (either collectively or on your own). A theory of action is a sequence of linked actions and reactions that are in the minds of people when they go about any kind of intervention or school-change process. It is the "if we do this, it'll shift this, which will lead to this" kind of thinking that shapes the actions you take. However, these theories of action often remain unspoken. Pushing yourself to articulate your theories of action may help you see faulty links in the chain or help you understand the causal links you expect to work for you. Being able to articulate it to yourself also makes it easier to explain it to others and possibly convince them that your plan is workable. As one teacher commented, "How can you pick a solution if you don't talk about the problem? We've never identified what the wound is, so how can we pick a Band-Aid?"

A theory of action goes something like this (in a simple form):

This problem is of concern...

We think if we do x, y and z...

It will result in these changes in how we go about doing things in school...

With this kind of student achievement outcome...

Sometimes the theory of action originates when an achievement goal is stated (e.g., we want to improve immigrant students' reading comprehension). The task, then, is to think through why you want that to happen and what has to change to get you there. Sometimes the theory of action starts with an idea people want to put in place or a change they'd like (e.g., let's do cooperative learning), and you have to push yourself to first state the problem you're trying to address and the goal you're trying to achieve. Sometimes the theory of action starts with the articulation of a problem (e.g., our students aren't reading) and you have to push to outline what activities might address that problem and what you are trying to achieve.

Example of a theory of action:

Problem: Our Hmong students are doing really badly in reading.

What do we think is the cause of this? What result do we want to see?

Result we want: We all agree we want to improve reading comprehension because we believe that is why they are doing really badly at reading.

What has to happen if you're going to improve reading comprehension?

Here, the group comes up with **four theories or interventions:**

- ☛ I think we need to improve home support for literacy.

☛ No, I think the issue is that we aren't really teaching reading comprehension or engagement with the text—so I think we need to improve our teaching.

☛ Well, I think the real issue is that the district has stuck us with a lousy curriculum series.

☛ We've got the strategies, but the kids just aren't motivated. They aren't engaged at all. They aren't interested. They watch too much TV.

We have four theories here. One is that reading comprehension requires a certain home environment and support that you think your students aren't getting. Another is that teaching strategies aren't adequate for teaching reading comprehension, a third is that the curriculum itself is at fault. The fourth is that the problem is student motivation, tied up in the fact that they watch too much TV. If you follow the first theory, you'd focus on family literacy or parent involvement. If you follow the second theory, you'd focus on professional development for teachers. The third leads us to a policy issue with the district. The fourth could end up having us searching for more interesting materials, engaging in motivational campaigns, or trying to develop policies about agreements with parents about how much TV our students should watch.

Strategy	*Result*	*Student Achievement Outcome*
Institute a family literacy project	More family support for literacy	Improved reading comprehension
Professional development	Build teacher capacity	Improved reading comprehension
Circulate petitions, get on district curriculum, council, etc.	New district policy	Improved reading comprehension
Develop agreements with parents about TV	Cut down children's time watching TV	Improved reading comprehension

But perhaps there's a problem with how you've envisioned the link between the challenge and the outcome—students may be doing poorly on tests not because they aren't comprehending what they read. Instead, it might be because of the time pressure on the tests. Or perhaps the strategies are not the most effective ones—maybe the best strategy might be to focus on improving motivation to read, not reading comprehension per se.

ACTIVITY 2.12
CONSTRUCT YOUR THEORIES OF ACTION

To articulate the links, engage in dialogue or reflection about different theories and consider a full range of options involves both constructing and questioning your theories of action. Your work is to push for deeper thinking and clear articulation of this theory of action, so that the actions you or your advocacy group take have the greatest potential for producing the outcome.

Once your group has determined some priority areas or concerns you want to focus on, be sure you spend some time constructing your theory of action. What is the problem? What are the outcomes you want to see? What sets of activities will change how you go about things such that the outcomes will be likely?

You can begin by filling in the chart below on your own or with others:

Problem or Challenge:	Activities:	Result:	Outcome:
This problem is of concern…	*We think if we do…*	*It will result in these changes in how we go about doing things in school…*	*With this kind of student achievement outcome…*

Reflect and assess, with your group or on your own, to probe each link in your chain of action.

☛ Is the analysis about why the challenge exists the right analysis?

☛ Is this the challenge area we most want to focus on?

☛ Are these the right activities to do? How will we know?

☛ Will these activities really lead to the desired outcomes?

☛ How will we know if we need to pursue other activities to get the impact we want?

It's good to revisit your theories of action over time as well. Whenever you find yourselves "stuck" or unsure whether you are doing the right thing, ask yourselves if the problem is still the right problem. If it is, are you actually doing the activities? If so, are they leading to the results you had hoped for?

(Based on the ideas of Kristin Geiser, Bay Area Coalition of Essential Schools.)

WORKING TO MAKE CHANGE AT YOUR SCHOOL

The activities in the previous section focused on ways to work with a group of advocates to build a home base for doing systemic advocacy. In this section, we explore ways you and your group of advocates can work with your particular schools to make change. To advocate systemically and effectively, you need an understanding of how hard change can be and how important diplomacy and strategic thinking are in the highly politicized contexts of most schools. You also need to know how to keep your work from being marginalized, to connect with others and to help others connect with your goals.

Any change is hard to pull off and hard for people to face. Yet the task of an advocate is to help other people make changes in their practice and often in their understanding and attitudes. Thinking clearly and thoughtfully about change is a critical first step. Change is particularly difficult for people when they feel coerced or pressured to make change, unsure of why they are supposed to change, or unclear on how to go about making a change.

There are added complexities to the kinds of changes advocates for English Language Learners must work for; these are issues about which you can bet there will be no consensus. There is still widespread ignorance

Colored pencil by Vay Duong, a high school student from Vietnam

among educators about the extent of the barriers to access for language minority students. There is misunderstanding and disagreement about how Limited English Proficient students learn. And resentment of immigrants, racism and classism still play out in our schools in subtle—and not so subtle—ways. The members of a school community hold different visions about the roles schools should play in addressing the specific needs of groups of students. For an advocate, to speak out for adding a course or any "extra" support for immigrant students means entry into a political arena. Being an advocate often means educating colleagues about the needs of immigrant students, grappling with what are often low expectations or hostile feelings towards the young people. It sometimes means insisting that the school do what is legally required and educationally indicated—whether or not everyone agrees that they want to make that change.

It is helpful to think, then, about what approaches and supports might be most productive as you seek to push the system and other teachers to change. The following activity is one way for you to reflect on the difficulties of change and ways different people, and yourself, react to change.

ACTIVITY 2.13
CONSIDERING REACTIONS TO CHANGE

Think about some changes you've gone through in your own experiences in schools. Think of one that was imposed from above or from outside—a change you would not have chosen on your own. Then think of a change that you yourself took on because you felt it was important. Spend some time analyzing each of these situations:

	An Imposed Change	*A Self-Selected Change*
What feelings did you have when you first encountered this need/demand for change?		
What forms of resistance were you aware of in yourself?		
What kept you moving to implement the change?		
What helped you?		

If we are to help our school colleagues develop more responsiveness to immigrant students, we have to think hard about what helps and hinders awareness, compassion and responsiveness for the specific students we strive to serve better. In learning about the challenges immigrant students face—the language barriers, the subtle forms of racism, the tracking, the discouragements, the lack of support, the differences in home and school cultures—educators can and do change. Take some time to think together about what you know will help open people up to the needs of the students you advocate for. Some of the activities in Chapter Five may be helpful in this endeavor.

BE DIPLOMATIC

Formal or unofficial advocacy often brings a person into conflict with others in the school who have the power to make changes and open doors needed to provide full access. For this reason, advocates need to hone the skills of diplomacy, build relationships with others in the school, know when to push and when to stop. It is not an easy dance, as another example from *Made In America* (1997) illustrates:

> In Lisa O'Malley's first year of teaching, she taught a class called ESL Skills. Two of her students seemed to know English well, and she considered them brilliant. She was also teaching a tenth-grade accelerated class and thinking these two students could easily do the work of an accelerated tenth-grade class. O'Malley went to the English Department Chair, saying, "I have a student and her brother who are very intelligent, write very well and need to be in an accelerated class." But she was faced with a policy which defined the progression out of ESL into skills-level classes first, followed by and regular level and then into accelerated. O'Malley argued, "They could die in the system before they make it to accelerated." Eduardo, the brother, was already a 12th grader, so she decided there was little hope for him. But O'Malley was angry. The Department Chair hadn't been willing to look at any of Luciana's writing samples as proof of the girl's abilities; she had simply insisted it was a matter of cut-and-dry policy. As she explains: "I went back to the department chair, to insist she look at the writing. But she still didn't budge. I offered to put Luciana in my own 10th-grade accelerated class. The answer was to go to the principal. Two days later, my Department Chair found me and said, "I've reconsidered and I think you're right. You can go ahead and put both kids into your 10th-grade accelerated class." I was mad. It wasn't right for Eduardo as a 12th-grader to be put in a 10th-grade class, but it was at least better than staying in a 10th-grade Skills class. I decided to take it a little battle at a time and not create a war we wouldn't win."

Choosing your battles and being diplomatic are part of effective advocacy. But to do so, you need a solid understanding of the politics at your school, some awareness of where the "landmines" are, where the battle lines are drawn, where faculty are open to new ways of thinking about their students. The following section provides tools for reflecting on your school's politics and structure.

WORK WITH THE POLITICS AND STRUCTURE OF YOUR SCHOOL

Every school has a unique history and a culture—a story, a path it has forged with regard to serving immigrant students. And these histories shape how responsive they are to the students themselves and to making changes to better serve those students. A teacher working in one school may be open to trying new instructional approaches to better meet the needs of her Latino students. That same teacher in another school might feel resistant to any inference that she needs to adopt some different approaches. She might be insulted if someone suggests she consider getting some training. One school, still smarting from a poor compliance review that resulted in a lot of public blame, may react with hostility if a new teacher tries to point out that English Language Learners aren't being adequately served, whereas another school might greet such a comment with open arms. Some schools support risk-taking and open examination of problems and challenges—others may discourage it.

One school may have a history of innovation, of supporting new programs, a culture of collaboration among the faculty. Another with the same student population may be characterized by teachers and administrators closing their doors in an act of resistance to change. These histories are important for advocates to know, understand and build from. What will work in your school will be strategies designed with full knowledge of the culture in which you work, and how that culture came to be.

Here are three key activities to encourage educators to examine together the history of their school in responding to groups of marginalized students. Such activities are especially useful when they set up participants for thinking about the next steps.

ACTIVITY 2.14
MAPPING OUR SCHOOL'S HISTORY

Take a large piece of wall-chart paper and colored pens. Your task is to map your school's journey. You can do these maps individually or in small groups and then share them with each other, or create the map together as one person draws what others are describing.

Draw a depiction of your school's history and journey (from as far back as there is memory in your group) in serving and building programs for immigrant students. Note major events or eras (e.g., the year we opened a newcomer center, the year we began serving a new neighborhood, the year the other high school closed, etc.). Note changes in the program or curriculum. Note when key people who've had an impact on services for these students came or left the school.

If your group is large enough and there are people present who entered the school in different eras, you may want to do mini fishbowls, inviting the group with the longest history to talk about how the school "felt" and how it dealt with the challenges of serving immigrant students in the early years. Then invite a group who arrived midstream to talk about what it felt like entering the school and what kinds of supports and challenges they saw. Then ask new teachers to talk about what they have seen and felt.

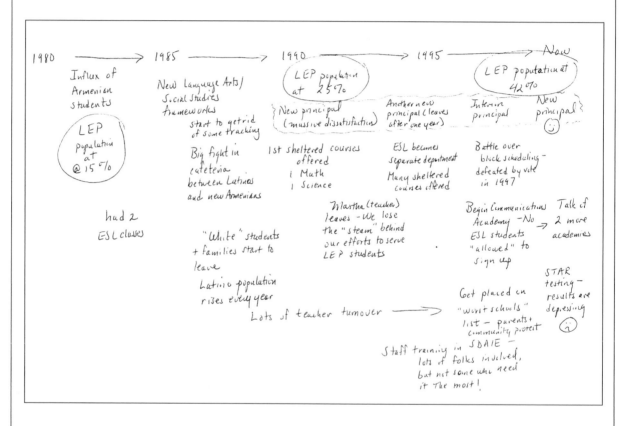

Once you have reviewed the history, depict where you are now and provide some symbolic or metaphorical graphic for how completely you are providing access and reaching achievement for immigrant students. Indicate how far you feel you have to go. What questions are you asking and what dilemmas and challenges are major right now?

Then discuss: What does our history tell us about tolerance for change in our school? About the pace of change? About the nature of change?

This activity will give people a sense of their own history, and a reassuring view that things change, that they are a part of the change and they can help shape the future.

There are two other kind of maps a group of advocates should use to become "smart" about how to go about crafting the most productive and appropriate strategies of change for their school. These encourage you to spend some time reflecting on the current social/sociological "lay of the land" and the politics of the school.

ACTIVITY 2.15
OUR SCHOOL'S SOCIAL/POLITICAL MAP OF REFORM

Your focus as an advocate may be on making schools more responsive to the needs of immigrant students. But most likely, this isn't the only change effort occurring in your school. There may be some teachers talking about instituting voluntary free reading across the school. There may be others interested in building a computer lab. There are lots of reform ideas. To gain a focus on a particular group of students who are not being well-served, you have to have a good sense of who is talking about what, how much energy is being expended on what kinds of change efforts, and how any of these relate (if at all) to your group of students. This mapping activity helps you lay out your school's social/political map of reform.

As a team, draw a depiction of the different reform ideas and efforts at your school. If it's a major thrust, make that idea big on your map. If it's a little idea of a few people and not much attention is focused on it, draw it on the margins, or make it small. Label each idea in terms of the kind of reform it is. Be sure the map includes all the reform ideas and changes being talked about in the school.

Add to your map any other major topics absorbing the faculty (it may the union contract, or the search for a new superintendent, or gossip about an affair between two district administrators), whether or not they have anything to do with reform. What do educators talk to each other about on your campus?

Once the map is drawn, discuss the following issues:

❧ What would each group need, what would appeal to them as a way of engaging them in caring about and getting active on the achievement problem you're concerned about?

❧ How might your work fit in with the other major planning and change efforts in the school?

❧ Which of those reform/change efforts hold the highest stakes for immigrant students? (Either because they would result in blocking access and widening the gap or because they could potentially result in truly improved access and achievement.)

ACTIVITY 2.16
OUR SCHOOL'S STRUGGLE MAPS

The purpose of this activity is to analyze together the kind of support and resistance there is in the school community for developing strong programs for immigrant students. It will stimulate dialogue about the political and social dynamics of the school in terms of serving these students.

As a school team, draw a picture or a "social/political map" of a major struggle you went through in the past or are going through now related to serving English Language Learners. What has been difficult for the school community to focus on? Has it been difficult to implement certain new support or instructional programs?

❧ What is the issue that is being fought over or creating tension?

❧ Who is where in this struggle? Include on your map or drawing the different "groups" or "camps" and their positions. Include those who may not be part of it at all because they choose to stay distant or are not aware, as well as those who are very involved. You may want to do this with actual names, or with general names (e.g., the veteran teachers in the English Department, or the union leadership, or the group of new teachers, etc.).

❧ What does the struggle look like and sound like? What are the typical actions, reactions, and comments (in the open and behind closed doors) that comprise the dialogue or argument?

❧ What is the relationship between the way people and groups have aligned on this issue and the major power groups in the school? Who in this struggle has power (formal or informal) in general in the school?

❧ Where would you each place yourselves on the map?

After studying your map, now come up with two metaphors or themes that describe the current dynamic within the school community related to improving and building the program for immigrant students.

SAMPLE SCHOOL STRUGGLE MAP

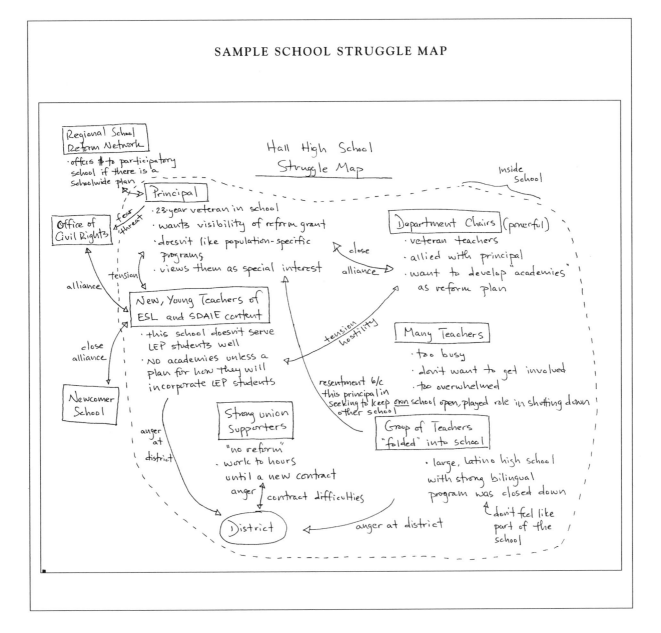

PUTTING THE MAPS TOGETHER

Putting all the reflections from your maps together, see if, as a group, you can come to some summary description of your school. What can be said about the school's history serving immigrant students, its reform energy and how serving these students falls within that? Who are your current and potential allies? What is the nature of how the struggle over serving immigrant students plays out? How does the struggle impact the vision of where you are trying to go?

Make for yourselves a list of reminders: landmines to avoid, strengths to build upon, good moments to evoke to give people a sense of hope, movement and pride. Such a list is the bedrock for developing a shared sense of vision about how you want to go about changing your school.

Here is one example of what a group of advocates focusing on LEP students came up with about their school:

🍃 Change at our school works best if we work through departments.

🍃 The bad feelings that still exist since Jack instituted the lawsuit against us mean that we probably shouldn't invoke the law as a threat unless we really, really have to.

🍃 People should be reminded that it's really only been a short time (just seven years) since Armenians started arriving here, and that we've made a lot of progress in building a program since then. We should feel good about that.

🍃 We've really done a lot in the past ten years. Now we have a Resource Teacher, we have ESL rubrics that our own teachers developed, we have a whole lot more courses offered by sheltered teachers. When we bring up the work still to be done, we should acknowledge that good work.

🍃 We keep getting caught in that cycle where the resentment about ESL classes having 18 students and other English classes having 24 gets in the way of any effort to call for attention to the needs of LEP students. We need to be creative about how to avoid getting caught in that anymore.

CREATING VISIBILITY AND LEGITIMACY— PREVENTING MARGINALIZATION

Maria Rodriguez, Bilingual Coordinator for Bayview Schools, had been my original contact leading to doing research at Madison High School. It was her work as an advocate for immigrant student issues that first drew my attention to this community almost ten years before. And, it was Maria who arranged for my lunch meeting with George Pereira, principal of Madison High School, to discuss the study I wanted to do of the school. She arranged the meeting as an off-campus lunch in a restaurant in downtown Bayview.

I approached the lunch nervously and was anxious to show that I had done my homework, and that my reasons for wanting to study Madison were based in an understanding of the student population at the school. I arrived early with a file full of demographic statistics about the community. Pereira arrived a little late to the lunch, a big smile, a warm handshake, a hug for Maria. He and Maria began what I came later to understand was the ritual greetings of high school principals: a conversation about what happened at the last Cabinet meeting, references to the latest political upheavals in the district, an anecdote about some frantic or crazy episode at the school site that morning that almost threatened to make him unable to get away from the school and was the cause of being slightly late. When Maria got up to go to the rest room, I used the opportunity of the break in their conversation to begin my explanation of why I wanted to study Madison High. In the first few minutes of this, I mentioned the swift and astounding growth of immigrant and limited-English-speaking students at the school to now being 24%—almost one in four. He seemed surprised. "You must be wrong. The numbers are off. We have a lot of diversity, but your numbers are wrong. We've had some growth, but it's nowhere near that high. It's more like maybe 12 or 15%."

I was embarrassed that I had my numbers wrong, but the conversation continued. The lunch was pleasant, Pereira was thoroughly agreeable about my doing the research. He liked the idea that someone was interested in the school and might write a book about it. By the end of the lunch we agreed that I would do research at the school over the next two years.

Later that day when I got home, I checked my files. Yes, I had recorded 24% LEP students in my notes. I called the Newcomer School to check the accuracy. They confirmed the 24%. I called Maria to debrief the lunch, and told her of the confusion over the percent of LEP students. "George should know that. For years the Language Census numbers have been shared with all the principals in the district. It just doesn't register."

I came to look back on that first lunch as an early warning and preview of the force with which the reality of population change is contested and resisted in this community, and the subtle efforts to maintain or reduce the invisibility of immigrant students as a point of struggle.

—From *Made in America: Immigrant Students in Our Public Schools* (1997)

There are some people on every school campus who just don't "see" that a certain group of students is there, don't consider them a significant enough part of the student body to pay much attention, and don't understand that there are needs that must be responded to across the school. They regard folks who are advocating for services and changes related to serving these students as a small special interest group, a fringe, that can be ignored, people making "much ado about nothing." The first battle, then, for advocates for immigrant students, is over visibility—establishing that these students are a part of the student body, that it is everyone's responsibility to serve them, that the needs are real.

The next battle for advocates is preventing marginalization and becoming viewed as legitimate. This comes not just as the luck of the draw, but as a result of hard work.

You must construct an ongoing campaign of visibility—for immigrant students and their needs, and for your reform efforts aimed at meeting those needs. When the California State Language Census was devised more than a decade ago, it was not only an attempt for the state to know how many students from which language groups were enrolled in the schools, but the census was also meant to be a tool that would lead school administrators and others to "see" the extent of impact that immigration was having on their schools, to know how many students were actually being served in programs designed to address the language barriers. Those simple numbers need to remain before people. How many LEP students are in your school? Which language groups? How many are "not being served"? See the following sample page from the Language Census—note column 5 in Section II for "unserved" students. In 1998, 223,730 students—16 percent of the state's 1.4 million LEP students—fell into this category (California Department of Education).

Advocates must find ways to bring about this visibility, through newsletters, bulletin board displays, memos, packets for department meetings and school site council meetings. Be sure that your school knows that the students are there. Then find ways to inform people about the implications of the presence of these students, what kinds of responses work, and what you are doing to address the needs of these students. The sample charts on page 82 are one way to draw attention to the presence of LEP students on your campus.

LANGUAGE CENSUS, SPRING 1999 (FORM R30-LC)
Fg. 3 of 3

School name

CDS code (from page 1 of this form)		
County # (2 digits)	District # (5 digits)	School # (7 digits)
I	I I I I	I I I I I I

II — Part II - English Learner (EL) Students Instructional Information

Row 01 - Number of English Learner (EL) Students enrolled in Specific Instructional Settings
Choose the column that most closely describes the placement of El Students as required by Education Code 300-400.
Count each EL student once. The total must match the total EL reported in Part I of this form.

	Structured English Immersion	Alternative Course of Study	English Language Mainstream Classroom		Other Instructional Settings	Total EL (Sum of Row 01)
			Students Meeting Criteria	Parental Request		
Row	(00)	(01)	(02)	(03)	(04)	(05)
01						

Row 02 - English Learner (EL) Students Receiving Instructional Services
Choose the column that most closely describes the services received by the EL Students reported in Row 01.
Count each EL student once in this row. The total must match the total EL reported in Part I of this form.

	EL Students Receiving Services from Teachers reported in Part V						
	English Language Development (ELD)	ELD and Specially Designed Academic Instruction in English (SDAIE)	ELD and SDAIE with Primary Language Support	ELD and Academic Subjects through the Primary Language (L1)	Instructional Services other than those defined in columns 00 through 03	Not receiving any English Learner Services	Total EL (Sum of Row 02)
Row	(00)	(01)	(02)	(03)	(04)	(05)	(06)
02							

III — Part III - Students Redesignated

[ ]	Enter the total number of English Learner (EL) students redesignated as FEP (fluent-English-proficient) since the last census (March 1, 1998). Include those who are no longer enrolled at the school (i.e., graduated or moved).

IV — Part IV - Oral English Proficiency   Check only one box.

Row Box	Status
01	Yes – This school uses one or more of the following oral language assessment instruments in English for initial identification of EL and FEP students: BSM I-II (K-12); LAS I-II (K-12); Pre LAS (ages 4-6); BINL (K-12); IPT I-II (K-12); Pre IPT (ages 3-5); QSE (K-6) and/or Woodcock-Munoz Language Survey (PreK-12).
02	No - None of the above tests have been conducted.
03	Other - The district has on file a current CDE approved waiver to use alternative instrument for initial identification.

V — Part V – Teachers (state authorized), Teachers in Training, and Paraprofessionals
Report teachers or paraprofessionals providing services set forth above in Part II, Row 02, columns 00-03. Count each teacher once.

Language of Instruction			Teachers providing Primary Language Instruction		Bilingual Paraprofessionals		Teachers providing English Language Development or Specially Designed Academic Instruction in English				
Code	Language name	Row	Teachers With a CTC Bilingual Authorization	Teachers in Training for a CTC Bilingual Authorization	Para Professionals (aides) teamed with teachers reported in Column 01	All other bilingual Para-Professionals (aides)	Instruction in English		Teachers with a CTC SDAIE or ELD Teaching Authorization	Teachers with SB1969 Certificate of Completion or District Designated with CDE approval	Teachers in Training for SDAIE or ELD Teaching Authorization
			(00)	(01)	(02)	(03)			(04)	(05)	(06)
01	Spanish	01					SDAIE and ELD	07			
		02					SDAIE only	08			
		03					ELD only	09			
		04									
		05									
		06									

SAMPLE CHARTS THAT CREATE VISIBILITY

Percent of LEP, FEP and English Only Students in California, 1998

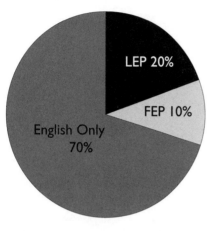

(Source: California Department of Education)

Major Language Groups in California Public Schools (Excluding English), 1998

Spanish	1,140,197	81%
Vietnamese	43,008	3%
Hmong	30,551	2%
Cantonese	25,360	2%
Pilipino (Tagalog)	20,026	1%
Khmer (Cambodian)	18,694	1%
Korean	15,521	1%
Armenian	13,584	1%
Mandarin	10,380	1%
Other languages	80,502	6%
Total	1,406,166	

(Source: California Department of Education)

Growth of LEP Students in California Public Schools, 1982-1997

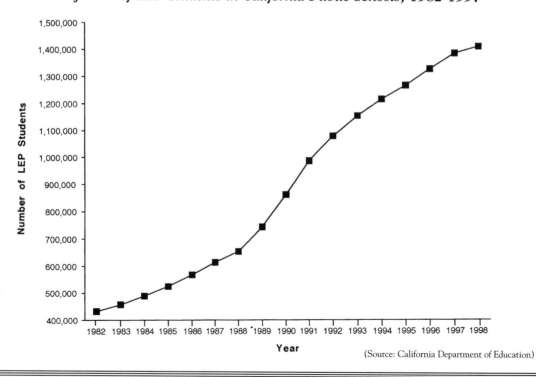

(Source: California Department of Education)

ACTIVITY 2.17
DISPLAYING AND SHARING DEMOGRAPHIC DATA
ON PARTICULAR GROUPS OF STUDENTS

Demographic data about a particular group of students can be very helpful in creating visibility. Begin by finding the data about how many Limited English Proficient students you have at your school. In California, teachers can look to CBEDS or the Language Census, prepared by your school or district for the California Department of Education. If you can't find copies at your school, request them from the State Department of Education directly. The Resources Section of Chapter Three describes where you can find data on the Internet, including Language Census data for California. Look back over the past six years, and construct a line graph of the growth of LEP students in your school, similar to the one on page 82.

Now construct a pie chart or other graphic showing the total student population in your school divided by groups. For example, depending on your purpose, you could show the spread of ethnicities/races, of students receiving Free and Reduced Price Lunch compared to the rest of the student population, or of English Only, Fluent English Proficient and Limited English Proficient students.

You can also find data that illustrates the level of access immigrant students experience in school. How many are enrolled in college-prep courses? How many are in the different tracks or levels of courses? How many are in courses specially designed to meet their needs? For example, California collects data on the number and percentage of LEP students enrolled in courses designed to meet their needs (ESL, sheltered, etc.). Use the data on access to construct a pie chart showing the percentage of students in particular programs or courses.

You may then choose to circulate this data to your school community, as part of awakening them to the numbers in your school. Find various ways to let people know what you're doing as a group. Put little notes in the daily bulletin or however your staff communicates with each other. Consider sending out a short, easy-to-assemble newsletter, by paper or electronically, presenting the kind of data you just constructed.

USING NEWSLETTERS TO CREATE VISIBILITY

At Alisal High School in Salinas, a core group of teachers working on literacy for their LEP students published a weekly one-page communications memo and placed it in the mailboxes of all faculty and staff. It was designed to keep people informed about their effort in the school, to provide enough tidbits of information to perhaps spark questions and discussion among other teachers and the core group and to provide some basic information about the student population.

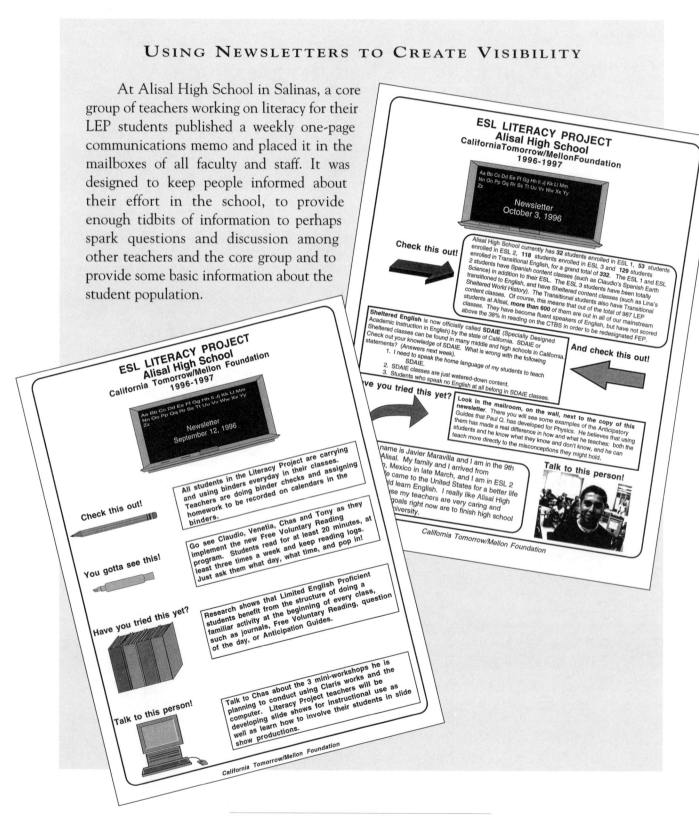

DELIBERATE, STRATEGIC OUTREACH

It is common in large schools for any self-developed working group to become viewed as a "clique." This becomes especially true as the work develops and a sense of excitement and unity grow within the group, and/or if the work they are focusing on is viewed by some others as "divisive." You may be able to become more visible through presentations, bulletins and newsletters, but unless you can avoid an "us/them" aura, it will be difficult to attract others to join you.

Once you are involved in inquiry and collaborative work for school change, it becomes very important to consistently "invite everyone to play." Keep inviting them in person and writing—and do it sincerely. Invite people formally and informally to come see what you're doing. Include the people you feel are poised to join you, as well as those who could get in the way if they feel they've been left out of the loop. Later, find ways to gently remind folks who may view your effort as cliquish that you have been inviting people to participate throughout the work.

Be deliberate and strategic in your outreach. Use the social/political map you developed together and figure out who amongst your core group of advocates can best talk to which other members of the school community. Divide up staff: Who connects with who? Talk to everyone about why the effort is important and what your process is. Determine which of you should be regular contacts with key stakeholders in the school. And think together about the best ways to make those contacts. Regular meetings? Deliberately-sought informal conversations? Written memos? Monthly open-luncheon briefings with food? At your school, which approaches are most likely to work with which groups?

REALIZE THE IMPORTANCE OF ONE-ON-ONE AND SMALL GROUPS IN MAKING CHANGE

Secondary schools are large, complex institutions. And to become responsive to the needs of students requires changes across the school, and throughout the program. But while the end result we seek is large-scale, the process for getting there needs to take place in smaller groups. The unfortunate tendency of high schools is to proceed in whole-faculty formations, for the sake of efficiency. The tendency of many people immersed in school reform efforts is that because they want to impact schoolwide, they believe they have to work in whole-group formats.

But change doesn't occur that way. It occurs best when people relate to each other as people in human-scale interactions. It occurs when people can really talk to each other and look each other in the eye, when they can share perspectives, raise concerns, speak their passions, ask questions and build relationships. Change occurs when groupings are small enough for each person to participate fully. This is particularly true when we must painfully confront data about underachievement, when examining beliefs about immigration, racism and classism. With one-on-one and small group interactions as the bedrock, whole-school votes and whole schools coming together becomes possible.

INFUSE YOUR WORK INTO OTHER EFFORTS: SEIZE THE OPPORTUNITIES

Strategize about how your group can be helpful to others in the school in a way that eases their burden, infuses knowledge and responsiveness to students into the life of the school, and begins to engage them. For example, if your school will be undergoing an accreditation process, perhaps some members of your core group could volunteer to work on the student voice aspects (see Chapter Five), and figure out ways to ensure that the voices of immigrant students are included—host focus groups, translate surveys, etc. Or, perhaps a powerful leadership group in the school has decided to go for a technology grant. Members of your group could volunteer to investigate the "technology gap" between Limited English Proficient students and others and collect some research about uses of technology to provide access to LEP students. You will, thus, build the proposal's strength to explain why and how your school would use the grant in ways that served all students.

Ironically, it is sometimes hardest to get recognition at home.

In this way, all of the reform energies at the school that seem to exclude immigrant students become not barriers, but opportunities. Use the school reform map you drew together to strategize how to infuse yourselves into the major reform conversations of the school, how to make yourselves helpful and connected to that dialogue in ways that insert the issues of the immigrant students.

CREATE OUTSIDE VISIBILITY AND SUPPORT FOR YOUR WORK

As you do your advocacy work, there will be times when it is essential that the people in your own school begin to view your efforts as special enough to warrant "saving" and responding to. Ironically, it is sometimes hardest to get recognition at home. One way to begin solving this is to look for recognition outside of your school. Think of ways to showcase your work at conferences. Let your school board, principal and others know (perhaps through your newsletters or regular memos) when you will be presenting.

At the conference, invite people to come visit your school. When they come, be sure to introduce them to key department heads and the principal.

BUILD COALITIONS AND ALLIANCES WITH ADVOCATES IN THE COMMUNITY

The universe of those concerned about the access and achievement of immigrant students is not confined to the school. In fact, the strongest advocates and proponents for access are the community. Building bridges between school-based advocates and parents and other members of the immigrant and language minority communities is essential. Keep your own efforts in tune with the community, and engage them in contributing to, understanding and supporting what it takes to actually produce that access and achievement within the school.

No movements for access in education have made changes without a strong community and public movement calling for the inclusion of a population. School-based advocates need to seek and build relationships with those people representing the students' communities and engaged in civil rights advocacy in the community. There are numerous ways to do this; some ideas are listed below.

Idea #1: Bring Together Community Groups with Educators Who Share Your Concerns

In Hayward Unified School District, Judy White, Zaida McCall-Perez and other advocates for immigrant and LEP students planned a series of community forums on topics related to immigrant student participation in school. Held after school, these forums were opportunities to share information and data about what was going on for the immigrant students. They included student panels so educators and community advocates together could hear and learn more about the student experience, and always included time focused on networking and sharing information about what supports, services and advocacy were available. The focus of the first forum, for example, was preparation for and outreach related to supporting immigrant students in the transition to higher education. The group heard from students about their dreams and aspirations for college and examined data about the huge disparities between these dreams and the actual course enrollment and preparation in high school the students were receiving. They talked about the impacts of new policies on financial aid for immigrant students. Then, they created a matrix of what kind of supports were available for which students and to analyze where the gaps exist, which is reproduced on the following page.

Building bridges between school-based advocates and parents and other members of the immigrant and language minority communities is essential.

SUPPORTS AVAILABLE FOR HAYWARD STUDENTS

Program	Schools Served	Target Group
Community College EOP Program	Hayward High	Low income
CSU High School Outreach	Hayward High, Mt. Eden, Tennyson	9th and 10th graders
CSU Mission Possible	Hayward High	12th graders—underrepresented African American and Latino males
CSU Upward Bound	Hayward High, Mt. Eden, Tennyson	Low income; first generation; neither parent has 4-year degree
Immigrant Students Support Project	Tennyson High	Immigrant students
Personal intervention of several teachers: college information, course advising, applications	Mt. Eden	Immigrant students
Prep for College	Tennyson High	Incoming 9th graders
Puente	All three high schools	Designed for Latino students
UC Early Academic Outreach	All high school and intermediate schools	Underrepresented Hispanics, Native Americans and African Americans; low income
La Familia Community Support Services	City-wide, Spanish-speaking families	Spanish speakers

(Co-developed by participants convened by Judy White for the community forum. The idea for the matrix activity was developed by Judy White, Carol Younglove, Laurie Olsen and Zaida McCall-Perez.)

After reviewing the matrix, the group planned how they might broaden their target populations and do more outreach to begin to serve students who were not included in the existing programs. Other community forums focused on the experiences of Latino/Chicano students, bilingual programs and language issues.

ACTIVITY 2.18
COMPILE A LIST OF COMMUNITY SUPPORTS

As a group, find out everything you can about what kinds of programs and supports are available in your community for immigrant and Limited English Proficient students. Look for programs that focus on transitions, outreach and preparation for higher education, academic support, and fostering of home language and culture. For each of these programs and supports, gather information about contact people and target populations. Compile a list and make this available to the faculty in your school.

Idea #2: Community Walks

Many teachers drive to work from a community that is not part of the school attendance area. The vast majority of teachers in our schools do not share a skin color, home language or cultural background with many of their students. Developing relationships with people in the community requires very proactive efforts to make connections.

In Watts, South Central Los Angeles, a group of students and parents forming the Academic Council of PASO (Parents and Students Organized for Harmony and Excellence in Schools and the Community) decided to create a way for educators to better understand their community. They began with some meetings with teachers and administrators in their schools who they knew were concerned about the low achievement of the Latino and African American students comprising the student population. As a group, the parents, students and educators in Markham Middle School decided to take "community walks." In teams, they walked through the housing projects near the school, greeting people, asking about their concerns for the education of their children and talking about what was going on in the school. These discussions were important eye-openers for the educators and rare opportunities for the community members to talk with the school people. It was a step toward joint understanding.

A high school in El Paso, Texas, sponsored a Community Walk after the faculty found traditional methods of attracting parents to the school to be unsuccessful. A volunteer from a community-based organization, who had conducted a successful community walk in New Mexico previously, suggested the idea. The main purpose was to acquaint teachers with their students' community; a secondary purpose was to allow parents and teachers to interact. The walk, which quickly got the principal's support, covered approximately thirty city blocks and included watching a group of *matachines* (ceremonial dancers of Aztec origin) dance at two of the stops. Afterwards, the Intercultural Development Research Association (IDRA) interviewed 15 of the participants, both teachers and parents. One parent commented, "There are many times when parents are afraid to speak to teachers. Maybe it's because of their English. But since the walk, I've seen a change. Since the walk, we've had a lot of success getting parents to come to the school" (McCollum, 1997, p. 5). Teachers got to know much more about the backgrounds of their students and recognized some of the gaps between the formal school curriculum and the practices of the community. Both new and veteran teachers benefited from the experience. As Pat McCollum notes, "The community walk was a first step in breaking home-school barriers and establishing school, family and community partnerships where parties teach and assist each other."

ACTIVITY 2.19
CREATE A COMMUNITY WALK OR FORUM

Once you have identified some community groups that share your concern with the participation, access and achievement of immigrant students in your school area, talk with them about working together on either community walks or forums that can spark conversations. Find other ways to begin to build relationships between those working for access in the schools and those who work for it from the community.

CONCLUSION

There is no straight line towards changing a school to meet the needs of immigrant students. New obstacles appear and plans have to be re-evaluated. New understandings emerge and call for different responses. Opportunities suddenly present themselves that you feel compelled to move on. The best laid plans sometimes don't work. And sometimes the data you uncover convinces you to go all-out for one single thrust or abandon some path.

Advocates cannot outline a single plan of action and simply proceed. It is essential to keep asking yourselves as a group: Given what is happening right now, which strategy makes most sense? Who is best situated for moving this piece? We call this an ongoing strengths-based analysis and reassessment process—examining what's working and why, putting heads together over new obstacles and what might dislodge them, adjusting strategies to match new opportunities. The remaining chapters delve more deeply into this process.

Whatever path you take, it will be essential for your group as advocates to be able to invoke the legal basis for the rights of language minority students to an education. You must know the law and how to access legal resources in your work to ensure access. That is why we end this chapter with a review of the federal laws, statutes and court cases related to the provision of programs to Limited English Proficient students.

Finally, at least annually, and preferably twice a year, it is important to take the time to reflect back on what you've done and accomplished, to revisit your goals and expectations and analyze why some things didn't happen or didn't have the impact you hoped for. This is also the time to redraw or revisit your maps. Update your school's history map, adding your own efforts to the story. Look again at your maps of reform and see if there are new dialogues you need to speak to. Revisit your struggle map and see if there have been any shifts in how efforts play out. Then examine the evidence and data on student participation and achievement that we will learn to gather in the coming chapters. It is in these reflections that you should also take a look at your theories of action and figure out where the strengths and weaknesses are in your plan.

Linoleum cut by Thoun Kheang, a high school student from Thailand

ADVOCATES NEED TO KNOW THE LAW

If you have a strong core group of advocates who support each other, if you are clear about your vision, and strategic in your approach to the school, if you use the strategies discussed in this resource book (student voice, data, etc.), you can make your school more accessible, open, inclusive and responsive to your LEP students. But sometimes in this effort, you will need to invoke or rely upon the law. Bottom-line civil rights laws have had to be instituted because there is not always a willingness to open doors to some groups. They exist because, without them, some people will resist fully serving language minority students and will refuse to do what is necessary to provide full access. Every advocate for language minority students should know what the law requires, how it works, how to access legal resources and how legal actions are initiated.

THE LEGAL BASIS FOR LANGUAGE MINORITY RIGHTS TO AN EDUCATION

All children in the United States have the right to a free public school education. School districts are required by law to develop a special program for children who need English language help. At a minimum, that program must provide special help through a trained teacher to assist your child to learn English and must provide special assistance to help your child learn what other children are learning, even if he or she does not speak sufficient English. This help must continue until the child no longer has a barrier to learning the content due to his or her English language skills.

The legal basis for the provision of programs to Limited English Proficient students stems from the Constitution and a series of federal laws, statutes and court cases. These are the major ones.

FEDERAL LAW AND STATUTES

The Equal Protection Clause of the Fourteenth Amendment to the Constitution reads:

"No state shall…deny to any person within its jurisdiction the equal protection of the laws."

Title VI of the Civil Rights Act of 1964 says:

"No person in the United States shall, on the grounds of race, color or national origin, be excluded from participation in, be denied the benefits of, or be subjected to discrimination under any program or activity receiving federal financial assistance."

The "May 25 Memorandum of 1970," issued by the Office of Civil Rights, interprets Title VI of the Civil Rights Act as follows:

"Where inability to speak and understand the English language excludes national origin-

minority group children from effective participation in the educational programs offered by a school district, the district must take affirmative steps to rectify the language deficiency in order to open its instructional programs to these students."

KEY COURT DECISIONS

In 1974, the Supreme Court decided in the case of a lawsuit brought by Chinese parents in San Francisco who argued that their children were being denied an education because they could not speak English. The landmark *Lau v. Nichols* decision states:

"There is no equality of treatment merely by providing students with the same facilities, textbooks, teachers and curriculum, for students who do not understand English are effectively foreclosed from any meaningful education…Basic English skills are at the very core of what these public schools teach. Imposition of a requirement that, before a child can effectively participate in the educational program, he must already have acquired those basic skills is to make a mockery of public education. We know that those who do not understand English are certain to find their classroom experiences wholly incomprehensible and in no way meaningful…"

In *Lau v. Nichols*, the court ordered "appropriate relief," although it did not specify a particular method. A later case sought to define a way of knowing whether or not "appropriate relief" was being provided. The Equal Educational Opportunities Act (EEOA) of 1974 states:

"No state shall deny equal educational opportunity to an individual on account of his or her race, color, sex or national origin by…the failure of an educational agency to take appropriate action to overcome language barriers that impede equal participation by its students in its instructional programs." (Section 1703[f])

In *Castenada v. Pickard* (1981), the court established a three-prong test to determine if the education services being provided constitute "appropriate relief." The three measures are:

- Is the program informed by sound educational theory?

- Is the program implemented effectively with sufficient resources?

- After a reasonable period of time, can the program be evaluated as being able to overcome the students' language barrier to education?

It also states that there is a "duty to provide limited-English-speaking-ability students with assistance in other areas of the curriculum where their equal participation may be impaired because of deficits incurred during participation in an agency's language remediation program." In other words, schools must do something to compensate for the fact that children tend to fall behind in other subjects until they learn English.

One other key court case governs the education of language minority students. This one speaks specifically to the requirement that these protections apply to all children, regardless of legal immigration or citizenship status. In the *Plyler v. Doe* (1982) Supreme Court Decision, it was determined that "All children in the United States have the right to a free public school education in the school district in which they live." The court noted that immigrant children do not need a green card, visa, passport, alien registration number, social security number nor any other proof of citizenship or immigration status in order to register for school.

A list of legal resources appears at the end of this chapter.

REFERENCES

Carrow-Moffett, P. (1993). Change Agent Skills: Creating Leadership for School Renewal. *NASSP Bulletin, 77*(552), 57-62.

Fullan, M. (1993). Why Teachers Must Become Change Agents. *Educational Leadership, 50*(6), 12-17.

McAloon, N. (1995). Advocacy in Schools. *Journal of Reading, 38*(4), 318-320.

McCollum, P. (1997). Two Innovative El Paso Schools Bring Together Teachers and the Community. *IDRA Newsletter*, vol. XXIV, No. 8, 3-6, 11.

Olsen, L. (1997). *Made in America: Immigrant Students in Our Public Schools*. New York, NY: The New Press.

Shachar, H. (1996). Developing New Traditions in Secondary Schools: A Working Model for Organizational and Instructional Change. *Teachers College Record, 97*(4), 549-68.

ADVOCACY
ANNOTATED BIBLIOGRAPHY

**Carrow-Moffett, Patricia. (1993). Change Agent Skills: Creating
Leadership for School Renewal. NASSP Bulletin, 77(552), 57-62.**

In this brief article, the author outlines the abilities and skills needed for
school leaders involved in a change process. Carrow-Moffett argues that
change agents not only need vision and purpose, but also need to set direction
and facilitate cooperation of those involved in overcoming the challenges of a
diverse world. Moreover, part of this process involves developing procedures
that allow advocates to be effective change agents. These include, but are not
limited to: identifying a vision; developing a logical outline for how a plan
should work, but keeping in mind that things don't always go as planned;
examining and understanding what advocates bring to the process; knowing
your values and identifying the nature of the change; and recognizing that
change requires learning new attitudes and behaviors.

**Fullan, Michael. (1993). Why Teachers Must Become Change Agents.
Educational Leadership, 50(6), 12-17.**

This insightful and concise article explores the reciprocal relationship
between moral purpose and change agentry. Fullan stresses that building
greater capacity for meaningful change, caring and commitment must be
accompanied by four core elements: personal vision; inquiry; mastery (of concepts); and collaboration. He also introduces a new paradigm emphasizing the
direct relationship between real improvements in the classroom and changes
in teacher learning and professional culture.

**Fullan, Michael. (1996). Turning System Thinking on Its Head. *Phi
Delta Kappan*, 77(6), 420-423.**

An informative and dynamic model for "reculturing" and restructuring
system reform, this article also advocates for an unequivocal change in the
nature of existing school cultures and structures. Fullan suggests five strategies
necessary for change: multiple ways of sharing information; integration of
school and district priorities; commitment to inquiry and assessment of
progress; a critical mass of school staff with the capacity to manage change on
a continuous basis; and linkages between schools to serve as support networks.

Margolis, Howard. (1991). Understanding, Facing Resistance to Change. NASSP *Bulletin*, 75(537), 1-8.

This article addresses teacher resistance to instituting change. Margolis examines the potential benefits of resistance and offers a framework for reducing it. Reducing resistance to change requires that the process be inclusive; focus on what stakeholders find most critical; have clarity of the goals; encourage innovation and experimentation; and generate ideas based on school-based norms, resources, and district responsibilities.

McAloon, Noreen. (1995). Advocacy in Schools. *Journal of Reading*, 38(4), 318-320.

This article outlines various manifestations of "advocacy" within schools and from the community. Examples are advocacy from teacher to teacher, from teacher to community and from teacher to parents for students. The author concludes that the common goal for all forms of advocacy is ensuring that students receive quality instruction.

McDonald, Joseph. (1989). When Outsiders Try to Change Schools from the Inside. *Phi Beta Kappan*, 71(3), 206-212.

This engaging guide is geared towards outside change agents involved in the school reform process. It reminds outsiders to always be cognizant that although they might help find solutions, they cannot provide them, and though they may help shape outcomes, they cannot determine them. It defines the attitude and methodology needed by change agents to create a "constructive space" between them and the school culture.

Olsen, L., Jaramillo, A., McCall-Perez, Z., White, J. and Minicucci, C. (1999). *Igniting Change for Immigrant Students: Portraits of Three High Schools*. Oakland, CA: California Tomorrow.

This book describes how advocates working with California Tomorrow created change in three high schools. Educators in Hayward worked district-wide to improve access and placement for immigrant students, while teachers in Salinas restructured their comprehensive high school and crafted an accelerated literacy approach. The book presents a partnership model for reform that is flexible and driven by powerful strategies. It details California Tomorrow's principles for equity in any school, lessons for their application, and an evaluation of the impact of the effort.

Shachar, Hanna. (1996). Developing New Traditions in Secondary Schools: A Working Model for Organizational and Instructional Change. *Teachers College Record, 97(4), 549-568.*

The article presents an international model of implementing cooperative learning for teachers and changing patterns of organizational behavior in secondary schools. The four-stage process incorporates a combination of strategies (a teamwork approach, ongoing inservice training, and use of outside consultants) to acquire new methods. The process also requires that leadership groups be developed, teachers and administrators learn and implement new traditions, and school staff "buy in" to the change process.

Tewel, Kenneth J. (1991). Promoting Change in Secondary Schools. *NASSP Bulletin, 75(537), 10-17.*

This brief article offers strategies advocates can use to make their schools more responsive to the change process. Tewel argues that successful change leaders set up systemic structures that nurture the change process. Building organizational capacity to respond to change includes: an opportunity for teachers to plan together and work collaboratively; the decentralization of decision-making; a redefinition of job descriptions; the establishment of a flexible management system; and the development of achievable goals.

Thurston, Paul, Cliff, Renee and Schacht, Marshall. (1993). Preparing Leaders for Change-Oriented Schools (Training for School Administrators). *Phi Delta Kappan, 75(3), 259-265.*

This insightful article reviews case studies involving change-oriented leadership. The case studies serve as examples for how administrator preparation is a key element of school reform. The authors argue in favor of training that prepares advocates to become the collaborative, visionary leaders needed to better serve the needs of school-age children.

Whitaker, Todd. (1995). Accomplishing Change in Schools: The Importance of Teacher Leaders. *Clearing House, 68(3), 356-357.*

Whitaker's article establishes "teacher leaders" as the essential link between site-based management and school collaboration. He emphasizes the degree to which informal faculty relationships and beliefs can affect school programs and curricular development during the change process. Whitaker also presents several techniques for identifying "influential" teachers and examines how they influence effective administrative leadership and subsequently affect change in schools.

ADVOCACY RESOURCES

California Association for Bilingual Education (CABE)

CABE advocates for positive bilingual education legislation by way of its Political Action Committee. Educators, parents and interested community members are welcome to join local chapters to participate in lobbying efforts. CABE hosts an annual conference (usually in February) focusing on all aspects of the bilingual education field. Their website offers news flashes, legislative updates and related publications. Membership includes a subscription to their newsletter and discounts on publications and conferences.

660 S. Figueroa, Suite 1040
Los Angeles, CA 90017
(213)532-3850
(213)532-3860 fax
WWW: www.cabe.org

California Latino Civil Rights Network

The Latino Network is a statewide network of Latino service agencies, individuals, professionals and religious and labor organizations. They serve as a clearinghouse for information gathering and dissemination, research, advocacy and policy development, and as a resource center for local organizations or individuals who want to promote civil and human rights for Latinos. The Latino Network's current projects include increasing civic participation, job creation in rural communities and creating a rapid response system that informs and mobilizes the Latino communities against potentially harmful political measures.

1605 W. Olympic Boulevard, Suite 9102
Los Angeles, CA 90015
(213)228-0220
(213)252-0560 fax
WWW: www.latinonetwork.org

1212 Broadway, Suite 1400
Oakland, CA 94612
(510)663-2020
(510)663-2028 fax

2115 Kern Street, Suite 103
Fresno, CA 93721
(209)498-7000
(209)498-7005 fax

National Association for Bilingual Education (NABE)

NABE is the national advocacy and professional organization for bilingual education whose members include educators, parents, community members and government and business people. NABE holds an annual conference and offers professional development in the field of bilingual education. Their website features legislative and policy links, as well as articles on bilingual education at the local and national levels.

1220 L Street
Washington, D.C. 20005
(202)898-1829
(202)789-2866 fax
E-mail: nabe@nabe.org
WWW: www.nabe.org

National Coalition of Advocates for Students (NCAS)

NCAS is a national advocacy organization focusing on school change to meet the needs of students who are not well served by public schools. Their effort to achieve equal access to a quality public education for all children includes advocacy work at the local, state and national levels to inform and mobilize citizens and help policymakers resolve critical education issues. Current projects include Mobilization For Equity (MFE), which trains and supports parents to participate effectively in local school improvement efforts; the Clearinghouse for Immigrant Education (CHIME), which provides research literature, referrals and other supports on issues regarding education services for immigrant children; and School Counseling in Today's Real World, which helps school counselors develop the capacity to work effectively with minority students and their families.

100 Boylston Street, Suite 737
Boston, MA 02116
(617)357-8507
(617)357-4703
E-mail: ncasmfe@aol.com
WWW: www.ncas1.org

National Coalition for Education Activists (NCEA)

NCEA is a membership network of families, school staff, community and union activists, and others involved in public school issues. NCEA members share a commitment to social justice, the elimination of bias, and creating quality public schools that serve all children well. NCEA supports local activists with a resource bank, newsletter and opportunities to discuss key issues and develop knowledge and advocacy skills.

P.O. Box 679
Rhinebeck, NY 12572
(914)876-4580
E-mail: RFBS@aol.com
WWW: http://members.aol.com/nceaweb

National Council of La Raza (NCLR)

NCLR, the largest constituency-based national Hispanic organization, focuses its advocacy efforts in two areas: 1) capacity-building to support and strengthen Hispanic community-based organizations; and 2) applying research and policy analysis with a Hispanic perspective to issues such as education, immigration and civil rights enforcement. The organization participates in innovative programs, catalytic efforts and coalitions. NCLR publishes a quarterly newsletter, as well as other issue-specific newsletters on education, poverty and HIV/AIDS and hosts an annual national conference.

(national headquarters)
810 First Street, NE, 3rd Floor
Washington, D.C. 20002
(202)289-1380
WWW: www.nclr.org

(Los Angeles office)
900 Wilshire Blvd., Suite 1520
Los Angeles, CA 90017
(213)489-3428

Rethinking Schools

Begun as a grassroots effort by teachers who wanted to improve education in their own classrooms, this organization has grown to become a national distributor of educational materials. Their goals have remained the same, with a vision that public education is central to the creation of a humane, caring, multiracial democracy. Resources, such as their quarterly journal and special publications on hot education topics, can be requested by fax, phone or E-mail. Their website offers a valuable list of related education links.

1001 E. Keefe Avenue
Milwaukee, WI 53212
(800)669-4192
(414)964-7220 fax
E-mail: webrs@execpc.com
WWW: www.rethinkingschools.org

LEGAL RESOURCES FOR LANGUAGE ACCESS

Multicultural Education, Training and Advocacy (META), Inc.

META, Inc. is a nonprofit national advocacy organization specializing in the educational rights of low income, minority and immigrant children. They work with public interest group, pro bono attorneys, as well as parents and community advocates, to advocate for the rights of these students at the local and statewide levels. META staff provide training, materials, advice and co-council on issues, including access to language programs for Limited English Proficient (LEP) students, so-called "zero tolerance" discipline policies, school uniform programs, and education reform practices, such as school-to-work.

785 Market Street, Suite 420
San Francisco, CA 94103
(415)546-6382
(415)546-6363 fax

Mexican American Legal Defense and Education Fund (MALDEF)

MALDEF is a national nonprofit organization dedicated to the protection and promotion of the civil rights of Latinos in the United States. MALDEF pursues its mission through community education, advocacy and, when necessary, litigation. MALDEF focuses on civil rights in the areas of education, employment, immigration, political access and public resource equity. MALDEF is particularly dedicated to protecting the rights of LEP students, including securing access to quality programs, and fair and accurate assessment.

182 Second Street
San Francisco, CA 94105
(415)543-5598
(415)543-8235 fax

634 South Spring Street, 11th Floor
Los Angeles, CA 90014
(213)629-2512
(213)629-0830 fax

California Rural Legal Assistance (CRLA)

CRLA is a statewide, rural legal services assistance organization with 16 field offices in California, from Marysville to El Centro. CRLA offers legal assistance in the areas of education, labor/employment, housing, health welfare and civil rights.

631 Howard Street, Suite 300
San Francisco, CA 94105
(415)777-2752
(415)543-2752 fax

Office of Civil Rights

The Office of Civil Rights investigates and records complaints by parents, community members, students and others for whom school districts are not providing equal educational access.

50 United Nations Plaza, Room 239
San Francisco, CA 94102
(415)437-7700
(415)437-7783 fax

Language Proficiency and Academic Accountability Unit

The Language Proficiency and Academic Accountability Unit is responsible for statewide monitoring of implementation of federal and state requirements for services for English Language Learners. In-house staff are available to answer questions regarding the rights and responsibilities of schools in providing students access to their curriculum.

California Department of Education
721 Capitol Mall
Sacramento, CA 94244-2720
(916)657-4674
(916)657-3112 fax

Categorical Programs Complaints Management Unit

Any complaints filed at the local school district level about language access problems should also be filed with this office. The Complaints Management Unit conducts an investigation or mediates when the local school district (where the first complaint was filed) has failed to act within 60 days, when an appeals has been filed, or when the Department of Education determines that direct intervention is necessary. This office also offers technical assistance on correct compliance and resource materials to parents and advocates.

California Department of Education
721 Capitol Mall
Sacramento, CA 94244-2720
(916)657-3630
(916)657-3443 fax

Immigrant Assistance Lines

The Immigrant Assistance Lines are available to answer questions concerning parent and student rights, immigration law and other accessible services. All calls are confidential, with multilingual operators who speak Spanish, Vietnamese, Mandarin, Cantonese and English.

c/o Northern California Coalition for Immigrant Rights
995 Market Street, 11th Floor
San Francisco, CA 94103
(415)543-6767 Spanish/English
(415)543-6797 Vietnamese/English
(415)543-6769 Mandarin/Cantonese/English

Lawyer Referral Hotline

With local offices in most California cities, this hotline offers free referral to attorneys. Referrals are also available for free or low-payment lawyers. Below is a partial list of telephone numbers. If your city is not listed, please call any listed office and ask for your city's Lawyer Referral Hotline number.
Sacramento: (916)444-2333
Fresno: (209)264-0137
San Francisco: (415)989-1616
Los Angeles: (213)243-1525
San Diego: (619)231-8585

Chapter Three:

OPENING THE DOOR TO DATA AND INQUIRY

The ten members of the Lincoln Middle School data analysis team gather around the library conference room table. Representing a cross-section of the staff and different subject matters, the team is meeting for the third time in two years. The principal, Armando Vigil, rushes in through the door, apologizing for being ten minutes late.

The first time this team came together, they were uniformly dismayed to find a disturbing pattern of failure among their Limited English Proficient students. More than 75% of these students had received an F in one or more of their courses; 45% had F's in two or more courses. The group decided to zero in on the failing LEP students as their major achievement challenge, and over the last two years, most of the staff at the school has been involved in one initiative or another to tackle the problem. For example, the Math Department started "Academic Homerooms," targeting LEP students who, after the first three weeks of school, appeared to be faltering. Here, students receive intensive pre-teaching of new material in Math and work on building skills in their weaker areas. The Math

Department also instituted a new curriculum aimed at getting all students into Algebra by the 8th grade. Several other departments have waded into their own efforts to target failing LEP students.

Mr. Vigil begins to pass out "data packets" that present the latest numbers for a whole series of achievement measures collected by the school over the last three years. The team members anxiously leaf through the pages, looking for the one titled "Students Receiving a D or F in Achievement by Number of Classes." As they peruse the data, small smiles begin to spread over some faces. Several "high-fives" are exchanged around the table. The rates of failing LEP students have gone down, in some cases significantly. Most recently, fewer than 40% of students received an F in one class, and fewer than 25% received an F in two or more classes. And it appears that the most dramatic improvement has come in Math.

As the team works through more of the data, although they are pleased with the progress, they are still not satisfied. They begin to dig into specifics, examining the Math Department as the model. What has the Math Department done that we could replicate in other parts of the school? What would it look like? What shall our goals be for this next year?

Data, when used effectively, is a crucial tool for advocates who seek achievement and access for language minority students. We need data to keep the needs of our students visible and to hold ourselves accountable, especially given the long history of excluding or poorly serving the language minority children in our schools. With the push for higher standards in education, we need data to indicate how well our English Language Learners are doing in attaining those standards. With bilingual education programs under attack, we need to know for ourselves and be able to prove to the public that our programs are effective in overcoming language barriers and helping our children reach high achievement.

In California, in 1998, a ballot initiative called English for the Children: Proposition 227 passed by a 2:1 margin. Its goal was to dismantle bilingual education programs throughout the state. During the campaign, public sentiment was aroused by a barrage of misinformation about bilingual education. But bilingual programs, although rich with evidence of students thriving academically under their wing, were not positioned to "showcase" irrefutable evidence and data—"the numbers"—about their effectiveness. This left them very vulnerable to attack. Unable to "see" the successes of many, many bilingual programs, the public bought into the single, narrow and untested program of 227, whose campaigners cited "data" about "the failure of bilingual programs" that were not even accurate. Bilingual education advocates were not prepared to demonstrate in multiple ways the impacts of their work to protect programs on the local level or to address the politicized public arena characterized by attacks on immigrants and language rights. Bilingual education advocates had not established the forums and structures in which data were being gathered, shared, known and built upon.

For all of the above reasons, we need good, timely data—data that answer our questions with measures we believe make sense—and we need strategies for how to use that data to improve our own practice, engage with others in examining our school and program effectiveness, build accountability and consensus and measure progress.

HOW AND WHY THE USE OF DATA HAS FAILED US IN THE PAST

Meaningful and thoughtful use of data, unfortunately, runs counter to the workings of most schools. Many of us have had bad experiences with data being used to blame or manipulate us for political ends. Few educators have had the time or training to learn how to use data effectively for their own purposes. As a result, too few advocates use data to develop responsive programs and focus their work. Far too many schools spin their wheels in ineffective reform attempts, never seeing or correcting the exclusion and inequities that exist (Johnson 1996; Olsen 1996). Consider these examples:

The principal, Mr. Starr, walks into the faculty meeting, flicks on an overhead projector and spends ten minutes running through the results of the latest standardized test scores. Chart after chart flashes across the screen. When it is over, Mr. Starr proclaims, "We have to do better," and they are on to the next agenda item. Few teachers in the room have even been able to absorb what the data actually said or meant, but the rest of the meeting is infected with an underlying resentment that judgment had been passed on their work. This school has other data, but it hasn't been studied or put into the hands of those whose work it sought to measure. It is unlikely that this faculty will eagerly seek the results of the next test.

Site-level decision-making and school-to-work academies (here called "houses") are the centerpiece of the reform plans at Southwest High. Because very few faculty are trained to work with LEP students, these students are not assigned into a house until they are proficient enough in English to participate in the curriculum. The faculty also has resisted cre-

We need good, timely data— data that answer our questions with measures we believe make sense.

ating a separate house for LEP students, citing a "philosophical" preference for heterogeneous as opposed to homogeneous groupings. As one student says, "We don't get a house yet. We're the homeless of the school until we learn English." Southwest High has also dismantled its ESL and primary language programs under reforms focused on heterogeneous grouping and integration. Since this restructuring, they speak of the overall improvements in student performance. But they are looking only at aggregated data—a single snapshot of the entire school population. They never disaggregate data to explore the impact of reforms on specific groups of students and to alert themselves to possible patterns of exclusion or differential impacts. In fact, in the name of reform, this school is creating new forms of exclusion—and never seeing it. They do not know that some students at this school—Limited English Proficient students—are being left behind and hurt by the reforms that seem to be such a good idea.

Schools usually think of student achievement and access data in terms of compliance, mandates and monitoring from the outside or above. Administrators have to worry about data, but certainly not teachers, we think. To make matters worse, a large number of educators have math anxiety. When a chart of numbers is presented, eyes glaze over. Numbers are boring. Math is hard and measurements are suspect. Those who don't tune out often react with resistance or anger about what the numbers imply.

In many schools, data have a bad reputation for good reason: data have been used against educators or to establish blame. As one administrator at a retreat noted:

"Let's face it—we're paranoid in schools. Data are used all the time to club us over the heads. There's very little sense that data can be useful to us in doing what we're trying to do. In short, it sure doesn't feel like a friend to us."

When the subject of the data is the differential treatment of specific language or racial/ethnic groups, this resistance and anger often deepens. We fear what the data will show, fear confronting the evidence of exclusion. Understandably, then, few school change efforts focus on using data as a cornerstone for exciting and engaging teachers.

How Data Can Help Us

Used well, however, data are powerful tools in moving schools to a new level of access and engagement for English Language Learners—indeed, for all students who have been traditionally frozen out of full participation in their own schools. Data can spur reflection, open eyes, spark dialogue, inform planning. Data can lead to professional development and help shape consensus about direction. Good data can build accountability and increase attention to equity issues by providing a stark picture of how your school is doing.

There is more. Data can prompt the very dialogues we need to be having as school communities about our goals, our beliefs and expectations and our understandings about each other. Data can stimulate inquiry into how the school community is educating all of its students and what it considers important.

We're not talking about simply collecting or reporting data. To promote access and achievement, data need to become part of the life of a school. Data need to be part of how schools work to improve programs, hold themselves accountable and deepen their understandings of teaching and learning. Ideally, such data use happens school-wide—but even in the hands of a core group of advocates or teachers, data can have the power to move a school.

Data can spur reflection, open eyes, spark dialogue, inform planning.

Schools that have made data central to the goals of equity and achievement use data to:

- Continually improve
- Surface inequities
- Identify weaknesses in the program
- Ensure accountability
- Make sure all students are achieving
- Prove programs are effective
- Protect effective but not necessarily politically popular programs.

ACTIVITY 3.1
GETTING A HANDLE ON
HOW DATA IS USED AT OUR SCHOOL

On your own or with your team, answer the questions below. They are designed to spark an opening reflection of the ways that data are currently used (and have been used) at your school site.

☛ Can you answer to your satisfaction how your ELLs are doing—whether they are achieving to high standards?
❑ yes
❑ no

☛ Can you answer to your satisfaction whether your programs are effective or whether some groups of students are being less well-served than others?
❑ yes
❑ no

☛ Does your school collect data about student achievement, access and participation, and then no one uses it?
❑ yes
❑ no

☛ Have you made an attempt to piece together some data to answer a concern, but found that they weren't quite the right data to answer what you're really asking?
❑ yes
❑ no

☛ Have you experienced one of the moments when someone presents data and there is simply no reaction? It fizzles? Or explodes?
❑ yes
❑ no

☛ Are you in situations where the data that are being used to evaluate you and your school aren't data that you trust, or are being used in ways that fingerpoint blame and don't support a change process?
❑ yes
❑ no

☛ Do you know your work is having an impact on students, but don't have the data that could defend it to an outsider?
❑ yes
❑ no

☛ Do your school reform discussions end up being a battle of preferences for different interventions with no way of weighing one against another?

❏ yes

❏ no

If you, like most educators in schools today, answered "yes" to one or many of these questions, you are sitting on a great deal of knowledge about what makes data use non-productive.

Now think about your positive experiences with data — times when they may have helped you understand something new, or made you realize the particular urgency of a problem.

☛ Do you currently use any assessment data about your students that are helpful to you in figuring how to target instruction or better teach?

❏ yes
❏ no

☛ Have you used data about student achievement to guide your decisions about professional development you might pursue?

❏ yes
❏ no

☛ Have you heard a statistic quoted that really stuck in your mind powerfully as a new realization of an urgent problem?

❏ yes
❏ no

☛ Are you in situations where the data being used to evaluate you and your school are used in ways that support individual teachers' change process and the change process of the school as a whole?

❏ yes
❏ no

If you, like many educators and advocates, answered "yes" to one or many of these questions, you are sitting on a great deal of knowledge about what makes data use work. To delve into the details of what does and does not make data use productive, try the following activity.

ACTIVITY 3.2
CONDITIONS AND APPROACHES FOR DATA USE

As a group or as a personal reflection, construct a list of what you know about the conditions and approaches that contribute to whether data end up being useful to you in understanding and improving practice and what make it counterproductive. Draw on some of the ideas above. Think about specific situations at your school site that have either promoted or inhibited the productive use of data.

These situations and approaches result in data being **non-productive** or **destructive** to school change	These situations and approaches result in data being **productive** and **supportive** to school change
1.	1.
2.	2.
3.	3.
4.	4.

THE HISTORY OF USING DATA TO IMPROVE SCHOOLS

The use of data in and by schools has a wide-reaching history. This history has involved five different movements within different fields, each varying in impetus, purpose and goals, how data are used and how the work has continued to evolve.

Although each of the five fields described below works with different purposes, audiences and methodologies, they all use data and inquiry as strategic tools for improving education. Depending on the purpose of a specific inquiry and the nature of a particular challenge, your school may draw upon the methodologies and models of one or more of these traditions.

TEACHER AS RESEARCHER: THE REFLECTIVE PRACTITIONER

In this tradition, teachers design and conduct research to improve their practice or improve the situations in which they work to help students achieve more. Teachers are seen as researchers and reflective practitioners who use data to fuel their own inquiries. Schools engaged in data-based inquiry seek to develop reflective practitioners able to observe, research and think deeply about their own practice. Teacher growth is, thus, seen as related to student growth (Barth, 1993). As teachers use inquiry as a tool of their own learning and professional growth, they become committed to creating classroom learning environments that support students in their inquiries (Short and Burke, 1996). Data of all kinds are used by these teacher-researchers to answer questions that have arisen out of their own teaching and observations.

PROGRAM PLANNING AND EVALUATION

The field of program planning and evaluation has contributed quantitative and qualitative models for assessing the effectiveness of educational programs. These models link research design and data collection more closely to those who need to use the data. So-called "stakeholder-based" models engage all interested parties in the planning of an evaluation and the framing of both the research questions themselves and the kinds of data that should be used to answer those questions.

Action research is one variation of a stakeholder model. The term "action research" was chosen to indicate that such inquiry and research would lead to actions that improve a program or organization. Educators have adopted this approach to identify problems in schools, collect data, shape action and then monitor whether and how well their reforms are

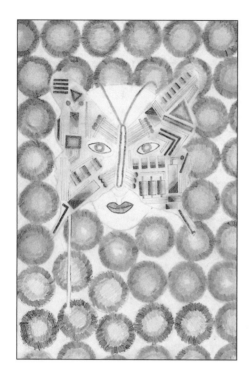

*Charcoal by
Katherine Estacio,
a high school
student from the
Philippines*

working. These models provide schools with valuable tools for investigating and assessing their own programs. Another model is often called a participatory model of evaluation. It is aimed at empowering communities (parents, community members, students) to take part in the evaluation process. This can result in a new set of relationships at the school site, a culture of inquiry and a legacy shared by everyone of asking questions about how the school is doing (Fine, 1997).

CIVIL RIGHTS AND PUBLIC ACCOUNTABILITY AND ADVOCACY

Another model of data-based inquiry has been developed by civil rights advocates since the 1960's. In this field, data and inquiry have been used to improve equity and access to a high-quality education. After the courts and federal government became involved in protecting the civil rights of language, ethnic, national and gender minorities to access to an education, a field developed to monitor and alert others about evidence of exclusion or inequities.

For example, the data documenting the wide gap in academic achievement separating low income children, African Americans, Latinos and Native Americans from other students is collected and sometimes reported by governmental agencies (National Center for Education Statistics, Office of Civil Rights, Office of Education Research and Improvement). But the analysis and use of these data to arouse public concern, demand public accountability and spark public dialogue have generally fallen to organizations like National Council of La Raza, the NAACP, Mexican American Legal Defense and Education Fund, National Coalition of Advocates for Students, the Achievement Council, California Tomorrow and others. As this example shows, because the very nature of these problems is comparative, the methodology often involves the analysis of standardized tests, standardized definitions and measurements, and seeking evidence of patterns of practice.

OUTCOME- AND STANDARDS-BASED EDUCATION REFORM

For more than a decade, national and state reform movements have called for the development of goals, standards and baseline indicators to assess educational improvement. The movement was spurred by the participation of governors, business leaders and others in the school reform movement. Drawing upon knowledge of strategic planning processes, they knew that a change process must begin by identifying goals, and they found that schools were characterized by a lack of consensus on desired outcomes and goals (Ravitch, 1992). They were concerned that changes were too piece-meal, uncoordinated and incremental. Standards-based reform was an attempt to push for clarity and consensus about the desired outcomes of education, in order to focus school change efforts.

Standards might include content standards for what students are expected to know in each subject area and by grade level. They might include performance standards of how students are expected to show they have mastered the content material. A third kind of standard is an oppor-tunity-to-learn standard, holding the school itself—resources, programs, staff training, personnel—accountable for delivering the support needed so that all students can reach high standards. The national standards move-ment has helped push schools to consider the adequacy of their goals, appropriateness of their assessments, and their approaches to data collec-tion. In the process, school sites seeking to maximize achievement and equity also found a useful new vocabulary and conceptual basis for answer-ing their own questions about the impacts of their program.

Once standards are in place, they are only useful to the degree that progress towards achieving those standards is measured—and then used to improve the program. And this is where the data-based inquiry process enters. Once a school has grappled with defining desired outcomes and standards, the quest for appropriate measures involves practitioners in con-ducting research, collecting data and considering the implications of what they have collected.

WHOLE-SCHOOL, SITE-BASED REFORM

Relatively recently, a movement has grown for whole-school reforms that are generated and renewed from within. Continuous inquiry and, thus, the use of data, are at the heart of this movement, along with collegial and collaborative relationships among educators developing a shared vision. Inquiry is used to build relationships and shared vision, as well as answer specific questions or fuel action plans. Processes of inquiry are school-wide, involving everyone.

School renewal recreates the organization from within—through changes that support continuous examination and improvement of the edu-cation process at every level (Joyce et al., 1993). The school is engaged in a life of inquiry (Schaefer, 1967) where there is continuous examination and improvement of teaching and learning, and where students are also engaged in continuous inquiry. By studying the learning environment, the school increases its inquiries, which in turn provide synergy, resulting in initiatives with greater effects on students (Joyce and Calhoun, 1995).

Researchers and educators in each of these fields have found that data and inquiry are powerful tools, especially in the hands of educators and advocates who want to make real changes. As those working in civil rights and standards-based reforms can attest, data-based inquiry is especially needed to attain high levels of achievement and equity. Without the right data, and a productive, ongoing process for examining data, schools would have a difficult time reaching their goals.

While you may choose to build on an existing tradition or start with one kind of data use, keep the big picture in mind: the best schools use data in all of these ways.

A PROCESS FOR ANALYZING DATA TOGETHER

If you are trying to figure out how to help your school improve access and achievement for its English Language Learners, you've got some serious data work to do. The following section outlines a comprehensive set of activities designed to engage a group in looking at achievement, access and equity data. Although the examples given here relate to English Language Learners, the same process has been used effectively with educators exploring data related to African-American, English-only Latino, and other groups of students for whom achievement and equity issues must remain in the forefront.

If your group has more experience with data, going through every step of the process may not be necessary. If, on the other hand, your group is newly formed or new to data work in general, you may want to have everyone experience each step with each other as one way to build common understandings. The process is designed to accomplish the following:

🖎 To discuss individual and group understandings of the meanings of the words "access" and "achievement," and how you might measure whether you've achieved them or not.

🖎 To give everyone concrete experiences with using and discussing data as a tool to generate consensus about the meaning of achievement and access.

🖎 To help people see how to use data to help the school identify work to be done and prioritize student needs.

❧ To model how to use data to deepen your thinking about what you can do and to figure out what interventions make the most sense.

❧ To experience ways to use data that help you see what else you need to know in order to shape your inquiries.

THE GROUP DATA PROCESS

Part I: Create Time and Space for People to Come Together

Part II: Set a Tone and Elicit Agreements on Purpose and Safety

Part III: Develop Group Definitions for Equity

Part IV: Consider Standard Definitions for Equity

Part V: Clarify the Purpose of the Meeting

Part VI: Present the Data Effectively

Part VII: Reach Agreement on What the Data Say

Part VIII: Record New Questions

Part IX: Prioritize Achievement and Participation Concerns

Part X: Brainstorm Theories and Explanations/Explore Interpretations

By the end of this process, your group will be ready to take on the next steps: constructing an inquiry to find out more about what you need to know; developing action plans; and checking back in on your theories of change. You may also realize that you need to do some work at your school to create the conditions for productive data use and to build the structures, including data systems, that support your needs. The final section of this chapter explores all of these next steps.

PART I: CREATE TIME AND SPACE FOR PEOPLE TO COME TOGETHER

In the beginning, some formal, facilitated sessions are helpful for leading people through a process of looking at and talking about data. The formal sessions will begin to get people used to working with data, assure them that the purpose really is reflection and deepened understandings, and sow the habits of asking questions of the data and deriving implications.

You need to keep the discussion groups small enough (ten to fifteen people) so real dialogue is possible. Fruitful data sessions are impossible with whole faculties or other large groups of people. Selecting the appropriate mix of people for these groups is key. Be sure you have people at the table who are major advocates and sources of expertise about ELL issues in the school, or at least assemble a group of people who might be interested in knowing more about ELLs. Sometimes it also helps to include teachers from different levels of the school (for example, across departments in secondary schools), as well as major "players" in the school. Having key players at the table, understanding the data about immigrant student achievement, can help make any future actions or plans easier to implement.

It is also important to devote sufficient time to delve into the issues. A minimum of several hours gives the group enough time to go through significant portions of the process described ahead. It takes several hours to work through a packet of data, have a meaningful discussion where people really get a chance to hear each other, and draw some implications for next steps.

ACTIVITY 3.3
CONSTRUCTING YOUR DATA GROUP

Take some time to think about the construction of a data group at your school. Remember, you want to limit the group to no more than 10 to 15 people—who would it need to include?

🌾 Who has real expertise about this population?

🌾 Who would comprise a good mix for getting a sense of LEP student participation and achievement across the school?

🌾 Who really needs to be part of this so that action can grow out of the discussion?

PART II: SET A TONE AND ELICIT AGREEMENTS ON PURPOSE AND SAFETY

In inviting people to the table, make it very clear that the purpose of examining student data is to help the school address the challenges of ELL achievement. You are gathering together to identify areas that need further inquiry, figure out your priorities, and structure the support, policies and programs students need to reach high standards. Many educators will need to be reminded that the purpose is not compliance or blame. When entering a data dialogue, educators need to know that the discussion is going to lead to a plan that there are resources available to support. Most educators have spent many hours filling flip chart sheets with ideas and plans, only to see these pages tossed in the recycling bin. The presence of school and district leadership can help assure them that this plan will be supported, backed up by adequate resources and followed up on.

Keeping a clear focus on using data to develop an action plan is crucial when examining issues of equity and exclusion. By definition, to examine LEP student achievement data means facing the kind of information that is the stuff of lawsuits against schools and is often used (and misused) in public dialogues to establish blame. It is the stuff that confronts teachers head-on with the relative weakness of their program.

It is just plain hard to spend time reflecting on evidence that things aren't working as well as we want for our students. This is made all the harder because most groups of educators don't have a reservoir of positive experiences with honest critiques and reflections about their program with each other.

To engage people productively in such a potentially "hot" topic, seek to find ways that paint a larger picture:

- Couch the task in terms of the larger challenge of designing schools that can work for all students.

- Stress the unprecedented challenges brought about by rapid demographic change and immigration.

- Focus on the problems of a schooling system that needs to re-tool itself to meet new challenges, not on the difficulties of individual teachers.

- Appeal to participants as responsible educators who are entrusted with crafting a solution.

- Remind participants that the purpose of looking at the data is to help them figure out what kinds of changes they need and want to make.

- Create a sense that change is possible, that they are part of creating that change and that they are not alone.

SHIFTING THE ATMOSPHERE FOR DATA DIALOGUE

To discuss data productively, we need to shift away from the atmosphere that often accompanies educational data and create a more supportive environment. One school community developed the following list of requirements for a supportive climate:

🌿 We need mutual trust and a belief that others are honestly attempting to find solutions and are committed to ending inequities.

🌿 We agree not to use data to humiliate or point fingers at others.

🌿 We need everyone to acknowledge that they play a role in reproducing inequitable patterns, but conversely, also have power to change the problems.

🌿 Everyone must be able to understand the data and how they were derived.

ACTIVITY 3.4
SETTING GUIDELINES FOR DIALOGUE

Everyone in this nation is heir to a deep and heavy history around racism and exclusion which evokes rage, guilt and fear of open discussion. The key is to focus on how, through your work together, your group can be part of the solution. To do this, it is crucial to think together about what kind of discussion about data you desire. To get full participation, it helps to brainstorm a set of guidelines that will describe the dialogue.

Here are examples of the sorts of guidelines that you might want to consider for discussions focused on "Sharing Perspectives and Deepening Our Understandings" (adapted from Kristin Geiser):

🌾 A "sharing perspectives" discussion is not a debate. This is not about one perspective winning over another.

🌾 Such a discussion assumes that the deeper our thinking, the better our understanding—and that we need to help each other think more deeply and invite each other's help in pushing our own thinking.

🌾 Assume that no one person has the full perspective and that we need each other's experiences and perspectives to get the fullest possible understanding of an issue.

🌾 Every interpretation or analysis should be viewed as a hypothesis that can and should be checked out further before it becomes the basis of action.

🌾 The basic guideline should be to focus on those aspects of a "problem" or "solution" that we, as educators, can do something about—and that are focused on student achievement or access.

🌾 It is everyone's responsibility to not retreat from the conversation, and to not write anyone else off. Stay in the conversation. Each person's perspective and input is essential.

🌾 Assume that everyone at the table is there because each wants to make schools a better place for English Language Learners.

It is also helpful to ask people to agree to confidentiality within the discussion. This means that they can ask questions or state tentative conclusions without fear that they will be quoted out of context later. It means that as they talk about the problems and obstacles to achievement at the school they can be honest without fear of something being repeated without their permission. At the end of the session, have people again visit the issue of confidentiality. You may decide to share what happened and the content of the discussion with others—but be clear about the parameters of this sharing.

The chart on the following page shows how to respond to several of the most common patterns that arise in discussions of data.

HOW TO AVOID COMMON DATA PITFALLS

Common Pattern	*What to Do*
Issues come up that the data do not necessarily raise.	• Chart data questions for later investigation.
Individuals and/or the group jump quickly from looking at a display of data into designing and planning interventions.	• Build in a way to keep track of the intervention suggestions, thereby capturing the ideas without getting sidetracked.
The discussion feels abstract and isolated from concrete next steps.	• Remind participants of the purpose of looking at the data—to address student achievement challenges—throughout the process.
Statements about the data blame young people and/or are based on an assumption that there's nothing that the school can do (e.g., "those kids just don't try, they don't want to learn").	• Pose strategic questions that seek understanding and clarification (e.g., What do you mean by "those kids"? Which students?). • Ask for evidence (e.g., How do you know? What makes you say that?). • Find the part of what is said that you can empathize with or validate, and then propose another interpretation.
The discussion keeps coming back to the data we need instead of the data we are looking at together.	• Chart the data questions that arise. • Continue to focus the group on "what is there" in the data. People will always find more if you are persistent.
The data are not disaggregated so it is hard to see how specific groups of students are achieving.	• Again, chart the data needs. Often there is a resource person in the school or district who may be able to help disaggregate data if you ask.
People want to see longitudinal data but the school has used different tests each year.	• Chart these data questions. Again, you never know what you can get if you don't ask.
The group is confused about how to use qualitative data.	• Qualitative data are useful for understanding some of the "why" questions that may arise. • Try to focus the group on asking effective questions about student achievement as a starting place for looking at all data.
The group is hesitant to say things which might be taken as blame. This is preventing honest dialogue and examination of the data.	• Re-connect to the norms you established with the group about being open and not blaming. • Emphasize that the purpose of looking at data is to help students. This is important work.
The group feels depressed by the patterns that emerge.	• Find positive patterns and recognize successes. • Remember that you are part of the solution.

(Developed by High Performance Learning Communities Consortium, RPP International. Collaborators include California Tomorrow and Bay Area Coalition of Essential Schools.)

PART III: DEVELOP GROUP DEFINITIONS FOR EQUITY

One of the important preparatory steps for a group looking at data is for members to share and discuss their definitions of equity. The people in your school or group need to define equity for yourselves so you have a shared understanding of what you hope to achieve. Usually these discussions reveal views along the following lines: equity involves providing equal treatment; equity involves providing whatever treatment and support is needed so all children have an opportunity to reach the same high standards; equity occurs when all children actually reach high standards and these outcomes are themselves the measure of whether equity exists.

The following excerpt from a discussion among one group of teachers illustrates the kind of dialogue that can occur around definitions of equity:

"For me, I think, equity will be when our kids in the flatland schools of Oakland get class sizes, teachers with as much training, labs for science and sports equipment equal to what kids in the hill schools are getting. That's equity—being sure that the neighborhood a kid grows up in doesn't define what they are given."

"I just think it's plain and simple—everyone having the opportunity to really fulfill their potential."

"But how do you know if that's happened? How do you measure? And anyway, we can't develop every bit of every kid's potential. That's not real. But we ought to be able to be sure every child leaves school with some basic level of skills they need to succeed. For me, I guess, equity would be everyone leaving school able to move on in some way that they can support themselves."

"Four-year college entrance. That's what we ought to be able to promise every student—that when they leave high school, they have the option of going on to college. It's up to them if they want to do that, but it's up to us to see that they are prepared and have that option."

"I think that's absurd. In this day and age, so few jobs require a college degree, it's a waste to mislead students."

As the example illustrates, most people do not share the same framework for thinking about these issues. Looking at data to uncover patterns of academic failure and achievement, or patterns of exclusion and access, can be confusing in a group unless the preparatory work is done to uncover individual beliefs about equity. You can apply multiple definitions and seek multiple forms of evidence, but if you avoid wrestling with talking about what you're looking for, you will miss rich dialogue and potentially set yourself up for frustration down the road.

ACTIVITY 3.5
WHAT DO WE MEAN BY THE WORDS
"ACCESS," "EQUITY" AND "ACHIEVEMENT"?

This activity is intended to get at the heart of the various meanings people bring to the words access, equity and achievement. It asks: What kind of data would provide evidence to tell you whether your have an achievement, equity or access problem?

Step 1: Divide into three groups: One group should take the word "access," another should take "achievement" and the third, "equity." Each group then brainstorms around the following questions:

☛ What does this word/concept mean?

☛ What evidence would we look for to see if we have attained it?

Step 2: Each group reports to the others on their meanings and evidence of access and achievement. While reporting, you might center the discussion around the following:

☛ Did you agree on measures?

☛ Were you talking about the same things when you spoke of "access" or "achievement" or "equity"?

☛ What were some of the complexities? Tensions? Difficulties in arriving at shared definitions and evidence?

USING LEGAL DEFINITIONS OF
ACCESS AND EQUITY TO SPARK REFLECTION

Several court decisions have profoundly influenced public policy and discourse around educating all students (see Chapter Two for further discussion). The decisions have, however, produced definitions that are sometimes posed as conflicting. In the *Brown v. Board of Education, 1954*, decision, the Supreme Court ruled to end racial segregation by stating:

"In these days, it is doubtful that any child may reasonably be expected to succeed in life if he is denied the opportunity of an education. Such an opportunity, where the state has undertaken to provide it, is a right which must be made available to all on equal terms…We conclude that in the field of public education, the doctrine of 'separate but equal' has no place. Separate educational facilities are inherently unequal."

The 14th Amendment to the U.S. Constitution, the Equal Protection Clause, and the Civil Rights Act of 1964 assure non-discrimination on the basis of race, gender and national origin, which the Office of Civil Rights used as a basis for protection of language minority children with limited English skills. The very fact that we can focus on English Language Learners and have programs designed to meet their needs is because civil rights law defines language as a barrier to accessing equal education.

Based on this legal framework, the U.S. Supreme Court issued the landmark ruling in the case of *Lau v. Nichols, 1974*, establishing the foundation for bilingual education. In their ruling, the justices stated:

"There is no equality of treatment merely by providing students with the same facilities, books, teachers, curriculum, for students who do not understand English are effectively foreclosed from any meaningful education."

They went on to say:

"Any grouping employed by the school system to deal with the special language skills and needs of national origin minority group children must be designed to meet such needs as soon as possible, and must not operate as an educational dead-end or permanent track."

The quotes from *Brown v. Board of Education* and *Lau v. Nichols* illustrate the tensions in "same" and "different" educational approaches as remedies for exclusion. Ask yourself the following questions about the quotes:

🖋 What does *Brown v. Board of Education* mean by…?

🖋 What does *Lau v. Nichols* mean by…?

🖋 Is there a conflict?

🌾 If so, what is it?

🌾 If not, why not?

In the *Lau* case, the court made no specific mandate or recommendations about bilingual education programs themselves, stressing only that schools must take affirmative steps to provide appropriate relief to rectify the language barrier. Later, in the *Castenada* case, a three-prong test was devised to determine whether schools were, in fact, providing affirmative steps to provide appropriate relief. A school must be able to show that its program is:

🌾 Informed by sound educational theory

🌾 Implemented effectively and with appropriate resources

🌾 Evaluated as being able to overcome language barriers

These cases provide a sound basis for formulating a set of questions that can help you determine whether you are providing access and appropriate programs for our English Language Learners:

🌾 Is what we are doing really based on the best research so that we can expect it will result in strong outcomes?

🌾 Are we devoting sufficient resources to the implementation of our program so it can be fully implemented? This requires data about teacher training, availability of books and materials, etc.

🌾 Are our English Language Learners making progress fast enough to catch up to their native English-speaking peers?

PART IV: CONSIDER SOME STANDARD DEFINITIONS OF EQUITY

You have now explored your own definitions of access, equity and achievement, and read the language contained in some of the legal frameworks connected to these concepts. It can also be useful for a group to spend time together reviewing the more commonly applied concepts of these words in education. These five common definitions are useful for looking at all sub-populations of students:

🌿 Proportionality

🌿 Progress over time

🌿 Size of gaps

🌿 Comparison to other locales

🌿 Meeting high standards

Two other frameworks for equity deal specifically with English Language Learners:

🌿 Reaching achievement in the ballpark of English-fluent students

🌿 Reaching and maintaining achievement at a par with English fluent students

For each, a definition and examples are provided below. Mull these over and talk about reactions and concerns. Once you have completed the steps in Part III and reflected on these definitions, you should then have enough common language with which to discuss your own data and the equity issues in your school.

Proportionality

From a civil rights perspective, most monitoring of access in education is based upon the notions of proportionality, representation and comparison to other groups. This perspective assumes, for example, that if all else were equal and there were no barriers or discrimination, if the students of one racial group made up 20% of the school population, they would then represent 20% of any achievement group (i.e., 20% of those students entering a four-year college after graduation would be made up of this particular racial group). Equity is achieved when any group is reflected in proportion to its representation in the larger population. Conversely, disproportionality means lack of equity.

PROPORTIONALITY

Our Latino students are 29% of our entering ninth graders. What happens to them proportionally as they move through our school?

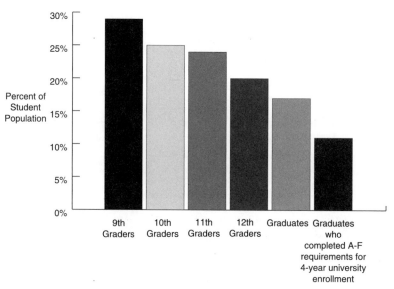

Latino students are 35% of our school. They are over-represented among those receiving disciplinary referrals, and under-represented in college preparatory courses and extracurricular activities.

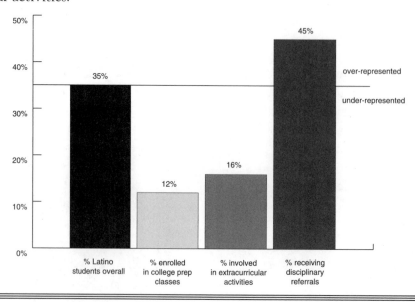

Progress Over Time

Another common measure used by courts and advocates is progress over time. Is a group doing better now than in the past? Does its progress mirror that of other groups? If we look at the progress of Latino students over time in a certain school district, we might conclude that they are doing better now than ten years ago. For example, one could say, "We are doing well; we are more equitable because there has been a 118% increase in Latinos over the past ten years in our university system."

Size of Gaps

Yet another measure of progress in serving LEP students is whether or not they are catching up with their English-speaking peers. Are we closing the gaps? For LEP students to catch up, they must make more than one year's progress in school in one year's time, because their English Only peers are also progressing in their English development, as the following chart illustrates. It may be that all students are improving, and that LEP students are improving at the same rates as their English-fluent peers, but the gap is still not closing. Attention to the size of the gap is crucial, as is attention to the need for accelerated learning for secondary students who have to make greater progress to close the gap.

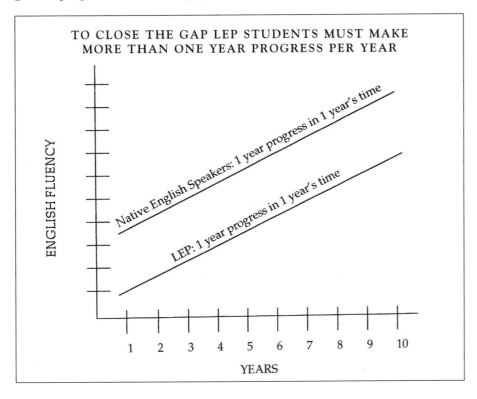

Comparison to Other Locales

The comparison of two schools in different neighborhoods, or of one county's schools to state or national averages, yields yet a different view of equity. For example, 33.8% of Alameda County's high school students complete the college A-F requirements, compared to a state average of 32.3%. Alameda could take pride in exceeding the state average. However, this comparison approach does not tell whether the state average is acceptable—merely how one locale compares to an overall average. Further, these kinds of comparisons tell nothing about how different racial/ethnic or language groups fare within Alameda County. In fact, vast discrepancies exist; for example, among the county's Hispanic students, 20.5% complete the college A-F requirements, compared to 51.5% of Asian students (data from California Department of Education).

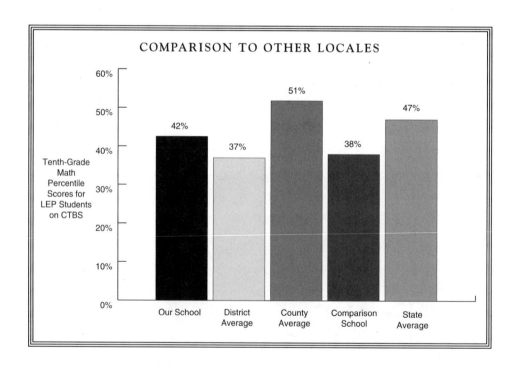

Meeting High Standards

An important element of this era of school reform is the emphasis on standards. Measuring whether our students are reaching those standards, and what percent of LEP students compared to English Only and FEP students can reach them, is important. A word of caution is required, however. Most district standards are minimum standards. Professional standards in curriculum areas are usually much higher. In determining whether our students are reaching high standards, we must always be aware of what the standards are and whether we consider them sufficient. Then we must define benchmarks for determining progress toward those standards.

Linoleum cut by Peng Lim, a high school student from Cambodia

Reaching Achievement in the Ballpark of English-Fluent Students

Currently, districts in California are required to define a set of measures that mark the point at which an English Language Learner has sufficiently caught up to English-fluent peers such that they can now be considered "Fluent English Proficient." Called the "redesignation" criteria, it marks the official point at which special instruction and support to overcome the language barrier ends. These criteria vary: from students scoring as low as at the 28th percentile on a standardized test of English, to as high as the 40th; from requiring that students receive a C or better in academic courses, to no assessment at all of how students are doing in classes. Redesignation is not a linguistic measure of a student having reached full English fluency—rather it is a somewhat arbitrary point at which a district determines the student needs no further special help. In no district is redesignation defined at the average (50th percentile) of English-fluent achievement. Therefore, redesignation measures only that a student is now "in the ballpark" of English-fluent students—not that he or she has caught up and overcome the language difference.

ACTIVITY 3.6
REFLECTING ON YOUR REDESIGNATION CRITERIA

Find out your district's redesignation criteria. How close to the English-fluent average does it come? What other criteria exist as evidence that the student is achieving "in the ballpark" or on a par with English-fluent students? What measures and standards do you think should be used?

Our district's redesignation criteria	What I think it should be...
Percentile achieved on standardized test of English:	
Other criteria:	

Reaching and Maintaining Achievement on a Par with English-Fluent Students

This measure of whether we have, in fact, helped our LEP students overcome language barriers is based on whether they reach and maintain achievement on a par with English-fluent students. In this case, for example, redesignation standards at third grade would only mean that LEP students have sufficient English language development to function close to a par with English-fluent students at that level. It would not be sufficient to inform us about whether the students' literacy base in English is strong enough to maintain the same level as English-fluent students as the academic English requirements become more and more complex over time.

Long-term data on LEP students have demonstrated that many students (particularly those who do not develop strong primary language literacy and were redesignated in elementary school) progress to a certain level academically and then fall further and further behind as they reach upper elementary school years and secondary school. The following graph illustrates this trend:

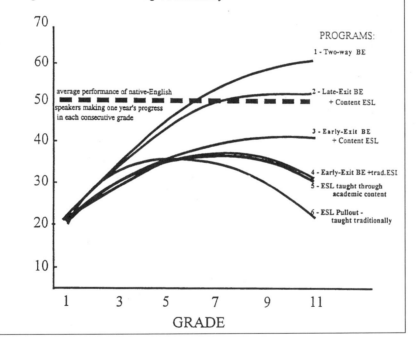

GENERAL PATTERN OF K-12 LANGUAGE MINORITY
STUDENT ACHIEVEMENT ON STANDARDIZED TESTS
IN ENGLISH READING
COMPARED ACROSS SIX PROGRAM MODELS

(Data aggregated from a series of 3-7 year longitudinal studies from well-implemented, mature programs in five school districts)
© Wayne P. Thomas & Virginia P. Collier, 1997

Program 1: Two-way developmental bilingual education (BE)
Program 2: Late-exit bilingual education + ESL taught through academic content
Program 3: Early-exit bilingual education + ESL taught through academic content
Program 4: Early-exit bilingual education + ESL taught traditionally
Program 5: ESL taught through academic content using current approaches
Program 6: ESL Pullout - taught traditionally

It is important for elementary school teachers to see what happens to their LEP students as they move on to the upper grades—and that secondary school teachers see the patterns that students experienced at elementary school. For many districts and schools, this may mean constructing a database that stores historical information and continuously tracks students across the full K-12 spectrum.

You might want to reflect on whether you know what happens to redesignated students after they become FEP. Do you have a way of tracking their achievement in comparison to English Only students?

PART V: CLARIFY THE PURPOSE OF THE MEETING

This next part of the process may or may not be necessary, depending on the amount of time your group has and the needs of the group. The idea here is to give you a chance to look and think together about what you want to try to change about your school and its program for LEP students.

Begin with some activity that will give the group a sense of what is on each other's minds. Before actually handing out any data packets, warm up the discussion with an "into" activity that evokes some of the concerns people have about ELL achievement. Three questions that might be helpful are:

- What concerns do you now have about how LEP students are doing at your school?

- What questions do you have about your LEP students?

- What challenges are you facing in serving LEP students that you would like new handles, approaches or supports for addressing?

You might write these questions on wall charts and give folks pens so that they can mill around and fill in their responses. It will give you a chance to reflect, to see what one another is thinking.

Exploring these questions together makes it clear that examining data will not subordinate or ignore group knowledge and that the discussion can build from where you are. It can also help you get a sense of each other's agendas and concerns.

PART VI: PRESENT THE DATA EFFECTIVELY

Before you hand out packets of any data, make sure that you know your data well. You should know where the data came from, how the data were collected, the tests and criteria, and other pertinent information. Make sure the data make sense and are accurate.

Everyone in the group should get a packet of data. It's too hard to try to examine data that is just on an overhead screen. Provide a good packet of data for each person—to write on, to examine, to take away. This makes it clear that it is "their" data—that it is meant as a tool for real work. Packets need to include multiple kinds of evidence and measures (achievement, program placement, redesignation, etc.) and good comparative information (allowing people to see comparisons over time, comparisons between LEP students and FEP and EO students, etc.).

SAMPLE TABLE OF CONTENTS FOR A DATA PACKET
LAS ALMAS MIDDLE SCHOOL

I.   Demographics
       Our school statistics
       Date first entered U.S. schools for children born outside of the U.S.
       Percentage of actual attendance, 1994/95
       Percentage of students with 20 or more absences, 1994/95

II. Achievement Test Results
       CTBS average NCE scores, 6th grade
       CTBS average NCE scores, 7th grade
       CTBS average NCE scores, 8th grade
       CTBS Spring 1993-Spring 1995
       1994 CLAS results
       8th grade proficiency results: reading
       8th grade proficiency results: writing
       8th grade proficiency results: mathematics

III. Redesignation Data
       Redesignated students by redesignation option
       Redesignation rates, 1991-1996

IV. Redesignation: What Does It Mean?
       District services for English Language Learners
       Redesignation options
       School district redesignation form

V.   LEP program services
       Oral language proficiency level and English literacy program

VI. Professional Development Plan and Glossary of Instructional Strategies
       Professional growth plan
       Glossary of instructional strategies

(The template and format for this data packet is based on the project SUCCESS model in Glendale Unified School District, developed by Suzanne Risse, Kelly King, Judy Sanchez and Laurie Olsen.)

SELECTIONS FROM A DATA PACKET:

EIGHTH GRADE PROFICIENCY RESULTS: PERCENT PASSING
LAS ALMAS MIDDLE SCHOOL

	Reading			Writing			Mathematics		
	LEP	FEP	English Only	LEP	FEP	English Only	LEP	FEP	English Only
1992-93	81.6%	99.2%	93.1%	78.9%	97.6%	92.4%	70%	98.4%	87.8%
1993-94	63.6%	95.8%	93.1%	78.5%	99.3%	91.2%	58.3%	95.8%	82.9%
1994-95	72.2%	98.8%	95.7%	59.5%	97.5%	91.4%	66%	95.7%	91.2%
1995-96	69.6%	98.3%	93.6%	57.7%	95.5%	85.7%	67.6%	95.5%	89.6%
1996-97	60.0%	97.7%	94.2%	42.9%	95.5%	91.9%	60.9%	97.7%	85.5%

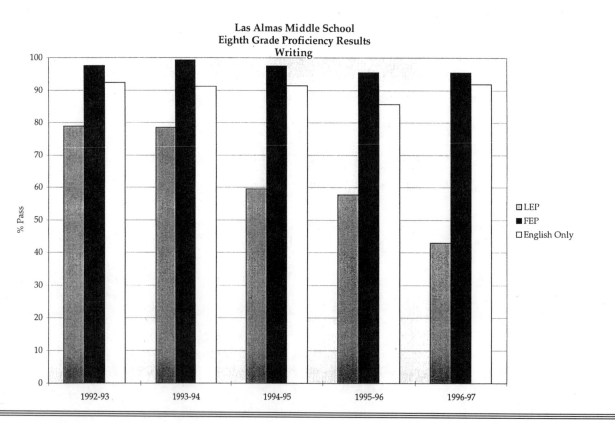

**Las Almas Middle School
Eighth Grade Proficiency Results
Writing**

STUDENTS RECEIVING A "D" OR "F" IN ACHIEVEMENT
LAS ALMAS MIDDLE SCHOOL

	LEP Students	FEP Students	EO Students	Total Students
# of Students	77	73	253	403
% of Students	49.6%	20.9%	37.3%	34.1%
# of Total Student Population	155	348	678	1,181
% of Total Student Population	13.1%	29.5%	57.4%	N/A

LEP STUDENTS RECEIVING A "D" OR "F" IN ACHIEVEMENT
BY NUMBER OF CLASSES
LAS ALMAS MIDDLE SCHOOL

	One Class	Two Classes	Three Classes	Four Classes	Five Classes	LEP Students Receiving a "D" or "F"	Total # of LEP Students at Site
# of LEP Students	41	8	16	8	4	77	155
% of LEP Students	26.5%	5.2%	10.3%	5.2%	2.6%	49.7%	N/A

Display the data so people can make sense of them. It helps to display data in multiple ways: as statements, charts of numbers or visuals, such as bar charts. Individuals learn in different ways and need to see data presented in different ways. It can also help to have printed explanations of each category of data (see examples in the box on the following page).

SAMPLE EXPLANATIONS FOR CATEGORIES OF DATA

ETHNICITY

The ethnic breakdown of the school's student population can be found in the CBEDS (California Basic Educational Data System) report of data compiled by the school and supplied to the district each October. These data reflect the numbers of students in different ethnic groups in the school; the information is compiled from student enrollment forms filled out by parents/guardians.

STANFORD ACHIEVEMENT TEST

The Stanford Achievement Test (also called the SAT-9) is an annually administered standardized test measuring achievement in math, reading and language. The scores are reported both as raw scores (number of items correct) and as "Normal Curve Equivalent" (NCE) scores separated by grade level, sub-test (such as Math, Reading and Language Arts) and language proficiency. The NCE is represented on a scale of 1 to 99 with an average score (mean) of 50. NCEs above 50 reflect better-than-average performance, whereas NCEs below 50 indicate less-than-average performance.

Explain the data in simple terms. Many educators have math anxiety which must be addressed in an effective data presentation. Complicating teachers' math anxiety is a healthy distrust many have for representing student work and achievement in quantitative, standardized and single measures. This distrust and anxiety can be addressed in many ways:

- Make sure people work through the data in small enough groups that they can help each other.
- Spread out people who feel comfortable with math across the groups.
- Do some work ahead of time so that the data are already arrayed in raw numbers, percentages and ratios.
- Have calculators available.
- Make sure you explain terms such as percentiles, ratios, proportionality and so on.
- Be explicit and clear about the mathematics and formulas involved. For example, determining whether a group is underrepresented in an achievement category requires a comparison of percentages.

❧ Remind people about how to calculate percentages. For example, if Spanish LEP students represent 47 out of 53 fifth-grade LEP students in the school, this means they are 88% of the LEP population at that grade level. Explain that this percentage was calculated in the following way:

$$\frac{47}{53} \times \frac{X}{100}$$

$$\frac{47 \times 100}{53} = X$$

$$53\overline{)4700} \quad 88\% \text{ (rounded up)}$$

Deal with educators' concerns about the use of standardized measures. When people raise these concerns, encourage the group to have an honest dialogue about the shortcomings of standardized tests and scores. Explain that these kinds of data should be used as a starting place for deeper-level exploration. By using multiple measures, you can compare them to each other and compensate for some of the shortcomings of a particular measure. For example, some teachers may be unhappy using the reading section of the SAT-9 as evidence of students' reading comprehension, because the test doesn't adequately measure how students apply what they know in the classroom and may not be aligned with the curriculum used at their school. Rather than throwing out the SAT-9 results, review them side by side with other measures of reading, such as district proficiency tests. Encourage teachers to provide their perceptions.

None of the data we have are perfect. But simply throwing data out or critiquing the measures at length can bog down the whole process of trying to understand student achievement. We don't have the data we need yet, but we can use what we do have to formulate the questions for our deeper inquiry. This is a crucial starting place for deeper reflection and dialogue.

If possible, don't restrict yourself to data about students only during their years at your school. Try to give an overview of their entire K-12 experience. Emphasize that while the real measures of our long-term impact will be found in the last years of high school, we need to know what happened earlier with our students. What data do we have about our students' achievement in the earlier grades? Where actual data aren't available, you might want to use general research data that show achievement over time for LEP students. This at least raises for people the benefits of taking longitudinal looks at achievement.

PART VII: REACH AGREEMENT ON WHAT THE DATA SAY

As soon as data packets are handed out, people start sifting through them, looking for something of interest. Immediately, one person wants to talk about the need for role models, someone else wants to argue about whether the redesignation data could possibly be correct, and someone else wants to talk about adopting new grade-level standards. To avoid this free-for-all, it is important to use a process for examining data that first immerses people in agreement about what each data element actually says. This is crucial before embarking on discussion about interpretation and intervention.

Step 1: Have everyone individually go through each chart in the data packet, giving them plenty of time to mull over the numbers and determine whether they can make some sense of what they see. Ask people to pay attention to the standard questions: What do you see that shows how our LEP students are doing in comparison to our EOs? In comparison to standards (national percentiles, standard attainment, etc.)? Is our LEP student achievement getting better or worse over time? Which subjects and areas of achievement are stronger? Weaker? As you go, be sure people are clear about the data represented in each chart in the packet.

Step 2: Bit by bit, work through the data, reaching agreement as a group about what the data actually say. For example, "On CTBS in fourth-grade language, our LEP students are scoring far below (about 20 points) our English Only and FEP students. By fifth grade, this gap has grown. Our LEP students are now 30 points below the English Only students, and 38 points below the FEP students in language." Only after the group has worked through all the data and agreed on a series of data statements should you move on to matters of interpretation, intervention or meaning. Make sure someone is charting the data statements as they are made.

PART VIII: RECORD NEW QUESTIONS

While agreement is being reached about what the data say, be sure to record new questions that the data are raising. This will become the foundation for possible later inquiries. For example, "The data show that as our LEP and EO students move up through the grades, the gap between them in language grows larger. How can we tell if the LEP group falling behind includes many students who have been at our school for some time or if this group is mainly characterized by newcomer students coming in at older ages with low levels of English fluency? How can we tell? Can we see the data separately for the students we've had at our school since 9th grade, and see SAT-9 in terms of length of time in the country?"

You might want to have a wall chart titled "Data Issues and Needs for Additional Data" as a running record and reminder that an important agenda item is to figure out what kind of data you need to track down.

Data Statements/Findings	Data Issues/Data We Need

PART IX: PRIORITIZE ACHIEVEMENT AND PARTICIPATION CONCERNS:

Usually, the data point to one or two student achievement and participation problems—for example, literacy in the content areas, few students completing requirements for higher education, or high failure rates in academic classes. But sometimes there is a long list of potential areas to focus upon. Then, you need to help the group prioritize. It's hard to prioritize if there is no sense of criteria. The question then becomes: What should guide us in determining what to focus on?

Sometimes, particularly if the group examining the data is small and somewhat marginalized within the school, it helps greatly to choose an area that is linked to a focus already prevailing in the school. For example, a group in a school whose district had adopted a new math curriculum knew they would be engaged in departmental meetings and trainings related to the new curriculum. They decided this was a good opportunity to bring attention to LEP student math achievement and the need to target instructional strategies in math for these students.

What should guide us in determining what to focus on?

At other times, you may specifically choose a focus area that affects many areas of the curriculum, such as reading comprehension. Always, a group should be encouraged to frame their priorities in terms of student achievement and access. This is why working from data about student achievement is so important. But sometimes other priorities will find their way onto the list: we need new textbooks, we don't have enough aides, the year-round schedule is a killer, etc. If this happens, the work of the group is to reframe these priorities in terms of achievement.

For example, a desire for new textbooks can be framed as: "Students are doing poorly on standardized tests in math. We think it is happening partly because we have outdated books or we don't have enough books for students to take home and study. The problem is poor achievement on standardized tests in math. The strategy is to get more textbooks."

Once you have the list of student achievement challenges to focus upon, and you have had some discussion about criteria on prioritizing, here are some helpful ways to prioritize:

- Everyone gets three votes. Go through the list and have people vote. The highest scoring item is the major focus.

- Go around the room and have each person say what he or she thinks is most important. Check the items. People can name as many as they wish. This approach takes time, but gives everyone a voice and allows for people to really hear what others' concerns may be.

🕊 Offer an analysis as the facilitator. "It seems that I heard the most concern about reading comprehension. Is that true?"

🕊 If it seems there is real disagreement about the magnitude of a certain achievement problem, consider using a fishbowl approach.

☛ Invite those who feel a specific problem really is most important to sit in a circle. For five minutes, have them discuss why they think the problem is so crucial, how they see it playing out in their own classrooms, and why they feel it is an area requiring change.

☛ Next, those who don't think this achievement problem should be a priority should sit in a fishbowl while the rest of the group listens to them. They should discuss why this problem doesn't seem so urgent, or what their concerns are about naming it as top priority.

☛ Afterwards, have people get in pairs, each including one person from the "urgent priority" group and one from the "not-so-urgent" group. Each person should share what he or she heard that led to some new perspective. The sharing is not to reiterate positions, but to reflect on what you heard and to try to understand differently.

☛ Finally, ask the group again to consider the question of priorities. If there are still major differences, suggest that two different focuses might be a good idea and allow folks to choose which they want to work on.

PART X: BRAINSTORM THEORIES AND EXPLANATIONS

Examine your theories

Once the data patterns have emerged, encourage discussion about theories and explanations. What do we think is going on to explain these patterns? Encourage people to think in terms of a chain of events. For example, if someone thinks that the increase in the number of "long-term LEP" students (students who have been LEP for 7 or more years) at the middle school level is due to a lack of primary language programs to develop literacy skills at the elementary level, encourage that person to trace a theory of action. What would need to happen in order to produce stronger language programs in elementary school in order to reduce the number of long-term LEP students in middle school?

The point of this part of the process is to show that there are many possible explanations for a single achievement problem. This makes a huge difference later, when the group decides on a plan of action. The differing beliefs about what "explains" low reading scores ("students do not read

enough at home" vs. "students are not motivated" vs. "Science and Social Studies teachers don't know how to teach reading") will compete against each other as people start to struggle with what to do about the problem.

Once the various competing theories are laid out, you can later develop a set of inquiries and dialogues that strengthen the chain of logic before interventions are actually put into place.

Explore your interpretations

Disaggregated data can unleash discussion and confrontation about responses, attitudes and beliefs. Differing interpretations of the data based on these factors lead to different proposed strategies. For example, if the data reveal that a certain population of students is failing in school, one interpretation of the problem may rest on the belief that this group of students is caught in a mismatch between their home culture and the school culture. The prescription, then, might be to try to draw some consistency between home and school, for example, by educating parents to support school learning at home or by training teachers to honor different cultural approaches within their classrooms.

In another interpretation, some educators may feel the school is failing this group of students because it is fundamentally ill-equipped to serve them. The prescription, then, might be to focus upon teacher preparation, funding or overcrowding—all requiring policy changes. A third analysis might focus upon the ways in which students' life experiences, such as poverty, abuse or family mobility, preclude their full participation in school. In this case, solutions might focus upon the school partnering with social services.

The broader the set of hypotheses and possible explanations, the more comprehensive and appropriate the solutions are likely to be. But drawing out such analyses opens precarious territory. There are those who still hold a deficiency view of their students, who assume that the failure of one group or another is a result of genetic or cultural inferiority. They will ascribe the failures not to what happens in school but to a set of "unchangeable" attributes they assign to "that community" or "that group." It helps to anticipate traditional, problematic interpretations such as the genetic or cultural deficiency model. Be prepared to challenge these interpretations and support the emerging inquiries with research that provides a basis for new thinking about student achievement and failure.

NEXT STEPS: WHAT TO DO AFTER THE GROUP DATA PROCESS

After you've examined achievement and access data together, it's time to take the next steps that will lead to action:

- ❦ Construct an Inquiry
- ❦ Develop an Action Plan
- ❦ Check Back In Regularly

As you begin to work with data and do your own inquiries, you may find that you are not operating in a school with the most optimal conditions for using data. You may need to take the lead or push for creating a stronger culture of using data. You may also discover that your data systems and the information they provide need to be improved. Thus, we end this chapter with suggestions for how to:

- ❦ Create the Conditions for Using Data Productively
- ❦ Take the Lead
- ❦ Build Effective Data Systems
- ❦ Design a Strong Student Information System

CONSTRUCT AN INQUIRY BEFORE TAKING ACTION

The point of immersing educators in data is not just to examine data. It is to deepen understanding about what needs to occur to produce higher achievement and fuller access for ELL students. It is to be sure that whatever effort goes into creating new programs or implementing new instructional approaches is based on the best understanding about what will make a difference.

So, once you have a sense of your major interpretations and hypotheses, it's time to figure out how to look a little deeper to confirm or alter those understandings. This is where having someone with real expertise on LEP issues is helpful—someone who knows what research exists and what resources are available. You may want to contact a district bilingual coordinator, someone from the County Office of Education or a professor from a nearby university. There may be faculty at your school who have taken (or taught) courses on LEP issues. A resource listing is provided at the end of this chapter which includes good organizations to contact for information. The basic question posed to the group should be:

What could we read to give us a deeper understanding of this issue?

Making the transition from looking at pages of numbers to figuring out what is really going on in a school requires investigation and a more formal inquiry process. The following process for conducting an inquiry can help:

Define the question: The inquiry begins when a group defines a question to pursue. For example, one school-site team examined their Language Census (R-30) and CBEDS data and constructed an inquiry focused around the following questions:

🖐 Why are so many of our LEP students "not in program"?

🖐 Who are these students?

🖐 How are they doing in mainstream classes?

🖐 Why can't they be redesignated as English fluent?

Decide what data to pursue: Beyond defining the question, you need to decide what kind of data to pursue. Are there more data you want to draw out of the student information system, such as getting an analysis of which language groups are failing in which classes? Are there some new assessment tools you want to use to get a better picture of which areas of writing are most problematic for students? Is there some aspect of the student experience you want to check out by talking with students? Might there be perspectives from other teachers about how this achievement issue plays out in other subjects?

Inquiries work best when they combine multiple forms of data: so-called "hard" (i.e., test scores) and "soft" (i.e., interviews) data, observations and achievement data, and so on. The larger patterns which are most apparent in quantitative or hard data can be given meaning and placed into a real context with the more "human" soft data. It helps teachers to see not only numbers but the actual list of student names the numbers represent. They can then put their own knowledge of those students to work in trying to unlock the puzzle of weak achievement. You can use the following form to construct an inquiry.

CONSTRUCTING AN INQUIRY

❧ **High Priority Access or Achievement Problem:**

❧ **The Question to be Pursued to Deepen Our Understanding of the Problem:**

❧ **Approaches to Answering the Question:**

Student Voice: What do we need to know from students? Which students?

Data Needed: What additional data do we need?

Research to be Read: What research might we read to shed new light on this problem?

Professional Development: What training approaches say they address this issue?

Observations: What do we need to observe to learn more?

Looking Outward: What models might we investigate for how others are grappling with the problem?

Seeking Other Perspectives: What kinds of dialogues might be helpful to get other perspectives? What other teachers, parents, etc. should we talk to for more information?

Policy Information: What policies exist that are affecting the problem?

Do some research on student needs: Often an inquiry requires actual research into the students and their needs. There are many different ways to elicit student experience, as described in Chapter Five: shadowing students, interviewing students, collecting student writing or student work. The more creative a group can become in listening to their students' experiences, the stronger their understanding will be around the larger patterns of underachievement. This kind of research forms a powerful counterpoint to achievement data, which can tell us a piece of how our students are doing, but not about our students' actual needs and experiences that might indicate what kinds of action we need to take.

The whole point of collecting data is to inform your school about what kind of programs it needs, what kinds of actions must be taken, and what changes in practice are needed.

Seek Professional Development Opportunities: There are often professional trainers and resource people who are working on instructional responses to particular achievement problems. It might be helpful for a small group to attend some of the trainings that are meant to speak directly to the achievement problem you are trying to understand. The purpose of attending such professional development is to glean as much as possible about how the achievement problem is understood and about the kinds of strategies that might be useful. Going as a group fosters the opportunity for deeper dialogue about what you learn together.

DEVELOP AN ACTION PLAN

Once you have become familiar with the relevant data and designed and pursued an inquiry into the issues raised by data, then it's time to develop an action plan. The whole point of collecting data is to inform your school about what kind of programs it needs, what kinds of actions must be taken, and what changes in practice are needed. An action plan should do the following:

- Summarize the data that show a problem exists.
- Define the change that the school is trying to bring about.
- Specify the measures that the school will use as evidence that the strategies in the action plan really result in improving the problem.
- List the actions the school will take.
- Describe your "theory of action" or "theory of change."
- Describe who will do what, when, and what kind of supports will be necessary to make it possible.
- Determine when the data will be examined to assess progress.

A "theory of action" is basically a statement of the problem, an interpretation of why the problem is occurring, the set of things you plan to do that you think will make a difference, and the evidence you will use to determine if you've had an effect. Each step has to be constructed well in order to have a real impact. Your interpretation of why the achievement problem exists has to be on target, or you'll be busy trying to fix the wrong thing. Your notion of what will improve that situation, likewise, has to be on target, or you will lose precious time and energy carrying out the wrong tasks, even though you appropriately identified the problem. You may have identified the right solutions, but you may not be implementing them fully or well. Finally, you could have the right analysis of the problem, a good, well-implemented plan that can really turn around that problem, but you might still not see the evidence of your impact if the right measures aren't being used!

The following is an example of an action plan which includes a clear theory of action:

Problem: Reading achievement is low on standardized tests, our LEP students are getting poor grades overall in Language Arts, and teachers note that many LEP students are "stuck" and not improving once they reach a certain basic level in reading.

Desired Change: Improve reading comprehension for our LEP students, and close the gap between English Only and LEP students in Language Arts.

Measures: SAT-9 reading scores, a new site-developed assessment of reading comprehension, and grades.

Our Theory of Action:

Problem	Activities	Results	Outcome
LEP students have low reading comprehension scores and low grades in Language Arts, especially compared to English Only students	Family literacy program; book-loan program; school-wide voluntary reading and professional development; talk to district about new upper-grades curriculum	More reading at home and in school; improved instruction and curriculum at the school	Increased reading achievement scores and grades in Language Arts for LEP students

Actions: Institute a family literacy program to engage parents in providing more home support for literacy; create a book-loan program for children and families; start school-wide voluntary reading; institute school-wide professional development in scaffolding, guided reading, reciprocal teaching and comprehension skills; and initiate dialogues with the district about adopting a new upper grades reading curriculum series.

Assessment Time Frame: At the end of the first year we'll check progress on our measures, investigate how teachers, parents and students are feeling about the new programs, and re-assess the action plan.

CHECK BACK IN REGULARLY

Once you begin taking action, it's important to check back in—reviewing the data at key points and rethinking the theory of action that guided your action plan. When you go back to revisit data the second, third or fourth time, it's important to go step by step, trying to figure out:

- Did we have the right interpretation?
- Were the steps we designed the right ones to address that problem?
- Did we choose the right action/intervention, but encounter trouble implementing it well?
- Did we implement our action/intervention well, but find that we don't really think it helped?
- Did we choose the right or wrong measures for evidence? Do we think we're having an impact but don't have the right tools to assess this for sure?

Here's an example of how one change group in a school looked back on their original theory of action to refine their efforts:

It's been two years now since a planning team from Roosevelt High School examined their data about LEP student achievement and developed a professional development plan aimed at reducing the high number of LEP students failing in their core academic classes. The staff had focused in those two years on getting intensive training in a score of literacy strategies for the content areas: reciprocal teaching, graphic organizers and mind-maps, reading for comprehension, etc. The first year was spent in inquiry, identifying who was actually failing and trying to figure out why. The educators had, as a result, established a special class for their "long-term LEP students with two or more F's." The data this year showed that while the students in that special class had, indeed, improved (F's were cut in half), the overall failure rates of LEP students had not changed.

To figure out what might be going on, staff from California Tomorrow (the school's "outside change partner") started by having the team members chart all of the things that had happened in the past two years that affected their focus on LEP students. The years had been profoundly difficult. A principal had died, two interim principals had passed through and now they had a new principal. The new district standards had been adopted and they were busy getting training for these changes in the curriculum. They'd been through an accreditation review. Earlier this year, a huge fight in the cafeteria between Mexican and Vietnamese immigrant students had occupied all the energies of the staff as they tried to mediate relations among the groups. It was real life in a real school approaching the year 2000. It was amazing any proactive effort to improve achievement was continuing—but the group was as determined as ever, and they wanted to figure out why there wasn't more evidence of impact on students after all the work they had done. Their task was to revisit their "theory of action" and analyze at what point the theory may have faltered. They broke it down into more steps than described earlier in this chapter, but the same "chain of events" thinking was evident:

Problem	*because...* (interpretation)	*If we do this...* (activities)	*then this will happen...* (results)	*so that...* (impacts)	*Evidenced by...(outcome measures)*
Too many LEP students are failing academic classes	because they have low literacy, and can't read the texts in class.	If we train teachers in literacy strategies to use in content classes	then teachers will promote more literacy in their classes	so that students will read better and fewer will fail.	Fewer F's given in academic classes and higher scores on SAT-9 in Reading.

When the Roosevelt teachers looked back, they felt sure that the failure of LEP students in their core academic subjects was still a major problem that needed addressing. There was still clear evidence of very high failing rates. A subgroup of the team had pursued an inquiry with LEP students getting two or more F's, and they reported their findings. They were now convinced that these students faced discouragement, disengagement and lack of motivation. While the staff had been pursuing their training in literacy, this subgroup was coming to see that the problem was bigger. All the good training they'd received didn't address concerns of student motivation. The team then decided to do some reading together about this issue. The subgroup secondly found from surveying teachers that while those who participated in the literacy staff development activities found them to be of very high quality, many were not actually implementing the instructional strategies in their classrooms because they found them difficult. Thus, the planning group decided their next step would be to invest in a "coach" and peer coaching approaches for their faculty.

This kind of continual investigation, revisiting of plans and seeking deeper understanding takes time and support. But it is exactly the kind of cycle that pays off in higher achievement, greater access, more engagement of faculty and deeper accountability.

This cycle does not happen without a serious commitment on the part of the people involved—and it helps if the school, the district and the community invest in creating the conditions to support such thoughtful and potentially transforming work.

CREATE THE CONDITIONS FOR USING DATA PRODUCTIVELY

Ideally, schools would have and use data in a continuing cycle: examining data, inquiring into issues raised by the data, developing action plans based on these new understandings, creating new interventions, and designing assessments to measure whether the interventions are working. Schools need to be set up in ways that support these uses of data. The conditions for using data productively include:

- Policies and practices that allow teachers and administrators access to the data
- A student information system (technology and staff) to produce the data
- Processes and habits of data-based reflection and inquiry
- Forums for discussing data together
- Time set aside for reviewing data
- Good facilitation by people who know the data
- Leadership that makes it known that looking at data, taking responsibility for ELL achievement, and reflection on practice are centrally important to the school.

Ideal Cycle of Data Use

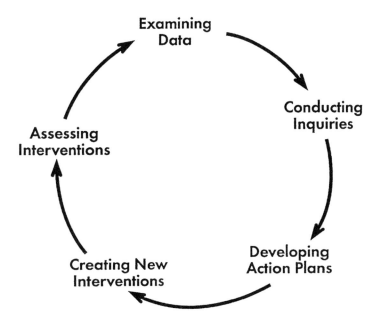

Your school, perhaps not yet ideal, may not have all of these conditions in place that make data use the most productive. Schools that want to support real data use have to deliberately create the conditions that allow for strong data collection, data access, the inquiry process and facilitative relationships. One place to begin moving in that direction is by assessing the current conditions at your school—and by taking the lead to move toward more responsive conditions.

ACTIVITY 3.7
ASSESSING THE CONDITIONS FOR DATA USE AT YOUR SCHOOL

Through our work with schools and districts, California Tomorrow has developed this assessment to examine how close your school is to having the conditions needed for effectively using data. The assessment allows you to gauge how up-to-date and effective your data systems are, who has access to data, whether data are discussed regularly, whether outcome measures are being used, and so on.

Any individual can sit and assess his or her school, but this assessment is particularly useful as a centerpiece for discussion. Each participant can comment on the school first and then everyone can compare their thoughts, thus, generating dialogue about high priority issues. The assessment serves as a vehicle to elicit people's varying perspectives and experiences within the school community about availability and access to data and the data "climate."

EFFECTIVE AND RESPONSIVE SCHOOLS ARE DATA-DRIVEN AND DATA-INFORMED

Not Supportive/Not Prepared	*Comments/Evidence*	*Supportive/Prepared*
• Student achievement and participation data are manually collected, exist in paper files or cumulative folders, are not aggregated, and do not appear in a system.		• The student data system centrally houses achievement and participation data, and provides for appropriate disaggregation of data to compare groups of students by race/ethnicity, language, LEP/FEP/EO status, gender and other key equity dimensions.
• Data are dated or unreliable.		• The data system provides accurate, up-to-date information.
• The data system generates reports for specific purposes only; reports are predetermined by expert users without collaboration with staff who might use the data.		• The data system is designed to respond to inquiries from multiple kinds of data users.
• Analytical report requests must be submitted to a centralized MIS unit or department; reports are generated based on a queue system.		• Access to the data system allows for individual and group inquiries for multiple users at the school site (teachers, counselors, administrators); equipment and training operationalizes this access.

Not Supportive/Not Prepared	Comments/Evidence	Supportive/Prepared
• No mechanisms exist to use data reflectively for school improvement; analysis of data occurs rarely, if at all.		• There are regular, formal mechanisms and forums through which staff can collaboratively reflect on data; analysis of data occurs on a regular, predictable basis.
• Data are used as a "hammer"; staff often feels guilty, fearful or ashamed when data are revealed; data use is generally avoided.		• The general culture of the school welcomes data as tools for school improvement and increased understanding.
• Staff does not use data; data are seen as unconnected to questions about student achievement or participation in school.		• The school is engaged in an ongoing cycle of inquiry—data lead to inquiries, to trying new practices or programs, to collecting more data, to more inquiries. The school regularly turns to data to illuminate current issues and problems or emerging issues.
• Student data exist in separated and unlinked systems.		• The data system links attendance, participation, background information, program services received, educational history, and academic achievement information; data can be produced on multiple levels—individual, subgroup, total group, and in comparison to district, state and national norms.
• Staff does not have the skills to work with data, and works in isolation to make sense of data.		• There are training sessions and technical assistance available to help staff analyze data.
• Data are not part of the planning activities of the school.		• The school uses data on student progress to identify problem points in programs, to trigger new program innovations and interventions, and as a part of every planning process.

TAKE THE LEAD

Data use doesn't happen on its own—it takes too much time and is counter to regular practices in schools. That means that if it is going to happen in your school, someone needs to take the lead. Anyone—a bilingual coordinator, a resource teacher, an "outside partner" to school reform, a teacher team, a project director on a reform initiative—can play this role of seeding the conditions to make data use an ongoing part of the school. It helps to be able to garner high-level support from people with formal authority in the school and district—people who make it clear they believe that site-based examination and use of student achievement data is centrally important. In this era, this shouldn't be difficult. Most administrators are feeling the pinch and pressure as a standards movement and accountability theme have heated up throughout the nation. The mission statements of most schools call for achievement for "all" students, and this kind of language should be used as a tool for working to ensure that LEP students "get there." Specifically, you need people in positions of power to establish the need for:

Data use doesn't happen on its own.

- Looking at data together in productive ways.
- Having everyone take responsibility for ELL achievement by reflecting on practice.

Support should be made manifest in the following ways:

- Quality training that supports educators in using the student information system to produce reports and respond to inquiries
- Policies that allow teachers and administrators access to the data
- A student information system (technology and staff) that is able to store and produce timely and accurate data
- Coordinated information systems that enable inquirers to link types of data
- Student information systems that are designed for disaggregation and achievement data
- Ways to provide release time or paid stipends for the time involved in data-based examination, planning and inquiry.

BUILD EFFECTIVE DATA SYSTEMS

An ongoing use of data for inquiry requires that you have infrastructures that support accurate, useful, easily accessible data. Much of what we've learned about effective data systems comes from our work with Catherine Minicucci, project evaluator for our work in Salinas and

Hayward. An effective data system includes not just excellent hardware and software, but also quality people who can provide access and training to others, quality data stored within it, and reasonable accessibility of the data. An effective data system:

- Contains good data on English Language Learners
- Is accessible to teachers and educators conducting inquiries
- Can easily answer questions about equity and access

Collect Good Data on English Language Learners

In many school districts, data on ELLs are often not reliable; data may be manually collected or maintained in separate systems that can generate reports only for specific reporting purposes. The data that are collected are not reviewed or monitored and, thus, are not part of any kind of inquiry. As difficult as it may be to change the way a district collects data, this is often an essential first step. Good data that are accurate and credible are essential, and a good database must be updated regularly to ensure timely, accurate information.

For English Language Learners, it helps to collect demographic, achievement, redesignation and program placement data. For comparison and context, it helps to have multiple years of data, to collect multiple measures of achievement, and to have data that enable you to compare Limited English Proficient students to English Only and Fluent English Proficient students. We recommend that school districts collect the following data for their English Language Learners:

- Nation of origin
- Prior schooling
- Interruptions in schooling
- Nations of prior schooling
- Length of time in U.S. schools
- Type of language access program
- Home language literacy
- Age in relation to prior school and to literacy in home language
- English oral fluency
- English reading comprehension, language skills, writing skills
- Course grades by type of class (such as: primary language instruction, primary language assistance, sheltered or SDAIE, mainstream)
- Tests: district and state proficiency tests (dates taken, pass/fail scores)

DATA TO COLLECT ON ENGLISH LANGUAGE LEARNERS

An ideal data system that would help you conduct inquiries on immigrant secondary students would include most of the following elements:

1. **Student Information**
   Demographic:
   Gender
   Birthdate
   Primary language
   Race/ethnicity
   Birthplace
   Date first entered any U.S. school
   Economic status (such as eligibility for Free or Reduced Price Lunches)
   Age at immigration
   Years in U.S.
   Years of schooling in home country or other countries of residence
   Age in relation to prior school and to literacy in home language
   Interruptions in schooling
   Years of schooling in U.S.

   Academic Status:
   Placement/ability-level classification (overall and by subjects)
   Grade level
   Enrollment in GATE or special education
   Grade point average, overall and by core subjects
   Number of courses taken (overall and by core subjects), coded by whether taken as specially designed instruction for language learners
   Course grades by type of class (such as: primary language instruction, primary language assistance, sheltered or SDAIE, mainstream)
   Number of courses enrolled in
   Number of advanced courses taken overall
   Completion of A-F course requirements
   Post-secondary follow-up (4-year college, 2-year college, trade or vocational school, no further schooling)

Language Development and Achievement:
  Language use at home
  Literacy in primary language
  Type of language-support program(s): primary language, pull-out, primary language support, sheltered or SDAIE, content-based ESL, mainstream, English Language Development
  English language proficiency level
  English language proficiency tests (e.g., SOLOM, LAS): dates taken and scores
  District proficiency tests in reading, writing and math: dates taken and scores
  Number of D's and F's by course
  Length of time from entry to redesignation as FEP
  Standardized tests: dates taken and scores
  Assessment of bilingualism
  Graduation date

Participation/Behavior Data:
  Number of suspensions and expulsions
  Attendance (number of missed days)
  Extracurricular activities
  Honors and awards
  Disciplinary referrals
  Community service
  Attitudes toward schools, teachers, English, peers (based on interviews, Rosenberg's Self Esteem Test, Seale Parent-Child Conflict Scale, Americanization Values Scale, School Climate Inventory)
  Dropout date
  Transferred out date

2. *Parent information*
   Demographic:
     Family income, race/ethnicity, number of years with a child in school, strongest language

School-Family Relations:
  Frequency of telephone contact with school
  Frequency of visits to school
  Response of school to initiated contacts
  Involvement in classroom
  Involvement in school-wide activities
  Parent satisfaction (Determined through surveys, interviews, focus groups)

3. **Teacher information**
  Demographic:
    Gender
    Race/ethnicity
    Fluent languages
    Years teaching
    Years teaching at this school
    Current teaching assignment
    Highest degree held
    Specialty certificates or credentials
    Most active areas of professional development

4. **School information**
  Course offerings:
    Method of instruction (sheltered English, primary language, etc.)
    Certification of teacher
    Required for graduation
    A-F college-preparatory course
    "Remedial" or skills course
    Average faculty/student ratio (by department and type of class)
    Average annual cost per student
    Special grants and funding
    Measures of student intergroup relations: in class, during free time, after school
    Number of certificated staff by type
    Total instruction FTE (overall and by class type)

5. *Aggregated information*

To be sub-aggregated by ethnicity, language group, LEP status and school:

Course enrollments

Attendance

Drop outs

Suspensions

Expulsions

Reclassifications/redesignations

Graduation rates

Grade point averages

Passage of minimum proficiency tests

(Based on data collected by Minicucci Associates and on Goodlab, J.L. and Keating, P. (1990). *Access to Knowledge: An Agenda for Our Nation's Schools*. New York: College Entrance Examination Board.)

Implementing Useful Language Proficiency Codes: One District's Story

The accuracy of data stored about LEP students' language proficiencies can make all the difference, as the following story illustrates. The Hayward Unified School District in Northern California decided to update its data system, purchasing a new system that came with English language proficiency codes already programmed in. Unfortunately, these codes did not match the ones used by the English Language Center (ELC), a center serving newly-arrived LEP students from all the district's secondary schools until they achieve an intermediate English proficiency. In fact, these pre-programmed codes were much less accurate and useful than the codes already in use at the ELC. The ELC, which had its own database, had developed a set of language proficiency codes which accurately identified a student's language status. It took two years of sustained effort, but eventually the district shifted from proposing halfway solutions that avoided writing a new program to focusing on the needs of the end-users of data. The new codes were implemented and are now listed on the student rosters that teachers receive.

Hayward's English Language Proficiency Codes

For Limited English Proficient (LEP) students:

LB: special education, unable to assess

LC: orally fluent in English, limited proficiency in reading and writing

LD: limited proficiency in English speaking, reading and writing

LE: no or very limited proficiency in English speaking, reading and writing

For Fluent English Proficient (FEP) students:

FF: no proficiency reported in primary language

FH: FEP upon initial assessment

FJ: initially LEP, redesignated to FEP

EO: For English Only students

These codes give teachers and counselors much more information about their students' English proficiency, which improves their placement. The codes also make it easier for staff who are conducting inquiries into English Language Learners to track students' English proficiency over time.

Make the Data Accessible for Teachers and Administrators

Good data is useless unless it is accessible to those who need it. A data-based program relies on data that teachers and administrators can access fairly easily to inquire into students' achievement. Administrators need to not only create policies for accessing data but help establish practices for how to do so on a regular basis. Access to data means that bilingual program coordinators and administrators, teacher research groups and planning groups have access to computers to generate the reports they need. It means that teachers and administrators are trained to use the data system and to conduct inquiries. It means staff have access to ongoing training so they become knowledgeable users of student data and a regular schedule of trainings is available to them throughout the year. Staff can access data in a timely way to see how defined groups of students are doing in grades, enrollment in classes, passage of proficiency tests, and so on. Access to data means that staff can easily design their own data reports to address their inquiries.

It also helps greatly when staff has an avenue to discuss any problems with the student data system. An orderly process should be explicit for review and resolution of data system problems as they arise. Staff who use student data need to know about this process and feel safe using it.

If you don't have an administrator pushing for an accessible data system, document each kind of data you identify to be necessary as you construct your inquiry (see page 147). Set up meetings with the data processing/student information system staff to talk about the data you need, how you plan to use it, and what it might take to access such information. Changing data systems requires instituting this kind of "consumer demand"—educating yourself about the barriers in the existing system and being able to articulate and illustrate to others the link between improving the data available and better serving students.

However, with all this said, don't ever let lack of the right data stop you from pursuing inquiries. Starting with whatever data is available is sufficient for sparking the kinds of dialogues and work together that can move a school forward. Standardized test scores or data available from state departments of education are starting points (see box on "Sources for Data" on page 170).

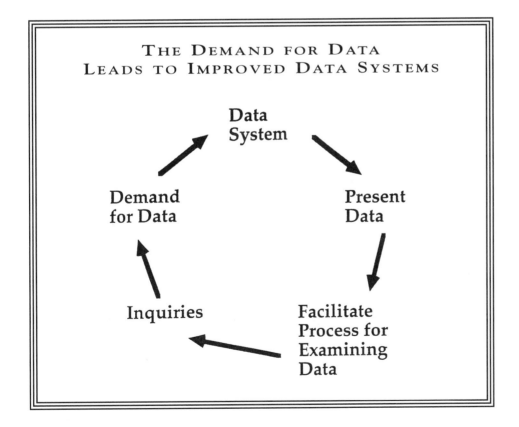

THE DEMAND FOR DATA LEADS TO IMPROVED DATA SYSTEMS

Data System

Demand for Data

Present Data

Inquiries

Facilitate Process for Examining Data

ACTIVITY 3.8
HOW MUCH ACCESS DO
PEOPLE IN YOUR SCHOOL HAVE TO DATA?

You may find it useful to do a school-wide survey to measure the extent to which faculty use data and the quality of the data available to them. This will identify what people want to know, how familiar they feel with the data systems in the school, and some possible new resources among the staff to help with data work.

A SCHOOLWIDE SURVEY TO MEASURE THE EXTENT AND QUALITY OF DATA ACCESS AND USE AMONG THE FACULTY

Please read each sentence and then circle the
answer that is the closest to how you feel about that statement.

	strongly agree	agree	disagree	strongly disagree	don't know
I have a good sense of what all the types of data are that our school collects about our students.	1	2	3	4	5
I have a good sense of what data on students are available to teachers and staff.	1	2	3	4	5
I know where to go or whom to ask if I want certain information about my students.	1	2	3	4	5
I know where to go or whom to ask if I want certain information about the whole student body.	1	2	3	4	5
I frequently want to know achievement/ background information about the students in my classes.	1	2	3	4	5
I have found it easy to find the information I want on students from the data gathered by the school.	1	2	3	4	5
I have gathered data on the students in my classes.	1	2	3	4	5
I have gathered data on the students in the whole school.	1	2	3	4	5
If the information I want is not collected by the school, I feel comfortable designing ways to gather that information myself.	1	2	3	4	5

DESIGN A STRONG STUDENT INFORMATION SYSTEM

The foundation for a school that opens the door to data and inquiry is a solid student information system, including the technology and staff necessary to maintain it. This system needs to be flexible enough that staff can get the data they need for their inquiries. It must contain the multiple kinds of data needed to track students' progress. Most schools and districts do not have a student information system sufficient to answer questions about equitable access. Increasingly, however, schools and districts are beginning to construct such systems. The following box, developed through California Tomorrow's work with numerous schools and districts, describes the key elements of a data system which supports inquiry.

ELEMENTS OF A DATA SYSTEM WHICH SUPPORTS INQUIRY

A good district-wide data system that supports inquiry and accountability has the following characteristics:

- Integrates or links databases: all electronic databases can communicate or interface with one another to share data.

- Allows disaggregation of all measures of achievement and participation by race/ethnicity, gender, language status (English Only, Limited English Proficient, Fluent English Proficient), and socio-economic class (e.g., Free and Reduced Price Lunch participation).

- Produces reliable, credible data that is updated in a timely fashion and available at key decision points in a school year.

- Is easily accessible to school sites, administrators and teachers; such access involves providing training as needed and creating a user-friendly system with the appropriate hardware and software.

- Responds to inquiries easily: new reports can be produced in a timely fashion to help school personnel find the answers to their questions about student achievement or equity issues.

- Maintains student information longitudinally, so student histories can be traced K-12 without having to resort to individual students' cumulative files.

- Links data to policies and standards set by the district and schools, so progress towards attaining those standards can be measured.

In addition to the ideal technological capability of a great student information system, there is an essential human side through which:

🌿 Training and technical support is readily available and effective.

🌿 District personnel who maintain the system or control access to it are willing to work with schools to help them get what they need.

🌿 Those who maintain separate databases (perhaps on a certain population of students) provide data willingly, and in a timely fashion, when requested.

Separate or Integrated Systems?

Ideally, each school and district would have a single student information system with all the information anyone might want to track progress and make inquiries about the participation and achievement of individual students or subgroups of students. Ideally, the teacher who wants to understand which students are getting failing grades in science classes across the school could simply ask a series of questions and get good quality printouts. How many are LEP? Which language groups do they represent? Are these low-English-fluency students or fully orally-fluent students? Are more girls than boys failing? Did these same students fail their science classes last year? Have these students received special tutoring services from the Computer Lab? Were these the students who didn't receive primary language instruction?

But the reality is that the different pieces of information that could help get to the bottom of such questions are seldom housed in a single database—and seldom accessible in ways that would enable someone to start formulating answers.

For people attempting to monitor and understand the progress and achievement of LEP students, it is especially difficult. The professionals who design student information systems for general district and school uses seldom understand any of the complexities about LEP students. They seldom include good fields or categories for levels of English fluency, for example, or for nation of birth, years in U.S. schools or years of prior schooling. For far too long, LEP students have been simply off the radar screen of accountability and information systems.

This has meant that in many, many schools and districts, the data that are available about LEP students is hand-collected or in a separate database developed by someone responsible for the categorical program for LEP students. "You want to find out the fluency levels of students who are failing classes? Go ask Elsie, I think she might have that information." And then Elsie sits down with the list of students getting F's and looks each up, one by one, to determine their fluency. This is a typical scenario in many schools. In some schools, the bilingual coordinator may have set up a database, but it often only includes the information she herself has entered, and it can't "talk" to the district database that houses attendance or disciplinary information. Getting large and fragmented student information systems to incorporate full and appropriate information about LEP students is an arduous and often political task.

ACTIVITY 3.9
MAP YOUR DATA SYSTEM

One way to begin understanding your data system is to "map" or inventory it to answer questions like: What kinds of information can you find where? How many separate databases store the data you might need? Can those databases link or "talk" to each other electronically? Who maintains the different databases? A data map is a document that includes:

❧ A visual that shows what data are stored where in the school and district

❧ An accompanying narrative on what types of data are stored in which systems; which systems are linked and which are not; the capacity of each system to disaggregate by race/ethnicity, gender, language status, etc.

❧ A list of the contact people who can access the data

❧ A list of the major data reports that are issued by which offices

❧ An overview of the capacity of the system to produce information about LEP student achievement and participation, such as:

 ☛ accessibility and ability to get training

 ☛ responsiveness to inquiries (can it generate new reports or only standard, pre-programmed ones?)

 ☛ reliability and accuracy

 ☛ longitudinal capacity (can you track individual students over time?)

To get this information, you will need to interview the people at your school and district who work with data and data systems regularly. Start with the person responsible for

LEP programs at your school (bilingual coordinator, etc.). Ask:

🌿 What data do you keep about LEP students?

🌿 How can people access it? Is training required?

🌿 Can your data system link with other systems in the district?

🌿 Can you disaggregate your data? In what ways?

🌿 Does your data system keep track of students over time?

🌿 Can your data system respond to new inquiries by generating new reports, or is it much easier to print out pre-programmed reports to get information?

🌿 Where do you go to find out information about LEP student achievement, participation, assessment or demographic information?

🌿 What regular reports do you put together about LEP student achievement and access?

Then ask the same set of questions of your principal, the District Student Information Systems Manager and the District Bilingual Coordinator. If there is anyone at your school who regularly uses a student database (the office manager or school secretary, perhaps), ask if they feel the data are regularly updated and if they have major difficulties in getting the data they need on a timely basis.

Once you've interviewed several people, put the information together in the format described above. You may want to share this data map with others interested in using data, or use it to lobby your school or district to improve your data system (e.g., establish links between databases, make more training available, store certain data, etc.).

(The idea of data system maps was developed by Laurie Olsen as part of California Tomorrow's participation in the High Performance Learning Communities Project with RPP International, 1998.)

Here's an example of the graphic from a data map:

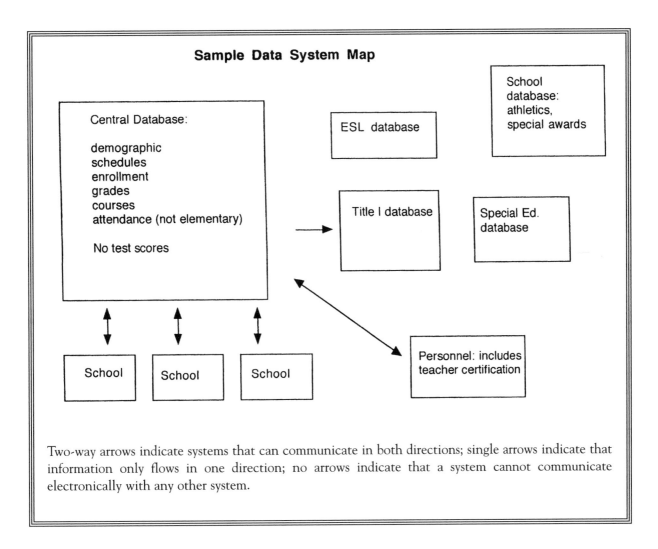

Sample Data System Map

School database: athletics, special awards

Central Database:

demographic
schedules
enrollment
grades
courses
attendance (not elementary)

No test scores

ESL database

Title I database

Special Ed. database

Personnel: includes teacher certification

School   School   School

Two-way arrows indicate systems that can communicate in both directions; single arrows indicate that information only flows in one direction; no arrows indicate that a system cannot communicate electronically with any other system.

SOURCES FOR DATA

Your school or district may have internal data (such as passage rates on proficiency tests, lists of students receiving D's or F's, etc.) readily available and already sub-aggregated by racial/ethnic group and other meaningful divisions. Most schools do not. Luckily, simple sources generated by every school in response to state or federal mandates should be available. These include:

- State and individual school-site dropout rates, disaggregated by racial/ethnic groups

- Suspensions and expulsions

- Eligibility for four-year colleges

- Enrollment in gatekeeping classes (such as Algebra, Lab Sciences)

- Reading scores or percentages of students at risk (below the 50th percentile) at grades 3, 6, 8 and 10

- Bachelor's degrees awarded in state university systems

Other standard statistics to seek include:

- Number of students by race/ethnicity and gender enrolled in different school programs (vocational programs, special education, "gifted" or honors classes, "skills" classes, etc.). Such data can indicate who and when certain groups are being steered into or away from these programs.

- Number of students entitled to a school service but not receiving it. For example, there could be students designated as Limited English Proficient who are not receiving language support.

- Number of facilities available in different schools and for different groups, for example, science labs, computer labs, lockers and showers for girls' and boys' athletics programs.

Educators in California can find the most recent Language Census (R-30) and CBEDS data on the website for the California Department of Education at: **goldmine.cde.ca.gov**.

Go to the demographics page to find data reports and to download data files on LEP and FEP students, by school district, grade, etc. Educators in other states can find links to state resources web pages on the homepage for the National Clearinghouse for Bilingual Education at: **www.ncbe.gwu.edu**.

CONCLUSION

We live in an era when schools are increasingly expected to produce data showing the impact of their work. And, the stakes are growing higher and the responses more punitive when schools cannot show evidence of high student achievement. It becomes imperative to the survival of effective programs in schools that each of us becomes familiar and proficient in defining what constitutes meaningful evidence of achievement and equity. We must become savvy at collecting and using data well.

Black-and-white X-Acto knife reverse by Thanh Truong, a high school student from Vietnam

In the scramble to meet external accountability demands, however, we can lose sight of the richer benefits that data can bring—as a guide for inquiry and planning, as a tool for deepening our understanding, and as a spark for the essential dialogues we need to have about what we are striving for and what we practice in schools. This chapter will hopefully help you clear the path to these benefits—to develop the data systems that can answer your questions about how students are achieving, to facilitate multiple forms of data use, to construct inquiries and develop action plans, and to advocate for the conditions that support data-based inquiry and planning. We hope these ideas will position educators and advocates to not only find their ground in the midst of what are too often meaningless and inappropriate data demands—but to instead use data successfully for the authentic purpose of improving schools.

REFERENCES

Barth, R. (1993). *Improving Schools from Within.* San Francisco, CA: Jossey-Bass.

Fine, M. (1997). *Participatory Evaluation Research in the Service of School Reform.* Unpublished manuscript.

Johnson, R. (1996). *Setting Our Sights: Measuring Equity in School Change.* Los Angeles, CA: The Achievement Council.

Joyce, B. and Calhoun, E. (1993). *The Self Renewing School.* Alexandria, VA: Association for Supervision and Curriculum Development.

Joyce, B., Wolf, J. and Calhoun, E. (1995). *School Renewal: An Inquiry, Not a Formula.* Educational Leadership, *52*(7), 51-55.

Olsen, L. (1996, Winter). The Data Dialogue for Moving School Equity. *California Perspectives.* San Francisco, CA. California Tomorrow.

Ravitch, D. (1992). National Standards and Curriculum Reform: A View from the Department of Education. *NASSP Bulletin, 76*(548), 24-29.

Schaefer, R. J. (1967). *The School as a Center of Inquiry.* New York, NY: Harper and Row.

Short, K. G. and Burke, C. (1996). Examining Our Beliefs and Practices Through Inquiry. *Language Arts, 73*(2), 97-104.

DATA AND INQUIRY
ANNOTATED BIBLIOGRAPHY

Calhoun, Emily F. (1993). Action Research: Three Approaches.
Educational Leadership, 51(2), 62-65.

This concise article provides an overview of action research, distinguishing three different applications for action research efforts in schools: individual teacher research, collaborative action research and school-wide action research. It's a useful article for a school community to read together to gain a general understanding of action research and its possibilities. Calhoun has written extensively on the subject and is a good resource for further reading.

Education Trust. (1997). *Education Watch: The Education Trust*
Community Data Guide. **Washington, D.C.: Education Trust.**

This guide is intended to help educators harness the power of local data to drive and sustain efforts to reform schools. Written for those seeking to analyze achievement patterns and identify needed changes in school practices, it also addresses parent groups and community-based organizations wishing to assess the effectiveness of their local schools. Focusing on the differential performance and attainment among students of various racial and ethnic groups, this book provides data templates that can be filled in with local data and then compared to national and state trends as reported in a companion volume, *Education Watch: The 1996 Education Trust State and National Data Book.*

Hopfenberg, Wendy S. et al. (1993). *The Accelerated Schools Resource*
Guide. **San Francisco, CA: Jossey-Bass.**

This practitioner-friendly resource guide introduces the Accelerated Schools Project model for school change resulting in high achievement for all students. One chapter focuses on the inquiry process and provides a step-by-step approach to engaging "cadres" of the school community in data-based problem solving. This five-step cyclical process includes: defining the challenge and framing hypotheses that explain why the challenge exists; brainstorming solutions and looking inside and outside the school for ideas; synthesizing solutions and developing an action plan; pilot testing and/or implementing the plan; and evaluating and reassessing student achievement to identify continuing or new challenges.

Johnson, Ruth. (1996). *Setting Our Sights: Measuring Equity in School Change.* **Los Angeles, CA: The Achievement Council.**

A rich, practical and informative resource book that provides a broad strategy and set of tools schools can use to create practices that result in high standards, equity and high achievement for all students. The book moves step-by-step through a process of engaging school communities in examining counterproductive and unequal school practices and developing the plans (and then monitoring the implementation of those plans) to remedy inequities in school practices and outcomes. Chapters explain how data can be used as a lever to achieve school change, with a focus on schools serving students most often left behind in "generic" reform efforts: low income, Latino, African American and Native American students.

McCarthy, Jane and Riner, Phillip. (1996). The Accelerated Schools Inquiry Process: Teacher Empowerment Through Action Research. *Education,* **117(2).**

The Accelerated Schools Inquiry Process is an approach to restructuring schools involving the school community in data-gathering activities to identify problem areas and assist in decision-making processes. This process of inquiry, called "taking stock," is a form of action research designed to empower members of the school community by gathering school data and using it to make collaborative decisions for change. Given the diversity of attitudes staff may bring to the process, the authors stress recognizing these varied reactions as important as they may affect the data collected, their analysis, and the nature of collaborative outcomes.

Olsen, Laurie. (1998). Using Data to Develop an Action Plan to Improve Program and Academic Achievement. *Data Collection and Program Improvement for English Language Learners.* **Los Angeles, CA: Southern California Comprehensive Assistance Center.**

This chapter focuses on using data to develop action plans that improve student achievement—by fueling inquiry, stimulating dialogue and building accountability for access and achievement into the life of a school. It answers the question: Once you have the data, what do you do with them? A rubric describes the structures, systems and practices that support the uses of data and inquiry, and the article describes a process for establishing the right conditions for developing a data-based action plan.

Slater, Robert O. (1993). Collecting and Using Information for Problem Solving and Decision-making. In Patrick B. Forsyth, Marilyn Tallerico (Eds.), *City Schools: Leading the Way.* Newbury Park, CA: Corwin Press.

A good resource for principals who want to improve the quality of information available to them, a necessary component for problem solving and decision-making. The article is clearly written and lays out the major components of a data-based, problem-solving and decision-making process, including framing the problem, deciding what to collect, collecting and caring for data, making meaning out of data, presenting the information to users, and creating a "value" around information within the school. While it is written explicitly for principals in schools engaged in whole-school reform with multiple people in leadership roles, the information is useful to a wide range of administrators.

Data and Inquiry Resources

The Education Trust

The Education Trust's goal is the high academic achievement of all students—kindergarten through college—with a special focus on serving low income, Latino, African American and Native American youth. The Education Trust works to shape educational policy and bring about educational change that benefits students. They are available for consultation with schools, parents and community groups in collecting, interpreting and using student data to drive K-16 reform. They publish resource materials and host an annual national conference.

> 1725 K Street, NW, Suite 200
> Washington, D.C. 20006
> (202)293-1217
> (202)293-2605 fax
> WWW: www.edtrust.org

The Achievement Council

This statewide nonprofit organization works to improve academic achievement among California's ethnic and low income youth. The Achievement Council creates opportunities for administrators and teachers to learn about practical and innovative strategies for their school change process. They are also available to work with schools wanting to know and understand more about their student data.

> 3460 Wilshire Boulevard, Suite 420
> Los Angeles, CA 90010
> (213)487-3194
> (213)487-0879
> E-mail: tacforall@aol.com
> WWW: achievementcouncil.com

California Tomorrow

California Tomorrow works with people working in schools, early childcare centers and community-based organizations to change their institutional practices so they are inclusive and respectful of diversity. Their mission is building a fair, inclusive, multicultural and multilingual society. California

Tomorrow is available to consult with schools on improving the use and collection of their student data. California Tomorrow can also assist schools in understanding what their data mean, establishing data-based inquiry and data-based planning processes and facilitate discussions on using data to improve student achievement.

436 14th Street, Suite 820
Oakland, CA 94612
(510)496-0220
(510)496-0225 fax
E-mail: generalinfo@californiatomorrow.org
WWW: www.californiatomorrow.org

The following websites are good on-line sources for data and research about English Language Learners and other students in public schools:

National Center for Bilingual Education: www.ncbe.gwu.edu

This website has state resources pages which link to data sources for the states; an on-line library; and access to databases, including research citations and abstracts.

National Center for Educational Statistics: www.nces.ed.gov

This extensive website contains on-line publications, research and statistics related to education. The annual Condition of Education is available on-line, as well as reports on Limited English Proficient students. There are links to national databases, including the Common Core of Data (which has data from public school districts across the U.S.) and the High School and Beyond longitudinal study.

California Department of Education: goldmine.cde.ca.gov

The demographics page on this website is a goldmine of statistical data about Limited English Proficient and other public school students, including data files based on the Language Census and CBEDS which can be downloaded by school, district or grade.

Chapter Four:

UNDERSTANDING THE COMPLEXITY OF OUR STUDENTS' EXPERIENCES

John sat at a table in the teachers' lounge, correcting papers from his sheltered World History class. He was banished from his own room everyday during his third-period prep by the need to share space with another teacher. Finding no other spot in his overcrowded, portable-laden high school, John was forced to spend these precious 48 minutes with a group of four other teachers who also had third-period prep and who habitually sat together drinking coffee, discussing the sorry state of the school and education in general. Bits of their conversation floated over to John's corner of the room everyday. Many of their gripes related to the "ineffective district administration" or the internal site struggle over a new disciplinary policy. Many days, John heard a whole litany of complaints about the seemingly endless pool of "unprepared, unmotivated and lazy" students arriving on the doorstep of the school.

The topic today drifted toward some mandated training for all teachers of Limited English Proficient students. Bitterness and resentment permeated each remark: "I don't know why I have to do this. I don't even have LEP kids in my classes," said a mainstream English teacher. "I might have a couple," replied the Economics teacher, "but they're Russian and they don't need anything special. They do fine." "Yeah, this is not what I signed up for when I came to this school. Let the ESL teachers take care of those kids. We don't have that many here anyway. I don't know what the big deal is. If they make me do this training, I will, but I'm not going to change anything I do," chimed in a longtime Biology teacher.

A third-year teacher at the school, John had hooked up in his first year with a small group of teachers struggling to rework the program for Limited English Proficient students in order to provide greater access to the core curriculum. Through this work and his own teaching, he knew he was just beginning to understand the nature and complexity of the students that many of the teachers at his school just called "those LEP kids."

He knew, for example, that the mainstream English teacher had a lot of English Language Learners spread throughout her classes, those that had become fluent speakers of English. How were they doing? he wondered. He knew that the Russian students in the Econ teacher's classrooms were representative of several groups of English Language Learners who had come with wonderful prior educational experiences, including the study of English. He also knew of at least eight or nine bright, motivated intermediate-level fluency students (three from Mexico, one Filipino, a couple of Armenian students and maybe two or three Punjabis) who would do great in a well-taught sheltered Biology class. But who would teach it?

Heavy on his own mind, however, was the work of a student he held in his hand at the moment. This was a 10th grader who had arrived in the U.S. only two years previously, with a mere three years of formal education. It would be a miracle if she made it through this sheltered World History class, not to mention high school. "They're all English Language Learners," John thought, "but they are as different from each other as night and day. How is it we can help teachers to see that? And how do we respond to those differences?"

The most effective advocates know "how to know" about their students. They know from their minds and they know from their hearts, and they use both ways effectively.

Understanding our English Language Learners is the key to responding effectively to their differing needs. The goal of this chapter is to help you create an interconnected web of understandings and insights about your English Language Learners, among advocates and school staffs. These understandings are the foundation for moving toward more responsive programs for your second language students—and ever-increasing levels of equity and access.

Knowing your English Language Learners involves a knowing on many levels and in many different ways. The most effective advocates know "how to know" about their students. They know from their minds and they know from their hearts, and they use both ways effectively.

❧ They know how to get all available hard data on their English Language Learners—they know where to go, whom to ask, what to look at, what to ask for, what is missing, what is relevant and what is irrelevant (see Chapter Three for more about using data).

❧ They become conversant with the technicalities of language proficiency issues, and with the socio/cultural/political issues related to acquiring a second language and can translate those into the day-to-day workings and conversations at the school in a way that all educators can understand.

❧ They know that all existing data are self-limiting—there is always the need to go deeper, look further, and understand more. They know that the students themselves often hold the answers, and all we have to do is ask the right questions in the right way (see Chapter Four for strategies to invite student voice).

❧ They take the responsibility to learn what they don't know—and then they take the responsibility to teach others all they know so the knowledge resides in multiple places in a school. They know that knowing is fragile, that people forget, that we often have to relearn what we once knew, or rethink what we thought we understood (see Chapter Six for more about how advocates can learn together).

❧ They know that who their English Language Learners are will change with time, and that this requires new insights and fresh perspectives in order to serve their students. They know not to assume—the students themselves are always more complex and confounding than any category, language proficiency code, ethnicity or score we might assign to them.

❧ They "know" from their hearts, from their day-to-day touching of the lives of immigrant students, from sharing their students' joys, sorrows, hopes and despair—and they use this knowledge to inform and help craft new ways of working with students.

❧ They seek ways to allow other educators to "know" from their hearts, too, to get them in touch with what inspired them to be teachers in the first place. They find ways for all teachers to see their immigrant students in new ways, so that there is a culture of wanting to know more about their students.

There is always a tension between wanting and needing to find out more about your students and directly addressing the challenges that exist. It helps if teachers have a sense that if they learn more, they will be better equipped to craft the right kind of response. There also should be an agreed-upon, not-too-distant time when action on behalf of the students will occur. All the activities outlined in this chapter are intended to build curiosity about your students and where they stand in the world—without building closure too soon about what ought to or might be done. The activities are also intended to provide a depth of understanding that might not have previously existed in the school so that any resulting changes rest on a deep bedrock of site-level knowledge about your second language learners.

THREE PATHS OF KNOWLEDGE

One of the most valuable things that a group of advocates can do together is make the time and space to talk about the interconnections among their own experiences and those of their students. The insights you generate together can be a powerful place to work from in creating a program that really works for your students. It all begins by constructing a plan that allows staff to connect and understand the lives of immigrant students in many ways, and on many levels, through many paths.

Although there are many ways "in" to knowing your immigrant students, the most productive paths are paved with complementary portions of the following:

🖐 Self-knowledge on the teachers' parts about their own or their family's immigrant and second language experience and how that is connected to their place in teaching and advocating for language minority students;

🖐 Knowledge about the immigrant experience in general—and in particular, about how the experience of being an immigrant relates to the schooling of language minority students;

🖐 Knowledge about their own particular students.

The sections that follow will give you a chance to explore each path in some depth. There is no absolute order to exploring the three paths listed above. One way "in" can lead to another. A group might begin by looking at an aspect of their students' experiences, and then move to thinking about their own personal realities. Or you could begin by looking at your own experiences and then finding out more about your students' lives. Each avenue can enrich teachers' understandings.

Before you take any of these paths, however, you might want to spend some time doing the following activity to assess how ready your school is to understand more about the LEP students you serve.

ACTIVITY 4.1
HOW SUPPORTIVE AND PREPARED IS
OUR SCHOOL TO UNDERSTAND THE COMPLEXITIES
OF OUR IMMIGRANT STUDENTS' LIVES?

The following assessment can be used as an individual or group activity to reflect on how ready and willing your school is to understand the many different English Language Learners you serve. Consider each element in terms of how close or far your school is from having the conditions that would support understanding your immigrant students. Use the center column to describe what you actually see in your school, your evidence for your assessment, and any comments. If you are working as a group, each person should do his or her own assessment first and then compare notes in a general discussion. Based on this assessment, select your highest priority in helping your school become more open to understanding the complexities of immigrant students' lives.

RESPONSIVE SCHOOLS DEVELOP THE STAFF'S CAPACITY
TO UNDERSTAND THEIR IMMIGRANT STUDENTS

Not Supportive/Not Prepared to Understand Students	*Comments/Evidence*	*Supportive/Prepared to Understand Students*
• Staff assumes that immigrant students as a group are uniform and uni-dimensional. Staff lumps all students together as "those LEP students."		• There is widespread understanding that the immigrant student population is multifaceted, diverse and complex.
• The school culture dismisses the implications of socio/cultural/political factors in acquiring a second language and student achievement. The problem is viewed only as a matter of learning English.		• The school culture actively seeks ways to understand the impacts of socio/cultural/ political factors on their immigrant students. The school uses these understandings to create more effective ways to educate and support their students.
• School plans, faculty dialogues and programs seem unaware of or ignore the existence of immigrant students.		• The school has a "heads-up" and proactive approach to changing student demographics. Multiple efforts are made to find information, understand, plan for and respond appropriately to the changing population of immigrant students over time.

Not Supportive/Not Prepared to Understand Students	*Comments/Evidence*	*Supportive/Prepared to Understand Students*
• A closed, fearful atmosphere exists around discussing issues of language and culture. Those staff attempting to open up discussion are shut down or ignored.		• There are structured opportunities for staff to explore and share the impact of immigration, language and culture on their own lives. They have the chance to relate their own personal experience to the lives of their own students.
• The staff displays little to no knowledge about language proficiency issues and their impact on access, achievement, and equity at the school.		• Many staff members understand how language proficiency issues affect their immigrant students. They understand the details of testing and placement and advocate for close monitoring of students to ensure access and equity.
• The school culture tends to stereotype immigrant students according to race, ethnicity, or language backgrounds. Program and class placement closely mirror stereotypical views of which students "can succeed" and which "cannot succeed."		• The school proactively seeks ways to ensure that particular groups of immigrant students are not favored over others. The school is self-critical and self-analytical about how students are placed and programs that are considered "appropriate."
• The school ignores the needs of different types of immigrant and Limited English Proficient students. No attempt is made to link educational needs of different types of immigrant students to program or curricular improvement.		• The school has a sound understanding of the types of immigrant students in the school. Every attempt is made to think through how to match the needs of different types of students with appropriate programs, classes, and curriculum.

GETTING TO KNOW EACH OTHER

One way to begin on this path is through an exploration of your own experiences related to second language learning or your family's immigrant experience. Good teachers often take the time to relate the content they're teaching to the personal lives of their students. Likewise, some time invested in teacher sharing can help teachers open up to one another, establish connections among staff, and give teachers an opportunity they don't often have—to know more about each other's lives and motivations for teaching immigrant students. Knowing your students ultimately means getting to know more about yourself and each other.

ACTIVITY 4.2
LANGUAGE HISTORY MAP

This activity focuses on exploring your own history and experiences with language and then sharing what you learn with other teachers or advocates.

Draw a picture or map of your own language history. You may choose to focus on your own personal history or you may decide to go back and explore several generations. Use words, phrases, colors, symbols and pictures to depict the history.

If you choose to do a language map for your family, it should include the languages spoken by your family as far back as you know, and then trace what happened. If your map is your own personal story, show what has happened to you regarding language gain or language loss. You may want to show the following on your map:

- Key events that show how languages have changed through your family moving to a new country, through marriage, wars, conquests, etc.

- When and how languages were lost or gained.

- What languages have been spoken in the home to children and others.

- How you might have learned a new language (studying in school, living in another country, developing friends who speak other languages, etc.).

- Show, if possible, the links between your own language history and your work in education on behalf of English Language Learners.

Find one or two other people, show your language history maps to each other and explain the history that you drew. Share general reactions, thoughts, comments or patterns as you consider the following questions:

❧ Were languages lost? How did it happen? What is it like for a family or person to lose a language?

❧ Were languages added? How? Is there bilingualism in your history?

❧ What conditions allow people to learn and maintain a language?

❧ What relationship is there between your own language history and your work with English Language Learners?

❧ Given the above discussion, where does your own school or district fall in terms of language loss, language gain, and other issues related to language?

GETTING TO KNOW ABOUT THE EXPERIENCES OF OTHER SECOND LANGUAGE LEARNERS AND IMMIGRANTS

Another way "in" to knowing about your students involves studying the immigrant experience as portrayed through literature. Rich accounts abound chronicling the lives of people, real and fictional, whose encounters with new languages and cultures can shed light on the challenges faced by your own immigrant and second language learner students. The box on page 191 lists suggested readings which portray immigrant experiences.

The following activity is one way of using such literature to enhance your understanding of some of the sociocultural and psychological factors that might affect your students.

ACTIVITY 4.3
READING ABOUT FOUR IMMIGRANT EXPERIENCES

Starting with fictionalized characters—one step away from your own students—is often helpful for everyone. The natural sorts of reactions—sadness, anger, blame, bewilderment, pain—that often arise when examining these stories of excitement, curiosity, loss and alienation are somewhat easier to handle when the story is not your own or your students' stories. Still, the pieces of literature function as windows into a teacher's or student's own experience, opening up a dialogue about where similarities and differences exist. The literary excerpts for this activity appear in Appendix A at the end of this chapter.

This activity, originally developed by Aída Walqui, is structured as extended jigsaw of text. As such, it is best accomplished when there is a group large enough to divide up into "home groups" and "expert groups" of three to four each.

Home Groups

❧ In the first step, divide the participants up into four home groups. Take about 10 minutes to have each person individually write on the following topic: What is the function and place of students' first language in the educational system? You may want to have participants share some of their thoughts to the whole group or share with a partner.

❧ Have each home group number off into fours.

Expert Groups:

❧ Re-form participants into expert groups by number: ones will read Richard Rodriguez, twos read Amy Tan, threes read Antti Jalava and fours read Luis Rodriguez. Ask the participants to look at the text organizer and answer the four questions for their text.

❧ Give the expert groups adequate time to read their selections and fill out the text organizer column for their piece. You may choose to either have them read aloud to each other, paragraph by paragraph, or to have them read silently and then discuss aloud together.

❧ After reading the piece, the responsibility of each expert group is to fill out their column. They will return to their home group and share what they learned, using the notes they've made.

Reconvene the Home Groups:

❧ Give members time to share what they read and how their expert group filled out the text organizer. Every home group member should have a completed chart at the end.

TEXT ORGANIZER

	Ones: A Chicano Experience: Richard Rodriguez	*Twos:* A Chinese Experience: Amy Tan	*Threes:* A Finnish Experience in Sweden: Antti Jalava	*Fours:* Another Chicano Experience: Luis Rodriguez
How do the protagonists view their native language (L1) and the family culture?				
How does society view their language and their culture?				
What are the major emotional, social and familial consequences?				
What are the implications for academic and cognitive development?				

(© Aída Walqui)

Whole Group:

🖊 Conduct a group discussion of the ideas generated from the readings. Here are some prompts for this discussion:

☛ What did you learn?

☛ What did these make you think of that you had not thought of before about immigrant students' experiences?

☛ What are the possible connections among the experiences of these characters and our own students?

☛ What does this lead us to wonder about in terms of our own students?

ADDITIONAL OR ALTERNATIVE STEP WHEN READING ABOUT IMMIGRANT EXPERIENCES:

Budget Tour: After the expert groups have read their selections (or at the end of the entire activity) you can give individuals time to complete the "budget tour" activity. This is a great way to summarize the key ideas of the text, and models for teachers an activity that they can use in their classrooms above and beyond the jigsaw. In this activity, teachers write on a poster sheet the text title, then create their own title for the text, pick out one key verbatim quote or statement from the text and say why they chose it, write a brief summary and create a graphic.

THE BUDGET TOUR

Text Title:

My Title:

Key Quote (Most Important Statement):

Why I Chose It:

Brief Summary in My Own Words:

Graphic:

SELECTED NOVELS
ABOUT THE IMMIGRANT EXPERIENCE

☛ Abinader, Elmaz. (1991). *Children of the Roojme: A Family's Journey*. New York, NY: W. W. Norton.
The story of a Lebanese family's immigration journey and eventual settlement in western Pennsylvania.

☛ Carlson, Lori. (Ed.) (1994). *Cool Salsa: Bilingual Poems on Growing Up Latino in the United States*. New York, NY: Ballantine Books.
A collection of poems in Spanish and English about the adolescent Latino experience, many of them about what it's like to be an immigrant.

☛ Jen, Gish. (1992). *Typical American*. New York, NY: Penguin Books.
A novel about a Chinese immigrant who comes to the United States to study, with hopes of becoming an engineer.

☛ Marshall, Paule. (1981). *Brown Girl, Brownstones*. New York, NY: Feminist Press.
Set in Brooklyn, New York, this is a story of a Barbadian immigrant family; the story focuses on the young daughter as she makes her way through school, dealing with poverty and racism along the way.

☛ Galarza, Ernesto. (1971). *Barrio Boy*. London, UK: University of Notre Dame Press.
The story of a Mexican boy who, with his family, emigrates from Mexico to Sacramento, California and tries to find his way to acculturate to the United States.

☛ Lee, Gus. (1991). *China Boy*. New York, NY: Penguin Books.
The story of a young Chinese immigrant boy growing up in San Francisco, California.

☛ Santiago, Esmeralda. (1994). *When I was Puerto Rican*. New York, NY: Vintage Books.
The story begins in rural Puerto Rico and follows a young girl as she immigrates to New York, finds her way through the public schools and goes on to Harvard.

GETTING TO KNOW YOUR OWN STUDENTS

Once you have taken the time to explore your own experiences and become acquainted with the experiences of other immigrant students, you will probably want to think of ways to better understand your own students in your own classes, in your own school. The activities in the rest of this chapter are aimed at getting to know your own students.

KNOWING YOUR STUDENTS: WHEN LANGUAGE PROFICIENCY IS THE ISSUE

This category of knowing revolves around whatever definitions might be out there that try to define what constitutes "ESL-ness" or "LEP-ness." Historically, the efforts made to protect the civil rights of language minority students have centered on access and equity for this group of students. What sets language minority students apart in the civil rights arena is the understanding that this particular group of students faces a language barrier, and that one key to knowing whether the barrier has been overcome or not is assessment of the English language proficiency of students.

Knowledge of language proficiency issues has often been related to compliance issues and often involves the administration of norm-referenced tests to determine levels of proficiency in speaking, reading and writing in English and the student's primary language. Strong advocates have a clear picture in their heads of how the different levels of language proficiency in English and the students' primary language play out in the identification and placement procedures at the school.

The most effective schools have a cadre of staff who understand the interplay of oral language proficiency with reading and writing. When a group of faculty and staff have adequate understanding of the complexities of their LEP student population, the right questions are asked more often, the right decisions made for each immigrant student. They are able to "eyeball" the test scores of a student and understand almost immediately what a good placement might be. They are not satisfied to let this program and curriculum information reside on a clerk's desk, in the district computer or at the testing center because they know they need to understand where their students are placed, or misplaced, and why.

An effective advocate can answer the following questions about this more "technical" side of knowing students:

❧ Where can you find pertinent language proficiency testing information for students in your school? What are the names of the tests used in your district to identify and place second language learners—oral, as well as reading and writing?

❧ How are tests scored and what do particular scores represent? How do different types of students tend to score on the tests?

❧ Can you explain to another staff member what a score means, and what the program and curriculum implications of a score might be? Can you explain the limitations of the testing, and what can a score tell you or not tell you about a student?

❧ Are the scores of second language students aggregated or disaggregated in meaningful ways so that staff can tell how many students there might be at different levels of language proficiency? What are the implications at your school of identifying particular groups of second language learners based on test scores? How does this information feed into program planning and the master schedule?

Mixed media by Thoun Kheang, a high school student from Thailand

Training a cadre of staff who have an intimate, working knowledge of language proficiency measures is a long-term project. Traditionally, a single teacher specialist or ESL teacher has had the responsibility of monitoring their students. As the numbers of students grow, and as the complexity of the immigrant student population becomes more apparent, so does the need to multiply the numbers of knowledgeable staff who can effectively advocate for appropriate programs and placement, someone who can take the information and act on it appropriately.

ACTIVITY 4.4
A METHOD FOR INTRODUCING STAFF
TO LANGUAGE PROFICIENCY ISSUES

The following is one way to introduce staff to the complexity of the immigrant student population, through the use of test scores and brief glimpses into the educational histories of students. This training was developed by an ESL teacher advocate who was constantly asked questions by other staff members, such as: "How did this student get in my class?" "Are you sure this student belongs in my mainstream science class?"

This activity can be completed in approximately two hours with staff. For this activity to work well, it needs to be set up by someone who really understands both the assessments given to LEP students at your site and the ways they're used to identify or place students in classes. The goal is to have the staff who participate walk away with a clear picture of the range of LEP students and some basic understanding of how the language proficiency scores are a part of that picture.

Preparing for the staff activity

❧ Select four to five "prototypical" immigrant students, that is, real students who represent different types of LEP students (newcomers, native-born, long-term LEP, etc.). The students should represent the range of students present at your school, from those who speak no English at all, to students who might have been schooled here since kindergarten or first grade. Gather testing data on each student; you will want to have:

  ☛ oral proficiency measures in English and the primary language,

  ☛ reading and writing in English and the primary language,

  ☛ prior education,

  ☛ and other pertinent site or district information.

Creating the prototypes will force you to sit down and really think about the kinds of immigrant students you have at your school. It will also force you to think about how you can make the student categories come alive for staff who have little to no understanding of this student population.

❧ Make a grid or chart similar to the one below with student names, and places to fill in all the information as the session progresses. ˙

As participants learn about the students, they will be filling in the data and constructing individual and joint understandings about the immigrant students at their school. The following example is site-specific to a certain degree, in that the immigrant student population is primarily Latino and Spanish-speaking, with a sprinkling of students from other language backgrounds. A blank version of this chart appears on page 198.

SAMPLE LANGUAGE PROFICIENCY PROFILES OF FOUR STUDENTS

Juan R.

Primary Language	Spanish
Years of Study in Primary Language	8 years
Primary Language Oral Proficiency	95 (LAS-O)
Primary Language Writing	4
Primary Language Reading	92%
English Oral Proficiency	15 (LAS-O)
English Writing	0
English Reading	0
Years in the U.S.	2 weeks

Hoa D.

Primary Language	Vietnamese
Years of Study in Primary Language	3 years (interrupted)
Primary Language Oral Proficiency	?
Primary Language Writing	Very limited
Primary Language Reading	?
English Oral Proficiency	32
English Writing	too soon to test
English Reading	?
Years in the U.S.	2 years

Blanca G.

Primary Language	Spanish
Years of Study in Primary Language	4 years
Primary Language Oral Proficiency	85 (LAS-O)
Primary Language Writing	2 (LAS R/W)
Primary Language Reading	30% (Aprenda)
English Oral Proficiency	74 (LAS-O)
English Writing	2 (LAS R/W)
English Reading	29% (SAT-9)
Years in the U.S.	4 years

Joe S.

Primary Language	Spanish
Years of Study in Primary Language	I year (kindergarten)
Primary Language Oral Proficiency	71 (LAS-O)
Primary Language Writing	0 (LAS R/W)
Primary Language Reading	Says he cannot read Spanish
English Oral Proficiency	85 (LAS-O)
English Writing	Not passed district proficiency
English Reading	25% (SAT-9)
Years in the U.S.	Since birth

Your own chart should reflect the kinds of immigrant students at your site; it need not be exhaustive in terms of possible categories of students, however. Keep it fairly simple and straightforward at first. For each student, you will want to have language proficiency testing data. First, make sure you have an English oral proficiency score for each student. Depending on the district, it might be the LAS (Language Assessment Scales), the BSM (Bilingual Syntax Measure) or some other standardized oral proficiency test. It is helpful to use the raw score (for example, a number from 1 to 100) rather than the level score (e.g., from 1 to 5) on something like the LAS because there is a huge range of proficiency within each level. Next, you will also want to have a writing proficiency score for each student. This might be a district writing proficiency score from a district rubric or again, it might be from something like the LAS Reading and Writing test. When possible, you should include a standardized reading test score, such as the SAT-9, as well as scores in the student's primary language if tests have been administered for those. Make sure you have the pertinent information related to years in the United States and years that the students studied in their primary languages, if applicable.

Conducting the staff activity

🖎 Begin by having participants think about what they already know about how the Limited English Proficient students are identified and assessed in their school. You may want to structure the conversation by having participants, in pairs or groups, discuss the following:

- ☛ What we know about identification and assessment of Limited English Proficient students

- ☛ Things we are not clear about or are unsure about

- ☛ The three most important questions for us

Generally, you will find that unless teachers are intimately connected with the testing procedures done at the school or district, they have limited knowledge about the whole process. It might be helpful to say, "By the time we finish today, you will be able to answer questions about the different kinds of Limited English Proficient students in our school, in terms of the range of language proficiencies. That way, when someone at your school says something about 'those LEP students,' you can reply, 'Which ones? The ones who might be sitting in your mainstream classes, or the newly-arrived immigrant student who just walked in the door? Our Korean speakers or our Spanish speakers?' These questions push for understanding the complexity of your student population."

🖎 **Primary Language:** Have participants look at the blank "Language Proficiency Profiles" chart that follows.

Tell them that you're going to use four real students to understand identification and assessment better and to see the broad range of students in the district who might be classified as Limited English Proficient. You may want them to look at the example we gave

LANGUAGE PROFICIENCY PROFILES

Name of Student: _____

Primary Language   _____

Years of Study in Primary Language   _____

Primary Language Oral Proficiency   _____

Primary Language Writing   _____

Primary Language Reading   _____

English Oral Proficiency   _____

English Writing   _____

English Reading   _____

Years in the U.S.   _____

Name of Student: _____

Primary Language   _____

Years of Study in Primary Language   _____

Primary Language Oral Proficiency   _____

Primary Language Writing   _____

Primary Language Reading   _____

English Oral Proficiency   _____

English Writing   _____

English Reading   _____

Years in the U.S.   _____

before, in which the students are all 9th graders.

First, have participants fill in the blank for each student next to "Primary Language." Of course, your own chart will differ from ours. In our example, Spanish is filled in for each student, except for Hoa, whose primary language is Vietnamese.

🍂 **Years of Study in Primary Language:** For this step, you will need to have gathered the educational history for each student. Oftentimes, students fill out an entering questionnaire or there may be information in their cumulative files. If you can, fill in the gaps of the data with other facts. In our example, you might say, "Juan went to school continuously in Mexico, in Guadalajara, so we'll put 8 years for him. Hoa, on the other hand, arrived in the U.S. with only 3 years of formal schooling. Even that, for her, was interrupted by her refugee status. Blanca attended school in Mexico through the 4th grade, and Joe had one year of study in his primary language, but that was only in kindergarten." The point here is to get participants to really focus on the prior history of the students and begin to think about how that might affect their current status in school.

🍂 **Years in U.S.:** This section is a great opportunity to have people consider what "years in the U.S." can actually mean. By realizing that Limited English Proficient students run the gamut from having a mere two weeks here (like Juan) to having been born here (like Joe), staff can begin to appreciate the fallacy of equating limited English proficiency with only recent-arrival students. It is also interesting to point out that some Mexican students who might have been born here also might have spent considerable time in Mexico. In the case of Joe, he was schooled completely in the U. S., but that is not always the case for native-born students of Mexican origin.

🍂 **English Oral Proficiency:** In this section, you want to give the participants some experience with whatever oral language proficiency test instrument you use in your district. First, you may want to show the various sections of the exam (vocabulary, listening, oral production) so people get a flavor for its components. The most important thing is to have participants actually score some oral language production samples, if possible. In our example in which the LAS is used, participants look at 5 to 6 student samples generated from listening to a story on tape (this is the oral production part of the test). They then actually score the story samples, in pairs, using the LAS scoring guide, discussing why they scored them the way they did.

At the end you will want to show the participants how the students scored on the entire oral proficiency exam, which includes oral production, vocabulary and listening. Have participants fill in the English oral proficiency scores for each student. In the sample, Juan scores a 15 (he probably knew a couple of vocabulary words), Hoa scores a 32 (she is still very limited orally despite having been here 2 years), Blanca gets a 74 (making her almost fluent orally in English), and Joe has an 85 (he is orally fluent in English).

🍂 **English Writing Proficiency:** This section is similar to the oral proficiency section above. The goal is to have participants look at several samples of student writing that represent the range of students. It might be the LAS R/W, which assesses reading and writing in English, or a similar instrument or a district writing sample. Again, if possible, you will want to have participants score some writing samples. In our sample, Juan, of course, cannot respond to any writing prompt since he is so new to the U.S. Hoa is still too limited orally in English to take the LAS R/W, Blanca scores a 2 and Joe (for whom the LAS is not appropriate because he is fluent orally) has not passed the district writing proficiency exam.

🌿 **English Reading Proficiency:** For reading, you can simply provide the scores of the students, with some accompanying background information. Most teachers are familiar with what these scores mean. Note that Juan would not be able to do much, if any, of the exam; Hoa also could do little to none; Blanca, after four years in the U.S. scores 32%; and Joe, despite having been here since birth, scores 25%.

🌿 **Primary Language Proficiency (Oral, Writing, Reading):** Now fill in the scores, dimension by dimension, for primary language proficiency. For some students, you may not have primary language information; for others it will be complete (e.g., for Hoa, there is a writing sample in Vietnamese, scored by a native-speaking instructional aide, but no reading measure).

🌿 **Discuss the Whole Assessment Picture:** Have participants look at the entire array of test scores and discuss the following:

☛ How are these students the same? How are they different?

☛ Where would these students typically be placed in our school?

☛ What level of bilingualism does each have at the moment? Who is most likely to become proficiently bilingual?

☛ What do you know now that you didn't know before about the different kinds of Limited English Proficient students in our school?

☛ What links might exist between prior schooling, years of study in primary language, and rapidity of acquisition of English?

☛ What don't we know about these students? What else might we need to know?

This mini-exploration into language proficiency of the various types of Limited English Proficient students can be a real eye-opener for many teachers and other staff members. It is one way to begin to tease out the differences that exist among immigrant students, and lets teachers begin to construct a multi-dimensional model for viewing their students.

KNOWING YOUR STUDENTS: DIMENSIONS BEYOND LANGUAGE

Twenty-six students file into Ms. Timberlake's third-block ESL 3 class. They are, by and large, appropriately placed by language proficiency: intermediate speakers of English, with varying degrees of skill in reading and writing. She knows they should be ready to study difficult content in English, in this case some selected core literature, but that she will need to scaffold her instruction so students can access the richness of the themes, characters, and language of the pieces. She knows, from past experience, that some will do their homework and some will not; that some will eagerly, and with a fair amount of ease, complete each assignment—and some will finish only by a constant barrage of reminders or threats on her part, and then only half-heartedly with little attention to quality or accuracy. She knows there are forces at work on her students—impossibly layered, subtle yet powerful pressures that ultimately affect their performance in school and their acquisition of English.

She thinks of three of her students, with nearly identical test scores in English coming into her class and how different they are. She knows a few facts about each, senses and guesses a few other things.

Sebastian is a ninth grader, a product of the feeder middle school where he had arrived as a total non-speaker of English in the sixth grade. He lives with his father and two older brothers—all of whom work in the fields to support the family here. His mother was left at home in Mexico to care for his ailing grandparents. Sebastian's father expects him to go to school and learn English, to help the family make entrees into American life through the language, and not to have to endure a hard life of backbreaking physical labor. Sebastian, however, longs for his life before coming to the U.S., with his friends, extended family, and meaningful, productive work on the family ranch. He regularly daydreams about going home to Mexico. Although he attended school in Mexico, there were several years when their pueblito simply did not have a teacher. Despite three years in school in the U.S., English still seems a mystery to him. He knows how to speak some, but reading and writing in English feel like almost insurmountable obstacles.

Juana, also a ninth grader, has breezed through the first two levels of ESL in less than a year. Though she knows her English is not perfect yet, she nevertheless is fearless about placing herself in situations with native

English speakers where she has to speak the language. She creates small, private challenges for herself in English, and mentally checks them off one by one as she goes: go talk to her counselor (who does not speak Spanish) about college, go ask her Geometry teacher about extra work, go talk to the clerk in the store about the style and color of shoes that would go with her new dress. She already knows she wants to be a teacher, although she has heard about the Health Careers Academy at the school and medicine as a career has crept into her consciousness. She attended school in Mexico and feels that school in the U.S. does not have the rigor or structure that most students really need. Though her parents are struggling to make ends meet in the U.S., Juana and her three younger sisters are expected to make school a priority and achieve academically.

Ricardo is the third. He lives with his sister and brother-in-law who are barely two years older than Ricardo, but who take their responsibility for him to heart. His mother died two years before and his father many years before that. He knows he is smart—Math has always been easy for him. He can't remember a time when he didn't know how to read. Even learning English requires few mental gymnastics on his part. He seems able to absorb it, to almost soak it up, although he can tell the language of his English Social Studies textbook is now beyond what he has been able to acquire in ESL. He worries secretly about whether he will be able to understand his Science class. Ricardo makes conscious decisions about which teachers he will "let see" that he is smart—with some, he doesn't care if they know or not, and, in fact, prefers a C, even a D or F if he doesn't respect the teacher. He also never reveals to his friends in the neighborhood the extent to which he likes school. Homework goes home carefully folded in his pants pocket; backpacks, textbooks, all other overt signs of "schoolboy" behavior are taboo where Ricardo lives. His favorite cousin belongs to one of the gangs loosely affiliated by a "Norteño" designation; a good friend who lives five blocks away regularly sports blue clothing, and hangs out with the "Sureños." Ricardo often thinks about the safety and protection he could get by joining up with his cousin. He most often imagines himself on one side or the other of a vast, deep canyon. The distance between the worlds that exists on each side of the abyss is infinite. It seems that if he chooses one side, or the other, there will be no going back, and no way of bridging the gap. And then he thinks that, despite his careful efforts to divide up his life, and hide one side from the other, maybe he doesn't really have a choice, anyway. Something will happen. He'll end up on one side of the canyon or the other, somehow. Does it really matter?

To some eyes, Juana, Sebastian and Ricardo are a somewhat homogeneous trio. On the surface, they are adolescent, Mexican immigrants, all at about the same stage of English language acquisition. They share the same language, the same culture, and don't differ vastly in socio-economic status. Under the surface, however, lie very different realities that help to govern their engagement in school, their speed of English language acquisition, their willingness to become a part of their newly adopted society. Their realities affect whether or not they will buy into commonly held notions of what makes for success or failure, whether or not they think they have choices about the paths they will take.

Thoughtful teachers and advocates of language minority students operate with an awareness of the sociocultural, political and psychological forces that affect their students' acquisition of English and engagement in school. One educator named this issue by saying:

> *"I'm concerned with the disjunction between the students' experience in their country of origin and their experience in the classroom. I think that's a major problem, but I don't know how to fix it or where to look to find evidence of it."*

Advocates know that to address these issues, they can look to the multiple efforts made by researchers and theoreticians to understand the complex sociocultural and psychological forces that shape their students' lives. They are familiar with research that explains why some language minority students prosper academically and socially in our schools and why some do not. Teachers need not have an encyclopedic knowledge of what's out there that attempts to explain the success or failure of their students—but it helps to be conversant with some key ideas that can get educators beyond blaming the students' cultures and families, or blaming the students themselves. The box on the following page examines some of these key ideas.

SOCIOCULTURAL AND PSYCHOLOGICAL FORCES AFFECTING LANGUAGE MINORITY STUDENTS

Each of the theories or ideas presented below can broaden and deepen teachers' understandings of their language minority students. A careful consideration of these extralinguistic factors provides fresh perspectives on your second language learners, helping you to see them from new and different angles.

The law focuses on language as the barrier to immigrant student achievement, but in the lives of students, language is just one part of the gap they must leap in trying to bridge cultures and nations. And learning the language is just a small part of what goes on for immigrant students in negotiating their place in school. The following are different ways for thinking about those "other factors" beyond language. These varying theories may help you consider what is going on in the lives of your students that help to shape their reactions to, and involvement in, school. Each is based on a different body of theory and literature and each poses its own set of questions.

THE ROLE OF CULTURE AND CULTURAL MISMATCH

Finding out what is going on in the lives of your immigrant students involves finding out about their home cultures. For instance, how are your students taught by the adults in their homes? How do they show respect for elders? What is schooling like in their home nations? What ways of learning work for them? What are the things that go on in school (in teaching and learning) that feel uncomfortable or "foreign" to your students? What kinds of behaviors or responses from students make us feel uncomfortable, disrespected or unfamiliar?

One teacher described her dilemma in recognizing cultural differences in the classroom:

> *"Part of our culture is different than other students' cultures. For example, having boys and girls sit and work together in groups, with my Islamic students, is not part of their culture. I have a student whose father came to me the other night for Open House and he would not shake my hand because he's Islamic. He said, 'I can't shake your hand, you'll have to shake my wife's hand.' And yet I feel conflicted — I'm not trying to say my culture is better, but this is the way we're doing it here, so how do I convey that this is not better but this is the way it's gonna be done here?"*

Immigrant students' lives and experiences have been shaped by another culture and set of norms. Our schools and the teachers in them, however, reflect a very different culture. This can lead to a cultural mismatch, where the possibilities for misunderstanding behaviors or attitudes between teacher and student are enormous and should not be minimized. The very processes of teaching and learning are different in other cultures, as are the expected roles and relationships between teachers and students. Whether or not students should express their opinions, ask questions or speak out in class differs from culture to culture. The ways in which teachers signal approval or disapproval differ from culture to culture. Very often, the more similar a child's home culture is to the culture of their teachers and the school, the smoother the learning process can be. The more they clash, the more likely there will be school failure (Delpit, 1995; Heath, 1983; Suarez-Orozco and Suarez-Orozco, 1995).

THE STRESSES OF IMMIGRATION

Knowing our immigrant students means educating ourselves about their immigration paths, the places and means by which their journeys occurred, and the kinds of stresses they face day-to-day in their lives.

All immigrants must adjust to a new culture and nation, but the size of the differences they have to bridge, the resources they bring to that adjustment, and their success in making the transition differ enormously. There is tremendous trauma associated with immigration for many children (Padilla and Duran, 1995). Some come from rural and isolated parts of the world, and the transition to our schools involves entering schools with more children in them than entire communities in which they lived—where the complexity of urban life, transportation, and technology presents a whole new world to them (National Coalition of Advocates for Students, 1988; Olsen and Chen, 1988).

Some of our immigrant students fled war and political oppression. There are almost two million worldwide refugees in need of protection or assistance, driven from their homelands by war and political or religious persecution. They must face a political ballgame over which nations will accept them. Many of our immigrant students are refugees who have lived with the confusion and upheaval of fleeing their homelands and some have experienced periods of serious dislocation or time in refugee camps. Their families have often been the victims of violence, the children themselves victims or helpless witnesses. Post-Traumatic Stress Syndrome and the stresses of this dislocation can be major forces in whether and how children adjust to school.

But there are other kinds of stresses involved with immigration. The "borders" immigrant students need to negotiate go beyond national borders and languages. Existing research literature can help identify many of these. The work of Patricia Phelan and her colleagues, for example, speaks of the difficulty immigrant students often face because the knowledge and skills they carry are more effective, valued and demonstrated in their homeland (Phelan, Davidson and Yu, 1993). In other words, once an immigrant student walks into a U.S. classroom, the rules and knowledge they received from their home culture do not readily apply.

Phelan et al. identify several "borders" that immigrant students must navigate in their new setting. One such border is linguistic, which results when communication between student worlds (home/school, peer/home) is obstructed—not because of different languages *per se*, but because one group regards the other group's language as unacceptable or inferior. Linguistic borders are created not only when immigrant students, limited in English proficiency, are taught in English so that their home language and culture are invalidated, but also because the serious emotional stresses of anxiety, depression, apprehension or fear blocks their ability to participate in school. These emotional stresses are often related to their home cultures being made invisible or criticized by schools and teachers.

EMPOWERING AND DISEMPOWERING STUDENTS

To know what is going on with our students means taking a hard look at whether they experience school as a welcoming and empowering institution, or one that devalues their language and culture. In California, where schools are the most ethnically and linguistically diverse in the world, our schools struggle over what their role should be. Is it to help maintain students' home cultures and languages, or to help "Americanize" and assimilate students to the dominant culture?

Immigrant students enter schools that have different climates and practices of including or excluding them. The prevailing attitudes in a school about students' languages and home cultures can heavily influence the curriculum, the ways teachers relate to immigrant students, and even how the school is structured. The attitudes can be quite subtle, too. One teacher at a California Tomorrow workshop spoke with concern about how "our school communicates to students that you can only be smart in English. You can't be smart in your home language."

Jim Cummins (1989) has described the ways in which schools can either empower or disable students to the degree their languages and cultures are valued, made visible and used in context. Cummins describes a disabling educational context as one that emphasizes "subtractive cultural and language incorporation," that is, the emphasis is on gaining English skills and "American" culture. As a result, immigrant students are forced to leave behind or neglect their home language and culture. A disabling context also emphasizes a "transmission approach" to teaching, where new information and culture are given to the student in a one-way process. An "enabling" context is "additive," supporting students in maintaining their home languages and cultures while helping them add the language, knowledge and skills they need in the U.S. In such enabling contexts, instruction is also more interactive and constructivist.

"THE INVOLUNTARY MINORITY" AND THE IMMIGRANT EXPERIENCE

Knowing our immigrant students means considering the ways in which they may "construct" how other immigrants like them succeed in the U.S. It means seeking to understand how immigrant students view schooling in terms of its "payoff," and considering whether, and in what ways, their reactions to school and teachers may be shaped by those experiences and perceptions.

Immigrants enter this nation as members of cultural groups that have a history in the U.S. Some theorists (Gibson, 1987; Ogbu and Matute-Bianchi, 1986) stress the importance of the position and history of that cultural group in the new nation and the ways in which opportunities are open or closed to that group. Many recent immigrants arrive expecting the U.S. to be the "land of opportunity," and most immigrant parents are willing to make enormous sacrifices for their children to realize these opportunities. Other immigrants are not really immigrants at all, but groups that have been incorporated into the U.S. involuntarily, such as Mexicans, Puerto Ricans and Native American Indians. Blacks are also an involuntary minority, having been enslaved and brought against their will from Africa.

The nature of their group history in this country makes involuntary minorities "caste-like." Their children see the impacts of a longstanding history of oppression: discrimination against and devaluation of their communities; the difficulty their parents and elders have in finding good jobs; and low wages and denial of basic benefits like healthcare to their families and countless other forms of injustice and exclusion. Theorists argue that witnessing these injustices makes immigrant students suspicious of claims that if they perform well in school, they can achieve "the American Dream." Therefore, these young people may resist acquiring the dominant group's culture and mentality; things like studying hard, speaking standard English, being liked by the teacher, getting good grades or other behaviors are identified as "acting white." And since some immigrant students do not believe their efforts or school achievement will pay off, there is no reason to study hard, speak standard English, or "act white." For these immigrant students, the world they see is extremely unjust and no amount of hard work will benefit them.

RACIALIZATION

Knowing our immigrant students means seeking to understand how they experience the process of being "racialized" in our schools and nation, and how their racial experiences in and at school affect their academic engagement.

The vast majority of immigrants and language minority students in the U.S. are also children and youth of color. They enter our country and have to learn our racial system—where they belong in it and what that means. This is a major part of the "Americanization" process for many immigrant students. The concept of "racialization" rests on the notion that "race" does not have a biological basis, but is a social construct that is constantly being taught, learned and negotiated in society. As people learn the expectations and beliefs that others have of them because of their skin color, they become racialized.

Many immigrant students of color learn in school the expectations and assumptions others have of their racial group (Olsen, 1998; Omi and Winant, 1990). This racialization process often includes taking on expected behaviors and attitudes towards school. Seen in the context of the "involuntary minority" concept described above, racialization may help explain why for some students, the longer they are in the U.S. (and despite learning English), the lower their school achievement. They have learned how "people with skin color like me" are "supposed to be" in this society and in school.

REPRODUCTION AND RESISTANCE THEORY

Knowing our immigrant students means examining the ways in which our schools track children of different classes, races, and languages to different kinds of futures—engaging with our students to understand what that looks like to them and what it means to them in terms of their feelings about school.

One way to understand this sorting process is by seeing how schools are political institutions serving the interests of the dominant group by reproducing economic, social and racial relations. This is called "reproduction theory." Reproduction theorists (Apple, 1982; Apple and Weis, 1983; Bourdieu and Passeron, 1977; Bowles, 1977) argue that schools imitate society's power relations, so that the children of wealthier and white parents receive the advantages and privileges many others do not. Essentially, even without the conscious intentions of educators, school practices result in sorting students into what are considered "appropriate" social positions for their racial or class grouping. Poor students are tracked into lower slots in schools where they learn to be good factory workers, follow rules, and do what they're told, while wealthier students learn the skills of management, control and critical thinking.

But many students, particularly those tracked into the lower slots, resist this process. A companion set of theories describes this resistance (Erickson, 1987; Fine, 1987; Ogbu and Matute-Bianchi, 1986); their work blends "caste-like minority" theory (when immigrant students don't believe their efforts will pay off) with the theory of how schools reproduce class and race relations. Resistance theorists say that students can see they are being tracked and sorted, and so find ways to resist schooling in general—by not cooperating, by losing interest, by not "playing along." They find ways to "not learn."

SEEING THE COMPLEXITIES OF THE IMMIGRANT STUDENT POPULATION

The following activities are some ways that educators can get themselves beyond the perceived homogeneity of certain groups of immigrant students or beyond the perceived heterogeneity of others. Educators can begin to see the complexity that is offered by the students sitting in their classes and walking their halls, in ways that go beyond the more surface features of language.

Watercolor by Susan Tran, a high school student from Vietnam

ACTIVITY 4.5
WHAT WE SEE, WHAT WE DON'T SEE

Reread the cases of Ricardo, Juana, and Sebastian outlined previously on pages 201-202 with your group. Individually, take some time to identify which facts, which characteristics of the students, which attitudes would be most apparent to their teachers—what we can see about each student in the daily life of school (such as, Ricardo refuses to carry a backpack; Juana is highly motivated). You might also want to take some time to construct what teachers might say about each of these students, based on the information in the case study. For example, "Juana is such a great student!" or "I don't know about Sebastian. He seems to be trying, but he's getting an F in my class."

Next, take some time to identify the things that would not be immediately apparent, the things you would only find out if you were to do some digging—what we can't see in the average daily interaction with students. Again, these might be facts, characteristics, or attitudes. For example, the average teacher in a secondary setting might not know that Ricardo does very well in some classes and poorly in others. Even if a teacher happened to know that (by seeing his report card), it's likely they would not know why that is the case.

As a group, share your ideas about each of the students. You might want to consider the following questions in your discussion:

1. How are the students, on the surface, the same?

2. What facts, characteristics, motivations, attitudes do you think would be most apparent, most visible to teachers?

3. What are some common assumptions that might be made about these students, based on visible, surface knowledge?

4. What facts, characteristics, motivations, attitudes do you think are the most hidden, the most invisible?

5. When you know more about the students, which of the assumptions made in Question #3 above fail to hold up?

6. How do you find out more about your own students? What are some ways that teachers usually find out about the "hidden" side of students' lives?

7. What difference could it make to know more about the "hidden" parts of the students' lives and feelings? How could knowing this inform what you might do for them academically?

ACTIVITY 4.6
REFLECT ON A STUDENT YOU KNOW

Think of an immigrant or language minority student you know fairly well, one that might typify a category of immigrant students at your school. It can be a student who does well in school, one who does not do well, or one who just plugs along in relative obscurity. It could be a student who is a recent arrival or one who has been here many years. Jot down any facts you know about that student—anything at all about test scores, grades, classes enrolled in, family, siblings, examples of the student's work, likes, dislikes, length of time in the U.S. Next to each fact, write how you found out, or how you know.

Now note what you don't know about the student. There are probably facts you don't know, as well as other issues that might affect how the student is doing in school.

Share with another teacher what you know about your student. Then share what you don't know.

Together, chart the following:

☛ Are there broad categories of "knowing" and "not knowing"?

☛ Where is it that most of the knowledge exists?

☛ How is it that most people found out what they knew about their students?

☛ How about the "not knowing" pieces?

☛ Are there important categories of information that people tend not to know that would be helpful in planning for equity and access for immigrant students?

☛ What difference does it make to know or not know?

As a group, discuss:

☛ When we "don't know," what happens?

☛ What did you find yourself doing when you "don't know"?

☛ Did you leap to any assumptions or interpretations based on what you knew?

☛ How can we decide when it is acceptable to go by guessing, intuition, hunches or common sense about our students, and when we need to develop a coherent view of what is really happening?

ACTIVITY 4.7
EXAMINING STUDENT PROFILES:
LONG-TERM LEP STUDENTS

The three profiles of immigrant students used in this activity were completed as a part of the California Tomorrow Immigrant Students Project. We were seeking to discover more about the immigrant student population at the secondary level. Through the process of interviewing many students, we heard fascinating, informative and compelling stories.[1] The profiles appear in Appendix B at the end of this chapter.

For this activity, we've chosen profiles of long-term LEP students—students who have been designated as LEP for 7 years or longer, who are no longer in the ESL sequence but, for a variety of reasons, are not yet able to redesignate as English-fluent. You can perform this activity with other types of LEP students, but we focused on long-term LEP youth because of the unique challenge schools face in addressing their needs.

Read the three profiles of long-term LEP students with your group. Depending on the size of the group, you may want to divide the profiles up so that two to three people can concentrate on each case. Or, if time allows, you may want to concentrate on one or two profiles per meeting. As you read and discuss the profiles, consider the following:

☛ What school responses seemed to help?

☛ What might have helped?

☛ Does your school have the kind of program or supports necessary for this student? If so, what are they? If not, what is missing?

☛ What might be possible appropriate programs or supports for these students?

---

[1] Interviewers included Amy Muckelroy, Gilberto Arriaza, Judy White and Zaida McCall-Perez.

CREATING TYPOLOGIES AS ONE WAY TO THINK ABOUT AND PLAN FOR YOUR STUDENTS

California Tomorrow's work in secondary schools throughout the state has revealed to us again and again the richness and complexity of the immigrant student population. As the student profiles for Activity 4.5 show, the lives and schooling experiences of our immigrant students vary vastly from one to another. They are not a homogeneous group and should not be educated as such. And yet it is also true that there are ways of "clustering together" students in roughly approximated groupings that can help you plan more thoughtfully and effectively for the individual students within those groups.

The four immigrant student typologies that follow have been developed by California Tomorrow, in partnership with Cathy Minicucci, Zaida McCall-Perez and Judy White, over the course of the last several years. They are still evolving, just as the student population changes with time. You can see by looking at the following chart that students might fit into more than one category. Like any attempt to "categorize" real human beings, the lines and distinctions often begin to blur or merge. To illustrate each typology, we include two cases, based on in-depth interviews with immigrant students.

You will probably also quickly see and begin to think about other typologies of immigrant students that exist at your school or in your district—ones that may not be adequately represented here. The intention of this sort of grouping is not to create definitive "types" of immigrant students, or to suggest that there are not other distinct, useful typologies, but rather to show how thinking about your students in this way can lead to better programs for immigrant students.

IMMIGRANT STUDENT TYPOLOGIES

Typology	Key Characteristics	Program Implications
Accelerated, College Bound	• In U.S. four years or less • Multiple countries of origin • Schooling in native country usually excellent • Rapid movement through ESL sequence • Academic achievement in terms of grades exceeds rest of school • Often highly motivated • Possibility to graduate in four years • Primary language content courses can assist many in credit accrual • Often successful in mainstream content classes, even with limited English proficiency	• Counseling to ensure appropriate college-prep course sequence • Credit offered for courses taken in native country • Acceleration through ESL sequence • Provision of primary language content courses whenever possible to aid credit accrual • Explicit, targeted instruction to help students meet grade-level standards
Newly Arrived, in the ESL Sequence	• In U.S. 3 years or less • Multiple countries of origin • Little English language proficiency on arrival • Some well-prepared in native language, on grade level; others below • Some arrive with many transferable credits, others with no transcripts or records • Steady progress through ESL sequence • If school offers native-language content courses, credit accrual toward graduation rapid • Difficulty passing minimum proficiencies within 4-year time frame • Academic achievement in terms of grades similar to rest of the school	• Need for content-based, literature-based ELD • Need to accelerate literacy across the content areas with consistency of approaches and strategies • Provision of primary language content courses to aid credit accrual • Credit offered for courses taken in native country • If arriving at 9th grade or beyond, many may need more than 4 years in high school—re-examination of traditional 4-year path
Underschooled	• In U.S. several years or less • Multiple countries of origin • Little to no English language fluency • Schooling in native country interrupted, disjointed, inadequate, or no schooling at all • Little to no literacy in native language • Three or more years below grade level in Math • Slow acquisition of English—tendency to repeat ESL levels • Tendency to struggle in academic content classes (D's and F's) • Lack of credit accrual over time • Unable to pass minimum proficiency exams	• Need for native language literacy instruction • Extended time for English language development • Extended time for acquisition of content subject matter • Extended time for passing minimum proficiency exams • Summer programs/after school/ other efforts to provide extra time in school • Attention to over-age issues, self-esteem of underschooled adolescents
Long-Term Limited English Proficient	• In U.S. 7+ years when entering high school • Multiple countries of origin • Usually orally fluent in English • Reading/writing below level of native English peers • Bi-modal academically: some doing well, others not • Some have literacy in primary language, others not • Some were in bilingual programs, most not • Mismatch between student's own perception of academic achievement (high) and actual grades or test scores (low) • Similar mismatch between perception of language ability and reality	• Need for programs designed to accelerate literacy in English • Native language instruction to "rebuild" mother tongue literacy—possible for some • Attention to authentic feedback to students on performance • Counseling crucial • 9th-grade interventions • Implementation of career paths, academies for all students • Need to disaggregate data on long-term students—don't make assumptions based on label

Thinking about your students from a typology framework also assists in confronting and breaking down the inevitable comments about "those LEP students." It is then that you can begin to ask the questions: Which LEP students are you talking about? The recently-arrived students who walked into the door of our school this year? The student who is sitting in my ESL class right now who cannot read or write in her native language? The one who waltzed through ESL in record time and is now in mainstream Physics, English, U.S. History? The struggling readers and writers who have been in our school system since first grade? School staff who have less experience with immigrant students tend to lump them all together, as if they are a homogenous group—often leading to the "those LEP students" comment. A typology approach to categorizing students can delineate how the various types of immigrant students might be the same and how they might be different—and how programs could be tailored to meet their differing needs.

FOUR IMMIGRANT STUDENT TYPOLOGIES

ACCELERATED, COLLEGE BOUND

The immigrant students who arrive in the United States with education and preparation that exceed the expectations of U.S. schools often have the ability to whiz through our typical high school curriculum with apparent ease. This is usually the case even if the students come with little to no English language proficiency. ELD teachers of accelerated students note the quick acquisition of English; their content teachers often point out their effective study habits and a wealth of background knowledge that facilitates learning of difficult content in English. Students in this group come from a broad range of family and socio-economic backgrounds; while some have well-educated parents, many have parents who have never completed elementary school. The one thing accelerated students hold in common is consistent, grade-level-appropriate (and often above grade level) instruction in their native language.

Of all the categories of immigrant students, accelerated students have the greatest possibility of graduating and going on to college within the typical four-year time frame. Still, several conditions can greatly enhance the chances of this happening. First of all, many of these students arrive with transcripts from their home country showing courses they have already taken that may be beyond what is expected for their grade level. This is especially true of Math. When a school gives appropriate credit for courses already taken—and follows it up with appropriate placement—students can proceed through an advanced sequence of courses with little interruption. Second, although accelerated students tend to be highly motivated, the U.S. school system is still new to them. Like any other student, they need help negotiating their way through the complex of courses they need to graduate and move on to higher education. Once they know what they need to do, these students are often more able to advocate for themselves— or seek out knowledgeable adults who can advocate for them.

Despite the advantages that accelerated students come with, it is still likely that they will need assistance to leap the hurdles of grade-level content standards. Explicit instruction, targeted at what the student needs to do to meet standards, is what accelerated students say is often missing for them in their U.S. educations. "Tell me what to do and how to do it and I will," might be their plea.

PROFILE OF AN ACCELERATED, COLLEGE-BOUND IMMIGRANT STUDENT

MICHAEL FOSU

Michael, a 17-year-old high school junior from Ghana, wears a wide and easy smile on his round face. When he talks, he appears friendly and thoughtful. Ask him about U.S. schools, which he has been attending for five years, and his enthusiasm will surface. "I just love school," he says in English, spoken with a thick Ghanaian accent. "I am never absent. I think if you come to school you are going to get some knowledge." He is a college prep student who likes Math and Science best because he likes to "play with numbers." There is nothing he does not like, he says, except maybe typing.

His love for schooling seems incongruous coming from a teenager. When asked why other students might not share his positive view of school, he replies:

"It probably [comes] from homes, their houses, because they didn't learn from their parents. They say in Ghana, an African expression, 'If a bear have a baby bear, the bear follow his mother footstep to get food.' So from their houses, that's who they want to follow."

Michael was born into an international family now scattered across four continents. His mother is Ethiopian and Italian. His father is a Brazilian citizen of Ghanaian heritage— a descendant of Ghanaian slaves that the Portuguese brought to Brazil. He is an airline mechanic who travels frequently and met Michael's mother in Italy. They married and lived in Brazil, where Michael was born. While he was still an infant, the family moved to Ghana.

After Michael came to the U.S., he once wrote about his Ghanaian hometown:

"I think the most beautiful place I've every (been) is Pokuase. Pokuase is a village located in the West Coast of Ghana. Pokuase is nest to hills and rivers. One of natural geif for Pokuase is the air and wind. If you vainf Pokuase first thing you would see was the most beautiful soil on the beach. The people of Pokuase are so very active to others...The village has many different ethnic backgrounds. I think Pokuase is home at everybody including white, black, yellow and grece. Therefore, Pokuase is place of family value. I think you should try to see Pokuase and see what I am talking about. I think it is good place to be."

Michael can speak English because it is Ghana's official language, but he also speaks Portuguese, French and regional or tribal languages, such as Ga and Ibo. Last summer, he spent two months visiting relatives in Brazil, Germany, Italy and Ghana. His mother still lives in Ghana, where she works as a bank teller. His father moved to the U.S. several years ago and arranged for Michael and his older sister to come in 1993, when Michael was 12.

Michael was excited about the move, but didn't know what to expect. "Everything was different," he says. "Different kind of people, different culture, different money, different school."

He misses Ghanaian schools. In secondary school, he earned good grades in classes such as English, Math, Social Studies, Ghanaian Languages, French, Technical Skills, General and Agricultural Science, Physical Education and Life and Vocational Skills. He recalls:

"They work us seriously. Here, I can make my grade just easy. I just do my homework and I will get a good grade. But in Ghana you have to prove it that you are smart to get a good grade, an A."

Although he likes school here, he doesn't feel he is being challenged as much.
In Ghana, a typical school day started at 8 a.m. He looks back:

"But you have to be in the school like seven o'clock to clean up the school. If you are late, you are written up for punishment."

Michael's courses were taught in English. After school, he says, "We don't go to movies, like the way people do here." Instead, Michael and his friends gathered to do homework:

"Something that I don't understand, [my friend] will teach me. Or me and my friend will be like competition, challenges, asking questions. Like science, I ask a question and he give me a definition, I give him some problems, he solve them, he give me a problem—that's how it is. That's all we do...[If a friend couldn't do the problem] we are not going to laugh at you, we're going to show how to do it."

When it was time to have fun, Michael and his friends would go fishing or play soccer.

When Michael arrived in California in the fall of 1993, he enrolled in 8th grade in intermediate school. By 9th grade, he was taking a combination of mainstream and sheltered courses, adding:

"When I came here my English is OK, it's good. Only my accent, you know. So if I say something, people really don't understand me. Also, we use Great Britain's system."

He attended a newcomer center through 8th and 9th grades, but says he found it a waste of time. "The school is for people who are from foreign languages, who never learn English before."

Despite Michael's opinion, he initially tested as a Level 1, non-English-speaking student on the Language Assessment Scales in oral expression, reading and writing. Now, as an 11th grader, he has improved on the LAS oral score—a level 4, or fluent. But he still lags behind on reading and writing, having scored only a Level 2.

At the end of 11th grade, Michael had a 3.24 GPA and earned 197 units, which is 30 credits ahead of what he needs to be on track for graduation. He has passed his math proficiency test, as well as reading and language tests. He says he enjoys engaging in class discussions. Each day, he spends about an hour and a half on homework and gets everything done. Michael also likes to read a lot:

"I like fictions, science fictions, and I like comic books. And I like to read sometime about history, people would do something good, like Martin Luther King, Mahatma Ghandi, and then Greek philosophers. I like to read the oral history about slavery. Most of the slave history was from Ghana."

He is now enrolled in all mainstream college-prep courses, except for one sheltered English class. His dream is to attend Morehouse College in Atlanta. He had heard about the school back in Ghana through pen pals:

"I asked [a friend in New York] about school systems, colleges. He tell me that the best school right now is an all-Black school, and I like that."

He hopes Morehouse will have a cultural richness that he misses, such as an appreciation for African music, dance and history. Maybe, he says, Morehouse would be "like going to school in Ghana."

In college, he wants to study to become a doctor. "My people would need more doctors," he says. With his mother still in Ghana, Michael believes he will return to live there someday, as his father also desires to do. But first, "My plan was go to high school and graduate successfully, go to college and get my degree, and make master degree." He knows, too, that a dollar goes a long way in Ghana. "I like the money," he says with a little laugh. "If I take a dollar to my country, I'll get rich. I like the opportunity [in the U.S.]," he says.

He has not found much of a Ghanaian community in the part of California where he lives. While he may miss being surrounded by people like himself, he seems to take the diversity he has found in stride. His girlfriend is an American of African-American and European-American descent. In high school, he has a multicultural circle of friends:

"For me, I don't care, so I just go for everybody. Most of my friends are, like, from Asian, and then Spanish people, and then Blacks…Because I wasn't taught to be a racist, so I think we are all the same."

But racial realities have intruded on Michael's life. He faces the challenge of adjusting to being Black in America. He faces expectations from all races to act and speak in a certain way that "corresponds" to his race and denies his national background—as is true for nearly all immigrant students. "Most people don't recognize me as from Africa. They recognize me as like an American, or Black American."

Michael has not connected with many African American students at his high school:

"Sometimes they laugh at you because of your accent. Sometime they make fun of you, where you came from, like Ghana, they think Ghana is poor. But if you take encyclopedia and find about Ghana, it says Ghana is rich, one of the richest country in West Africa. So they make fun of, like, Africa…If you say you're from Africa, they don't know the difference between continent and country, so they laugh at you. I don't try to do something to make them understand me where I came from. Like, if the person is observing me, how I walk and how I talk, he can tell that this guy is from different country, or different land."

PROFILE OF AN ACCELERATED, COLLEGE-BOUND IMMIGRANT STUDENT

MARTA FIGUERAS

Before Marta emigrated from Peru in 1993, she had taken only one "very basic" English class at her school in Lima. When she enrolled in eighth grade in California, she was assessed as a non-English-speaker and placed in sheltered Math and Science classes. Her only mainstream class was U.S. History. A very hard worker, Marta soon earned all A's.

Today, four years later, she is a 17-year-old high school junior and she takes only college-prep, mainstream classes. With her 4.0 grade point average, she hopes to attend UC Berkeley, UC Davis, Stanford University or Cornell University to start her on the path to becoming a pediatrician.

Several factors contributed to Marta's impressive academic success. Her enthusiasm for learning has taken her a long way, enabling her to achieve despite the language barriers and cultural adjustments that confront so many newcomer students. She says she has always liked school, especially Science, Math and English. "It's fun," she says. "I like everything."

Marta also arrived with a strong school background, in contrast to many immigrant students who come underschooled. In Peru, she attended an all-girls school. Her teachers in Peru were strict, she says. Students never showed disrespect, and most of the children worked hard. Marta remembers the nightly routine of eating dinner, then diving into homework. By the time she left Peru, she had built a solid academic track record up to seventh grade.

Compared to Peru's demanding school system, it's easier to earn good grades here, Marta says. "In my country I got C's, and here I get A's and B's." She confesses that sometimes she thinks U.S. students don't try hard enough:

"Very few people try here. Sometimes they do and that's good. But I don't know. For example, I have a friend who dropped a class because most people spoke English and she has a second language. I mean, I don't think I would have dropped it."

Family support and her parents' own educational achievements have had a lot to do with Marta's positive attitude toward school. In Peru, both of her parents worked in a hospital, her mother as a radiologist and her father, a lab technician. They came here to seek better opportunities because the economy in Peru was poor. Marta's aunt, who lives in California, brought them to the U.S. Currently, Marta's father is looking for work and her mother is an in-home adult caregiver. Now that the family is here, Marta's parents want her to succeed. "They support me," she says. Her success, she adds, "is very important for them, too." Marta's twin sister, Liliana, also excels in school.

Marta's strong academic background and her literacy in Spanish may have helped her to learn English quickly. Marta herself credits reading as the key:

> *"I began reading my first English book in the first ESL level. I just read a lot of books. And I just did my homework and paid attention in class."*

Her conscientiousness extends beyond the classroom. She spends two to three hours per night on homework and usually completes all her assignments. "Sometimes I get lazy and I watch TV first. Then I have to stay up late," she says with a laugh.

Marta benefits from strong teacher interest in her progress. "My teachers help me a lot. Most of my teachers are really nice." She is enrolled in an Early Outreach Program, through which she took courses at a local junior college. In 1997, one teacher referred her to the Pre-College Academy, a six-week summer academic enrichment program sponsored by UC Berkeley. Marta took Calculus and a Biomedical Science class that included topics such as biotechnology, anatomy, physiology and bioethics.

Through the summer program and Saturday classes at Berkeley, Marta has learned about colleges and how to apply to them. She has taken the SAT once, in 10th grade, but did not do as well as she had hoped. She is taking a preparation class and plans to try again.

Despite her success in the classroom, she's still adjusting to life in the U.S. Before she came here, she had never met anyone who was not Peruvian. People in this country often mistake Marta for being Mexican or Indian. She tells them she's Peruvian. She says she wasn't surprised to be surrounded here by people from so many different nations and languages, but "Mostly, I hang around with Hispanics."

Sometimes she misses Peru and her family members there. But she adds, "I like it here, too. For example, if I go back to Peru, I will miss the things here, too." She's philosophical about adapting to wherever she lives. "Wherever you go, you have worries," she says. She wants to maintain her links to Peru, perhaps by visiting after graduation. She observes:

> *"Some people, when they come here for a long time, they forget their culture and everything like that, and they become Americanized."*

She still speaks mainly Spanish at home, but sometimes speaks English with her twin and two other sisters. She speaks English with all her friends except those who are Spanish-speaking. She watches telenovelas in Spanish and listens to traditional Peruvian music, but she doesn't read or write much in Spanish anymore. She doesn't worry about losing her first language, but she says, "Sometimes I kind of forget some words."

In the U.S., Marta enjoys playing badminton and field hockey, watching American sit-coms and listening to soft popular music. But achieving in school is never far from her thoughts. She says:

> *"I don't have my mind on other things right now, just on getting a career and being a good person. Wherever we are, we have to keep on being good persons and good students."*

RECENTLY ARRIVED, IN THE ESL SEQUENCE

When any person not necessarily connected with schools thinks about "immigrant" students, recently-arrived immigrants are the students that probably spring to mind. By and large, these students arrive on our doorsteps with little to no English language proficiency. The implications for this one characteristic are many. At the secondary level, even if the student arrives in the middle school, the challenge of gaining enough proficiency in English in order to pass high school minimum proficiencies is enormous.

When you add on the new requirement of reaching state or district-adopted standards in English Language Arts (not to mention math and other subject matters), the matter of time emerges as the most important. Time here refers to two dimensions: how time is actually spent in ELD instruction—what the content of that instruction is—and the time that is usually needed, in years, to become fluent enough in English to compete with native-English-speaking peers. Reaching grade level standards in English Language Arts would be evidence of the ability to compete with English Only students. Research seems to suggest that it takes a minimum of five to seven years.

One great help for students who fall in this typology is offering native language content courses that provide college-prep as well as high school graduation credits. This can greatly assist the acceleration of some students through some content sequences. For example, if a 9th grader is ready to take Algebra in the 9th grade—but not ready to tackle Algebra in English—then taking the course in the native language provides not only access to that valuable content, but opens the doors of opportunity for that student to be on track with college-prep Math throughout high school. A sheltered Geometry class might follow, with mainstream Advanced Algebra or Calculus later on.

The further along in the typical ESL sequence students are, the greater chance they have of becoming fluent enough in English to meet graduation standards. The implications for secondary schooling here seem obvious. Schools need to make sure that what happens inside of ELD classrooms is focused on literacy, that it is content-based and absolutely topnotch. Additionally, a four-year sequence in high school may simply not be enough time for the majority of newly-arrived students. Secondary schools need to take a long, hard look at the traditional four-year approach. If four years does not provide an extended enough window of opportunity for newly-arrived students to graduate, what then are the responsibilities of the school to inform the students that that is likely to be the case? And how can a school go about providing for and educating the significant numbers of newly-arrived immigrant students who, by and large, will not be able to meet grade level standards in a traditional four-year model?

PROFILE OF A RECENTLY ARRIVED ESL STUDENT

ALEJANDRA ORTEGA

Alejandra, a 17-year-old high school sophomore, moved to California from Mexico only a little more than a year ago. She entered high school as a freshman, and in the short time she has been here, she has adapted readily to her new life. Not only has she progressed through the ESL sequence quickly, but she now has a 3.87 GPA, which makes her an "A" student.

What accounts for Alejandra's success? At first glance, she appears confident, intelligent, and academically inclined. She said she enjoys school and is a good student. She also may have a natural ability to adapt to new circumstances. The interviewer from California Tomorrow observed that Alejandra looked very stylish. Her clothes, hair and makeup reflected the MTV style of American teens everywhere: baggy jeans, a small knit T-shirt, and clunky shoes. Her straight, dark hair was combed back and fell below her shoulders. Her pretty face was adorned with black eye makeup and dark red lipstick.

Alejandra says she has been happy with her school experience so far. Being able to take some classes in Spanish during her first year in high school made a big difference, she notes, because she doubts that she could have done the coursework in English. Even though she had taken some English in Mexico, she never really learned it, she says, although the familiarity probably helped her to pick it up quickly once she came to the U.S.

Many other advantages may have contributed to her academic success and social adjustment. Alejandra comes from a relatively stable family background. Her father, a migrant agricultural worker, has spent part of the year in Salinas and part of the year with his family in Mexico ever since he was in his early twenties. Although the separations have been hard, his U.S. wages have enabled his wife to care for Alejandra and her three sisters full-time.

The four daughters grew up in a small town in the state of Zacatecas where Alejandra attended primary and secondary school. When she came to the U.S., she had nine consecutive years of schooling behind her. In Mexican secondary school, she took courses such as

Economics, Accounting, Business Administration and Office Skills. She received high marks in her classes, equivalent to A's in this country. Her favorite classes have been Math and Science.

When Alejandra learned that she would be moving to the U.S., she felt excited but apprehensive. She heard that living here could be scary and dangerous. But moving here proved to be an "unforgettable moment of my life," she says, and not nearly as frightening as she had expected. Aunts, uncles and cousins already living in California met her family at the airport and helped them to adjust to life here.

When Alejandra arrived in California at the beginning of the 1995-96 school year, she found the school campus to be very different from what she had known in Mexico. She felt scared and confused, but soon found a friend to show her around. Students and teachers have been a great help to her. Newcomers should know that there are a lot of people to help them, she says.

Alejandra had completed 9th grade in Mexico and had earned enough credits to become a 10th grader, which would have placed her in class with peers of her age. But the school decided to place her in 9th grade to give her one extra year of schooling to improve her English before entering the work world or college. Many immigrant students are over-age for their grade for this reason.

When she started high school, she took ESL 1 and content classes, such as Algebra and Earth Science, in Spanish. One year later, she had progressed to sheltered English and content classes. By the second half of 10th grade, she had switched to some mainstream classes, such as Advanced Algebra.

Alejandra feels that classes are easier here than in Mexico, where teachers were stricter and assigned more work. Here, Alejandra is able to complete all her homework in half an hour each day, she says.

She spends her free time hanging out with her boyfriend or other friends. Sometimes she watches TV, listens to music, or plays basketball or volleyball at home. Her friends are both recently-arrived immigrants like herself or those who have lived in the U.S. most of their lives. She mingles with both groups, but has noticed tension at school between newcomers and those who were born and raised in the U.S.

Alejandra speaks mostly Spanish to her friends, and only Spanish at home. She does not read or write very much in Spanish anymore, but does not feel that she is out of practice.

Her English is hesitant and her vocabulary is limited, but she comprehends a great deal. Besides ESL classes, she is also learning more English by watching TV.

She is motivated to succeed, but says that some of her friends here do not value school as much. Sometimes they tell her not to do homework, but Alejandra says she always does her work, even if it means staying up late.

She studies hard because she wants to attend college and become an accountant. Her parents tell Alejandra and her sisters that they have an opportunity to get an education—something her parents did not have. Alejandra's mother was 18, her father, 22, when they had their first child. Her father has worked in the fields for most of his adult life, which has meant months of separation from his family each year. Alejandra's parents have told her that they truly hope their children will have a better life.

PROFILE OF A RECENTLY ARRIVED ESL STUDENT

CINDY TRAN

To her teachers, Cindy poses a difficult challenge. She emigrated from Vietnam two years ago and is now a sophomore ESL student at a large, comprehensive high school. On one hand, she is making consistent progress and has earned a C+ average. She is not disruptive in class and doesn't appear to have obvious problems outside of school. But she isn't motivated academically. Her dissatisfaction with school shows up in tardiness and several cuts. She says, through a translator:

> *"I know school attendance is mandatory, but some days it seems too hard to get up and go. I tell myself I need to do it, but I have to force myself to go a lot of days."*

The school's sheltered Math teacher has noticed Cindy's ambivalence. She comments:

> *"She is real interesting. I haven't quite got a handle. She has now decided that maybe she should try to go to college, but she wanted to know if that means she has to take more Math. I told her yes, and she wasn't sure she wants to push that part."*

The Math teacher is frustrated because she knows Cindy can do better:

> *"She's not a bad student, but not terribly motivated to push herself at all. I don't know if she'll make it to college at this point because she's not willing to do the extra work to get there."*

Does she participate in class? "As little as possible," the teacher says. "She'll sit at the back, and it's sort of like, 'Please don't call on me.'" Culturally, Cindy may feel uncomfortable speaking out in class, but because she is quiet it's easy for teachers to overlook her. She seems to have little teacher support.

Adding to Cindy's problems, her academic program falls short of a full curriculum. During the first semester of 9th grade, her program included no Math at all and somehow she was misassigned to a regular mainstream English class instead of ESL—a mistake that was not corrected until eight weeks into the semester. Her other courses included P. E., Keyboarding and Design.

She cannot afford to miss out on any ESL. Although Cindy is getting by in her classes, she cannot move forward in her content courses until her English improves. She thinks it will take her ten years to become fluent in English. As Cindy admits:

> *"Even in my P.E. class it's hard sometimes to understand the teacher or the other students. I'm not sure I can learn English fast enough. I wish I had more than four years in this school."*

Despite her struggles with English, Cindy wants to keep up her Vietnamese. She speaks

Vietnamese at home with her family, a fact that she is proud of:

"Many of my Vietnamese friends at school who have been here longer can't speak it that well. I think they're a little jealous."

Although Cindy attended school in Vietnam, she says the classes were large and there were times when she had to work instead of go to school. Still, by the time the family left to rejoin their father who had come to the United States five years earlier, Cindy had managed to squeeze in the equivalent of six years of schooling. And despite her lack of English proficiency, Cindy says that school in the U.S. is easy compared to Vietnam.

As a newly-arrived immigrant student in the 8th grade, Cindy took ESL, P.E., Home Economics, sheltered Math, and sheltered Science. Her ESL teacher noted:

"Cindy made Honor Roll the first quarter, but it has been difficult ever since. She is staying to herself more and more, not completing her assignments, not interacting with other students. I am concerned because she has shown that she can learn quickly."

Her grades fell from A's and B's in the first quarter to B's and C's the rest of the year. Cindy's high school ESL teacher echoes the concerns of Cindy's other teachers, explaining:

"She misses some school, but that's not really the problem. It's almost like she has already given up. I've seen that she can learn and do the work and her oral English is really improving. But she's very discouraged by how little she can understand any reading in English, and she's particularly frustrated by the errors she makes in writing. We did an assignment in class where students wrote and drew about their dreams for the future. Cindy drew a college diploma, but it seemed to me like it was an exercise for her and not real."

After one year at high school, Cindy is on target to graduate in terms of earning enough credits. But she still needs to successfully maneuver taking about three more years of required courses, most of which are not offered in a sheltered mode, not to mention courses required for college. Next year, she is signed up to take sheltered World History, mainstream Pre-Algebra, ESL, P.E., mainstream Earth Science and Art. Cindy is worried:

"I know in some of those classes the students don't work very hard, and I don't know if my English is good enough yet for Science."

And Cindy's ESL teacher adds:

"These classes will be a real stretch for Cindy's English, but it's what we have to offer here. I hope she gets a couple of sympathetic teachers who understand about immigrant students. If she doesn't, I don't know how it's going to go for Cindy."

Despite the very real challenges for Cindy, she says, "School is really, really important...because I want to get a good job."

UNDERSCHOOLED

The immigrant students who come to us with little to no prior schooling offer immense challenges at a secondary school. Some "underschooled" students come to us at the secondary level never having attended school at all in their native country; others may have one or even several years of inadequate instruction. Others may have significant gaps in their schooling, having attended school only sporadically. Underschooled students either cannot read at all, or read far below their grade level in their primary language. Their math skills often mirror their low literacy skills. Experienced ELD teachers often note that underschooled students tend to acquire all forms of English slowly; the acquisition process is laborious and uncertain. This is frequently the case in spite of excellent, intensive ELD instruction.

This particular group of students requires an intensity of approach and focus that other groups may not. The implications of not knowing how to read or write in your native language at the age of fourteen or sixteen are enormous. For some students, instruction has to begin at the level of learning how to hold a pencil and understanding what are appropriate and inappropriate school behaviors. Not only do these students often have difficulty learning English, they also have similar problems in their content area classes. It is often challenging to provide an appropriate sequence of courses for underschooled students, as their progress can be slow and unpredictable.

On the other hand, when underschooled students are offered the opportunity to become literate in their native language, they can make surprising academic leaps. Every effort should be made to teach underschooled students to read and write in their native language. Learning English and other content becomes problematic, if not an insurmountable task, without this basic skill. This is a group for whom extra time at the secondary level is necessary, not optional.

PROFILE OF AN UNDERSCHOOLED STUDENT

JUAN DIEGO

Juan is fifteen years old and carries himself with an air of self-assurance. His height and build resemble a twelve-year-old, and his dark brown eyes mirror his abundant straight black hair. He does not wear clothes that indicate any kind of group affiliation; in fact, he makes sure that people know he's not a *cholo*, who, in his words, "is a criminal person who means a threat to everybody."

From Guadalajara, Mexico, Juan is going into the 8th grade, a year or so older than his classmates. He completed 5th grade in Guadalajara, but missed a year of school after moving to California. Though he says he learned to read in third grade, he tests as non-literate in Spanish and English and only knows a little basic Math. He is not yet orally fluent in English.

He's also currently enrolled in a special summer program for underschooled students. He says:

> *"This summer program is teaching me how to read and write better. I learned to write whole words. I know that if I learn Spanish well, it's going to help me learn English."*

Juan likes school, especially Science—a course he's taking for the first time this year—and History. He's an eager student in class, often raising his hand and participating. He gets help with his homework from his sister, who's in the ninth grade, his mom and dad, and his friends. "All my friends are Latinos and we help each other with homework," he says in Spanish, noting that he could not do well in school without this help. Like him, his friends are recent arrivals; most of them had classes together last year. He says:

> *"I know they like school also. Them and me study very hard to get good grades. Echamos muchas ganas (we try hard)."*

Compared to Guadalajara, he feels he learns much more in Hayward, where all his classes except P.E. are in Spanish. Teachers here, he says, "have a lot of patience and teach you little by little." But in Guadalajara, he adds:

> *"Teachers get mad and shout at you. These gangs beat you, steal and even kill you. The kids are very violent there."*

Here, he says, "I like my classes, teachers treat me well, they explain if you don't know or if you don't understand."

There are gangs and fighting here, too, but Juan steers clear. "I don't like gangs because they hit and even kill each other." He notes that this year is better than last year, because "it's more quiet—last year there were lots of fights among gang members." He knows how to tell who's in a gang by the clothing style and hair style. He notices tension between Black and Mexican students, and between rival gangs, but notes that last year, "the fights were among everybody—Black, Mexican, Chinese—not only between Black and Mexican kids."

When he grows up, he wants to be "a lawyer to help people get out of trouble, like jail. I want to help the community. I like to resolve cases. Becoming a lawyer is a decision I just made, my mom and dad still don't know, but I decided to do it because I want to help the community." He has some idea of what it'll take to become a lawyer—he knows he needs to study "a lot" and plans on first improving his grades, then going to high school and graduating, then going to the university.

But even though he studies many hours and participates willingly in his classes, his sketchy skills in Basic Math and lack of literacy in any language will make his goal of becoming a lawyer extremely difficult to attain for this fifteen-year-old 8th grader.

PROFILE OF AN UNDERSCHOOLED STUDENT

JULIE SCOTT

Julie, a 17-year-old sophomore, is a newcomer to the U.S. public school system, having arrived in this country only three years ago. With her straight, waist-length black hair, oval face, tan skin, full lips and almond eyes, she is often mistaken for being from the Philippines. But she's actually from the Marshall Islands, located in the Pacific Ocean halfway between Hawaii and Indonesia's Papua New Guinea and populated mainly by people of Polynesian and Malaysian descent.

Julie is often homesick. Ever since she arrived at age 14, adjustment to the U.S. and its school system has been extremely hard. Her grades have reflected the struggle. By the end of 10th grade, Julie had earned a 1.62 GPA and was 15 credits (3 classes) behind the average progress toward graduation. Fifteen credits is not a large deficit—she should have time to make them up before her class graduates. The real problem is that Julie is barely even able to earn poor grades. Without intervention, it is likely that she will continue to struggle in school, fall further behind, or drop out.

A California Tomorrow interview with Julie reveals inconsistent attendance at a Marshallese-speaking parochial elementary school. When she entered seventh grade in California, she had only four years of schooling behind her.

Her background holds the possibility of neurological damage as well. Julie said that when she was eight, she had an accident or illness that took her out of school for two years. She recalls her mother saying that she almost drowned. Although there's no concrete evidence of brain damage, at times Julie's thoughts seem scattered. Should she have been screened as a possible special education student?

One of her English teachers considered this possibility after noticing that Julie has trouble understanding her reading, even though she makes an effort. Julie also attempts to participate in class, but her answers to questions often miss the mark. On the other hand, she just might not be fluent enough in either English or Marshallese to express herself well. Without adequate screenings, it's hard to know what lies at the root of Julie's academic troubles.

Julie's language problems, however, became evident almost from the start. She considers Marshallese her primary tongue. Because English is the official language of the Marshall Islands, she must have grown up hearing it all around her, too, although she never took an English class back home. She's able to speak with a perfect American accent, but her incorrect word usage and struggles with vocabulary reveal that she is not orally fluent.

When she entered U.S. public schools, she was assessed as a non-English-speaker and enrolled in a newcomer program, concurrent with her attendance at a local middle school. Julie feels that she couldn't speak English at all when she arrived in the U.S., but her first Language Assessment Scores (LAS) showed a beginner's understanding of English. Here is a quote from her writing sample, "My Story About My Family":

> *"My family was feel great and my country is hard word [work] and I like to come here and see how to they doing and I play vollyball and I have friend alots of friend and I was mak somethings for English and…I like to write this story about myself and I was fun and I went to my school. My school is easy but my speech Marshall and I don't understand what she, and went come her I was feel great or have fun and now I like to be on school because to remember how school to an my mother name is diana. Parker and I have older sister and brother I have 3 brother and I have 2 sister."*

Although she has progressed through the entire ESL sequence in four years, beginning with level 2 and currently at level 5, standardized test scores show that she has only marginally improved her English reading and writing skills. She failed ESL 4 in 8th grade and had to repeat it when she entered 9th grade.

Despite her language difficulties, she says she likes to read fiction in English. Even though her teacher expresses concern, Julie feels her reading skills are adequate, but adds, "I can't really pronounce that good. Like the long words, people's names." Clearly, though, she feels her writing "is not OK." She thinks in Marshallese and has a hard time translating thoughts into English. Spelling also gives her trouble.

Sadly, Julie is also aware that she is losing her first language, in which she may not have been fully competent in the first place. In fact, she exemplifies the student who does not have a strong grasp on any language. When her mother and stepfather brought her to the U.S., they told her to stop speaking Marshallese. Now, she speaks only English at school and at home. Compounding Julie's struggle is that she comes from an isolated language and cultural group. There is no one to whom she can speak her native language. Her four younger siblings used to speak Marshallese when they were little, but they no longer remember it.

Julie continues to fall behind in school. No mechanism is in place to alert the school to her needs. She is already over-age for her grade level—18 by the end of 10th grade. By the time she graduates, she will be 20. Her course work in middle school included an ESL 2 Reading, Writing and Survey, sheltered Math 7, mainstream Math 8, Art, Physical Education, and Industrial Technology. She earned many C's, but also D's in Math. In the spring of 7th grade, she scored a 3.9 grade equivalency on a standardized test, corresponding to her four years of schooling in the Marshall Islands.

During 9th grade, she was placed in basic skills classes. During the first semester, she took sheltered Science, ESL 4, and Art—but no Math. The second semester, she took Physical Education, Fundamentals of Math, and Computer—but no English. Such scheduling, in which she does not learn English and Math all year long, poses a problem because she needs intensive catch-up in these two important subjects. Julie spends about an hour a day on homework and doesn't always finish. She says she wants extra help.

She is barely making it through school. Unless she begins to progress in English and Math, she will continue to fail or barely pass her courses. As a result, she may not be able to make up her 15-credit deficit in order to graduate on time. Furthermore, she still has not passed all her proficiency tests, which are required for graduation.

By themselves, Julie's school problems are overwhelming. But family adjustments and dramatic cultural changes complicate her plight. Julie's parents were both from the Marshall Islands, but her father left the family when Julie was very young. Her mother remarried, this time to an American living on the islands. Julie was raised by a great aunt, but had some contact with her mother and four new half-siblings. When her mother and stepfather decided to move back to the U.S., they invited Julie, by then a teen-ager, to come with them. Julie probably feels like an outsider in her family. She seems emotionally distanced from her stepfather—she's not even sure where he works.

She appears lonely and admits to being very homesick for the Marshall Islands, for the people and the way of life there. She speaks of the importance of extended families and the welcoming, respectful way in which people treated one another. She remembers it as a diverse place in which many languages were spoken. Because people respected differences, racism did not seem to be a major problem, she says. In contrast, she dislikes the U.S., its schools, and its students. She detests her classmates' "bad" behavior and disrespect toward teachers. At times, they pick on her. In 9th grade, she was suspended for almost three days for fighting with a Chinese girl who had been teasing her.

Julie is losing the battle to maintain a connection with her home country. Although she wants to return to the Marshall Islands, she also knows she'll find more opportunity here. She expresses a desire to succeed. She wants to graduate, get out into the world, have a career, "and all those things," she says. When asked why school was important to her, she responds that it is the way to college and to a job. She adds that she wants a job to help contribute to her family, to show her parents that she is "valuable." She has considered going into nursing because she believes herself to be good at Science, or maybe she'll become a doctor or lawyer. But unless Julie receives the help she needs, these dreams may just be fantasies.

Colored pencil by Moises Orozco, a high school student from Mexico

LONG-TERM LIMITED ENGLISH PROFICIENT

The long-term Limited English Proficient students represent a growing sub-population of immigrant students. They are a puzzling and diverse group. In this particular subgroup, the word immigrant is often not applicable. Many of these students have been born in the United States and most have been schooled here their entire lives. Others entered in early elementary school as "typical" immigrant students. For a significant number of them, ESL class is a barely-remembered part of early elementary school.

Long-term Limited English Proficient students do not fit one particular profile. Some have been in bilingual programs (for widely varying amounts of time, with widely varying quality and consistency); others have never been in a bilingual classroom at all. They appear to be split academically as well: a good many are surviving academically at the secondary level (in grades, if not in standardized test scores); many others are struggling academically, earning a preponderance of D's and F's and seriously behind in credits. In our interviews of long-term students, many seemed overly optimistic about their prospects of graduating. The actual performance of this group of students often does not match their perceptions of how they are doing in school. They view themselves as doing far better than reality suggests.

Because most long-term LEP students have become orally fluent in English, they are frequently "hidden" in mainstream classes. What is clear about long-term Limited English Proficient students is that they frequently read and write significantly below grade level. Up to now, little attention has been paid to investing in instructional approaches and curricula that will address the gap that exists between these students and their English-fluent peers. Like the other groups of immigrant students, long-term students have little chance of meeting grade-level standards without rethinking what it will really take to get students to high standards.

PROFILE OF A LONG-TERM LEP STUDENT

HUGO ROSAS

With fears for his safety constantly on his mind, it's no wonder that Hugo has trouble focusing on school. Somewhere along the way, the 18-year-old high school sophomore became involved in a gang. On and off campus, he faces the threat of violence, he said. Despair permeates his circle. Only weeks earlier, one of his best friends killed himself. "I don't know if he was just tired of life," Hugo says. "One day, his cousin went into his room and he had the gun in his mouth." Hugo feigns pulling the trigger.

Another friend in Hugo's neighborhood was shot to death. "I'm trying not to go outside that much, 'cause where I live, it's just like, lots of things happen," Hugo says. His friends do not care about school because "they don't think about the future." Hugo's afraid for his own future, but hasn't figured out how to change his circumstances. "I don't know what's going to happen," he admits.

It's easy to want to hope for Hugo. His face is youngish, his stature small and thin. Instead of making him appear tough, his slicked-back hair, baggy pants and oversized shirt seem almost like a disguise. He's polite, soft-spoken and sweet. It's not hard to imagine that under other circumstances, he could have flourished.

Hugo has loved sports ever since elementary school when he was captain of his baseball team. He also enjoys art, evidenced by the fact that he has taken Art every school year, with good marks. Despite his overall failing grades, he says that school is important to him and his family. His father, a construction worker and roofer, and his mother, a homemaker and laundress, never graduated from high school. Both want Hugo to get his diploma. On a "Sophomore Counseling Plan" form, he indicated that he wants to go to a four-year college or university, although he marked his career areas "undecided."

But high school records for Hugo, a native-Spanish-speaker classified as LEP, chronicle a downward slide. In the middle of 9th grade, his first year in high school, he had a 2.0 grade point average. By the beginning of 10th grade, it had fallen to 1.45. By the end of sophomore year, it stood at 1.11. The credits he has earned are overwhelmingly in elective classes, such as Art, Industrial Technology and Physical Education.

His teachers blame excessive absences for his failing grades. Both his parents are from Mexico, and most summers and Christmas breaks, the family returns to visit relatives. Several times, they have traveled to Mexico during the school year, once for as long as a month when Hugo's grandfather died during his 9th-grade year. But Hugo readily admits that even when he is in town, he often cuts classes, sometimes because he's hungry and wants to go eat. As for failing to finish his homework, he complains that he finds it boring.

Some of his teachers have commented, "assignments not turned in" or "not prepared for class."

But Hugo's story is more complicated than chronic absences and incomplete assignments. His schooling history illustrates the desperate need for triggers within the school system to identify and help students who are steadily declining—those who stay in the system, but become more lost with each passing year.

No obvious interventions show up in Hugo's files. He spent his early childhood in Mexico, moving to Los Angeles when he was four. Because he spoke no English, he began kindergarten in L.A. in a Spanish-speaking class. Then during the school year, his family moved to Northern California, where Hugo's English as a Second Language teacher in elementary school deemed him too poorly prepared to begin first grade.

Early on in elementary school, Hugo's records raised the specter of health or special education needs. One bilingual classroom teacher referred him for a health, speech and academic screening, with notations of "possible epilepsy and hearing problems." Under the "Behavior" checklist on the referral form, the teacher had marked "inattentive/overly active." No records show what actions resulted from this referral, although Hugo's file shows numerous screenings for vision, hearing and scoliosis problems. Although nothing in the school files pinpoints a concrete health problem, the unusually high number of screenings and further tests suggest that Hugo might have needed special attention to succeed in school.

Hugo himself says that writing has been particularly hard. "It's been a problem all the time. I can't write. I can't spell."—this, despite extra attention from teachers. Could Hugo be suffering from undiagnosed learning disabilities?

Regardless, Hugo's grades started off well enough—satisfactory throughout elementary school. Grading reports also painted a picture of a boy who got along with most peers, was sociable, participated in the classroom and was physically active. But teacher comments also mentioned that Hugo was sometimes unruly, often failed to turn in homework, and "could apply himself more."

Hugo's homeroom teachers did not try to teach him English until 3rd grade. He did receive ESL instruction in a pull-out program, but he says it did not help much. He began to learn English, "mostly with help from friends," and from watching TV. Not until 5th grade did he feel he was making significant progress in English, he adds. He earned mostly C's in grades 4 through 6, with several A's and B's and a few D's.

The picture changed drastically when Hugo went to Intermediate School. He was enrolled in sheltered content classes, including a reading class and the lowest level of Math. His grades started to deteriorate from a solid C average in elementary school as D's and F's began to pile up. Both years of middle school, Hugo took the CTBS (in English) and scored well below grade level. On the 7th grade CTBS, he scored in the 22nd percentile in Math and the 2nd percentile in Reading and Language.

Hugo says he liked elementary school, but a sense of alienation began to settle in during middle school. His behavior worsened. In 7th grade, he was suspended for one day for stealing a classmate's wallet. In 8th grade, Hugo was suspended three days for fighting, "a physical altercation on his way home from school with another student," according to the disciplinary report.

In high school, the behavior problems persisted. Sometimes, racial tensions flared between Hugo's friends and other students. He identifies himself as Chicano or Mexican. His girlfriend is Puerto Rican and Mexican, and his friends date Filipina girls and Black girls, he says. But, for the most part, students of different races stay away from each other. Why? Sometimes, "we get in a fight with the Blacks...so we have to stay apart," Hugo explains. What causes the fights? Hugo couldn't give any clear reasons, although he told of one big fight that started when a Black student struck Hugo's friend on the head with a bottle.

Hugo's pattern of academic failure has also persisted. In almost every quarter of high school, Hugo failed at least two of his classes. Now, in the last quarter of 10th grade, he has failed every class, leaving him with too few credits to be promoted to 11th grade. To graduate on time, he would have to make up one semester of work, as well as pass every class in the next two years of high school. Given his academic history, the challenge seems insurmountable.

Hugo shows glimmers of his true abilities, but his social environment overwhelms him. His sheltered Math teacher says:

"Hugo has worked really hard with me, and he's done really well, but Hugo is a really poor student. His sheltered Science class, he cut repeatedly, because he's out with his friends. And frequently I'll see them; they cut and stay on campus. He's on the borderline of being sent to continuation school. He's not bad, but you've got to push, push, push, all the time. He really needs a lot of one-on-one encouraging attention, which isn't always available in a classroom."

She alludes, too, to the most serious and frightening of Hugo's problems—his gang involvement:

"He's not a bad kid, but again, he's got a whole lot of outside influences, peer pressures, that are keeping him out of class. And I'm afraid it'll do him in."

PROFILE OF A LONG-TERM LEP STUDENT

MARIANA HERNANDEZ

Mariana, a high school senior, is tall, strong and athletic—a student who exudes energy and confidence. At school, she plays on the girls' basketball team and boasts a 3.6 cumulative GPA. She hopes to attend UC Santa Barbara or UC San Diego—whichever has the better basketball team—so that she can become a high school teacher, perhaps at her old high school, someday. She rounds out her school schedule by volunteering to help with freshman orientation and the health academy at the school, and she serves with the leadership group for her class.

Mariana is also a long-term LEP student, despite her success as a college-prep, "A" student. She started attending U.S. schools seven years ago, when she came from Mexico, but she still has not been reclassified as English fluent because she has not met all the official requirements. In her case, she has not passed the district writing minimum proficiency test. She says:

> *"I still don't know how to write yet. I always think of the word in Spanish before saying it in English. And I spell it wrong, I guess."*

Fortunately, despite these limitations, Mariana has continued to make big strides in her education. In 9th grade, she earned all A's and several teachers gave her outstanding citizenship marks. In 10th grade, she began taking mainstream classes even though she was still classified as LEP. By senior year, English was the language of instruction in all her classes.

Mariana has liked U.S. schools from the start, but her adjustment has been rocky at times. She was born in California, but her mother raised her and three brothers in Zacatecas, Mexico, while her father remained in California to work in the fields. Mariana attended school in Mexico consistently from kindergarten to the beginning of sixth grade. She remembers little about school in Mexico, but recalls liking elementary school and feeling sad at leaving her friends there.

When Mariana was in sixth grade, her mother moved the family to California to reunite with the children's father. The parents also sought better education and work opportunities for their children. In February 1990, Mariana entered sixth grade at a local elementary school. Designated a non-English-speaker and migrant education student, she was placed in a Spanish bilingual classroom and received ESL instruction for part of the day. Her teacher's notes show that Mariana was succeeding, but that the adjustment had been difficult:

> *"Mariana has in four months here made progress. She is more comfortable and successful. She participates in most activities but does not get along with all students. She is quite immature, low academically, and should benefit from another year in elementary school. She has*

many nervous habits (eye, nose, neck pain) but improved with time in classroom. She likes school and seems motivated."

The school wanted Mariana to repeat 6th grade, and her parents agreed. The following year, she was again placed in a bilingual classroom with a new teacher. Mariana credits this teacher with helping her to adjust to school, to get involved with activities, to succeed academically, and to land a spot on the girls' basketball team. She won an "Athlete of the Year" award and her grades improved. Mariana's confidence increased, and her natural competitiveness and willingness to take risks helped her to shine. Her teacher commented:

"Mariana is very serious about her studies, likes school and works hard. She is a leader in group activities and assertive."

Supportive teachers continued to influence Mariana when she went on to middle school for 7th and 8th grades. She kept playing basketball and continued to like school, particularly English and History. She said her English teacher was helpful and patient, and her History teacher "wasn't only my teacher, but she was also my friend. And that time I had a lot of problems at home, and I talked to her like a friend and she was really helpful." As for other classes, she says:

"I was really comfortable because some of the classes were in Spanish and all the students were just the same as me. They were from Mexico."

One of her ESL teachers in middle school remembers Mariana as being "very smart" and "very obstinate." She recalls:

"She was a girl who had trouble with being a middle school kid and with authority, and I was an authority figure as far as she was concerned. So we had a few clashes."

This teacher also saw Mariana's confidence, assertiveness and strong will as an advantage. Mariana "is one of those people who's willing to put herself out there…she's a risk-taker," she said. She was impressed that even though Mariana spoke little English, she played on the basketball team with kids who were fluent English speakers. "That didn't phase her one bit. Mariana is one of those students who will be fine. She's obviously going to make it."

In middle school, Mariana took ESL classes, while her content classes—Social Studies, Math and Science—were in Spanish. By the end of 8th grade, Mariana scored a level 3 on an English LAS R/W test—almost fluent in reading and writing—and a level 2 score on an English LAS Oral test—not yet fluent in spoken English. Her grades were excellent during middle school—all A's.

When she went on to high school, she spent her first year enrolled in sheltered college-prep courses, including sheltered English, and she continued to play on the basketball team. While still in middle school, she had spoken Spanish almost exclusively, even though she was learning English basics through her ESL classes. She feels that she did not really start to practice her English until 9th grade, when she began taking more classes in English.

In high school, Mariana worked hard for her good grades, spending two to three hours per day on homework. She took English, Chemistry, Economics, U.S. Government, Mexican American History—all college-prep courses, along with Art and Computer Keyboarding. She gets as much help as she can from teachers. She named Chemistry as her hardest course and said she stays after school or visits her Chemistry teacher at lunch to get her questions answered.

Mariana thinks school is easier here than in Mexico, where teachers are more strict. She also believes that U.S. students do not appreciate the opportunities they are given, commenting:

"The students just mess around a lot, and they just don't take advantage of the education they have here. In Mexico, there's all kinds of students who really want to go to school, but they can't because they have to work."

Education is important to Mariana, she said, because she wants to go to college and realize her dream of becoming a high school teacher:

"Since I came here, I met a lot of good teachers and they helped me a lot. And I know there's a lot of students that need help, and I just want to be a teacher to help those students."

She watches her own teachers closely to see if she would like the work. She is also articulate on what makes a good teacher—patience, kindness and the willingness to give lots of homework. "Some teachers, they don't give you homework, or they don't care if you do good or not." She praises one teacher because "he's all into it, he's so energetic and he gives a lot of examples. He uses a lot of methods to teach, like movies, drawing pictures. It's not like other teachers is boring. They talk and talk and talk." Mariana has also considered becoming a doctor "to help the people who is sick." She once wrote in an essay, "In my future I only want to do good thing for everyone and to feel important in the life."

Making a little money would be a good thing, too. Mariana says:

"If my little brother wants to study, I going to pay his studies. I want to buy a big house and a beautiful car and maybe get married and have children."

Her parents, she says, "are the ones that keep pushing me, hard and hard, to get a good education, because that was the purpose of coming to the U.S. And they're really helpful and understanding. They help me a lot...sometimes with homework, like History. My dad knows a lot of history."

She has attended college presentations at her high school, so she understands how to apply. When she gets to college, she hopes to continue playing basketball. She is excited at the prospect of leaving home, but she is a little worried that she won't be ready. She thinks that some of her classes haven't prepared her for college work, but she is most worried about her mastery of English:

> *"That's one of my biggest problems, because I don't feel ready to go, but I also don't want to stay here in the community college. Last year, my thought was to stay at [the local community college], but a lot of teachers have told me that I'm ready to go for it. My brother, he's already in college and I read a couple of his books, and it's like really good English."*

To help her prepare for college, she gets help with her writing and has taken a developmental reading class to improve her English reading and writing skills. Sometimes she reads novels in English. She expects to find tutoring when she gets to college.

Mariana is confident that even though she has improved her English, she has also maintained her Spanish skills. She speaks only Spanish to her parents, and mostly Spanish with her brothers. In 9th and 10th grades, she took Spanish for Native Speakers. The only weak area is that she does not read much in Spanish anymore, she said, because she no longer takes Spanish in school.

Mariana identifies herself as "Chicana, I guess. Mexican, sometimes." She has been back to Mexico only once, four years ago. She wrote after the trip that it was unforgettable (*"inolvidable"*) and that she saw her grandparents, cousins, friends and her old school. Her friends in the U.S. are mostly "like me," she said, immigrant teens who have lived in this country since they were children. They mostly call themselves Mexican American "because they were born in Mexico, but they have lived here their whole lives." But she added:

> *"I just don't understand the labeling of different student groups. It's like, Sureños and Norteños are the same people. Why so many names...I don't know."*

But she did acknowledge distinctions between newcomers and those who have lived here a long time. Newcomers, she noted, are often shy and less involved in school activities, perhaps because they're still unsure of how they fit in. "It's always the students who have been living here for a long time who does all the school activities, and the rest."

Not one to take care of just herself, Mariana has attempted to make newcomers feel welcome. While participating in her high school's Ambassador Program for newcomer orientation, she told a group of Spanish speakers to get involved in groups, activities, sports. Part of the problem, she thinks, is the poor dissemination of information on activities to newcomers:

> *"This year, we're doing the announcements in Spanish and English and we try to spread all the information involved so they can all understand. So I hope that's helping."*

ACTIVITY 4.8
CONDUCTING YOUR OWN IN-DEPTH INTERVIEWS

The previous profiles were constructed based on in-depth interviews with students. One way for you to get such an in-depth view of your own students is to conduct your own interviews with a selection of students representing a "typology"—one like ours or a typology of your own. See Chapter Five for more information about how to go about conducting interviews.

🌿 **Step 1:** First take some time with your colleagues to figure out, broadly, the types of language minority and immigrant students that you have at your school. You may want to designate some common categories that you know exist—categories that have enough students in them to warrant a closer look. Categories might include designations such as: ESL students here two years or less; mainstreamed ESL students; 9th-grade ESL students with multiple D's or F's; 8th-grade ESL students with mostly A's and B's; students with three or fewer years of prior schooling before coming to the U.S., etc. The categories should be meaningful for you and your school site.

🌿 **Step 2:** Develop a set of interview questions that will get at what you wish to investigate. You may want to use some of the questions in the long-term LEP student interview protocol in Chapter Five.

🌿 **Step 3:** Interview a representative sample from each category of students. Again, you will want to follow the procedures outlined in Chapter Five about getting permission, using a tape-recorder, transcribing, taking notes, etc.

🌿 **Step 4:** Based on the interviews, write up short case histories for a couple of students from each category or type. They need not be as long as the cases we have presented. Actually doing the write-ups may be something you want to share among the group. You will want to end up with a piece that is readable and highlights the important findings from the interview.

🌿 **Step 5:** Present the cases to the group.

🌿 **Step 6:** Spend time charting and mapping the programmatic implications of your findings. Some questions to consider include:

  ☛ What did we find out that was surprising, or an "aha" moment for us?

  ☛ What did we find out that confirmed some of our ideas from before the interviews?

  ☛ What do we have in place right now for each type or category of student? How well is it working or not working?

☛ What do we not have in place for these students? Where are the biggest gaps?

☛ What are the biggest equity, access or achievement issues that surfaced through the interviews?

☛ Did developing the typologies produce any important new categories that would be useful to incorporate or track in our data system?

ACTIVITY 4.9
CONDUCTING A CENSUS

Whether or not you have the time or the resources to interview students from each of your typologies, it can be valuable to spend some time doing an approximate count of each type of student you have. Because students do not always fit neatly into a single category, you may have to make some arbitrary decisions for some of them.

First, decide on the categories of types of students you hope to count. Then brainstorm where you can find the information that would help you identify these students. For example, year of entry to the U.S. would be helpful in sorting out the recently-arrived students, or you could simply count all who are still in the ESL sequence. Data on the year students entered your district or were first assessed as LEP would be useful in determining who is still LEP after 6 or more years and, therefore, a long-term LEP student. You might need to examine students' cumulative files to find those with gaps in their schooling. Course lists from Advanced Placement or college-prep courses could help you identify the college-bound students. Use all the data you know about to help you identify the types of immigrant students so you can count how many of each you have at your school.

This mini-census can prove enlightening to a lot of the staff. They may not realize, for example, that the school actually has more than 300 students who could be categorized as long-term Limited English Proficient; they may be unaware that there are 45 students who have been in the United States less than three years, but who are accelerated academically and are already out in the mainstream. For example, the evaluator of our project in Hayward, Catherine Minicucci, found the following breakdown for ninth-grade LEP students:

NINTH-GRADE LEP STUDENT TYPOLOGIES IN ONE HIGH SCHOOL

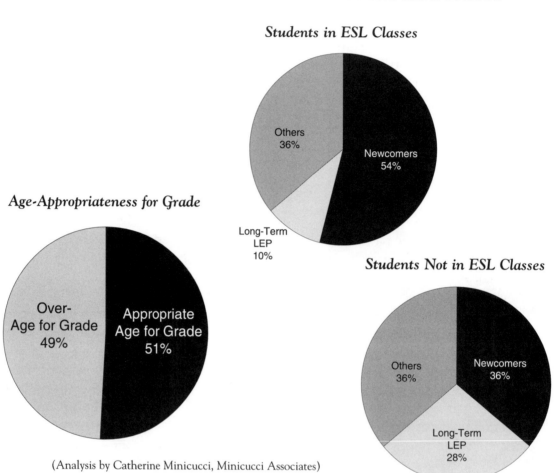

Students in ESL Classes

Age-Appropriateness for Grade

Students Not in ESL Classes

(Analysis by Catherine Minicucci, Minicucci Associates)

Minicucci and the project team used the following definitions for these typologies:

❧ over-age students turned 15 before December 1 of their ninth-grade year;

❧ newcomers entered U.S. schools in the 7th grade or later;

❧ long-term LEP students arrived between kindergarten and 2nd grade and have been designated LEP since arrival.

This kind of comprehensive picture will be helpful in thinking about what sort of programs you already have, where the gaps might be, where the areas of greatest need are and where students are indeed being served well.

CONCLUSION

The ultimate goal of knowing your immigrant students well is to create schools where that knowledge becomes a catalyst for designing programs that respond to the students' needs. The knowledge becomes a solid base for questioning current practice, providing the basis for creative new ways of educating immigrant students.

Advocates for immigrant students are always negotiating their way through a complex maze of competing interests: district funding and staffing allocations, teacher availability and certification, rapidly shifting demographics, particular school cultures and traditions. Advocates who possess a deep knowledge about their immigrant students can more effectively find their way through this maze. They know how to talk about the language proficiency issues that impact LEP students' schooling. They know how to bring up and discuss the issues of race and culture that affect the everyday lives of immigrant students. They can articulate not only how the school contributes to the distance students often feel from school but also ways in which the school can begin to bridge that gap.

Most importantly, effective advocates understand the need to pass on their knowledge about immigrant students. They know how crucial it is to continually build and rebuild a core of people who will carry the torch. Creating a program for immigrant students based on need and dedicated to access and equity is a fluid, dynamic and often unpredictable task. The potential for erosion—"forgetting" why and how successful ideas were implemented, underestimating the complexity of the need—all are immense. It is only through constantly learning together and seeking the truth about our students that a firm foundation can remain. And it is only when many teachers know their students well on many levels that we can create schools with the heart and will to respond effectively to their needs.

REFERENCES

Apple, M. (1982). *Education and Power*. Boston, MA: Routledge.

Apple, M. and Weis, L. (Eds.) (1983). *Ideology and Practice in Schooling*. Philadelphia, PA: Temple University Press.

Bourdieu, P. and Passeron, J. C. (1977). *Reproduction in Education, Society and Culture*. London, UK: Sage Publishers.

Bowles, A. (1977). Unequal Education and the Reproduction of the Social Division of Labor. In J. Karabelt and A.H. Halsey (Eds.), *Power and Ideology in Education*. New York, NY: Oxford University Press.

Cummins, J. (1989). *Empowering Minority Students: A Theoretical Framework*. Los Angeles, CA: California Association of Bilingual Education.

Delpit, L. (1995). *Other People's Children: Cultural Conflict in the Classroom*. New York, NY: New Press.

Erickson, F. (1987). Transformation and School Success: The Politics and Culture of Educational Achievement. *Anthropology and Education Quarterly, 18*(4), 335-356.

Fine, M. (1987). Silencing in Public Schools. *Language Arts 64*(2), 157-174.

Gibson, M. (1987). The School Performance of Immigrant Minorities: A Comparative View. *Anthropology and Education Quarterly, 189*(4), 262-275.

Heath, S. (1983). *Ways with Words: Language, Life and Work in Communities and Classrooms*. New York, NY: Cambridge University Press.

National Coalition of Advocates for Students. (1988). *New Voices: Immigrant Students in U.S. Public Schools*. Boston, MA: National Coalition of Advocates for Students.

Ogbu, J. and Matute-Bianchi, M. (1986). Understanding Sociocultural Factors: Knowledge, Identity and School Adjustment. In *Beyond Language: Social and Cultural Factors in School Language Minority Students* (pp. 73-142). Los Angeles, CA: Bilingual Education Office, California State Department of Education.

Olsen, L. (1998). *Made in America: Immigrant Students in Our Public Schools*. New York, NY: New Press.

Olsen, L. and Chen, M. (1988). *Crossing the Schoolhouse Border*. San Francisco, CA: California Tomorrow.

Omi, M. and Winant, H. (1990). *Racial Formation in the United States: From the 1960s to the 1990s*. New York, NY: Routledge.

Padilla, A. and Duran, D. (1995). The Psychological Dimension in Understanding Immigrant Students. In R. G. Rumbaut and W. A. Cornelius (Eds.), *California's Immigrant Children* (pp. 131-160). San Diego, CA: Center for U.S.-Mexican Studies, University of California, San Diego.

Phelan, P., Davidson, A. L. and Yu, H. C. (1993). Students' Multiple Worlds: Navigating the Borders of Family, Peer and School Cultures. In P. Phelan and A. L. Davidson (Eds.), *Renegotiating Cultural Diversity in American Schools* (pp. 52-88). New York, NY: Teachers College Press.

Suarez-Orozco, M. and Suarez-Orozco, C. (1995). The Cultural Patterning of Achievement Motivation. In R. G. Rumbaut and W. A. Cornelius (Eds.), *California's Immigrant Children* (pp. 161-190). San Diego, CA: Center for U.S.-Mexican Studies, University of California, San Diego.

UNDERSTANDING THE COMPLEXITY OF OUR STUDENTS' EXPERIENCES ANNOTATED BIBLIOGRAPHY

California Department of Education/Bilingual Education Office. (1986). *Beyond Language: Social and Cultural Factors in Schooling Language Minority Students.* **University of California, Los Angeles, CA: California Department of Education.**

This book is an early classic in the field, a compilation of seven articles by major theorists in social and cultural studies related to language. Authors include: Carlos Cortes, Stanley Sue and Amado Padilla, John Ogbu and Maria Eugina Matute-Bianchi, Shirley Brice Heath, Stephen Dias and Luis Moll and Hugh Mehan, Spencer Kagan, and Mary McGroarty. Together, the articles explore various factors, aside from language, which could affect the lower achievement of some minority students and which have implications for how educational programs can be improved.

Crandall, JoAnn, Jaramillo, Ann, Olsen, Laurie and Peyton, Joy Kreeft. (in press). Diverse Teaching Strategies for Diverse Learners: Immigrant Children. In H. Hodges (Ed.), *Educating Everybody's Children: More Teaching Strategies for Diverse Learners.* **Alexandria, VA: Association for Supervision and Curriculum Development.**

This chapter explores the challenges immigrant students face in making the transition to secondary schooling in the U.S., such as living in transitional families, acculturating, arriving as adolescents, learning a new educational system, recovering from war trauma, dealing with discrimination, etc. It also examines the kinds of instructional strategies that are effective with them and what schools can do to "cultivate resiliency."

Cummins, Jim. (1996). *Negotiating Identities: Education for Empowerment in a Diverse Society.* **Ontario, CA: California Association for Bilingual Education.**

This new version of Cummins' *Empowering Minority Students* offers an impassioned rationale for why educators should become aware of how power relations in society influence the interactions that occur between teachers and students in classrooms—and how these interactions can either empower or disempower students. Cummins delves into the evolution of xenophobia and ways in which cultural and language diversity have been viewed as detrimental rather than advantageous to our society. He also delivers an extensively researched defense of bilingual education, with specific critiques of the claims of the "academic critics" of bilingual education. This book is extensively footnoted—and the footnotes make for reading that is just as interesting as the text itself.

Gibson, Margaret and Ogbu, John (Eds.). (1991). *Minority Status and Schooling: A Comparative Study of Immigrant and Involuntary Minorities.* **New York, NY: Garland Publishing, Inc.**

A collection of international case studies on the experiences of different groups of students which comparatively and systematically examines the forces that promote or impede student success. The book critiques and compares differing school adaptation patterns for "voluntary" and "involuntary" minorities as they confront discrimination and unequal opportunity. The authors present ethnographic findings on the schooling experiences of different minority groups to address the question of why some minority groups perform better than others in school.

Leyba, Charles F. (Ed.). (1994). *Schooling and Language Minority Students: A Theoretical Framework (Second Edition).* **Los Angeles, CA: Evaluation, Dissemination and Assessment Center, UCLA.**

This recently updated version of this classic text on the schooling of language minority students provides the basics that every teacher needs to know. Articles by Jim Cummins and Stephen Krashen provide the theoretical foundation for teaching language minority students. Of special importance are Cummins' eloquent defense of the importance of primary language instruction and Krashen's presentation of his second language acquisition theory and its links to bilingual education. The second part of the book describes strategies for implementation, including communicative approaches for second language teaching, reading instruction, primary language instruction, and designing and monitoring program delivery.

Lucas, Tamara. (1997). *Into, Through and Beyond Secondary School: Critical Transitions for Immigrant Youths.* **Washington, D.C.: Center for Applied Linguistics.**

In this first volume, Lucas suggests four principles for schools to base their efforts to increase immigrant student achievement. The author also presents schools, programs and organizations that use the four principles with positive impacts. Contact information for programs is available in this volume.

Mace-Matluck, Betty, Alexander-Kasparik, Rosalind, and Queen, Robin. (1998). *Through the Golden Door: Educational Approaches for Immigrant Students with Limited Schooling.* **Washington, D.C.: Center for Applied Linguistics.**

This guidebook for secondary school administrators and teachers of students with little or no prior schooling paints a vivid picture of the challenges their students face in school, the labor market and their communities. Using case studies, the authors chronicle the diverse experiences of five low literacy, immigrant students from Haiti, El Salvador, and Vietnam. The book also profiles four different programs (in Illinois, Texas and Virginia) that have successfully increased access and opportunity for students with limited schooling.

McDonnell, Lorraine and Hill, Paul T. (1993). *Newcomers in American Schools.* **Santa Monica, CA: Rand Corporation.**

This nationwide study of immigrant education policy in nine districts and fifty-seven schools examines the schooling needs of immigrant students, assesses instructional curricula and programming, and suggests strategies for improving student outcomes. The authors present four major conclusions from their research: immigrant students constitute a growing proportion of the student population; they have different needs that are an invisible policy issue not often recognized or accepted by school districts; the quality of education received depends on the resources of the districts in which they reside; and one way to serve the unmet needs of the immigrant student population is to strengthen the entire school system.

McKeon, Denise. (1994). When Meeting "Common" Standards is Uncommonly Difficult. *Educational Leadership, 51(8), 45-49.*

This informative article explores the cognitive and linguistic challenges faced by LEP students during language acquisition. McKeon discusses various types of LEP students and how variation can complicate learning content standards. The author stresses the need for greater opportunities to learn standards and increased access to high-quality instruction for second language learners via access to: positive learning environments; appropriate curricula; full services; and equitable assessment. The article provides a useful resource for educators (administrators and teachers) concerned with enhancing LEP student achievement and meeting the unique needs of this student population.

Nieto, Sonia. (1992). *Affirming Diversity: The Sociopolitical Context of Multicultural Education.* White Plains, NY: Longman Publishers.

This very readable book explores how personal, social, political, cultural and educational factors interact to affect the success or failure of subordinated group students in our schools. While the focus is not exclusively on immigrant or language minority students, Nieto speaks directly to language issues as they interact with race, ethnicity, gender and class—and the suggestions for what needs to happen to provide fully multicultural education are powerful and appropriate for teachers of English Language Learners. The book is punctuated with case studies of a selected group of successful students from a variety of backgrounds, speaking about their families, school and community experiences and how these have affected their academic achievement.

Olsen, Laurie. (1997). *Made in America: Immigrant Students in Our Public Schools.* New York, NY: The New Press.

This book is an ethnography of a single high school in which over 20% of the students were born in another country and over a third come from homes in which English is not spoken. Through the stories of the teachers, immigrant students and U.S.-born students, Olsen describes the contemporary version of the "Americanization" of immigrants. The book paints a portrait of how students give up their national identities and languages to be accepted in an academic and social world that does not allow them full participation, and how students learn their "racial place" in our society. The voices and stories in the book explore what it looks and feels like to go to school as an immigrant adolescent.

Rumbaut, Ruben and Cornelius, Wayne (Eds.). (1995). *California's Immigrant Children: Theory, Research and Implications for Educational Policy.* San Diego, CA: Center for U.S.-Mexican Studies.

A collection of resource articles addressing the challenges of educating children from geographically and culturally diverse immigrant communities. This book explores the heterogeneity of immigrant experiences: the diversity of cultural and family practices they bring with them and the variability of opportunity, access, and discrimination they encounter. The book also discusses the rapid growth of the immigrant population and the corresponding growth of the number of Limited English Proficient students in California schools. Articles review the implications this growth has for school finance, teacher training and curriculum development. An interdisciplinary project, the book blends field-based empirical research on different ethnic communities, as well as multiple theoretical and policy perspectives that identify and/or suggest strategies for improving educational outcomes for immigrant children.

Rumberger, Russell W. and Larson, Katherine A. (1998). Toward Explaining Differences in Educational Achievement Among Mexican American Language Minority Students. *Sociology of Education, 71.*

In this article, the authors critique the common belief that English language proficiency will improve achievement for immigrants and language minority students, specifically Latino students. Using a case study in Los Angeles, the authors examine why English proficiency does not always improve student performance. To clarify the outcomes of the study, two theoretical constructs (socioeconomic perspective and sociocultural perspective) serve as the basis for acquisition and use of English by language minorities and immigrants. Neither construct alone is sufficient to explain the educational achievement of Latinos. They conclude that student engagement and educational achievement are influenced by students' educational commitment, educational background and attitudes, as well as characteristics of their families, schools and communities.

Smith-Maddock, Renee and Wheelock, Anne. (1995). Untracking and Students' Futures: Closing the Gap Between Aspirations and Expectations. *Phi Delta Kappan, 77(3), 222-228.*

This brief article addresses the schooling experiences of adolescent, non-college bound, low-track students, particularly African Americans and Latinos. It outlines a "coaching" approach that schools can use to open new career alternatives for students.

APPENDIX A
READINGS FOR ACTIVITY 4.3
READING ABOUT FOUR IMMIGRANT EXPERIENCES

Excerpts from:

Always Running: La Vida Loca. Gang Days in L.A.

by Luis Rodriguez. (1993). Willimantic, CT: Curbstone Press. Used with permission.

First day of school.

I was six years old, never having gone to kindergarten because Mama needed me then to take care of La Pata and Cuca so she could work. When La Pata became old enough to enter kindergarten, it became time for me to go. Mama filled out some papers. A school monitor directed us to a classroom where Mama dropped me off and left to join some parents who gathered in the main hall.

The first day of school said a lot about my scholastic life to come. I was taken to a teacher who didn't know what to do with me. She complained about not having any room, about kids who didn't even speak the language. And how was she supposed to teach anything under these conditions! Although I didn't speak English, I understood a large part of what she was saying. I knew I wasn't wanted. She put me in an old creaky chair near the door. As soon as I could, I sneaked out to find my mother.

I found Rano's class with the retarded children instead and decided to stay there for a while. Actually it was fun; they treated me like I was everyone's little brother. But the teacher finally told a student to take me to the main hall.

After some more paperwork, I was taken to another class. This time the teacher appeared nicer, but distracted. She got the word about my language problem.

"Okay, why don't you sit here in the back of the class," she said. "Play with some blocks until we figure out how to get you more involved."

It took her most of that year to figure this out. I just stayed in the back of the class, building blocks. It got so every morning I would put my lunch and coat away, and walk to my corner where I stayed the whole day long. It forced me to be more withdrawn. It got so bad, I didn't even tell anybody when I had to go to the bathroom. I did it in my pants. Soon I stunk back there in the corner and the rest of the kids screamed out a chorus of "P.U.!", resulting in my being sent to the office or back home.

In those days, there was no way to integrate the non-English-speaking children. So they just made it a crime to speak anything but English. If a Spanish word sneaked out in the playground, kids were often sent to the office to get swatted or to get detention. Teachers complained that maybe the children were saying bad things about them. An assumption of guilt was enough to get one punished.

A day came when I finally built up the courage to tell the teacher I had to go to the bathroom. I didn't quite say all the words, but she got the message and promptly excused me so I didn't do it while I was trying to explain. I ran to the bathroom and peed and felt good about not having that wetness trickle down my pants leg. But suddenly several bells went on and off. I hesitantly stepped out of the bathroom and saw throngs of children leave their classes. I had no idea what was happening. I went to my classroom and it stood empty. I looked into other classrooms and found nothing. Nobody. I didn't know what to do. I really thought everyone had gone home. I didn't bother to look at the playground where the whole school had been assembled for the fire drill. I just went home. It got to be a regular thing there for a while, me coming home early until I learned the ins and outs of school life.

Not speaking well makes for such embarrassing moments. I hardly asked questions. I just didn't want to be misunderstood. Many Spanish-speaking kids mangled things up; they would say things like "where the beer and cantaloupe roam," instead of "where the deer and antelope roam."

That's the way it was with me. I mixed up all the words. Screwed up all the songs.

The opportunity for me to learn something new became an incentive for attending Taft High School. At Keppel and Continuation, I mainly had industrial arts classes. So I applied for classes which stirred a little curiosity: photography, advanced art, and literature. The first day of school, a Taft High School counselor called me into her office.

"I'm sorry, young man, but the classes you chose are filled up," she said.

"What do you mean? Isn't there any way I can get into any of them?"

"I don't believe so. Besides, your transcripts show you're not academically prepared for your choices. These classes are privileges, for those who have maintained the proper grades in the required courses. And I must add, you've obtained most of what credits you do have in industrial-related courses."

"I had to—that's all they'd give me," I said. "I just thought, maybe, I can do something else here. It seems like a good school and I want a chance to do something other than with my hands."

"It doesn't work that way," she replied. "I think you'll find our industrial arts subjects more suited to your needs."

I shifted in my seat and looked out the window.

"Whatever."

The classes she enrolled me in were print shop, auto shop and weight training. I did manage a basic English literature class. I walked past the photography sessions and stopped to glimpse the students going in and out, some with nice cameras, and I thought about how I couldn't afford those cameras anyway: Who needs that stupid class?

In print shop I worked the lead foundry for the mechanical Linotype typesetter. I received scars on my arms due to splashes of molten lead. In auto shop, I did a lot of tune-ups, oil changes and some transmission work. And I lifted weights and started to bulk up. The one value I had was being the only Mexican in school—people talked about it whenever I approached.

One day at lunch time, I passed a number of hefty dudes in lettered jackets. One of them said something. Maybe it had nothing to do with me. But I pounced on him anyway. Several teachers had to pull me off.

They designated me as violent and uncontrollable; they didn't know "what to do with me."

The leading members of ToHMAS, an on-campus student group, were mostly women, among them Esme, Cha Cha, Amelia, Yvonne, and Flora. A few dudes helped, such as Ysidro, Alex, Chuy and myself. But the women ran everything. It was through ToHMAS, and through the example of Mrs. Baez, Blanca and Carmela, that the women from Lomas found a place to address some longstanding grievances. Their leadership found shape and form through ToHMAS, as they took to heart the battle for their respect, and that of their people.

We dealt with two dominant aspects. One was something called Project Student, with Carmela as our sponsor, which targeted the physical deterioration of the school: walls were cracked, stairwells in disrepair, and the freeway behind the school drowned out lessons from second-floor classrooms. In the summer, the air conditioning system rarely worked, making for long, sweltering days. In the winter, rain accumulated in buckets from roof leaks. Project Student, in fact, involved more than just Chicanos; whites and others also had to endure these conditions.

The other aspect involved the issue of dignity for the Chicano students.

"You don't mind if I don't call you Chin, do you?" Mrs. Baez asked.

"*Chale*, what's up?"

"We'd like to propose you and Esme try out for Joe and Josephine Aztec."

I looked over at Esme and then back to Mrs. Baez.

"You're joking, right?"

"We're very serious," Esme said. "We're tired of them paddies—excuse me—but them Anglos putting down our culture. They make the mascots look like Pocahontas with tommy hawks and then prance around like fools."

"That's true, but what are our chances—I mean, how are we going to win when the Anglos do all the judging?"

"We plan to do an authentic Aztec dance, in authentic Aztec dress," Esme said. "If they deny us, then everyone will know how racist this school is."

"But I don't know any Aztec dances."

"We have somebody willing to teach you," Mrs. Baez said. "He's an instructor for a *folklórico* dance troupe at one of the colleges. You look Indian enough with your long hair. And I think it would help involve some of the hard-core Lomas students in what we're doing if you tried out."

"What do you say, Louie?" Esme asked.

They knew they had me. I accepted as a formality.

Esme and I went to East L.A. College and met with a Señor Franco, the *folklórico* dance instructor. He taught us some basic steps and helped us find the material and designs for our dancewear. To get it right, we dedicated hours of our evenings to rehearsal.

Esme choreographed the dance routine, based on Señor Franco's instruction. Our mothers created the costumes, and they were so strikingly beautiful, even Señor Franco was impressed. We added some non-Aztec touches too.

The rehearsals were secret. When the time neared for the tryouts, we walked into the activities office and signed up. A couple of the white students there gave us funny looks. Esme and I signed our names and then left.

The day of the tryouts, all contestants were to meet in the gym. Parents, teachers and students took up some of the bleachers. A row of judges, including some teachers and students, stayed near the performance area.

I entered the gym area in Aztec dress; I had on a leather top, arm bands and loin cloth, with a jaguar-imaged headgear propped on my head and bells strapped around my ankles. And I must have been a sight with tattoos on my arms and an earring. I saw a couple of rows of bleachers filled up with Chicanos; Mrs. Baez had organized the students to attend. As I entered, they cheered and hollered. I considered getting out of there but Esme came up behind me and held my hand. We were both nervous.

Esme and I were the last ones to perform. We suffered through a number of tumbling acts and screwball routines. Then an announcer came on the speaker:

"Now we have the team of Esmeralda Falcón and Luis Rodríguez."

Silence saturated the gym area. I walked up solemn and straight, a wooden chair in one hand and a conga drum in the other, and sat down in the middle of the basketball court. I paused for 10 seconds, then began the beat. Esme came in slow, purposeful, with a turquoise sequined-and-feathered garment and multicolored headgear that arced around her head like a rainbow; she also had bells.

Esme could have been a priestess from Tenochtitlán, her face pure and brown, with slight make-up that accented her already slanted, indigenous eyes. She danced around me, as if calling forth a spirit; the bells on her ankles swirling around the beat, in time with the rhythm of the drum. At one point, I arose and danced with her in unison, round and round through various steps, leading up to the climax.

We had to be serious—no laughing, no smiling, in keeping with the integrity of the dance.

A murmur swept through the bleachers when Esme and I crossed our feet together and swung around and around, hooked by our ankles, going faster and faster, the force of our swirling keeping us locked, letting the motion pull and embrace us at the same time, like in a battle. When we finished, one of my knees fell to the floor as Esme stood above me, the victor.

A few seconds passed, then an uproar of applause and cheers burst out of the bleachers. None of the other contestants received the response we did. I even saw white students and some judges clapping. They had never seen anything like it.

Esme and I waited by Mrs. Baez as the judges mulled over their decision. Finally:

"The winners are—and the new Joe and Josephine Aztec mascots of Mark Keppel High School—Esmeralda Falcón and Luis Rod. . ."

The yells drowned out my last name. Esme shrieked, threw her arms around my neck and hugged me. Other ToHMAS supporters came over with smiles and handshakes. In other people's eyes, this may have been a small victory. But for the Chicanos at Mark Keppel High School, this meant another barrier had been torn down and an important aspect of our culture recognized. I surprised myself and felt warm inside. I tried to shake it off, but couldn't. A flush of pride soon covered my face. *We won!*

More Chicanos became involved in ToHMAS. We started our own *folklórico* group in which Carmen San Juan taught the students some basic Mexican and Flamenco dances. Esme and I started a *teatro* group, based on what the *Teatro Campesino* of Cesar Chávez's farmworkers union were doing in rural California. Our *teatro* group, however, had an urban slant.

I wrote the three plays we performed. One involved a dramatic verse monologue of a Chicana about to be arrested by the cops. Another involved a one-act about being proud of our culture. But the most controversial one dealt with getting Lomas and Sangra to stop fighting each other.

This play began with someone from Sangra crossing out Lomas on a huge piece of white paper pasted on a wall. Then the action moved toward a point when the dudes from both neighborhoods go at each other. The upshot is as the two *barrios* fight, local government officials are on the side determining the site of a new mall or where the next freeway will go while making plans to uproot the very land the dudes were killing each other for.

"Who wants to play the dude crossing out Lomas?" I asked. Nobody raised their hand.

"What's the matter, it's only a play."

"I finished reading all the work you gave me a while back—remember, your poems and stories?" Mrs. Baez asked.

"Yeah, sure—they're no good, right?"

"Luis, how can you say that! They're wonderful. We should get them published."

"Great—but how?"

"Well, I picked up a newspaper the other day where they announced a Chicano Literary Contest in Berkeley. It's from Quinto Sol Publications. Let's send them the work. But it has to be retyped—your typing is terrible."

"I know, I know—but who's going to retype it?"

"I'll find some help. I'm sure there are people willing to do something. What do you say?"

"I guess okay—I mean, it's worth a try."

About the same time, the California State College at Los Angeles offered me an Economic Opportunity Program Grant—despite my past school record, lack of credits and other mishaps. Chente, Mr. Perez and Mrs. Baez teamed up to help me get accepted.

And a Loyola-Marymount University art professor asked me to paint a mural for the school; he offered some pay and student artists to work with.

My head spun with all the prospects.

But the kicker was when Mrs. Baez returned the newly-retyped versions of my writing; I couldn't believe I had anything to do with it. The shape of the words, the forms and fragments of sentences and syllables, seemed alien, as if done by another's hand.

The fact was I didn't know anything about literature. I had fallen through the chasm between two languages. The Spanish had been beaten out of me in the early years of school—and I didn't learn English very well either.

This was the predicament of many Chicanos.

We could almost be called incommunicable, except we remained lucid; we got over what we felt, sensed and understood. Sometimes we rearranged words, created new meanings and structures—even a new vocabulary. Often our everyday talk blazed with poetry.

Our expressive powers were strong and vibrant. If this could be nurtured, if the language skills could be developed on top of this, we could learn to break through any communication barrier. We needed to obtain victories in language, built on an infrastructure of self-worth.

But we were often defeated from the start.

In my case, though I didn't know how to write or paint, I had a great need to conceive and imagine, so compelling, so encompassing, I had to do it even when I knew my works would be subject to ridicule, would be called stupid and naïve. I just couldn't stop.

I had to learn how, though; I had to believe I could.

From:

Nobody Could See That I Was A Finn

by Antti Jalava

Published in *Bilingualism or Not: The Education of Minorities* by Tove Skutnabb-Kangas. (1981). Clevedon, England: Multilingual Matters Ltd. Used with permission.

My parents were welcome, sure enough, but as far as we kids were concerned, matters were altogether different. After all, we were not useful, productive, and on top of everything else, we couldn't even speak Swedish. The principal of my new school did not really know what to do with me when I was admitted; she was just as embarrassed and at a loss as I was, and when she escorted me to the elementary third-grade classroom we walked hand in hand. Holding hands was the only language we had in common. There was a vacant seat in the rear of the classroom. The boy I was put next to protested vehemently, but I was ordered to stay put anyhow. The flush-faced fellow whose bench I had to share was called Osmo. It was a Finnish name and he came from Finland, but even so for some reason he refused to speak a word of Finnish. Later I came to understand why he behaved as he did; and if I had only guessed that his fate would also be mine, I would have taken to my heels and run for my life.

My new classmates were curious: they watched my every movement closely, they walked in circles around me, they sniffed in my presence, and they felt the muscles on my arms. After that they began to call me Finnbiscuit, and that was my nickname until I learned to speak Swedish as well as Osmo did . . . or, more precisely, until I had adjusted to their ways to the extent of my passing in their eyes for a real Swede.

Adjusting was not, however, at all simple. To what did one have to adjust and how? There was nobody to explain things, there were no interpreters, no Finnish teachers and no kind of teaching of the Swedish language. And I was no chameleon either, for I only wanted to be myself, out of habit and instinct. When the others wrote in Swedish, I wrote in Finnish. From the time I had learned to spell, it had given me pleasure to put together sentences on paper. But that was something that just couldn't be done. The teacher grabbed my pencil and angrily shook his finger at me. In spite of everything, I continued to fall back on my mother tongue. There was a row at my desk. The teacher tore up my paper and stamped on my words he had thrown on the floor. He scolded me loudly. I pulled a wry face and muttered, "Damn fool!" (in Finnish). Osmo pulled at my sleeve and shook his head in warning. But I felt indignant and hurt, and I went into a tantrum. In the principal's office, I got my hair pulled and a Finnish boy from an upper grade was brought in to tell me writing compositions in Finnish was prohibited. I asked him why and he whispered in my ear in his Savoian dialect that he didn't know.

That night I threw a stone through the window of the principal's office. I never again wrote in Finnish. I just sat idly at my desk, silent and bewildered. What the dickens was this all about? Where have I ended up? Has everybody gone crazy? If Grandma hears that I've stopped writing Finnish, she'll die.

By the time I was promoted to the junior grade, I had picked up quite a lot of Stockholm slang. The language of my textbooks and teachers, on the other hand, was middle-class Swedish, to me quite incomprehensible and hard even for my classmates to understand, for most of them belonged to the working class and were accustomed to a totally different way of speaking. Their parents, just like my own, knew a lot, but the bourgeois school system despised that kind of knowledge. As time passed, I fell more and more behind my class; school seemed totally meaningless. Somehow I felt as though I didn't exist and the teacher's eyes would always look over my head. I started to daydream and to play hooky. My homesickness was fierce and seared my mind. I went frequently down to the Finnish terminal for Finnish boats, I wept secretly, recollected faces and voices, and in my imagination I was back home. In my sleep, too, I dreamed of familiar faces and voices, of tall pines with trunks a rusty red and the shimmering waters of great Lake Saimaa; and every morning without fail I felt compelled to curse reality and to confront it in a rage or with sobs.

When the idea had eaten itself deeply enough into my soul that it was despicable to be a Finn, I began to feel ashamed of my origins. Since going back was out of the question—and this thought was what had sustained me—there was nothing for me but to surrender. To survive, I had to change my stripes. Thus, to hell with Finland and the Finns! All of a sudden, I was overwhelmed by a desire to shed my skin and smash my face. What could not be accepted had to be denied, hidden, crushed and thrown away. A Swede was what I had to become, and that meant I could not continue to be a Finn. Everything I had held dear and self-evident had to be destroyed. An inner struggle began, a state of crisis of long duration. I had trouble sleeping, I could not look people in the eye, my voice broke down into a whisper. I could no longer trust anybody. My mother tongue was worthless—this I realized at last—on the contrary, it made me the butt of abuse and ridicule. So down with the Finnish language! I spat on myself, gradually committed internal suicide. I rambled by myself through the woods of Årsta and talked to myself aloud in Swedish. I practiced pronouncing words to make them sound exactly like the ones that come out of the mouths of Swedes. I resolved to learn Swedish word-perfect so nobody could guess who I was or where I came from. They still laughed at my Finnish accent—but after a while, never again!

My tongue was still limber and flexible. At the age of thirteen, I was just about ready. As long as I was a wee bit careful, nobody could tell I was a Finn, neither my speech nor by my ways. The only thing that betrayed me was my name. But, for some reason, I did not dare to change my name. I kept it.

I spoke Finnish only when it was absolutely unavoidable. "Why are you always so quiet?" my parents would ask me at mealtime. "Why don't you talk to us anymore?" For an answer they would get an evasive glance. I was incapable of anything else; my tongue had run dry, its power of speech depleted.

When word came from Finland that Grandmother was dead, I merely shrugged my shoulders in indifference and went over to see Åke. He was one of my bitterly won-over buddies. I did not want to remember, I would not allow myself to think of Grandma, who had existed once upon a time, long ago, when I used to live in another world. But that night I dreamed about Grandma: she was out on the pier washing clothes and she called out my name. In the morning I woke up feeling treacherous and filled with longing. I did not go to school but lay in bed all day, staring at the ceiling and remembering, as if in secrecy, what I did not otherwise dare to remember. Then the act continued, that of self-denial, of pretending ever more completely. In short, in order to live in harmony with my surroundings, I had to live in perpetual conflict with myself.

I never told anybody about the old times in Finland, not even by a slip of the tongue. I had cut off part of my life, and this caused me inexplicable distress, which later developed into a sense of alienation. My distress then turned into a longing for sincerity and spontaneity.

In the upper grades, one had to apply oneself to one's studies in earnest and compete for the best marks. Others were way ahead of me in knowledge, so I had to study as hard as I possibly could. But it was no use, no matter how hard I tried—the meaning of words eluded me; I had to read lines over and over again and still I could not understand. My examinations turned out badly; I always got the worst marks. This again put me in low spirits and made me think I was stupid. Paradoxically, however, deep down inside me I had a feeling I had a head for books. But words mocked me, refused to open up for me; they gave off no odour and seemed to be totally barren; I recognized words but failed to grasp their sense. The depth and diversity of language were lost; this matched the loss of my mother tongue, my Finnish.

Continuous failure at school forced me to search for something else. Those sliding downhill could always find pot down around the subway stations, or they might seek diversion in pilfering or acts of mischief. For my part, I was attracted to sports. At least, on the athletic field, I had a chance to engage in honest competition; the stopwatch ticked away at the same rate for everybody, all you had to do was to run like hell and stay in your own lane...It helped a bit to salve my wounds and restore my self-respect...What it did not give me was a healthy soul, and a healthy soul was my deepest desire, for my mind was in a chaotic state, on the verge of a breakdown. I was troubled by a growing sense of emptiness and alienation. I was conscious of never—hardly ever—using the words "our country" or "us Swedes." It never crossed my mind to speak of "us Finns" or, with reference to Finland, "my country." I was without a people, without ties. Perhaps this is what made me feel empty. Or maybe the reason could be found in the dismal face flitting in the mirror of my soul.

I was sixteen years old when one June day I stood in the sun-drenched schoolyard and looked at my graduation diploma. My ears burned red with shame. Then I let out a hysterical laugh and headed for home. In front of the stairs little Timo was sitting and playing marbles. He had come from Joensuu, Finland, three weeks before, but could already say 'låt pli' (don't touch). I folded up my diploma to make a paper swallow and lured Timo to accompany me up to the attic. There I lifted him up to the window and I let him fling my swallow into the air. Timo shrieked in delight as the paper swallow spun down toward the ground. As for myself, I was no longer capable of yelling Finnish—even though, down in my heart, I might have had the desire to do it.

(translated by Paul Sjöblom)

Excerpts from:

Hunger of Memory. The Education of Richard Rodriguez
by Richard Rodriguez. (1982). Boston, MA: D.R. Godine. Used with permission.

With great tact the visitors continued, "Is it possible for you and your husband to encourage your children to practice their English when they are home?" Of course, my parents complied. What would they not do for their children's well-being? And how could they have questioned the Church's authority which those women represented? In an instant, they agreed to give up the language (the sounds) that had revealed and accentuated our family's closeness. The moment after the visitors left, the change was observed. "*Ahora*, speak to us *en inglés*," my father and mother united to tell us.

At first, it seemed a kind of game. After dinner each night, the family gathered to practice "our" English. (It was still then *inglés*, a language foreign to us, so we felt drawn as strangers to it.) Laughing, we would try to define words we could not pronounce. We played with strange English sounds, often over-anglicizing our pronunciations. And we filled the smiling gaps of our sentences with familiar Spanish sounds. But that was cheating, somebody shouted. Everyone laughed. In school, meanwhile, like my brother and sister, I was required to attend a daily tutoring session. I needed a full year of special attention. I also needed my teachers to keep my attention from straying in class by calling out, "*Rich-heard*"—their English voices slowly prying loose my ties to my other name, its three notes, *Ri-car-do*. Most of all I needed to hear my mother and father speak to me in a moment of seriousness in broken—suddenly heartbreaking—English. The scene was inevitable: One Saturday morning I entered the kitchen where my parents were talking in Spanish. I did not realize that they were talking in Spanish, however, until, at the moment they saw me, I heard their voices change to speak English. Those *gringo* sounds they uttered startled me. Pushed me away. In that moment of trivial misunderstanding and profound insight, I felt my throat twisted by unsounded grief. I turned quickly and left the room. But I had no place to escape to with Spanish. (The spell was broken.) My brother and sisters were speaking English in another part of the house.

Again and again in the days following, increasingly angry, I was obliged to hear my mother and father: "Speak to us *en inglés*." Only then did I determine to learn classroom English. Weeks after, it happened: One day in school I raised my hand to volunteer an answer. I spoke out in a loud voice. And I did not think it remarkable when the entire class understood. That day, I moved very far from the disadvantaged child I had been only days earlier. The belief, the calming assurance that I belonged in public, had at last taken hold.

Shortly after, I stopped hearing the high and loud sounds of *los gringos*. A more confident speaker of English, I didn't trouble to listen to how strangers sounded, speaking to me. And there simply were too many English-speaking people in my day for me to hear American accents anymore. Conversations quickened. Listening to persons who sounded eccentrically pitched voices, I usually noted their sounds for an initial few seconds before I concentrated on *what* they were saying. Conversations became content-full. Transparent. Hearing someone's *tone* of voice—angry or questioning or sarcastic or happy or sad—I didn't distinguish it from the words it expressed. Sound and word were thus tightly wedded. At the end of a day, I was often bemused, always relieved, to realize how "silent," though crowded with words, my day in public had been. (This public silence measured and quickened the change in my life.)

At last, seven years old, I came to believe what had been technically true since my birth: I was an American citizen.

But the special feeling of closeness at home was diminished by then. Gone was the desperate, urgent, intense feeling of being at home; rare was the experience of feeling myself individualized by family intimates. We remained a loving family, but one greatly changed. No longer so close; no longer bound tight by the pleasing and troubling knowledge of our public separateness. Neither my older brother nor sister rushed home after school anymore. Nor did I. When I arrived home there would often be neighborhood kids in the house. Or the house would be empty of sounds.

Following the dramatic Americanization of their children, even my parents grew more publicly confident. Especially my mother. She learned the names of all the people on our block. And she decided we needed to have a telephone installed in the house. My father continued to use the word *gringo*. But it was no longer charged with the old bitterness or distrust. (Stripped of any emotional content, the word simply became a name for those Americans not of Hispanic descent.) Hearing him, sometimes, I wasn't sure if he was pronouncing the Spanish word *gringo* or saying gringo in English.

Matching the silence I started hearing in public was a new quiet at home. The family's quiet was partly due to the fact that, as we children learned more and more English, we shared fewer and fewer words with our parents. Sentences needed to be spoken slowly when a child addressed his mother or father. (Often the parent wouldn't understand.) The child would need to repeat himself. (Still the parent misunderstood.) The young voice, frustrated, would end up saying, "Never mind"—the subject was closed. Dinners would be noisy with the clinking of knives and forks against dishes. My mother would smile softly between her remarks; my father at the other end of the table would chew and chew at his food, while he stared over the heads of his children.

My mother! My father! After English became my primary language, I no longer knew what words to use in addressing my parents. The old Spanish words (those tender accents of sounds) I had used earlier—mamá and papá—I couldn't use anymore. They would have been too painful remainders of how much had changed in my life. On the other hand, the words I heard neighborhood kids call their parents seemed equally unsatisfactory. *Mother and Father; Ma, Papa, Pa, Dad, Pop* (how I hated the all-American sound of that last word especially)—all these terms I felt were unsuitable, not really terms of address for *my* parents. As a result, I never used them at home. Whenever I'd speak to my parents, I would try to get their attention with eye contact alone. In public conversations, I'd refer to "my parents" or "my mother and father."

My mother and father, for their part, responded differently, as their children spoke to them less. She grew restless, seemed troubled and anxious at the scarcity of words exchanged in the house. It was she who would question me about my day when I came home from school. She smiled at small talk. She pried at the edges of my sentences to get me to say something more. (What?) She'd join conversations she overheard, but her intrusions often stopped her children's talking. By contrast, my father seemed reconciled to the new quiet. Though his English improved somewhat, he retired into silence. At dinner he spoke very little. One night his children and even his wife helplessly giggled at his garbled English pronunciation of the Catholic Grace before meals. Thereafter, he made his wife recite the prayer at the start of each meal, even on formal occasions, when there were guests in the house. Hers became the public voice of the family. On official business, it was she, not my father, one would usually hear on the phone or in stores, talking to strangers. His children grew so accustomed to his silence that, years later, they would speak routinely of his shyness. (My mother would often try to explain: Both his parents died when he was eight. He was raised by an uncle who treated him like little more than a menial servant. He was never encouraged to speak. He grew up alone. A man of few words.) But my father was not shy, I realized, when I'd watch him speaking Spanish with relatives. Using Spanish, he was quickly effusive. Especially when talking with other men, his voice would spark, flicker, flare alive with sounds. In Spanish, he expressed ideas and feelings he rarely revealed in English. With firm Spanish sounds, he conveyed confidence and authority English would never allow him.

The silence at home, however, was finally more than a literal silence. Fewer words passed between parent and child, but more profound was the silence that resulted from my inattention to sounds. At about the time I no longer bothered to listen with care to the sounds of English in public, I grew careless about listening to the sounds family members made when they spoke. Most of the time I heard someone speaking at home and didn't distinguish his sounds from the words people uttered in public. I didn't even pay much attention to my parents' accented and ungrammatical speech. At least not at home. Only when I was with them in public would I grow alert to their accents. Though, even then, their sounds caused me less and less concern. For I was increasingly confident of my own public identity.

I would have been happier about my public success had I not sometimes recalled what it had been like earlier, when my family had conveyed its intimacy through a set of conveniently private sounds. Sometimes in public, hearing a stranger, I'd hark back to my past. A Mexican farmworker approached me downtown to ask directions to somewhere. "*¿Hijito...?*" he said. And his voice summoned deep longing. Another time, standing beside my mother in the visiting room of a Carmelite convent, before the dense screen which rendered the nuns shadowy figures, I heard several Spanish-speaking nuns—their busy, singsong, overlapping voices—assure us that yes, yes, we were remembered, all our family were remembered in their prayers. (Their voices echoed faraway family sounds.) Another day, a dark-faced old woman—her hand light on my shoulder—steadied herself against me as she boarded a bus. She murmured something I couldn't quite comprehend. Her Spanish voice came near, like the face of a never-before-seen relative in the instant before I was kissed. Her voice, like so many of the Spanish voices I'd hear in public, recalled the golden age of my youth. Hearing Spanish then, I continued to be a careful, if sad, listener to sounds. Hearing a Spanish-speaking family walking behind me, I turned to look. I smiled for an instant, before my glance found the Hispanic-looking faces of strangers in the crowd going by.

I grew up victim to a disabling confusion. As I grew fluent in English, I no longer could speak Spanish with confidence. I continued to understand spoken Spanish. But for many years I could not pronounce it. A powerful guilt blocked my spoken words; an essential glue was missing whenever I'd try to connect words to form sentences. I would be unable to break a barrier of sound, to speak freely. I would speak, or try to speak, Spanish, and I would manage to utter halting, hiccuping sounds that betrayed unease.

When relatives and Spanish-speaking friends of my parents came to the house, my brother and sisters seemed reticent to use Spanish, but at least they managed to say a few necessary words before being excused. I never managed so gracefully. I was cursed with guilt. Each time I'd hear myself addressed in Spanish, I would be unable to respond with any success. I'd know the words I wanted to say, but I couldn't manage to say them. I would try to speak, but everything I said seemed to me horribly anglicized. My mouth would not form the words right. My jaw would tremble. After a phrase or two, I'd cough up a warm, silvery sound. And stop.

It surprised my listeners to hear me. They'd lower their heads, better to grasp what I was trying to say. They would repeat their questions in gentle, affectionate voices. But by then I would answer in English. No, no, they would say, we want you to speak to us in Spanish ("*en español*"). But I couldn't do it. *Pocho* then they called me. Sometimes playfully, teasingly, using the tender diminutive—*mi pochito*. Sometimes not so playfully, mockingly, *Pocho*. (A Spanish dictionary defines that word as an adjective meaning "colorless" or "bland." But I heard it as a noun, naming the Mexican American who, in becoming an American, forgets his native society.) "*¡Pocho!*" the lady in the Mexican food store muttered, shaking her head. I looked up to the counter where red and green peppers were strung like Christmas tree lights and saw the frowning face of the stranger. My mother laughed somewhere behind me. (She said that her children didn't want to practice "our Spanish" after they started going to school.) My mother's smiling voice made me suspect that the lady who faced me was not really angry at me. But, searching her face, I couldn't find the hint of a smile.

Embarrassed, my parents would regularly need to explain their children's inability to speak flowing Spanish during those years. My mother met the wrath of her brother, her only brother, when he came up from Mexico one summer with his family. He saw his nieces and nephews for the very first time. After listening to me, he looked away and said what a disgrace it was that I couldn't speak Spanish, "*su proprio idioma.*"

Excerpts from:

"Joy Luck Club," "Double Face" from The Joy Luck Club

by Amy Tan. (1989). New York, NY: Penguin Putnam Inc. Used by permission of Putnam Berkley, a division of Penguin Putnam Inc.

"But you must stay! We have something important to tell you, from you mother," Auntie Ying blurts out in her too-loud voice. The others look uncomfortable, as if this were not how they intended to break some sort of bad news to me.

I sit down. Auntie An-mei leaves the room quickly and returns with a bowl of peanuts, then quietly shuts the door. Everybody is quiet, as if nobody knew where to begin.

It is Auntie Ying who finally speaks. "I think your mother die with an important thought on her mind," she says in halting English. And then she begins to speak in Chinese, calmly, softly.

"Your mother was a very strong woman, a good mother. She loved you very much, more than her own life. And that's why you can understand why a mother like this could never forget her other daughters. She knew they were alive, and before she died she wanted to find her daughters in China."

The babies in Kweilin, I think. I was not those babies. The babies in a sling on her shoulder. Her other daughters. And now I feel as if I were in Kweilin amidst the bombing and I can see these babies lying on the side of the road, their red thumbs popped out of their mouths, screaming to be reclaimed. Somebody took them away. They're safe. And now my mother's left me forever, gone back to China to get these babies. I can barely hear Auntie Ying's voice.

"She had searched for years, written letters back and forth," says Auntie Ying. "And last year she got an address. She was going to tell your father soon. Aii-ya, what a shame. A lifetime of waiting."

Auntie An-mei interrupts with an excited voice: "So your aunties and I, we wrote to this address," she says. "We say that a certain party, your mother, want to meet another certain party. And this party write back to us. They are your sisters, Jing-mei."

My sisters, I repeat to myself, saying these two words together for the first time.

Auntie An-mei is holding a sheet of paper as thin as wrapping tissue. In perfectly straight vertical rows I see Chinese characters written in blue fountain-pen ink. A word is smudged. A tear? I take the letter with shaking hands, marveling at how smart my sisters must be to be able to read and write in Chinese.

The aunties are all smiling at me, as though I had been a dying person who has now miraculously recovered. Auntie Ying is handing me another envelope. Inside is a check made out to June Woo for $1,200. I can't believe it.

"My sisters are sending me money?" I ask.

"No, no," says Auntie Lin with her mock exasperated voice. "Every year we save our mah jong winnings for big banquet at fancy restaurant. Most times your mother win, so most is her money. We add just a little, so you can go Hong Kong, take a train to Shanghai, see your sisters. Besides, we all getting too rich, too fat." She pats her stomach for proof.

"See my sisters," I say numbly. I am awed by this prospect, trying to imagine what I would see. And I am embarrassed by the end-of-the-year-banquet lie my aunties have told to mask their generosity. I am crying now, sobbing and laughing at the same time, seeing but not understanding this loyalty to my mother.

"You must see your sisters and tell them about your mother's death," says Auntie Ying. "But most important, you must tell them about her life. The mother they did not know, they must now know."

"See my sisters, tell them about my mother," I say, nodding. "What will I say? What can I tell them about my mother? I don't know anything. She was my mother."

The aunties are looking at me as if I had become crazy right before their eyes.

"Not know your own mother?" cries Auntie An-mei with disbelief. "How can you say? Your mother is in your bones!"

"Tell them stories of your family here. How she became success," offers Auntie Lin.

"Tell them stories she told you, lessons she taught, what you know about her mind that has become your mind," says Auntie Ying. "You mother very smart lady."

I hear more choruses of "Tell them, tell them" as each auntie frantically tries to think what should be passed on.

"Her kindness."

"Her smartness."

"Her dutiful nature to family."

"Her hopes, things that matter to her."

"The excellent dishes she cooked."

"Imagine, a daughter not knowing her own mother!"

And then it occurs to me. They are frightened. In me, they see their own daughters, just as ignorant, just as unmindful of all the truths and hopes they have brought to America. They see daughters who grow impatient when their mothers talk in Chinese, who think they are stupid when they explain things in fractured English. They see that joy and luck do not mean the same to their daughters, that to these closed American-born minds "joy luck" is not a word, it does not exist. They see daughters who will bear grandchildren born without any connecting hope passed from generation to generation.

"I will tell them everything," I say simply, and the aunties look at me with doubtful faces.

"I will remember everything about her and tell them," I say more firmly. And gradually, one by one, they smile and pat my hand. They still look troubled, as if something were out of balance. But they also look hopeful that what I say will become true. What more can they ask? What more can I promise?

They go back to eating their soft boiled peanuts, saying stories among themselves. They are young girls again, dreaming of good times in the past and good times yet to come. A brother from Ningbo who makes his sister cry with joy when he returns nine thousand dollars plus interest. A youngest son whose stereo and TV repair business is so good he sends leftovers to China. A daughter whose babies are able to swim like fish in a fancy pool in Woodside. Such good stories. The best. They are the lucky ones.

And I am sitting at my mother's place at the mah jong table, on the East, where things begin.

My daughter wanted to go to China for her second honeymoon, but now she is afraid.

"What if I blend in so well they think I'm one of them?" Waverly asked me. "What if they don't let me come back to the United States?"

"When you go to China," I told her, "you don't even need to open your mouth. They already know you are an outsider."

"What are you talking about?" she asked. My daughter likes to speak back. She likes to question what I say.

"Aii-ya," I said. "Even if you put on their clothes, even if you take off your makeup and hide your fancy jewelry, they know. They know just watching the way you walk, the way you carry your face. They know you do not belong."

My daughter did not look pleased when I told her this, that she didn't look Chinese. She had a sour American look on her face. Oh, maybe ten years ago, she would have clapped her hands—hurray!—as if this were good news. But now she wants to be Chinese, it is so fashionable. And I know it is too late. All those years I tried to teach her! She followed my Chinese ways only until she learned how to walk out the door by herself and go to school. So now the only Chinese words she can say are *sh-sh, gouche, chr fan,* and *gwan deng shweijyau.* How can she talk to people in China with these words? Pee-pee, choo-choo train, eat, close light sleep. How can she think she can blend in? Only her skin and her hair are Chinese. Inside—she is all American-made.

It's my fault she is this way. I wanted my children to have the best combination: American circumstances and Chinese character. How could I know these two things do not mix?

I taught her how American circumstances work. If you are born poor here, it's no lasting shame. You are first in line for a scholarship. If the roof crashes on your head, no need to cry over this bad luck. You can sue anybody, make the landlord fix it. You do not have to sit like a Buddha under a tree letting pigeons drop their dirty business on your head. You can buy an umbrella. Or go inside a Catholic church. In America, nobody says you have to keep the circumstances somebody else gives you.

She learned these things, but I couldn't teach her about Chinese character. How to obey parents and listen to your mother's mind. How not to show your own thoughts, to put your feelings behind your face so you can take advantage of hidden opportunities. Why easy things are not worth pursuing. How to know your own worth and polish it, never flashing it around like a cheap ring. Why Chinese thinking is best.

No, this kind of thinking didn't stick to her. She was too busy chewing gum, blowing bubbles bigger than her cheeks. Only that kind of thinking stuck.

"Finish your coffee," I told her yesterday. "Don't throw your blessings away."

"Don't be so old-fashioned, Ma," she told me, finishing her coffee down the sink. "I'm my own person."

And I think, How can she be her own person? When did I give her up?

⁕

My daughter is getting married a second time. So she asked me to go to her beauty parlor, her famous Mr. Rory. I know her meaning. She is ashamed of my looks. What will her husband's parents and his important lawyer friends think of this backward old Chinese woman?

"Auntie An-mei can cut me," I say.

"Rory is famous," says my daughter, as if she had no ears. "He does fabulous work."

So I sit in Mr. Rory's chair. He pumps me up and down until I am the right height. Then my daughter criticizes me as if I were not there. "See how it's flat on one side," she accuses my head. "She needs a cut and a perm. And this purple tint in her hair, she's been doing it at home. She's never had anything professionally done."

She is looking at Mr. Rory in the mirror. He is looking at me in the mirror. I have seen this professional look before. Americans don't really look at one another when talking. They talk to their reflections. They look at others or themselves only when they think nobody is watching. So they never see how they really look. They see themselves smiling without their mouth open, or turned to the side where they cannot see their faults.

"How does she want it?" asked Mr. Rory. He thinks I do not understand English. He is floating his fingers through my hair. He is showing how his magic can make my hair thicker and longer.

"Ma, how do you want it?" Why does my daughter think she is translating English for me? Before I can even speak, she explains my thoughts: "She wants a soft wave. We probably shouldn't cut it too short. Otherwise it'll be too tight for the wedding. She doesn't want it to look kinky or weird."

And now she says to me in a loud voice, as if I had lost my hearing, "Isn't that right, Ma? Not too tight?"

I smile. I use my American face. That the face Americans think is Chinese, the one they cannot understand. But inside I am becoming ashamed. I am ashamed she is ashamed. Because she is my daughter and I am proud of her, and I am her mother but she is not proud of me.

Mr. Rory pats my hair more. He looks at me. He looks at my daughter. Then he says something to my daughter that really displeases her: "It's uncanny how much you two look alike!"

I smile, this time with my Chinese face. But my daughter's eyes and her smile become very narrow, the way a cat pulls itself small just before it bites. Now Mr. Rory goes away so we can think about this. I hear him snap his fingers. "Wash! Mrs. Jong is next!"

So my daughter and I are alone in this crowded beauty parlor. She is frowning at herself in the mirror. She sees me looking at her.

"The same cheeks," she says. She points to mine and then pokes her cheeks. She sucks them outside in to look like a starved person. She puts her face next to mine, side by side, and we look at each other in the mirror.

"You can see your character in your face," I say to my daughter without thinking. "You can see your future."

"What do you mean?" she says.

And now I have to fight back my feelings. These two faces, I think, so much the same! The same happiness, the same sadness, the same good fortune, the same faults.

I am seeing myself and my mother, back in China, when I was a young girl.

⁂

My mother—your grandmother—once told me my fortune, how my character could lead to good and bad circumstances. She was sitting at her table with the big mirror. I was standing behind her, my chin resting on her shoulder. The next day was the start of the new year. I would be ten years by my Chinese age, so it was an important birthday for me. For this reason maybe she did not criticize me too much. She was looking at my face.

She touched my ear. "You are lucky," she said. "You have my ears, a big thick lobe, lots of meat at the bottom, full of blessings. Some people are born so poor. Their ears are so thin, so close to their head, they can never hear luck calling to them. You have the right ears, but you must listen to your opportunities."

She ran her thin finger down my nose. "You have my nose. The hole is not too big, so your money will not be running out. The nose is straight and smooth, a good sign. A girl with a crooked nose is bound for misfortune. She is always following the wrong things, the wrong people, the worst luck."

She tapped my chin and then hers. "Not too short, not too long. Our longevity will be adequate, not cut off too soon, not so long we become a burden."

She pushed my hair away from my forehead. "We are the same," concluded my mother. "Perhaps your forehead is wider, so you will be even more clever. And your hair is thick, the hairline is low on your forehead. This means you will have some hardships in your early life. This happened to me. But look at my hairline now. High! Such a blessing for my old age. Later you will learn to worry and lose your hair, too."

She took my chin in her hand. She turned my face toward her, eyes facing eyes. She moved my face to one side, then the other. "The eyes are honest, eager," she said. "They follow me and show respect. They do not look down in shame. They do not resist and turn the opposite way. You will be a good wife, mother, and daughter-in-law."

When my mother told me these things, I was still so young. And even though she said we looked the same, I wanted to look more the same. If her eye went up and looked surprised, I wanted my eye to do the same. If her mouth fell down and was unhappy, I too wanted to feel unhappy.

APPENDIX B
READINGS FOR ACTIVITY 4.7
EXAMINING STUDENT PROFILES:
LONG-TERM LEP STUDENTS

PROFILE OF A LONG-TERM LEP STUDENT:
YUSEF ABDUL

With his friendly, open personality and warm smile, Yusef, a 17-year-old high school sophomore, makes a pleasant first impression. After he arrived here at age 8 from the Fiji Islands, his elementary school teachers noticed his sweet nature. "He is a very kind and considerate boy. I really enjoy him," his third-grade teacher wrote. Teachers also recognized that Yusef struggled academically, but each year, he passed to the next grade level, with admonitions to work harder on his reading and writing.

Now, after 11 years as a Limited English Proficient student, Yusef still has trouble learning, even though he is on target for graduation with a solid C average. He understands the value of a diploma, but wonders how useful his high school courses have been.

Yusef emigrated from the Fiji Islands with his parents and younger sister in February 1988. Although citizens of Fiji, the family is ethnically Indian. Fiji has about 700,000 inhabitants, most of them descended from laborers brought from British India between 1879 to 1916 to work on sugar cane plantations. Most ethnic Indians in Fiji are Hindu, but a minority, including Yusef's family, are Muslim. To a smaller degree, the islands are populated by native Fijians of Melanesian, Indonesian and Polynesian descent. English is the official language of Fiji, but many people speak Hindi and Fijian languages. Yusef's first language was Hindi.

Yusef's family prospered in Fiji. His father, a bus driver, also owned two or three taxis. The family rented out property, which they still own. In the U.S., Yusef's father drives a truck and his mother is a homemaker. Yusef says, "She never worked in her whole life. I will never let her, too." Yusef's grandfather, after living in the U.S. for about 27 years, sponsored the family. During the past decade, most of Yusef's relatives have also immigrated, so he is surrounded by family.

Yusef is tall and thin, with a narrow face, short hair and a tan complexion. Many people assume that he comes from India, so he has to assert that as a Fijian, his experience is different:

"I don't know why, but if you say 'Fijian,' most of the time kids over here, I mean, the guys from India, they think we're the same. But we're totally different."

He also feels different from other Muslim students: "It's like the guys from Iran and

Iraq, they say we're the same. I mean, it's the same thing, but it's different." Rarely do American-born kids know anything about his country or its history, he says: "It depends on the parents. Sometimes the parents don't tell their children about the world."

Yusef's own experience as a newly-arrived immigrant in the schools began in elementary school. In the spring of 1988, at age 8, he was placed in the first grade because he spoke no English and had only attended school for one year in Fiji. For this reason, Yusef is a year or two older than his classmates.

He recalls being quiet and scared on his first day of school because in Fiji, teachers would hit children to discipline them. He was relieved to find out that U.S. teachers don't strike their pupils: "After quite a while, after all that you see, I feel better."

He says he was able to follow many of the class activities, but had a hard time understanding the teacher. He had heard English spoken in Fiji, but had never learned it. Instead, he learned to read and write in Hindi, although now he has forgotten much. He still speaks Hindi with his parents, but English with his sister.

During first grade, Yusef received ESL instruction through a pull-out program. School records don't reveal how much ESL he took in elementary school, but Yusef remembers only one year. Almost every one of his elementary school teachers gave him high citizenship marks, but he was not achieving academically. His grades throughout elementary school were mostly C's, with some B's and a few A's.

Each year, he was promoted to the next grade level. But shockingly, his scores on standardized tests such as the CTBS (California Test of Basic Skills) and Language Assessment Scales tests show that Yusef never improved academically. For example, in second grade, he had a reading score that was equivalent to the second grade level. In fifth grade, three years later, his reading score still stood at second grade level. He progressed better in Math, but by sixth grade was still below grade level.

As the years passed, he fell behind his peers as his test scores declined relative to theirs. He attended class regularly and participated, yet failed to learn. He was not a special education student—he was simply promoted from year to year with teacher reminders to read and write more.

When Yusef went on to middle school, he found academics to be harder, especially classes that required writing, such as English and History. On a 7th-grade Language Assessment Scales Reading and Writing test, he showed that he still struggled with the basics:

"The beautiful place I went was this park it is so, so beautiful. It had lake and duck it had bird. There are people walking around it was a big park. There are people riding there small boat and I also saw some people riding their horuse and they also let the litter kids ride them. Me and my family we stey there and we eat lunch then we walke around then we went home."

He scored a level 2 on that test, which meant he was "limited literate."

When Yusef entered 9th grade, teachers began to cite him for behavioral problems. Perhaps his frustration at his lack of academic skills was starting to take its toll. He was disciplined for stealing a former student's work and trying to pass it off as his own; forging his father's signature on rules and regulations; throwing blocks in class and encouraging other students to fool around; and making disrespectful remarks about a teacher. The school contacted his parents several times.

In 9th grade, Yusef earned C's and D's in courses such as sheltered Science, sheltered Math, and Physical Education. He took no English in the fall semester, and failed a spring sheltered English course. In 10th grade, he earned similarly poor grades in sheltered classes, such as English, Pre-Algebra and World History.

Despite Yusef's poor performance on standardized tests and school courses, he is on track for graduation with 110 units at the end of 10th grade and a solid C average (2.0 GPA). In 1995, Yusef passed the district minimum proficiency language test, but still has to pass the reading and math minimum proficiency tests.

Remarkably, Yusef has remained socially confident—a strong personality indeed. He says he loves school and is determined to graduate. "I think education is important," he says. In part, he is reflecting the weight of his immigrant parents' expectations—they came to this country hoping their children would have opportunities for a good education. Yusef has a hard time describing his performance as a student, though. "I don't do only the bad stuff, like smoke and stuff like that," he says. He adds that he participates in class and hardly misses classes unless absolutely necessary. Each night, he spends 30 minutes to an hour on homework and "mostly" finishes. If he has no homework, "I'll read the paper—the car dealer papers. I love to see that."

Yusef is a self-taught mechanic—with a lot of help from his father. On the weekends and some weeknights, customers bring cars to his parents' house and Yusef and his father work on them. Yusef loves cars and says he makes good money doing repairs.

He dreams of attending an automotive mechanic technical school. He looked into a car shop program through his school's Regional Occupational Program, but found out he had to be in 11th grade to sign up. Yusef didn't feel like he could wait one more year to enroll in the progam, as he was already self-conscious about being older than the other 10th-grade students. Instead, Yusef transferred from high school to adult school. To him, the utility of a high school degree is what's most important. He feels that his course content has not been that useful, but he needs a diploma to get into certain programs and jobs.

He doesn't have much interest in college right now. "I don't want to waste another four years," he says. He acknowledges that people can earn more if they get a college degree, but notes the exceptions:

"A lot of people don't [earn more money]. They stay at McDonald's. That's it. Spend their whole life. So I don't want to do that. I never want to [make] five, six dollars an hour."

What's in store for Yusef? He wants to stay in the U.S. for now, although he says that eventually he and his parents may move back to Fiji. Even though school has been tough for him, he has gone to class consistently, and now he harbors a strong vocational interest in auto mechanics. His perseverance, along with his burgeoning repair skills, may serve him well in the work force as he leaves the public schools.

PROFILE OF A LONG-TERM LEP STUDENT
MOHAMMED KHALILI

Mohammed is an enigma. He is a long-term Limited English Proficient (LEP) student, born in Afghanistan, who attends classes and passes most of his courses. But his school records show worrisome behavior. He has been disciplined with numerous detentions and suspensions for infractions ranging from fighting to setting off a firecracker. And, although he is making consistent progress, Mohammed himself is the first to admit that he's losing interest in school.

Mohammed, a high school junior, thinks his troubles may have started in middle school. He started hanging out with a friend who criticized him for being a good student. Mohammed remembers his friend saying, "You don't do nothing for fun." The teasing got to Mohammed. "I guess I slipped off towards the side a little bit," he admits. "I messed up." Soon, his grades dropped and he started to get into trouble in class.

During 8th grade, he started cutting classes and was suspended three times—for setting off a firecracker, bringing a cap gun to school, and shooting staples in class. When he went on to high school, he kept cutting classes and misbehaving. In 9th grade, he was suspended twice, once again for setting off a firecracker and another time for fighting in class. In 10th grade, he was caught forging notes to excuse his cuts. In 11th grade, he was written up for incidents such as "horseplaying in class and spraying a student with liquid cleanser" and for leaving class without permission to go to the library. He was suspended twice in 11th grade for failing 10 times to appear at Saturday detention and for repeated unexcused absences.

Despite these problems, Mohammed is passing in school, although his grades are far from good. By the end of 11th grade, he had a 2.27 cumulative GPA and had earned 160 credits, which meant that he was close to being on track for graduation. His Language Assessment Scales (LAS) scores have shown some improvement in reading and writing skills over the years. In 9th grade, he passed the reading and writing minimum proficiency tests, but still needs to pass the math test.

He seems capable of doing good work, as evidenced by some A's and B's in academic classes. But he feels his teachers "don't like me for some reason." Even if he gets a good grade, they often tell him he isn't doing his best. He knows they are telling the truth. It frustrates him to know that he could do better, but he feels he can't motivate himself to do the work.

He remembers a time, though, when he enjoyed learning:

"From second grade to seventh grade, I really used to love school. I used to do work and I used to be done before everybody, right? I was like, really, really smart."

He recalls reading just for fun. "Whenever I got bored, I'd just open a book...but then, after awhile, it just didn't amuse me anymore. I don't know what it is."

What went wrong?

Despite Mohammed's optimistic descriptions of his early schooling years, there are clues in his records of potential sources of trouble, such as family upheaval, as well as Mohammed's short attention span and unruly behavior. One California Tomorrow interviewer wondered whether he should have been tested for Attention Deficit Disorder.

Mohammed's early life was marked by major changes. He was three when his family fled the war in Afghanistan in 1984. They traveled to India, where they had relatives. After more than two years there, Mohammed's family moved to the U.S. Mohammed is the youngest child in a family with seven sisters, two who now live in Pakistan. Mohammed's parents settled in California in 1987. His father, now retired, owned a body shop in the U.S. for many years.

Because he has lived in several countries, Mohammed is orally fluent in four languages: Farsi (his first language), Hindi, Iranian and English. He reads and writes, however, in English only. With his family and friends, Mohammed speaks both English and Farsi. Most of his friends are Afghan, but he has some Indian friends with whom he still speaks Hindi.

Mohammed started first grade in California in the middle of the 1986-87 school year. He was five and the only student from Afghanistan in the class. Because he spoke no English, he was placed in a bilingual classroom with a teacher who spoke Iranian, which is similar to Farsi.

His first-grade teacher wrote promising comments: "Mohammed has adjusted well to his new country, school and language. He is not yet fluent in English but does well in Math." And, "Mohammed had a successful year adjusting to his new environment. He should continue to do well next year."

He was promoted to a second grade bilingual classroom, even though his lack of English skills had prevented him from achieving all first-grade skills. His teacher noted that he was making great strides in learning English and working at grade level, but she also noted, "Behavior is very immature. Often does not follow rules."

Mohammed's school performance was inconsistent. Although elementary school teachers sometimes praised him for being a hard worker and good student, behavioral problems continued to surface each year. He was an active boy with a short attention span who was easily bored. He continually frustrated his teachers by not following the rules or completing assignments. He maintained his grades at a C+ or B- average, and he mostly got low marks in citizenship and study skills.

His fourth-grade teacher wrote, "He tends to be verbally abusive to some of his peers without considering their feelings. Was chosen conflict manager, but because of his behavior in and out of class was dropped from the program." In sixth grade, he received 13 citations during the year.

Academically, from third grade on, it is unclear whether Mohammed was receiving ESL instruction or whether he was in a bilingual or sheltered classroom. When asked when he really began to feel comfortable speaking English, Mohammed said it wasn't until 4th or 5th grade. In 4th grade, he took his most recent Oral LAS test and scored a level 4, indicating oral fluency in English. At the same time, he took the LAS Reading and Writing and scored a 2 in reading and 1 in writing, indicating that his English reading and writing skills lagged far behind his speaking ability.

When he reached middle school, he was enrolled into all mainstream classes and maintained a 2.5 GPA during those two years. Not only did his behavior problems continue, but he also started cutting classes.

When Mohammed entered high school, he made lots of friends, he says:

"I'm cool with everybody. I have Black friends, Mexican friends, you know? I have Vietnamese friends, I have everybody."

But he also comments that students tend to stick with others of their own race:

"At lunchtime, I just like to kick it with Afghans, because I enjoy it more. You won't feel comfortable with Mexicans as you will with Afghans…You speak the same language, you know."

Students do get into fights, and Mohammed has joined in at times:

"We don't get along with a lot of Fijians, right? If I have to start something I will handle it, you know? Like I'll try to avoid it, but if I can't…it's like that."

His loyalty to friends also pulls him into fights:

"I'm going to back up my friend, whether he's Black, Mexican, Afghan or whatever, right? But they'll do the same for me because I've kicked with them long enough to earn their trust."

Perhaps the one thread of hope, the main reason that keeps Mohammed in school, is his dream of becoming a physical therapist. Through the Regional Occupational Program, he takes medical occupations courses and works at a physical therapy clinic from 7 a.m. to 10 a.m. every morning, administering heat packs, performing ultrasound and helping patients learn correct techniques for lifting weights. To gain a work permit and permission to participate in ROP, he signed an "Academic/Attendance/Behavior Contract" with his high school, in which he pledged to observe school rules, attend all classes and complete homework. He gets school credit for his clinic work and has done well at the job.

"I think I'm really interested in that career," he says. He can become certified to be a physical therapy aide by completing a certain number of hours of work by the time he graduates from high school. He wants to continue to study physical therapy in college but he has not yet looked into schools.

What's in Mohammed's future? Besides having a goal and skills, he has been responsible enough to perform well at work. He is a sociable person who does not seem intimidated by school, despite the continual discipline problems he has faced. And he does enough work to pass and graduate on time. That's not to say he couldn't do better—some teachers have noted that he's a bright person who isn't working at his best. Given this confusing picture, will Mohammed's dream of becoming a physical therapist be enough to keep him engaged in schooling for a few years longer?

PROFILE OF A LONG-TERM LEP STUDENT
LUISA MIGUEL

Luisa Miguel, an 11th grader, appears bright, creative, hopeful and optimistic—just the opposite of the stereotypical disengaged student. Her face is friendly, with a quick smile, large expressive eyes, and curly dark brown hair that falls below her shoulders. Despite her openness, she is a bundle of contradictions. She seems happy to tell her story, talking easily about her life, interests and aspirations in rapid, fluent English punctuated by frequent laughter. Nevertheless, she is failing school.

Superficially, Luisa's story is similar to that of many of her peers, who have attended U.S. schools for most of their lives, but languish academically. Despite their long years in this country, many are still classified as Limited English Proficient. Luisa, now 17, was born in Michoacán, Mexico, and immigrated to the U.S. when she was eight. Her family settled in California, where she began attending school as a first grader. In elementary school, Luisa seemed full of promise, a good student who worked hard and loved to sing and dance, read and write. But at some point during middle school, her interest in academics waned. Now, several years later, her high school teachers know her as a student who fails to do her work and is often late or absent.

Throughout high school, Luisa has been enrolled in mainstream classes at the general education level (as opposed to college prep), despite being classified as LEP. Her attendance has been spotty. In her first term of 9th grade, for instance, she was absent 20 days. When she comes to school, she often arrives late, especially to her first class of the day. Her first-period History teacher admits that her continual tardiness is annoying and disruptive. Although he is a young, energetic and caring teacher, he says that being responsible for 45 other students prevents him from investigating why one student is chronically late. He says:

> *"If people don't come to my class, I really don't have time. I see her—she's trying hard. But nothing is penetrating. In my class, if you miss one day, you're going to be behind."*

He says he feels extremely frustrated because she seems bright, but "I don't even know if she is capable or not because she hasn't shown me anything to base [a judgment] on."

Luisa's grades have been dismal. At the end of 9th grade, her GPA was .67. In 10th grade, Luisa continued to rack up absences and receive D's and F's. By spring of that year, her progress report warned that she would fail all her classes. Teachers admonished her about missing class, not turning in homework or participating in class, and not suiting up for physical education classes.

Her high school teachers would be surprised to learn that Luisa was once a girl who earned the frequent praises of her elementary school teachers. Luisa's earliest years were spent in Mexico. She is the second of six children and the eldest daughter. When Luisa was small, her father was a migrant farmworker in California. When she was 6, her mother left Mexico to join him. Grandparents and family friends in Mexico took care of the children for about two years. Luisa stayed with a woman who had taken care of her father when he was a child. The woman taught her how to read and write in Spanish, as well as to paint, cook and wash clothes.

When Luisa was about 7, she and the other siblings received word from their father that they'd be joining their parents in the U.S. Luisa said she felt sad to be leaving Mexico:

"But when my dad told us that we were going to come to school, we were happy because I wanted to learn—and I wanted to learn English."

An uncle brought Luisa and her siblings to California in 1987.

When Luisa arrived in elementary school in November 1987, she was 8 years old, spoke Spanish only, and had never attended school before. Because she was assessed as non-English-speaking, she received ESL instruction and tutoring in Math and Spanish, and was placed in bilingual classes or sheltered classes until 6th grade. She progressed quickly and earned high marks. She was even promoted over parts of third and fourth grade. Her success is even more impressive given that she completed 1st through 6th grades in five years—at five different schools. During those years, her family moved three times within the same school district.

Luisa's teachers commented on her outgoing personality, intelligence and creativity. Her second-grade teacher wrote that she was a "fast learner and excellent reader." Others noted that she had strong artistic skills, got along well with others, and enjoyed the support and attention of her parents. She finished 6th grade with many A's, including ones for completing classwork and homework, and only a few B's—in Math and "listening." She had very few absences throughout elementary school and high marks for citizenship.

At first she felt uncomfortable at school and found it hard to make friends:

"When I started school, I didn't like it because I just heard everyone speaking English, talking to each other, and I didn't understand what they were saying. The most hard thing for me was to ask a question. I couldn't ask [the teacher] because I knew she wasn't going to understand me."

Soon, though, she found some Spanish-speaking students who helped her ask questions or take care of details, such as asking permission to go to the restroom or take medicine. Her new friends taught her easy English words, as well as the alphabet and numbers. She explains:

"So then when I started making new friends, I started liking school. It started becoming easier."

Luisa's disjointed school experience continued in her middle school years, but this time, she was not as successful. She lost interest in school, her grades slipped, and she has not recovered.

The timeline during middle school is confusing, but it appears that Luisa was 13 years old at the start of 7th grade. Her records show that she dropped out of 7th grade for a short time, perhaps to take a job as a Spanish-English interpreter at a health clinic, and that her 8th-grade classes were taken through an independent study program.

In 7th grade, she was enrolled in sheltered classes. But at this point in her life, Luisa began to have other things on her mind. She discovered a passion for music. She says that during that time, "Everything was listening to music." She spent endless hours learning to play the guitar. By 7th grade, she had written many poems in English and Spanish that she set to music.

She met four other musicians. They formed Sentimiento, a band that still performs together today, mostly at parties. Luisa sings and writes the songs while the others play instruments. She says that as a middle school student, she wanted to be able to do everything—perform, work and go to school. At some point, she decided that school was less important and began to attend irregularly, sometimes missing weeks at a time.

Her absences and distractions took a toll. In 7th grade, she received C's, D's and F's in all her classes—the second semester GPA lower than the first. Her parents told her it was all right to pursue music, but they wanted her to keep up with school. She says: "My dad said that he didn't want us—none of my brothers or sisters or me—to work on the fields like he was working." Apparently, the pep talk worked. In 8th grade, Luisa enrolled in an independent study program and bounced back with her previous A's and B's.

Despite this rebound, standardized tests throughout middle school showed that Luisa's English and Math skills lagged behind grade level by about two years. In 7th grade, her CTBS results ranked her in the lower third of all students who took the test—native speakers and second language learners alike. By 8th grade, her CTBS score was at the 17th percentile in Math, two years behind the average, and her English skills were uneven. She was almost at grade level in language expression (33rd percentile) and reading comprehension (42nd percentile), but scored poorly in reading vocabulary (1st percentile) and language mechanics (3rd percentile). As an LEP student, every year that she slips behind her native English-speaking peers adds more than a year she has to make up in order to catch up to them.

Sadly, as Luisa failed to thrive in English skills, she was also losing her first language. In first grade, when Luisa underwent her initial assessment of Spanish proficiency, she scored above average. Her grading of 5 on a scale of 6 indicated she was a fluent Spanish speaker. But she lost ground over the years. Her early SABE (Spanish Assessment of Basic Education) tests showed an initial jump in achievement that then levels out. By 6th grade, her Spanish skills are a little below average.

When Luisa was promoted prematurely to 9th grade, she fell behind her peers. Her grades plummeted and have remained poor throughout high school.

A deeper look into Luisa's story reveals that not only do her school and personal life pull her in different directions, fragmenting her energy and attention, but her home life also loads her with numerous responsibilities. Her parents work in the fields, which means long days and back-breaking work. As the eldest daughter, Luisa is the primary homemaker and caregiver to four younger sisters, ages 14, 11, 9 and 7 months old. She explains:

> *"I wake up in the morning at 6 a.m., and I get my little sisters ready for school. I prepare them something to eat. And then I get ready myself, and my materials, so when I come [to school], I come late and I don't get to hear the whole instructions."*

When she returns home at 3 p.m., she cleans the house and cooks dinner. From 5 to 6 or 6:30, she does homework. Afterwards, she spends half an hour on songwriting, then does aerobic exercises. She adds:

> *"Then I get tired and I go have some dinner with my family or have sandwiches outside with my neighbor (a close friend), and then start writing again or reading. So that's most of the day. I do most of the same things every day."*

And although she is close to her family and credits her parents with encouraging her education, she expresses frustration that her brother, two years older, did not have to shoulder domestic responsibilities. She comments:

> *"He didn't have to do anything at home. He could go out playing basketball, hang out with his girlfriend, and have time for his homework, whereas I can't."*

At the same time, she respects him. A year earlier, he graduated from her high school and moved to Phoenix, Arizona, to take courses to become a mechanic. She says he inspires her to graduate and find a good job, too.

Although she is failing classes, Luisa is surprisingly positive about school and optimistic about her future. She says she gets "everything" she needs from her teachers and that all her teachers are good teachers. Luisa also says that she is able to get her homework done, and that she gets help from teachers when she needs it.

She wants to be an interpreter because of her work as a clinic translator during middle school. While she still spends as much time as she can on her music and art, she sees those pursuits as hobbies. It's more important, she says, to graduate and pursue a career. Even though Luisa has not talked to a counselor about getting into college, she believes she has all the information she needs to get into college and that she is taking the right courses. Clearly, there is a significant reality gap between her performance and her expectations, a common phenomenon among LEP students.

Chapter Five:

STUDENT VOICE: INVITING, USING AND HONORING OUR STUDENTS' PERSPECTIVES AS WE ENVISION CHANGE

"I just can't keep up, you know. Every teacher thinks she is the only one and gives us so much homework. I go to work after school. I want to be a good student, but I can't."

"When I came here, my only problem was with English. I knew how to do the work and, if it was in Spanish, I could do it well. We know the answers, but we cannot express the words."

"I just have to say it straight out—my classes are boring. Sorry, I know the teachers are probably nice people and all. But when's the last time you tried sitting through a whole long day of boring school? In the morning you can start out thinking it's gonna be okay today, but by lunch you just know, no way. It's another boring day."

"The most important thing of all is if the teachers could get to know us and care about us. I don't think most of my teachers really know my name or anything about me."

"The ESL students are all isolated and categorized into a group by themselves. No one else talks to you. You can't make American friends. It's like three different schools here. There's the ESL school, the college-prep school, and everyone else."

—STUDENT PANELISTS SPEAKING BEFORE AN ASSEMBLY OF THEIR TEACHERS, ALISAL HIGH SCHOOL, SALINAS, CA

With these truthful and unadorned words, students at Alisal High School helped their teachers understand how their school needed to change. In fact, teachers on the school's restructuring team recalled the presentation as being pivotal:

"I'd heard over and over about how low our test scores are at Alisal. Frankly, you just hear that so often—I would just tune out. It wasn't until I heard our own students, kids I knew, telling me how hurt they were that the work we gave them seemed 'dumbed down,' hearing them talk about the way low expectations get communicated to them everyday, that I realized I needed to do something. You don't just walk away."

—SCIENCE TEACHER, ALISAL

"What can I say? I just had no idea. I didn't realize so many kids work everyday after school. I'd just assign homework and mark them down for not turning it in. I just assumed they were lazy or didn't care or didn't try. The student panel really gave me something to think about."

—ENGLISH TEACHER, ALISAL

Throughout three years of school reform at Alisal, the echoes of students' words inspired teachers as they switched to a block schedule, with fewer, longer classes and built-in academic tutorials. Under this new structure, students could concentrate more on each subject and get more academic help; teachers could also spend more time with fewer students and, thus, get to know them better.

As Alisal has shown us, student voice can help shape school reform so that it truly addresses students' academic and social needs. Student voice activities aim to create a culture in which adults understand how their students experience school, then use this information to improve the school. Student voice also helps build a climate of inclusiveness by involving students who have traditionally been "silent." Immigrant students, in particular, may be reluctant to speak because of differing cultural norms for when speaking up is appropriate, different habits from prior schooling in another country, or difficulty in speaking English.

Listening to students is more important now than ever before, as teachers increasingly face classrooms of students with whom they share neither a culture, national or ethnic background, or community experience. Without a doubt, students can shed light on their experiences in school related to achievement and access and can help faculties understand the cultural complexities of their lives.

But student voice doesn't just happen, particularly for students who feel excluded or unwelcome, especially those who have trouble expressing themselves in English or who come from traditions in which students and parents do not criticize schools or have felt poorly served by them. Schools committed to learning from historically excluded or underserved student populations need to deliberately invite student voice—and consciously create the climate in which student voice can be heard.

California Tomorrow's use of student voice for equity-centered reform, while unique in many ways, also builds on traditions of involving students in their education. In the following section, we explore these traditions, then present strategies for inviting and using student voice. We illustrate many of these strategies with examples of how real schools have used them. As powerful as student voice can be, we need to approach the process with care and an awareness of how student voices have been heard or ignored in our particular schools.

Listening to students is more important now than ever before.

STUDENT VOICE TRADITIONS IN EDUCATION

YOUTH DEVELOPMENT

In the late 1970's and early 1980's, attempts to build youth leadership became prominent, along with job training and federal programs related to youth development. Student voice in this tradition focuses on building the individual skills of "disadvantaged" young people, with a larger goal of producing a generation of young leaders equipped to participate in society (Johnson, 1991). Job training programs, schools and recreation centers started "student involvement projects" aimed at giving young people the experience of speaking out, participating, and planning together for action. But student voice in this tradition is not about changing institutions or about the specific messages conveyed through student voices.

CRITICAL PEDAGOGY

In the late 1980's, a second tradition of student voice focused on shifting the power dynamics of classrooms, schools and communities to allow disempowered groups to voice their experiences. One dimension of oppression is lack of acknowledgment that certain systems oppress groups of people. Thus, one way to combat powerlessness and to become liberated is to name oppressive conditions and realities (Freire, 1970, 1998).

Within the field of education, a substantial body of literature emerged about legitimizing student voice in a classroom setting. This approach rested on the realization that entire realms of experience fail to become legitimized by school curriculum and practice. Individual teachers would try to equalize the power relationships between their students and themselves by using a problem-posing or critical pedagogy (Darder, 1991; Díaz-Greenberg, 1997; Shor, 1992, 1996). A body of literature on "silence" and "silencing" was accompanied by the development of classroom pedagogies for inviting student voice, building upon student experience in the curriculum and legitimizing the experiences and traditions of students (Cummins, 1989; Fine, 1991). These pedagogies were allied with the movement for multicultural curriculum and for constructivist models of instruction. Many teachers approach their curriculum and classroom teaching through these lenses (Olsen and Mullen, 1990).

THE DEMOCRATIC SCHOOLS MOVEMENT

A third kind of movement for student voice grew from the democratic schools movement and the movements for responsible citizenry on social issues (Allen, 1995; Kreisberg, 1992; Olsen, 1986; Wood, 1992). For most people in this movement, student voice is an essential component of preparing students for participation in a democratic society, often by involving them in studying and acting upon the most pressing social issues of their time. Sometimes, these issues are linked to curriculum about the Holocaust, nuclear arms race or the environment. Students engage in critical thinking, explore how they can "make a difference" and seek to become activists. This movement often cites public schools as vehicles for developing an educated citizenry, but interestingly, this branch of the student voice movement has been strongest in private and suburban public schools.

STUDENT VOICE AND SCHOOL CHANGE

Even with two decades of traditions of student voice behind us, the school reform movement has suffered from a remarkable lack of activity in seeking and using student voice. As JoBeth Allen (1995) notes:

"Rarely is the perspective of the student herself explored. Nowhere is this silence more ringing than in the area of decision-making...children must be encouraged to voice their concerns, opinions and plans as learners; to discuss decisions; to talk and act like citizens in a democracy."

California Tomorrow's approach to using student voice for equity-centered reform draws upon elements of all of the above traditions, then adds an additional component: student voice is used to inform and develop the capacity of our teaching force, the majority of whom simply do not have the knowledge they need about their students' lives and experiences. Our strategies aim to create opportunities for students to speak and teachers to hear. Then, we help design ways in which teachers and students can work together to create schools that will result in higher achievement for all students.

In fact, we believe that student voice can counteract some of the failures of reform, such as efforts that have fallen flat because reformers didn't understand enough about their students to shape the most effective strategies.

Students can be a powerful force for reform if their voices are brought to bear at the right time and in the right ways. Schools that employ regular, multiple, formal mechanisms and forums in which teachers and administrators invite student voice will reap multiple benefits over the long-term. Drawing students into the conversation will shift planning and decision-making from adult-centered talk to a more inclusive way of viewing school reform.

Students can be a powerful force for reform if their voices are brought to bear at the right time and in the right ways.

GETTING STARTED

To use the strategies in this chapter effectively, you need to start with a solid understanding of your particular school context. Before you start organizing a student panel or interviewing students, reflect on your school's culture and history—factors that shape your campus' capacity for inviting and responding to student voice. If you haven't been at your school long, enlist the help of those who have. Use the following activities to assess your school's history with student voice, the current climate around student voice, and the kinds of skills your school community possesses for deepening work on student voice.

ACTIVITY 5.1
OUR SCHOOL'S HISTORY WITH STUDENT VOICE

Think back over your own history with the school or assemble a small group of people who have been at the school for a long time who are willing to talk openly with you. First, think about what events, mechanisms or approaches the school has used in the past that involved inviting or using student voice. List these efforts, then ask these questions of each effort:

- Which types of students did this effort involve? Student leaders? Language minority/immigrant students? Students of color?

- What was the effort's main purpose(s)? Skill-building among students? Decision-making? What kinds of decisions allowed for student involvement? Input for faculty? Informing the faculty?

- What impact did the effort have?

- What was the response from teachers and students at the school?

Then, consider, in general, whether or not your school had positive experiences with student voice:

- What made student voice work?

- Are there lessons to be learned from failed experiments in student voice?

- Which types of students were drawn into the process?

ACTIVITY 5.2
OUR SCHOOL'S CLIMATE FOR STUDENT VOICE

To assess your school's current climate around student voice, use the following prompts. This activity can be done as an individual reflection, think-pair-share activity, or small group discussion.

☛ The percentage of our faculty eager to hear student voice in order to better understand student experience is...

☛ What most teachers at our school would say about eliciting student voice is...

☛ We often don't consider our students' experiences when...

☛ The best ways to find out about student experiences is...

ACTIVITY 5.3
ASSESSING OUR READINESS:
HOW SUPPORTIVE AND PREPARED IS OUR SCHOOL TO RESPOND TO STUDENT VOICE?

As an individual reflection or group activity, use the following assessment to check how ready and willing your school is to invite student voice and to respond positively. Consider each element in terms of how close or how far your school is from having the conditions that will support student voice. Use the center column to describe what you actually see in your school, your evidence for your assessment, and all comments. If you are working as a group, each person should do his or her own assessment first and then compare notes in a general discussion. Based on this assessment, select your highest priority in creating a school that seeks, listens and responds to student voice.

RESPONSIVE SCHOOLS INVITE AND RESPOND TO STUDENT VOICE

Not Supportive/Not Prepared for Student Voice	Evidence/Comments	Supportive/Prepared for Student Voice
• Student voice is not elicited.		• There are regular, multiple, formal mechanisms and forums where teachers are able to hear students speak about their concerns and experiences in school.
• When teachers hear student comments or voices, they generally discount them, consider them irrelevant, too biased or "obvious."		• Student voice is listened to with respect and consideration; there is basic trust that students are being honest and authentic.
• Adult/staff concerns and viewpoints shape the agenda for decision-making and planning.		• Student voice is an integral part of the improvement process at the school; student voice is a form of data that is systematically cycled into decision-making and planning.
• Students do not generally receive information about school reform options, deliberations and decisions.		• Students routinely receive information about considered changes, reform options and decisions; material is available in their primary language.
• Individual teachers may use constructivist teaching approaches or student involvement in classroom decision-making, but this is up to the individual teacher and such activities do not go beyond the classroom.		• There is a collaborative emphasis on constructivist teaching approaches across the curriculum; professional development and support in using such teaching approaches is ongoing.
• Immigrant and language minority students are not involved in decision-making bodies at the school; such students face significant barriers to involvement in student leadership.		• Formal processes exist to recruit and support the involvement of language minority students in student government and other student decision-making bodies.

ACTIVITY 5.4
IMAGINING STUDENT VOICE IN OUR SCHOOL

When educators imagine doing student voice activities at school, they often think about what could go right and what could go wrong. Articulate these nightmares and fantasies early on, either individually or in a group, so that you can consciously aim to create the fantasies and avoid the nightmares.

To begin, draw a line down the center of a sheet of paper. Label one column "Nightmares," the other, "Fantasies." Imagine what could go wrong as you explore student voice, as well as what positive changes could take place if student voice really worked. Think about the concerns people at your school have about student voice, the kinds of protections you might need to create, and the possible pitfalls you might face. If working within a group, share these thoughts and discuss the implications for how to invite student voice for your school. Hold onto your list of nightmares and fantasies so you can keep them in mind as you proceed. A sample list:

Nightmares	*Fantasies*
We would tune out student voices.	We would really listen to students and hear new things.
Some or most of us would disbelieve or dismiss what students said.	Student voice would make a positive difference in our school.
We'd believe students—but not know what to do next.	Students and teachers would feel empowered.
Actions would backfire and set us back in the change process.	Actions would move us forward in obvious ways.
Students and teachers would close down and tune each other out.	Student voice would change hearts and minds.
We wouldn't ask the right students, or all the students, or ask the right questions.	We would start to use student voice all the time—not just once.
The work would not be worth it, or it would be irrelevant to our other efforts.	Our change efforts would truly address students' needs.

ACTIVITY 5.5
BUILDING AN APPETITE FOR STUDENT VOICE

To brainstorm questions to ask students, use this activity to spark your own thinking or promote discussion within a faculty group. Have each person write or reflect on the following prompts:

☛ Think about a student you know fairly well who is an English Language Learner. Choose, perhaps, a student who did particularly well, one who troubled or worried you because he/she didn't do well, or one that you befriended.

☛ Write a little about your student. Why did he/she come to mind? What is special about that student? What "worked" or "didn't work" for him/her in school?

☛ What do you wish you could ask that student? How has his/her school experience been disappointing? Conversely, how has school been a good, supportive experience?

☛ Share what you wish you could ask that student with each other.

USING STUDENT VOICE STRATEGIES

How does a school begin to include student voice in its decision-making and planning processes? How can the results of student voice inquiries be systematically cycled into school-wide examination of data?

To answer these questions, you need to understand your school context: what will move one school to change might only create resentment at another; what works for a high school might need to be modified for a middle school; while one school seeks to work on whole-school issues, another may want to explore students' classroom experiences in depth.

Several approaches for delving into student experience are outlined ahead. Advocates in all schools should have them at their fingertips. You can use multiple strategies to invite and respond to student voice. Your choice should be deliberate—the right method for the right time—and should take place when the "listeners" are prepared to act upon what they hear.

When should you invite student voice?

🌿 As part of every inquiry process, as a means of deepening understanding.

🌿 Whenever you or a faculty group are considering making changes in the school.

🌿 As part of or a prelude to professional development, to set the context and provide some new information.

🌿 As part of program evaluation.

🌿 When faculty members seek a focus among many reform ideas.

Begin with a map: which students do you want to hear from?

For any of the above purposes, you must first consider which students you need to hear from. For example, which students will be affected by the plans you are considering? Which different student perspectives will give you the broadest understanding?

To discover which students you need to reach, you may want to work with a small group to "map" the student population as it relates to the problem or challenge you hope to understand.

Here are two examples:

Marshall High School wanted to address low grades, dipping test scores and poor attendance among its 9th graders. Because teachers were well aware that the 9th grade is a problem year because of the transition from middle school, they tried adding some counseling components. But a small group of teachers felt they needed to dig deeper to understand why achievement patterns were chronically poor. They wanted to hear from the students themselves, so they used the mapping technique to figure out which students they needed to reach:

> *"Some 9th graders are doing well and others are not. We need to hear from those who are doing well to get a sense of whether they have some supports that the others don't. We also need to hear from those who are not doing well to find out what is going on with them."*

> *"African American and Latino students are scoring particularly low in the 9th grade. We need to be sure to hear from them."*

> *"Maybe we should find out whether kids from one of our feeder middle schools are doing better than kids from the others—maybe the answer had to do with differing preparation for high school."*

"We may need to talk with 10th graders, who can look back on the 9th-grade year to give us perspective about what they were dealing with then and what happens as they move on to 10th grade."

The teachers ended up designing a set of fishbowls (discussions among a small group of students that teachers would listen in on) and focus groups to hear from these different groups of students.

Alisal High School wanted to move forward with reform, but faculty had little focus among the many circulating ideas. Teachers decided that they needed to hear from a cross-section of students to get a sense of which issues were most important.

"We certainly need representation across the 9th through 12th grades."

"We also should have college prep students, and jocks, and student government students—those are three really different groups."

After the teachers used a prompt that asked students to write about the different kinds of students on campus, the faculty was able to add several new categories to the list:

"There's like three different schools here: the college kids, the regular kids, and the ESL kids."

"You have to get some kids who have just come here, and some kids who were born here."

"The different gang kids—Norteño, Sureño…and the cholos."

Based on these responses and others, the faculty designed a set of focus groups to explore the range of students' experiences.

CONSIDERING WHICH APPROACHES TO USE

While all approaches to inviting student voice are useful, each has distinct drawbacks and benefits. Besides weighing the pros and cons, you'll need to think about how to protect students and ensure confidentiality, particularly if they'll be addressing subjects that arouse adults' anxiety or hostility. Consider, too, the level of intimacy or direct contact you'll need between students and teachers if one of your primary considerations is to inspire and motivate the faculty to change. The following chart may help you select the best approach in terms of student safety, intimacy and adult receptivity:

COMPARING DIFFERENT STUDENT VOICE APPROACHES

Student Voice Approach	*Benefits/Drawbacks*
Focus Groups	**BENEFITS:** Students feed on each other's comments, and you can get more depth than in written forms of response; can get responses from many students in the time it would take to interview just one; students like to talk. Great way to get overall themes and patterns, to get sense of priorities, to get reactions to ideas, to hear students' words. **DRAWBACKS:** Time- and labor-intensive to set up; lose individual stories and detail; sometimes unusual experiences don't get expressed because of peer pressure to discuss shared concerns.
Surveys and Questionnaires	**BENEFITS:** Relatively easy to administer; can get responses from many more students than through interviews or focus groups; anonymous responses can provide more protection for students and sometimes more honest response. Good for finding out the extent of a problem, for getting responses across large numbers of students. **DRAWBACKS:** Any written form of response is harder for students and often yields less depth and "meat" than formats where they talk; surveys often not taken seriously by students; restricted to forced choice or relatively simple responses. Can be difficult to design a good questionnaire.
Quick-Writes (quickly and informally written responses to a given prompt)	**BENEFITS:** Easy to administer; takes little time; can get lots of students' responses; encourages writing; can be done across multiple classrooms without any particular teacher skill; responses are in students' words (compared to surveys in which they choose prewritten responses). Good for getting responses to specific prompts. **DRAWBACKS:** Sometimes what students have to say is filtered and limited by their writing ability and comfort; restricted to a single prompt.

Panels	**BENEFITS:** Real students talking to real teachers—the face-to-face contact can be powerful; somewhat protected format for students; responses are in the voices of students.
	DRAWBACKS: Students can become shy or intimidated by the face-to-face "in-front-of-the-room" format; teachers need to be prepared to listen respectfully.
Shadowing and Observing	**BENEFITS:** Allows teachers to really see and feel what a student's day and life are like in a school; offers more holistic cues into student experience than a report from a student about their experience.
	DRAWBACKS: This is a one-on-one activity, very labor-intensive; hard for many teachers to participate or for any teacher to shadow or observe numerous students.
Fishbowls (when a few people have a discussion, often in response to a prompt, while others listen in)	**BENEFITS:** Less structured and less scary than a panel, but allows teachers to see students and hear them talk; the discussion nature of a fishbowl allows students to feed off each other and for the facilitator to probe for deeper responses; requires less preparation than a panel.
	DRAWBACKS: Allows less depth of individual stories than interviews or panels.
Interviews	**BENEFITS:** Good for getting individual stories and perspectives in depth, for reconstructing someone's experiences and history, for eliciting perspectives about an issue, etc. Can be more comfortable and often powerful for students because they are talking to a real person (compared to surveys); more revealing than surveys or questionnaires because of depth of response and opportunities for follow-up questions; more chance for individual voices than focus groups or panels; can create powerful connections between the teacher and student.
	DRAWBACKS: Very labor-intensive; interviews take a lot of time to prepare, conduct and analyze.

CONDITIONS FOR SPEAKING AND LISTENING

On the surface, student voice activities seem relatively benign and straightforward. In truth, they tap into deep feelings within students and teachers—feelings rooted in the power dynamics of schools, in the frustrations of being a teacher or student in public institutions that are not structured to support either, and in the overwhelming nature of a system that often tracks and warehouses students.

Mixed media by Iris Arrieta, a high school student from Peru

It can be risky for students to speak out about what they experience in school. What they have to say may not be easy to hear. There are real power dynamics at work. In school, students' behavior is regulated, their work is graded, and support is meted out by teachers. Students can be disciplined, suspended or flunked. Inviting student voice may be painful and risky for teachers as well. Teachers, for their part, are evaluated by their administrators. For student voice to be a powerful tool in improving our schools, we have to carefully structure conditions that make it safe for students to speak and teachers to listen. When one student was invited to be part of a fishbowl in front of teachers, he said:

> *"Honest? I don't believe they want to hear what I have to say about discrimination and stuff, 'cause then they have to do something about it. They won't listen. I get up there and try to say this shit, and they'll cover up their ears, you wait and see! It's like a wall, built to keep out what we got to say. And if we break through that wall, all hell could break loose. Naw, I have to stay in this school. I have to come back tomorrow. I'm not going to put myself out there like that."*

Remember, too, that voice does not exist simply because someone speaks. Real "voicing" depends on being heard. Teachers, too often blamed for schools' shortcomings, can only hear what students say after measures have been taken to make them feel safe, too. Many teachers know there are students they have failed or been unable to reach; many are aware they've made mistakes but don't want them known publicly. What's more, teachers who work hard, who pour their lives into teaching, feel even more overwhelmed when confronted with what is still wrong in schools. All these burdens can make teachers resistant to student voice.

It's crucial to establish guidelines that ensure safety and respect. For starters, a school may want to use an outside facilitator or an insider whom students trust to pose the question: What would help make you feel safe, respected and supported in speaking to teachers about your experiences at school? Teachers, too, need a trusted person to ask them what conditions would help them to feel safe and respected during sessions in which students speak about school.

What students and teachers need in terms of safety will help you determine whether you are better off pursuing one-on-one interviews, surveys or Quick-Writes with their relative anonymity, or panels and fishbowls in which teachers and students have face-to-face contact.

In interviews, assurances of confidentiality are always important. Students must be told that they have the right to not answer a question. Before students are even invited to be part of an interview, they should know its purpose and that it is different from the normal adult-student relations in school (for example, the interview is not a counseling session, a means to monitor behavior, etc.). When students understand how their voices can inform adults about a problem, they are generally eager to help.

In California Tomorrow's work, we always ask teachers who go into a student voice forum to keep their hearts open for at least one truth or idea that touches them. After students stop speaking, we immediately ask teachers to pair up with one another to share that revelation. This exercise sets a tone of legitimacy for student voice and begins the response session with a sense of connection.

Here are some ways that schools have set conditions of safety and respect:

At **Alisal High School,** students who presented to faculty felt that several ground rules would help:

🕯 Teachers would be instructed to simply listen; students would be allowed to share their reflections and focus group findings without being interrupted.

🕯 Students who spoke about student concerns would be understood to be reporting on aggregate findings from the focus groups, not necessarily their own opinions.

🕯 Students would have a chance to practice what they wanted to say in the actual room so the setting would feel familiar.

In return, Alisal faculty asked that the following conditions be set for their own protection:

🕯 Individual teachers would not be identified. Instead, a student could say "an English teacher" or "a teacher I once had."

In **Hayward**, immigrant students presenting as a panel during a community forum had different concerns. Students asked that:

❧ The panel would be in a question-and-answer format and they would be given time beforehand to reflect and brainstorm as a group about their responses to the questions.

❧ They would have the choice to answer in Spanish or English, knowing that a translator was available.

❧ There would be an adult moderator whom they trusted, in case questions from adults seemed hostile or compromising.

Remember, students often need encouragement that you indeed want them to tell you what isn't working. Once they believe that, they often open a floodgate of information that will touch you and deepen your understanding in ways that little else can.

GIVING THE FINDINGS LEGITIMACY AS DATA

California Tomorrow believes that student voices are an accurate and powerful form of data. But we're aware, too, that some audiences dismiss students or believe that their stories are "moving but anecdotal." Faculty who are supportive of the student voice approach can counter by treating student voices as "real data."

Here's how: Some forms of student voice—focus groups, panels, or interviews—seem less like "data" than others, such as surveys (which can be tallied and presented as numbers). Thus, it is critical that the findings from these less quantitative forms of student voice be presented as data in the form of trends, patterns or themes. One way to emphasize findings as data is to produce a handout that lists the findings along with sample quotes and some indication of how widespread each finding appears to be.

PRESENTING STUDENT VOICE FINDINGS: A SAMPLE HANDOUT

The following handout shows how the results of student voice activities—in this case, a set of focus groups at Alisal High School—can be presented as "real data."

FINDINGS OF THE FOCUS GROUPS

We held twelve focus group discussions in classrooms throughout the school. A total of 260 students participated. The opening prompt was: What do you want your teachers to know about the student experience at this school so that they can help improve our education?

Major Finding: A Cycle of Low Expectations

The most common thing students spoke about in every focus group was a destructive cycle of lower and lower expectations. Many students blamed students and teachers equally for the low performance in this school. Teachers are not demanding and students are not motivated. The more students feel that teachers don't care, the less they are motivated to work. The less they work, the less teachers care and the less they expect from students. Some sample comments:

"Students are lazy here and teachers don't take teaching here seriously. It's one big problem."

"Students at our school just think about getting by and being average. We're also treated like we're barely average—or worse. It's what they expect of us."

"The students and the teachers here just give in to the reputation that our school sucks."

"Our school's like a big factory assembly line—huge crowds just moving through school. And if you need a little extra time for something, or a little extra help, too bad. Just move right along. And no one notices you unless you do something really bad, really out there. It just makes you feel like no one cares. And then you stop caring."

"When you get a teacher that really cares about whether you are learning it's so great— you learn so much. Caring means that he makes us stay after school if we are getting below a C in his class. But it's not punishment. When we stay after school he helps us catch up. He really believes we can do it."

HOW STUDENTS CONTRIBUTE TO THE CYCLE

We heard many, many comments about how students have low expectations for themselves and what they can do in life. They don't seem to understand the implications of not going to school or of not doing well. Many students talk about feeling despair and no hope.

"Some students feel that we [Latinos] could make it without school."

"Students don't feel like they have a future. They really feel there is nowhere to go, so why try?"

"The students here don't believe that they ever could go to college. They don't ever really believe they can graduate."

HOW TEACHERS CONTRIBUTE TO THE CYCLE

Many students commented on low teacher expectations, teachers who don't push students or check on how they are doing, and teachers who just give up or don't try to teach.

"I have a teacher who says, 'Oh well, this is just Alisal. What do you expect?'"

"Teachers don't push enough and check enough. They let kids lag. It's not OK to just let students lag and fail."

"We have tutorials, but many of my teachers have not used the tutorials to help students catch up or push them. I have some who just sit and read the newspaper."

STUDENT VOICE APPROACHES

The following six approaches—student focus groups, panels and presentations, shadowing and observing students, in-depth interviews, surveys and questionnaires, Quick-Writes and Tea Parties—can all be used to invite student voice. The rest of this chapter focuses on how to use these approaches, with examples of how schools have used them effectively.

STUDENT FOCUS GROUPS

Student focus groups are a powerful if somewhat complicated approach that can provide far more depth than questionnaires or surveys. Creating focus groups also captures more diverse perspectives than relying on input from an already established student leadership group. Two kinds of focus groups exist: the first type helps you to identify and prioritize issues; the second helps you mine issues for deeper meaning.

Unlike a survey, in which results can be tabulated and shared on paper, a focus group is basically a form of discussion. You'll need to think about how to combine the findings from all the focus groups in order to communicate the information to others. A small group of students is often the best means to communicate with school faculty. While the focus groups themselves should include a wide range of students, select those student "communicators" who seem most capable of hearing, reflecting upon, and then articulating what their peers have told them. We also recommend that a faculty sponsor or other adult oversee the complex process of creating student focus groups.

HOW TO CREATE A FOCUS GROUP

🖜 *First, clarify your purpose for doing a focus group.* For example, do you need help in deciding on a proposed change within the school (e.g., a move to block scheduling)? Are you aiming to inform teachers about how students feel so that teachers can be more responsive? Or are you trying to identify problems that might need specific attention?

🖜 *Figure out how you are going to present findings from the focus groups.* If you simply want a list of concerns or issues, you need not worry about writing down students' actual words. But if you want some kind of "alive" presentation that presents findings in students' own voices, you may need to follow up with a panel presentation, slide show or a written report with students' quotes. If you need a clear picture of priorities or some idea of how widespread certain perspectives may be, you'll need to supplement the focus group with a survey or other quantifiable approach.

🖜 *Select and prepare a small group of students who will attend all group meetings, help lead discussions, summarize what they've heard and present the information.* An ideal group should be small (3-6 students). Pick students who are interested, articulate, good listeners who are also able to miss class. These student "leaders" have a big job to do; California Tomorrow often pays a stipend or honorarium for their time. In some cases, schools have arranged extra academic credit as a research or leadership project.

Make sure your student group represents the spectrum of students affected by whatever issue you're probing (e.g., students at different grade levels, from both genders, or from different ethnic or academic backgrounds). The outcome of your focus group will be more authentic if its participants come from different sectors of the student population.

Before your students begin leading the focus groups, you may want to engage them in a one- or two-hour discussion, a small-scale focus group of sorts, about the issues. This "preview" gives students a chance to talk about the roles they'll play in the focus group, for instance, leading, listening or documenting. Here are some examples of how students can fill their roles during this trial run:

☞ One or two student leaders may start off by presenting the purpose, process and questions for discussion.

☞ One student may assist the faculty sponsor in charge of facilitating the discussion.

☞ At least two student leaders should take notes during the discussion.

Furthermore, all students are free to ask questions at any time to clarify or get more information.

To prepare for the actual groups, have your students brainstorm a list of ten possible questions for each major topic. Also, ask them to brainstorm strategies for what to do if students don't talk. Reassure them that if discussion slows, you (the adult/teacher) will help out.

✿ **Now it's time for the actual student focus group discussions.** Arrange for a class session in at least four or five classrooms that differ from one another in grade level or student composition. The teachers should tell students in these classes ahead of time about the topics and purpose of the discussion. To get the class discussion going, here's what focus group leaders can do:

☞ Introduce the student focus group leaders.

☞ Describe the purpose of the focus group, for example, "You can help us (the teachers, administrators, school district, community, etc.) to understand what school is like for students and what needs to be changed." To keep discussion on track, hang a poster that lists the topic's major questions.

☞ Describe the process and how you'll run the class session (e.g., first a discussion about four major topics, then a survey).

☞ Start with the first question. Ask it generally, then use follow-up questions for more depth. Encourage the class to give lots of detail by saying, "Tell me more," or "Can you give me an example?" After about ten minutes, go to the next topic. If a really great discussion is going on, it's fine to stick with one topic and not get to the others. Be sure to stop the discussion when you have ten minutes left in the period so you have time to wrap it up.

➤ Thank the teacher and students in the class. Tell them that after the process is complete, you'll be back to inform them of the conclusions you'll be presenting to the faculty, district, committees, and so on.

🍃 *Figure out how you want to document the student discussions.* Because taking good notes is hard for most students, they will need help in learning what is important to write down. For the first two discussion groups, an adult should take "wall notes" to show by example. Then two students can take notes after that in their notebooks. These sets of notes, all together, will serve as the main record of the discussion.

It's a good idea for an adult to also keep notes of the discussion so that he or she can prompt the student communicator team in a debriefing session. Taping the session is discouraged for several reasons: students often become self-conscious; recording quality of a classroom discussion is frequently poor; and it can be time-consuming to transcribe the tape.

After *each* discussion group, ask the student leaders to spend about ten to fifteen minutes away from class to debrief what they heard in their own group. What were the major concerns raised? What really stood out? Are certain themes emerging? You might want to ask students to write in a journal about what they heard, especially memorable or unexpected comments that people made.

🍃 *Analyze what you've found across the student focus groups.* Work with the student leaders to go back over their notes and journal entries. Quantify the surveys, if you did any, and agree on the major findings.

🍃 *Supplement the focus group with a survey of the entire student population*, if you wish. For example, if the focus groups revealed real tensions between newcomer students and others, a school-wide survey could reveal how commonplace certain experiences are, or whether all grade levels are affected equally. Or you may want to supplement the focus group with a Quick-Write activity in classes throughout the school. Such an exercise will provide the student communicator team with more quotes to illustrate the findings.

🍃 *Prepare the presentation.* If student leaders present their findings on a panel, they should have written notes that include major findings and quotes from other students. Practice is important. Allow students to practice their presentation in the actual room where the event will occur. If they have never used a microphone, they will need practice. To create visual aids, choose some favorite quotes from the student discussions or Quick-Writes and post them on large charts.

VARIATION ON FOCUS GROUPS: AN APPROACH TO BRAINSTORMING AND PRIORITIZING

Using the same general format described above, student focus group leaders can ask a classroom to generate a list of answers to a question, then have everyone vote for various answers to prioritize issues. Here's how this variation works:

☙ A student leader or facilitator poses a question and asks students to brainstorm all the answers they think are important. Students simply state a response and it gets listed, with no accompanying discussion at this point.

☙ After the list of answers has been compiled, the facilitator goes through the responses one by one. For each answer, the facilitator asks the class to explain or discuss until everyone feels he or she understands.

☙ Once all the items have meaning for the group, the facilitator goes through the list and simply asks for votes for each item. Ideally, every student casts three votes, but don't worry if someone votes for four or only two. The answers that garner the most votes can be considered the highest priorities or strongest answers to a problem.

EXAMPLE: A faculty committee on student achievement was puzzled over why so few students complete the required number of books needed to pass 10th-grade English. They posed this question to a focus group of students in four English classes. Here's how one class responded:

"Kids don't know about the requirement until it's too late."

"The English level of the books is too hard for the kids who aren't fluent English readers."

"Too much homework collectively from all the subjects."

"A lot of kids have to work after school."

"Kids are lazy."

"The books are boring and kids don't like them."

"There aren't enough copies of the books in the library."

In clarifying meaning, the students discussed in detail what they meant by "The books are boring and kids don't like them" and "Kids are lazy." In the process, they generated very important information for the teachers about what students feel is relevant in curriculum and their feelings of invisibility and lack of connectedness to the curriculum. They also engaged in a spirited discussion with each other about student "laziness" that unlocked perspectives about students who "get away with doing nothing," as well as a desire for teachers to push students more.

By the end, the three answers with the most votes were: "The books are boring and kids don't like them," "Kids don't know about the requirement until it's too late," and "There aren't enough copies of the books in the library." Needless to say, the session gave important direction to the faculty.

STUDENT FOCUS GROUPS: ONE SCHOOL'S EXPERIENCE

Student focus groups at Alisal High School in Salinas, California, helped spark a three-year comprehensive reform effort. For many years, the faculty, which numbered more than eighty, entertained lots of innovative ideas, but shared little coherent vision. One idea seemed as good as another—until these adults stopped to listen to their students.

As part of a California Tomorrow project to assist the school in becoming "immigrant responsive," project staff decided to create focus groups and a student panel to engage the faculty and administration in listening to students' experiences. Specifically, we wanted the conversation to center on student achievement and educational programs.

A group of six students was selected to represent the range of students at Alisal: immigrant newcomers and students born in Salinas, as well as college-track students and students who were marginally connected to the school. We also chose ninth through twelfth graders. These student focus group leaders conducted sessions in classrooms ranging from Advanced Placement to mainstream to ESL. They took notes, analyzed their findings and presented their peers' concerns to teachers and counselors, who were instructed to simply *listen*.

The students shared a litany of hopes and fears. Many of Alisal's young people felt overburdened by outside duties, such as afterschool jobs, that often kept them from completing homework. Others were disappointed that teachers had low expectations of them. Some lamented intergroup relations on campus, with ESL students feeling especially isolated from the rest of the students.

Visibly moved, teachers left the session determined to address the concerns raised. The school forged a new 98-minute block schedule format that included tutorials, as well as an advisory period that grouped students across grade levels and language proficiency levels. To provide more opportunity for important human connections to form between students and teachers, students switched to having three teachers each semester, instead of six. The school also began systematic efforts to incorporate ESL students into all aspects of school life.

School staff credit the student focus groups and panel for motivating them. Paul Quiggle, a science teacher and reform leader at the school commented:

"Something shifted. The talk about students became much more positive. More of us began looking at students from the perspective of what they need and what we should do. Before the project, the talk was more about teachers."

The power of student voice really took at Alisal. A year after the formal project work with California Tomorrow ended, the school decided to use student focus groups again, along with surveys, to solicit student insights into the school's poor student achievement and the low number of graduates prepared for higher education. Mamie Chow-Wang, a California Tomorrow staff member working with the students for the first time, was impressed:

"The students had so much to say when given the chance to speak without judgment."

"The students had so much to say when given the chance to speak without judgment. They were willing to share their personal struggles with home, family, friends, even school. I was deeply impressed by their desire to achieve academically and personally."

This time, the students prepared for focus groups by looking at well-known theories about minority student achievement. They talked about how some students of color resist behaviors commonly associated with being "white," such as carrying books, doing all your homework or running for student council. They talked about bilingualism and the process of "Americanization." They moved from there to examining data which compared Alisal with other predominantly Latino schools as well as with "white schools." Finally, they saw data for their own school that showed how few students were fulfilling requirements to get into college and how many freshmen were not completing credits and were, thus, not able to graduate in four years. Dismayed by what they learned, the students decided that "every student should see this data." So they did—every student in every classroom they worked with received real data on Alisal.

As the students prepared for their panel, it was clear they were proud and excited to be part of the process of change in their school. They led

focus groups in classrooms across the school and also surveyed students. Before the panel presentation in front of their teachers, they were nervous. But, in the end, they eloquently and passionately conveyed the voices of their peers. The faculty listened with some apprehension and a great deal of compassion. It was clear that the seven young people on the panel had become aware of the compelling power and presence of their voices.

STUDENT PANELS AND PRESENTATIONS

Student panels and presentations can also be done without a lengthy focus group process beforehand. During a panel, 3 to 6 students sit in front of a group of faculty to respond to prompts or questions on a particular issue. Panels are powerful face-to-face formats for students to address their teachers, but preparation is essential because of the intimidating, high visibility, high stakes format. Students must feel that they'll be able to speak freely without risk.

As with focus groups, student panels should have an adult sponsor who works with the presenters, then moderates the panel or presentation. Some guidelines for creating a panel:

- Select students who are willing to take the risk of speaking before adults about their experiences.

- Meet with the students before the panel to review the purpose of the panel and think about the kinds of questions they want posed to them.

- Ask the students the type of questions that will be used on the panel and let them talk privately as a group about their responses. Then give them an opportunity to jot down some notes about what they want to say.

- Give the students a chance to see the room where the panel will be held, to practice with a microphone if needed, to sit on the stage or in the front and get a feel for the space before the actual panel begins.

- Check with the students about whether they'd be willing to take questions from the audience. If so, decide beforehand upon a signal students can use with the moderator if they feel attacked, undermined or uncomfortable. The moderator, normally an adult working with the students, should commit to intervening in case such a situation occurs.

❧ Set up the panel so students are allowed to speak fully before they take any responses or questions from the audience.

A STUDENT PANEL HELD AT A COMMUNITY FORUM

Community forums were held in Hayward as part of a multi-year project to create more immigrant-responsive high schools. These evening meetings brought together community organizations that serve the immigrant population in Hayward, the colleges and universities in the region, and people from throughout the school district. At several of these forums, we also used student panels to showcase student voice.

The first community forum highlighted a panel of nine high school students, ninth to twelfth graders, assembled to share their experiences in Hayward schools. Their lives differed, ranging from that of a Chicano born in Hayward to an immigrant who arrived in the United States only nine months ago.

The panel was organized and moderated by project staff member Zaida McCall-Perez, who had spent hours working with the students. The students were honest and articulate in sharing their thoughts and experiences regarding learning English as a second language, the relations between Chicanos and immigrant Latino students, the help they have received from teachers, and the frustrations they have endured.

Early in the panel, Carolina, an articulate high school student, set the tone by speaking honestly about the frustrations of not knowing English:

"I spent six years in Mexican schools and it was difficult to come here. I was in higher classes in Mexico than here because I can't read English. We come, we know the subject but we don't get put in the class where we can learn something new. It's not fair. There are some teachers here who really do a good job and help students get a good education. But there are some who think that because we don't understand their English, we do not know anything. That we are stupid. It is hard that they think we are stupid."

Evangelina, another student from the same school, added:

"When I first came here, it was so hard to explain things to the teacher. I couldn't say what I think, and I thought then that my dreams could never be. When I came, everyday, I felt anguish. People from our own country just see us as lower and if you ask someone who knows Spanish and English to help, they don't. They just turn their backs because they are afraid to speak Spanish and think their friends won't like them. Now that I have learned their language and customs, they want to be with me, but that's very sad what I went through before."

The panel pondered the split relations between Chicanos and Latino immigrants. Corinna, a leader in the Latino Club at her high school, has tried to organize activities that involve both immigrants and Chicanos. She said:

"It's really hard to get Latinos and Chicanos together. Immigrants have different points of view from Chicanos and don't get along with them, and Chicanos don't get along with immigrants. Immigrants and Chicanos don't understand that we are on the same side. We need to get together."

All nine students considered what has helped and hindered them in school. Hector, a 12th grader, remembered how difficult it was for him to speak in class and have students laugh when he mispronounced English words. He then gave a wonderful tribute to the difference a teacher can make in these situations:

"The thing that helped me survive and helped me to learn English was Ms. White, sitting over there. She used to tell me I have to keep reading books and to learn English, and she kept helping me so much. It helps when a teacher has patience for us if we don't speak English."

"It helps when a teacher has patience for us if we don't speak English."

The group spoke of wanting classes to help them maintain and develop their Spanish language skills, and to learn Spanish literature and Latino history. One student, Juan Pablo, looked directly into the face of a room full of teachers and said, pointblank:

"We would like our teachers not to be absent."

Amidst the laughter, he went on to explain:

"When substitute teachers come, we just turn in our assignments and we have no explanations and it is hard to learn. Please come to class so we can learn."

The particular challenges facing undocumented immigrant students came up as one student spoke of her friends:

"For some reason it is discouraging. I hear other students saying it is hard to work hard in classes when they are not legal here. They are afraid they will finish high school and will not be able to go to college. So they say, 'Why should I work so hard? What is my future here? I cannot do what I really want to do.'"

A university representative in the audience responded that undocumented students can attend college but are precluded from tuition waivers and financial support that is given to residents. She spoke of a growing network of Latinos and others in the college teaching system that want to help all students to attend college so that they can reach their dreams.

By the end of the forty-five-minute panel, the entire community forum had learned a great deal about the lives of immigrant students in Hayward high schools and were deeply moved—all thanks to the brave students who spoke their minds and shared their lives.

Shadowing and Observing Students

Shadowing a student for an entire school day can be an eye-opening experience for adults involved in a targeted change effort. Viewing school through a young person's eyes often enables you to confirm your beliefs or forces you to reconsider long-held notions about student life in and out of the classroom.

Guidelines for Shadowing Students

These suggestions for student shadowing, which is usually done as part of a larger inquiry, should help you to gain a deeper understanding of what works and what doesn't inside your school.

Shadowing a student for an entire school day can be an eye-opening experience.

❧ First, focus on which group of students to shadow, depending on the nature of your inquiry. Your target group might be large, e.g., all ESL students or all students who are still LEP after six years. Or it could be more narrow, for instance, all 9th graders currently getting D's or F's in Math, or recently mainstreamed Filipino students who are in a pilot, heterogeneous 10th-grade English class.

❧ Select specific students to shadow. Try to have one student and one back-up student (in case the first student is absent) for each adult or teacher who will be shadowing. If more than one adult will be shadowing, choose students who have different class schedules in order to view a wide range of classrooms. Have each teacher meet with their "shadowees" to ask their permission to do the shadowing. (Be sure you've checked first about any district requirements for asking for permission to interview students.) Explain to your student that you aren't shadowing to check on how he or she is doing, but that you want to get a sense of what it is like being a student at the school for a day. Often, students' initial mystification turns into curiosity and happiness at being selected to be shadowed.

❧ Pick a day to do the shadowing, arrange for teachers to substitute for you, and make sure teachers whose classrooms you will be visiting are aware that you will be coming, agree to the visit and understand your purpose (not to observe them, but to shadow the student).

☙ Interview your student briefly in the morning on the day of the actual shadowing. You will want to ask questions that will let you become acquainted with the student, as well as give you some idea of his or her experiences about school. Some examples:

➤ *Feelings about school:* How do you like school? What do you feel when you wake up in the morning and realize it's a school day? Do you usually eat before you get to school? What kind of student are you? What kinds of things are usually on your mind these days on your way to school? During the day? After school?

➤ *Friends:* Tell me about your friends in your classes this semester. What kinds of kids do you hang out with? What do you and your friends like? Do you participate in school activities/clubs? Sports?

➤ *Identity:* How do you describe who you are?

➤ *Personal immigration background:* Where were you born? Where did you emigrate from? How long have you been in the U.S.? Why did you come? How is school here different from school in your native country?

➤ *Language background:* How well do you think you understand and speak English? Do you prefer classes taught in English, or in your native language? What language do you speak mostly with your friends? Your family?

☙ Resist the temptation to shadow a student for only one or two periods or half a day. There is no substitute for a full-day observation, in which you truly get a feel for the ebb-and-flow of your student's day. Anything less will rob you of a chance to see your student at work and play.

☙ Follow your student through all parts of the day, including classes, lunchtime and breaks. Try to walk in your student's shoes as much as you can (eat what they eat, follow the rules for students, sit in the part of the classrooms where they sit, etc.). Your goal is to be as much like a fly on the wall as possible—not to interact with the student, but to witness the day.

☙ Think about what types of observations you'd like to record for later reflection. You may want to use a format for taking notes like the ones on pages 318-319. A few suggestions for what to note:

➤ Draw a picture of how each classroom is arranged, how students sit, and where your student is sitting.

➤ What is it like to sit through the class as a student?

➤ How physically active are students able to be?

- Did you or your student seem to be distracted or disturbed by other students?

- How much were you able to focus on the lesson? How focused did your student and other students seem to be?

- Which language(s) did the teacher, your student and other students mostly use?

- How hungry did you get? How much eating was going on in the classroom?

- Did your student seem to comprehend the lesson or to follow what was happening? Where did the comprehension break down? What seemed to help (if anything)?

- Did your student seem prepared, such as having homework done, bringing a notebook, etc.?

- How varied were the activities and types of instruction or interaction in each class?

- What kind of direct interaction did the student have with the teacher? With other students?

✤ Spend time with your student at the end of the day, when the shadowing has ended, to find out how he or she felt about the day. A short list of questions can help you put the day in context. You might want to ask:

- Was this a typical day? How was this day the same or different from other days?

- How do you usually feel at the end of a school day? Now?

- What was interesting to you today? Boring? Tell me what you learned today.

Discuss, too, any incidents during the day that struck you as exciting, distressing or disruptive—did your student notice and have any reactions?

STUDENT SHADOWING PROJECT
IN-CLASS NOTES

Student Name _____   Period _____
Date _____   Subject _____
Teacher (Shadower) _____   Teacher _____

CLASSROOM INTERACTION ELEMENTS

Sketch the classroom on a piece of paper. Note where your student sits, how other students are seated or grouped.

What does your student bring to class? What materials does he/she have? Does she/he have homework finished, or unfinished? Does he/she have binder, pencil, paper, etc?

What kinds of interactions does your student have with other students? Social interactions? About what? Interactions about the class activities? What is the balance between social and academic interactions? Which languages does your student use? Write verbatim examples, if possible.

What kinds of interactions does your student have with the teacher? Personal? Behavioral? Academic? What is the balance among the interactions? Write verbatim examples, if possible.

How focused were you able to be on the lesson? How focused did your student seem to be on the lesson?

LITERACY ELEMENTS

List the kinds of literacy activities or tasks your student engages in during the period. Also note for how many minutes your student does each. Be specific. For example: "Student reads silently out of text for about 10 minutes" or "Student works on writing a poem for 20 minutes."

How actively engaged is your student in the literacy tasks? What evidence is there for the active engagement?

What other evidence is there in the classroom that literacy is a focus? (Look on walls, in portfolios, in your student's binder, folders, etc.)

STUDENT SHADOWING PROJECT
OUTSIDE-OF-CLASS NOTES

Student Name _____

Date _____

Teacher (Shadower) _____

Before School Notes: Remember to explain to your students that you aren't shadowing them in order to check up on behavior, but just to get a sense of what it is like being a student at this school for a day. Encourage them to do what they would do on any other day, to act natural, and behave as they normally do. Remind them that you really will be with them all day, during class, passing periods, lunch, etc. You might ask the students how they are feeling this morning, what time they went to bed last night, what they ate for breakfast, if they had homework. Note the answers in the space below. You might also describe what the students look like, what they are wearing, how they appear to be feeling—nervous, excited, sleepy, etc.

Lunch and Passing Period Notes: What does your student eat? Drink? With whom does your student talk? Whom does he/she greet? What languages does your student use with friends? Who does he/she hang out with? What else do you notice about this time that is different from the class time for your student?

After School Notes: Spend a little time with your student at the end of the day to find out how the student felt about the day. Things you could ask the student: Was this a typical day? Are most school days like this one? How do you usually feel at the end of a school day? Now? Was anything especially interesting to you today? Boring? What did you learn today? Ask about any incidents in that day that you noticed as possibly particularly exciting or horrible or disruptive. Ask if the student noticed, how they reacted, what they thought, etc.

As with all other methods for eliciting student voice, the key to the utility of the experience lies in how the data from the shadowing is compiled, analyzed and used. After the shadowing experience, take time to reflect on what you saw, using the following questions. If other teachers did shadowing, too, convene as a group for at least two hours to discuss experiences in depth. Groups of shadowers should chart any major themes that emerged. Begin by allowing each person to describe what it felt like to be a student for a day.

General questions to reflect on include:

- What did you see/experience that was a surprise to you?

- What did you see/experience that you expected to see?

- What can you say about student life at the school that you couldn't have said before?

- What did we see in common? What did it tell us about the school?

- How can this information be transmitted to other staff?

- Would you like other staff to shadow, too? If so, why? How could you arrange this?

- What are the next steps?

- How do the results of the shadowing affect the school's reform efforts?

SHADOWING: ONE SCHOOL'S EXPERIENCE

One middle school decided to embark on a shadowing project to investigate literacy on campus. The faculty's concerns centered around a large group of students who had been in U.S. schools since first grade, but who were still struggling with reading and writing in English and were not yet ready to be redesignated as "Fluent English Proficient." The teachers were curious about the classroom experience of these students in relation to literacy. How and where during the day were these students being asked to read or write extensively? How were students reacting?

In this case, teachers who did the shadowing looked at two things: students' experience in the classroom and literacy elements in the classrooms. The previous shadowing form shows how these two factors interacted. In the end, the shadowing led teachers to request intensive training in explicit instruction in reading strategies, such as Reciprocal Teaching. In essence, the shadowing showed teachers that the instruction they had hoped their students were receiving simply wasn't happening.

IN-DEPTH INTERVIEWS

In-depth interviews, which are often part of a larger inquiry or concern at a school, are helpful when your goal is to understand the meaning and complexity of a person's experiences—motivations, perceptions, and viewpoints, for example. Interviews can be helpful in these situations:

🖎 Reconstructing a history of someone's experiences: "What happened...?"

🖎 Eliciting someone's perceptions about an issue: "What do you think...?"

🖎 Understanding someone's experience: "What's it like...?" "Describe..."

🖎 Gaining a sense of someone's emotions about an experience: "How does it feel...?"

If you or your inquiry group chooses to interview many people, analyze the results for common themes and patterns. You may uncover a new set of questions about a "problem" or "challenge" that can be explored through further kinds of data collection, such as surveys, questionnaires or focus groups.

Bear in mind: on the plus side, students are usually far more comfortable and revealing in interviews than in questionnaires or surveys (which require writing) or panels (which are more public). On the minus side, though, interviews are labor-intensive. They require lots of time to prepare, conduct and analyze. In addition to the guidelines for doing interviews that we provide, you may also want to use the guide for student interviews presented in *Through the Golden Door: Effective Educational Approaches for Immigrant Adolescents with Limited Schooling* (Mace-Matluck, Alexander-Kasparik and Queen, in press). You can also refer to the sample interview protocol for long-term LEP students beginning on page 326.

WHOM TO INTERVIEW

🖎 Articulate succinctly (in writing if possible) what challenge or problem you're trying to understand by doing this interview. What will the information help you to do?

🖎 Chart the major concerns that you want to explore as they relate to the problem at hand.

🖎 Think carefully about the types of students you'd like to know more about. Then select students to interview who fit these typologies or characteristics. If working in a group, assign a teacher to interview each type of student. To find students, the teacher may need to collect some data first, such as obtaining a list of all 9th-grade students getting D's and F's, with information about gender and ethnicity included.

❦ Always get parental permission to conduct interviews, even if the information will remain confidential rather than being presented or published. Getting permission also notifies parents that their child may be interviewed. That way, they can step in if they object.

BEFORE THE INTERVIEW: DEVELOPING THE PROTOCOL

❦ Brainstorm several hypotheses that could explain the problem you face. For example, if the problem is low attendance, maybe students have heavy responsibilities at home or work long hours and, thus, have trouble getting to school. Or maybe they find classes too boring and don't see the usefulness of attending regularly.

❦ Draft a set of questions organized by subtopics and hypotheses. Arrange questions in an order that seem to "flow," perhaps from easier to more difficult or thought-provoking questions.

❦ Avoid leading or closed questions. Instead, construct open questions that allow the person maximum freedom to answer from his or her own experiences and perspectives. An example of a closed question: "Many people feel teachers get burned out because of disruptive students in their classroom. Do you agree?" The likely answers are short and closed: "Yes" or "No." Change the question to an open-ended one, such as, "Many people feel that teachers get burned out because of disruptive students in the classroom. What do you think?" Not only does this form of questioning invite more meaningful responses, but it also may lead you to think of additional questions.

❦ Avoid multiple or combination questions. An example of a multiple question is: "Why did you drop out of school and what do you think is the main reason most kids drop out?" Be sure to ask one question at a time.

❦ Decide whether you want a direct, personal question or an indirect, general one. Direct: "Are you satisfied with the help you get from your teachers?" Indirect: "Are teachers doing a good job helping students?"

❦ Think about a way to begin the interview so that the student can frame the problem from his or her own point of view before you start to pursue the questions that probe specific hypotheses. You could start off, for example, by noting that attendance is an issue you're exploring and elicit the student's view, which might be "many kids don't come to school all the time because they have to work."

🌿 Review your questions and ask someone else to check them, too, to make sure there are no leading questions and that you have a sufficient variety of questions (e.g., What's happening...? What do you think...? How do you feel about...? What is it like...? etc.). Revise the interview protocol accordingly.

🌿 If you plan to take notes during the interview (instead of taping), create a protocol sheet that leaves room after each typed question for you to jot down answers.

DURING THE INTERVIEW:

🌿 Explain to the student why you are doing the interview and what you hope to learn.

🌿 Clarify your role in the interview. Especially when teachers interview students, the student may expect the teacher to act as an advisor, monitor, authority figure checking up on the student, and so on. Explain at the beginning that this interview is to help you understand what it's like for that student (and/or students in general), and that you want to do the interview to learn more about what the student experiences and thinks because you feel it will help you to be a better teacher.

🌿 Set guidelines about confidentiality and be sure the student understands them. Will you change the name of the student in talking about this information with other teachers? Does the student have the "right to pass" on any questions asked? Can the student ask for something to be "off the record"?

🌿 If you are taping the interview, ask permission to tape and explain that the student has the right at any point to ask that the tape recorder be turned off. Check that the tape recorder is working properly and test it with the student's voice level.

🌿 Ask your questions, then listen closely. Appreciate this opportunity to get a new perspective on the "challenge" or "problem" you are studying.

🌿 If a student raises some aspect of the topic that you don't have in your interview protocol, be encouraging—he or she may be offering some connection that you haven't thought of yet. Don't be afraid to veer from the protocol.

🌿 Avoid interrupting. Let the student finish before going on to the next question.

🌿 Allow for pause and reflection time after a question has been asked.

Ask your questions, then listen closely. Appreciate this opportunity to get a new perspective on the "challenge" or "problem" you are studying.

❧ Students often give short answers when interviewed by adults. You need to give some guidance and encouragement for how much detail you want. It is helpful to use some probes, such as, "Say more about...", "Can you tell me more..." or "Can you give me an example of..."

❧ Be flexible. You want to cover all your areas of questioning, but the exact order doesn't matter. The interview will work better if you allow the topics to "flow" naturally.

AFTER THE INTERVIEW:

❧ Immediately afterwards, try to jot down your thoughts and reactions to the interview, what really "hit" or "moved" you.

❧ Soon afterwards, review your notes to make sure that major ideas are clear. Fill out your notes as needed. If you used a tape recorder, play the tape and review the interview protocol. Jot down key themes next to each interview question.

ANALYSIS:

When you analyze your interviews, look for patterns, ideas, explanations and understandings. Decide whether you want to do the analysis with the full interviews or with summaries of major themes. If you choose to prepare summaries before the actual analysis, you can categorize them in several ways: 1) by student (a student profile); 2) by theme across the interviews you conducted, or 3) by question. If you go the route of doing summaries, be sure to have your notes from the full interview to refer to during your analysis. If you're working with a group, bring your summaries or notes to an analysis session—when others raise issues, you'll be able to check your own interviews for responses. In this way, the members in your group can build on each other's work to gain a fuller understanding of the issue.

IN-DEPTH INTERVIEWS: ONE DISTRICT'S EXPERIENCE IN RESEARCHING LONG-TERM LEP STUDENTS

When secondary teachers in Hayward realized that many students were still classified Limited English Proficient (LEP) after seven or more years in the district, they dubbed these students "long-term LEP" and partnered with California Tomorrow to inquire into this group. The teachers asked: "Who are our long-term Limited English Proficient students? What do we really know about them? Why are so many of them still LEP after so many years in our schools? What kind of program would best meet their needs?"

A turning point came during a two-day, California Tomorrow-sponsored retreat. A dialogue among English Language Development (ELD) teachers sparked a decision to begin a teacher research group for the purpose of looking at issues affecting long-term LEP students. At the group's first meeting, teachers hypothesized about who the long-term LEP students were and why they remained LEP-designated for so long. The following are some of these theories:

- Students may have been placed initially in inappropriate programs, so they didn't get proper instruction to achieve basic literacy.

- Students may have been placed in English language development programs that did not adequately prepare them in reading and writing.

- Students may have perceived sheltered and ESL classes as "dummy" classes and opted out.

- Some students may suffer from undiagnosed learning problems.

- Some students may have poor school attendance and low grades.

- Some may have little academic support at home.

- Students and families who are struggling to survive in a new country may have other priorities besides school.

- Cultural conflicts, such as a belief that speaking out often, if at all, in class is not appropriate, might impede language acquisition.

- Students may pick up bad habits, such as watching lots of TV and devoting less time to homework, as they become "Americanized."

- Finally, students may know enough English and fare well academically, but can't be redesignated from LEP to FEP because they don't perform well on standardized tests.

The teachers' group, organized by Carol Younglove, did not want to make assumptions. After creating the long list of possible explanations, the teachers decided to gather the facts by interviewing some of their long-term LEP students about their schooling experiences. With California Tomorrow's help, the group came up with questions about the students' past and current education, their study habits, their friends and family, their hopes and dreams (see protocol beginning on the following page).

Each participant in the teacher research group committed to interviewing one long-term LEP student enrolled in her school each month. For the purpose of the study, the teachers agreed to focus on secondary LEP students who had attended Hayward schools since the early primary grades so that the teachers could evaluate the effect of programs and bilingual support services they knew had been available in the district.

INTERVIEW PROTOCOL FOR
LONG-TERM LEP STUDENTS

This is not a questionnaire. It is an interview guide that raises issues and ideas you may want students to discuss with you. Feel free to ask additional questions as they occur to you during the interview. If students answer briefly, try asking them to clarify or expand on their responses.

Tape these interviews and place the tape recorder very close to the student for clearest sound. Allow roughly 45 minutes per interview.

I. Background

a. Find out the nation in which the student was born, as well as where he or she grew up: Tell me about your background. Where were you born? Where did you grow up?

b. Ask about where the student has attended school. Probe for when they came to the United States and when they entered U.S. schools. Find out whether they have moved back and forth between the U.S. and their home nation. If so, ask if they attended schools in both countries.

c. For each grade level through which the student progressed, ask: Where were you in school during kindergarten? In first grade? In which nation? How many different schools have you attended? etc. For each year that he or she attended a U.S. school, ask whether the student was in a bilingual class. (Students may not know the formal designation for the class, so you'll need to ask in specific terms: Did your teacher speak to you in Spanish? Did you learn to read in Spanish? etc.)

II. Feelings and Attachment at School

a. When you were in elementary school, did you like it? How did you feel about school? What did you like? What didn't you like?

b. In elementary school, what kind of student were you? Was your schoolwork hard for you? Easy for you? Which things were easy? Which things were hard? What kinds of grades did you get?

c. When you were in middle school, how did you feel about school? What did you like? What didn't you like?

d. In middle school, what kind of student were you? Was your schoolwork hard for you? Easy for you? Which things were easy? Which things were hard? What kinds of grades did you get?

e. Here in high school, how do you feel about school? What do you like? What don't you like?

f. In high school, what kind of student are you? Is your schoolwork hard for you? Easy for you? Which subjects and kinds of assignments are easy for you or hard for you? What kinds of grades do you get?

III. About Classes

a. Do you feel you are placed in the right classes for you? Do the classes seem about the right level for you?

b. Tell me about your classes. Do you feel that you understand most of what your teachers are saying in class? Do you participate in class discussions? If not, why? Is it because you don't feel comfortable speaking in English? Do you feel that you understand most of what you read in your school texts? What don't you understand? Tell me what makes it easier or harder for you to understand a book or text.

c. About how much homework do you have every night? Do you mostly get it all done? If not, why?

d. Describe a really good teacher you've had. What is it that he or she did that helped you? Are most of the teachers you have now like that? How are they helpful or not helpful?

e. How important is school to you in general? If school is important, why?

f. If you didn't have to go to school, would you choose to? If not, what do you wish you could be doing instead of going to school?

IV. Ethnic Identification/Social Friendships

a. How do you identify yourself primarily—by race, nationality or some other aspect? If someone asks you to describe yourself, or asks, "What are you?", what do you say?

b. What nationality are you?

c. What race are you?

d. Do you hang out with friends who are mostly of your own race and nationality and language? Has this changed from the kind of friends you mostly had in the past? Tell me about the kinds of friends you have now.

e. How do most of your friends feel about school? Do they like it? Do they get good grades?

f. What are relationships like at school between students who are new immigrants to this country and other students?

g. If another immigrant student (Mexican, Fijian, etc.—match this to the ethnic background of the student being interviewed) had just moved here and asked you to tell him or her what this school is like for a new student from (Mexico, Fiji, etc.), what would you say?

h. Do you date or have a boyfriend/girlfriend? Is he/she also (Mexican, Fijian, etc.)? How do you feel about people dating someone of a different race or religion?

V. Career and Future

a. What might you want to do when you've completed high school? What kind of work do you hope to be able to do?

b. Are you taking classes now that you think will prepare you for college or a vocation (or whatever plans the student has for after high school)?

c. Do you want children someday? When do you want that to happen?

d. Do you think you will ever return to your home country to live? Do you want to? If you marry and have children, where would you want to raise them?

VI. Language Use

a. In what language do you speak the most?

b. Do you speak English in places other than school? Where, and why?

c. What language do you use the most at home? At work? With your friends?

d. Do you read much besides your schoolwork? About how much each day? When you're reading books other than schoolbooks, in which language do you read the most?

VII. Work and Other Responsibilities Besides School

a. Besides going to school, do you have other responsibilities? Do you have a job? How many hours a week? Why do you work? At what age did you first begin to work?

b. Do you take care of your sisters or brothers? About how many hours a week? Are you responsible for household duties? What kinds of duties? How many hours a day do you put into such work?

When the teachers discussed the data from the first three students interviewed, they found interesting similarities. The students, who came from Fiji, El Salvador and Mexico, each felt good about school and were progressing toward graduation. Their supportive parents monitored homework and report card grades. Each student had someone in their family with higher education. Students reported feeling comfortable with people from other cultures; they also indicated that they had difficulty in certain teachers' classes when instructions were not well explained.

The students differed, though, in the kinds of services they had received in the Hayward schools: one had participated in a Spanish bilingual program for the first three years of schooling; another had been in a sheltered magnet program and received some support in his primary language for one year; and the third student had been in sheltered classes throughout elementary school, but had not received any primary language support. When teachers reviewed the students' cumulative folders, they noticed some mismatches between what the students remembered and what really happened on their academic path. Two of the students reported no problems with completing homework assignments, but their teachers had noted that they often failed to turn in work. One student's record also indicated that she had been retained in the first grade, but she had no recollection of repeating the grade. The teachers realized there would be no easy answers.

The teachers met again to share data about three more students who seemed more "at risk" than the first group. They had potential special education issues, family problems, severe emotional problems or gang affiliation. These students, from Nicaragua, Mexico and Afghanistan, had yet to be hooked into support services that would adequately meet their needs. The parents of these students were less involved in their children's education. Still, all three students stayed in school and expressed a desire to continue, although two had poor attendance and often came unprepared for their classes. School records for one girl showed that her school had considered referring her to special education during third grade, but apparently held off in order to monitor whether her learning difficulties were language-related. Yet there was no follow-up. Perhaps the girl's easygoing personality had fooled subsequent teachers into thinking that her academic problems were related to language.

The teacher research group continues to explore the issues of long-term LEP students in Hayward. Each interview and discussion reminds them of how complex the issues really are, how educators must continue trying to understand their students as individuals with unique experiences. The search for patterns among the students, the sharing of knowledge and the exploring of options—all have deepened the teachers' understanding of their students as they attempt to make Hayward schools more responsive to the district's multicultural population.

SURVEYS AND QUESTIONNAIRES

Surveys or questionnaires are a good way to get direct information from large numbers of students in an efficient manner. They're especially helpful if you need to get a sense of overall patterns and how widespread certain issues are in your school. And they certainly don't take as much time to conduct as in-depth interviews or focus groups.

As far as content, surveys and questionnaires are most effective in finding out students' thoughts, priorities and opinions. They're less useful for gathering facts or information on incidents or academic performance. Nor do surveys and questionnaires allow you to understand students' experiences in depth. For these purposes, in-depth interviews, assessments and observations work much better.

WHAT DO YOU WANT TO KNOW?

Just as with an interview, be sure you have a firm purpose in mind before you create a survey. A survey should be relatively short, one that allows students to write brief responses to questions or to check responses so they can be tallied later. Surveys run the risk of easily boring students, and because students respond on paper instead of to another human being, many students don't take surveys very seriously. To motivate your students to cooperate, help them to understand what you want to know and why, and what will happen with the information.

HOW SHOULD YOU CRAFT QUESTIONS IN ORDER TO GET CLEAR ANSWERS?

Make your own job easier by phrasing questions in a way that best suits your purposes. First, decide whether the questions should be open or closed. Open-ended questions do not provide answer choices. Instead, students write brief responses in their own words. On the plus side, open-ended questions allow students to voice answers that you haven't considered, but on the minus side, compiling the results is much harder than with close-ended questions.

☛ *Example of an open-ended question:*

Think of good teachers you've had. What qualities made them good?

Close-ended questions make sense when you need to survey many students. They provide students with multiple choice answers or simply the responses, "Yes" and "No." While responses are fast and simple to tally, be aware that they often don't give you enough information to fully understand the student experience. If you decide to use close-ended questions, brainstorm possible answers first. Then test or "pilot" the survey on a group of students to see if they think the answers provided are sufficient and the questions make sense.

☛ *Example of a closed question with multiple answers:*

Think of the "good" teachers you've had in this school. Check all of the following characteristics that you think are true of most of these good teachers:

   ___ *Teacher is interested in the subject*
   ___ *Teacher understands students*
   ___ *Teacher controls the class well*
   ___ *Teacher gives regular feedback to students*
   ___ *Teacher has a sense of humor*
   ___ *Teacher communicates clearly*
   ___ *Teacher is available and willing to give extra help*

☛ *Example of a closed question with single response:*

Many people believe that teachers get burned out because of disruptive students in the classroom. What do you think of this statement?

   ___ *Definitely agree*
   ___ *Somewhat agree*
   ___ *Somewhat disagree*
   ___ *Definitely disagree*
   ___ *Don't know*

TIPS FOR CLOSE-ENDED QUESTIONS:

☛ Simplify the questions.

☛ Don't mix issues together. Suppose you ask, for example: "Do you think good teachers are strict, fair, fun and interesting?" If a student answers "yes," did he or she agree with all the qualities you listed or just some? To avoid confusion, break the long question into four short separate ones.

☞ Phrase the questions as closely as possible to how students actually speak. Avoid jargon.

HOW ARE YOU GOING TO ADMINISTER THE SURVEY?

Are you going to survey in classrooms? Send surveys home with students and have them returned? How can you ensure that you'll get surveys back from most students? Think carefully about what will work best to give students the chance to answer thoughtfully. Also, be sure to translate the survey into the languages of the students, or you will end up excluding the voices of English Language Learners and getting biased results.

On the following page is a sample portion of a student survey that combines open- and close-ended questions and is written in two languages.

QUICK-WRITES AND TEA PARTIES

Quick-Writes are another fast, easy way to get a sampling of students' written responses to a specific prompt. Because they are written in students' own words, Quick-Writes allow you to take a powerful "pulse" of students' perspectives in a way that eludes close-ended surveys or questionnaires. And because they are simple and fast to administer, Quick-Writes can be done with many students.

To do a Quick-Write, simply prepare the prompt and ask teachers across the school to allocate 15 minutes for students to write a response. Once you collect the Quick-Writes, you can use them in various ways. You can analyze them for content (for example, arranged thematically so that all student comments reflecting a similar response are put together; arranged by type of student to compare responses of 9th graders to 11th graders, or ESL students to English Only students, etc.). Or you can use the responses to set the tone for subsequent faculty discussions.

One format for faculty to use Quick-Writes or other student writing is the Tea Party. Each teacher is given one or two cards that contain Quick-Write responses from students. Then teachers mill around the room, like at a Tea Party, but instead of making small talk, they read to each other what students wrote. Only the students' words from the cards can be voiced during the Tea Party (usually ten minutes). No reactions, no comments, just the students' words.

STUDENT SURVEY
CUESTIONARIO PARA LOS ESTUDIANTES

Note to students: Please answer all questions as completely as you can. Your responses will help all of us to look at how the changes we have made in the school are going. It will also tell us what we still need to do to make our school even better.

Nota a los Estudiantes: Por favor contesta todas preguntas completamente. Nos ayudará a determinar como van los cambios en escuela y que todavía necesitamos hacer para mejorar nuestra escuela.

Block Scheduling/*Horario Block*

1. Has it been a positive or good change to institute block scheduling? *¿Ha sido un cambio positivo o bueno el establecer el horario "block" de tres cursos?*

   (Circle one/*encierra uno en un círculo*)   Yes - *Sí*   No - *No*

2. If your answer is YES, circle below all reasons why you like block scheduling. *Si contestaste afirmativamente, encierra en un círculo todas las razones por que te gusta cursar tres clases bajo el horario "block."*

   A. I have fewer classes to worry about. *Tengo menos clases de que preocuparme.*

   B. The school feels calmer. *La escuela se siente mas tranquila.*

   C. I can get all my work done. *Puedo hacer toda mi tarea.*

   D. There is more time in class to do labs and other activities. *Hay mas tiempo en la clase para trabajar en el laboratorio y otras actividades.*

   E. Other/*otro* _____

   Please write other reasons why you like block scheduling. *Favor de apuntar otras razones por qué te gusta el horario de tres clases.*

3. If you do not like block scheduling, why not? *¿Si no te gusta cursar tres clases en el horario "block," por qué no?*

In the Glendale Unified School District, the Tea Party put a human face on school data. The district wanted to create a systemwide professional development plan for all teachers in the district who served LEP students. Working groups from each school spent time with California Tomorrow staff to take an intensive look at LEP student achievement and access. But the data they were relying on was "hard" data—grades, standardized test scores, and numbers. California Tomorrow decided to try Tea Parties that used student Quick-Writes as a welcome break from looking at hard data. Some prompts that had been given earlier to students at their schools included: What is difficult for you about learning English? What helps you in learning English?

Here are some students' responses:

The students' words reminded teachers of the human reality behind the data they had been studying.

"*The think that is difikilt for me about lerning English is the words. My moth wants to say them in Farsi. My tong wants to say them in Farsi. And my mind has to make them in English.*"

"*TV help me learn English. I watch and figur out what it means.*"

"*I feel so sad and cry ever day because I cannot speak English right. My techer help me a lot. She give me books to take home, and she smiles at me and gives me time to answer. When I learn English good it will be becaus of her.*"

Each teacher was given a card containing one student quote. They moved through the room reading their student's words to others and listening to their colleagues voicing the words of students. The Tea Party never failed to move people. The students' words reminded teachers of the human reality behind the data they had been studying. The students' words reconnected teachers to the fact that these were their kids. As a result, the teams felt reinvigorated for the afternoon sessions. They also felt more urgency to shift from studying the data to planning action that could make a difference.

CONCLUSION

Student voice is powerful when students are supported to speak out and when faculty is ready to listen and act. Seeking student voice requires resources: staff time to plan the protocols, forums and materials, and staff time to listen and reflect. Often, schools may feel they don't have time for such a "luxury." But for student voice to work, a school's leadership must insist on the need to listen to and learn from students. Whenever there is hesitancy about time—for instance, "We'd like to do focus groups, but don't really have the time to"—revisit the different benefits that various approaches give you. If you need a force to motivate, push and inspire teachers to make a change, then a survey probably will not be enough, but something in a student's voice will be. If you need a much deeper understanding of some issue, you will only get it if you invest time in eliciting it.

Unfortunately, school curriculum isn't arranged in a way that creates time for student voice. This is one of the silencing aspects of schools. But there are ways to fit various aspects of student voice into the normal functioning of a school. Quick-Writes can be done in English classes throughout a school since writing for numerous purposes is a part of the curriculum expectations of language arts and English. Civics classes and social science classes can do a unit in which students use survey and questionnaire methods to gather data, then analyze it in response to political or social issues of the school. Math classes can do surveys and quantitative analyses. Student government and leadership classes can conduct focus groups and take the lead in a variety of formats to check the pulse of student attitudes and experiences. These are only a few of the creative ways to seek student voice within the structures and goals of a school.

When student voice succeeds in being heard, the payoff is tremendous—in stronger relationships between faculty and students, better focused reform plans, more informed and motivated faculty and more appropriate interventions that ultimately benefit the students themselves.

REFERENCES

Allen, J. (1995). Friends, Fairness, Fun, and the Freedom to Choose: Hearing Student Voices. *Journal of Curriculum and Supervision, 10*(4), 286-301.

Cummins, J. (1989). *Empowering Language Minority Students.* Sacramento, CA: California Association of Bilingual Educators.

Darder, A. (1991). *Culture and Power in the Classroom: A Critical Foundation for Bicultural Education.* New York, NY: Bergin & Garvey.

Díaz-Greenberg, R. (1997). *The Emergence of Voice in Latino Students: A Critical Approach.* Los Angeles, CA: California Association of Bilingual Education.

Fine, M. (1991). *Framing Dropouts: Notes on the Politics of an Urban Public High School.* Albany, NY: State University of New York Press.

Freire, P. (1970). *Pedagogy of the Oppressed.* New York, NY: Continuum Books.

Freire, P. (1998). *Teachers as Cultural Workers: Letters to Those Who Dare to Teach.* Boulder, CO: Westview Press.

Johnson, J.H. (1991). Student Voice: Motivating Students through Empowerment. *Oregon School Study Council, 35*(2).

Kreisberg, S. (1992). *Transforming Power: Domination, Empowerment, and Education.* Albany, NY: State University of New York Press.

Mace-Matluck, B. J., Alexander-Kasparik, R. and Queen, R. (in press). *Through the Golden Door: Effective Educational Approaches for Immigrant Adolescents with Limited Schooling.* Washington, D.C.: Center for Applied Linguistics.

Olsen, L. (1986). Youth Activism and Empowerment. In B. Berger Gould, S. Moon and J. van Hoorn (Eds.), *Growing Up Scared: The Psychological Effect of the Nuclear Threat on Children* (pp. 119-135). Berkeley, CA: Open Books.

Olsen, L. and Mullen, N. (1990). *Embracing Diversity: Teachers' Voices from California Classrooms* (p. 18). San Francisco, CA: California Tomorrow.

Shor, I. (1992). *Empowering Education: Critical Teaching for Social Change.* Chicago, IL: University of Chicago Press.

Shor, I. (1996). *When Students Have Power: Negotiating Authority in a Critical Pedagogy.* Chicago, IL: University of Chicago Press.

Wood, G. H. (1992). *Schools That Work: America's Most Innovative Public Education Programs.* New York, NY: Dutton.

STUDENT VOICE
ANNOTATED BIBLIOGRAPHY

Allen, JoBeth. (1995). Friends, Fairness, Fun and the Freedom to Choose: Hearing Student Voices. *Journal of Curriculum and Supervision*, 10(3), 286-301.

Allen believes that preparing students to be active in a democracy requires schools to model democratic processes and encourage student voice in decision-making, at both the classroom and school-wide level. In one network of elementary schools which are working to involve students more at these levels, students were interviewed about how they felt about having more of a role in decision-making. The results showed that students liked the increased involvement; many also commented on better relationships with teachers and a heightened sense of community in their school.

Bryant, Coralie and Benjamin, L.E. (1997). Developing Student Voice: A Follow-Up Study with Students as Researchers. Paper presented at the Annual Conference of the American Educational Research Association. Chicago, IL, March 24-28.

The authors describe how involving students as researchers in a survey of recent high school graduates helped develop student voice. Students from a school in Winnipeg, Canada learned research skills and earned credits; the process strengthened their sense of the importance of student voice. The results of the study, and the research process itself, became a part of the community's dialogue about education.

Clark, Carolyn and Moss, Pamela. (1996). Researching With: Ethical and Epistemological Implications of Doing Collaborative, Change-Oriented Research with Teachers and Students. *Teachers College Record*, 97(4), 518-548.

This case study examines the implications of using a student-centered research group to examine literacy practices. It follows a project as it shifts from a teacher-centered group which examines student writing for assessment and accountability purposes, to a partnership with students as co-researchers exploring how students perceive and use literacy. In choosing a student voice methodology, the researchers encountered issues of inclusion, authority and development.

Darder, Antonia. (1995). *Culture and Difference: Critical Perspectives on the Bicultural Experience in the United States.* Westport, CT: Bergin and Garvey.

Most of this book presents a theoretical exploration of how power relations in society and schools lead to the subordination of bicultural students in U.S. schools. Darder argues that bicultural students—speaking other languages or dialects of English in their home communities, living in both the mainstream and home culture—need to develop their "bicultural voice" and experience empowerment in classrooms. The development of student voice in the classroom becomes fundamental to the struggle for democracy; this voice is developed through dialogue and critical reflection. The author explores how to create true democratic environments in classrooms which integrate the experiences of bicultural students. One chapter discusses a bicultural development program which was part of a college's teacher education program.

Díaz-Greenberg, Rosalía. (1997). *The Emergence of Voice in Latino Students: A Critical Approach.* Los Angeles, CA: California Association for Bilingual Education.

This work, informed by Paolo Friere's "problem-posing" education and need for dialogue to transform oppression, presents the findings of a study of Latino student voices. These students discuss how their voices become silenced in schools, how breaking this silence can lead to acquiring power, as well as the home and school factors that shape their ethnic identities and the role of reflection in education. The author turns to these students as the experts about their school experiences and about what happens when their voices emerge. She stresses that student voices need to be acknowledged in the classroom, and that by doing so, power dynamics shift, which enhances students' education.

Fine, Michelle. (1991). *Framing Dropouts: Notes on the Politics of an Urban Public High School.* Albany, NY: State University of New York Press.

In this accessible book, Fine reports on her six-year qualitative study of dropouts from one urban high school. She analyzes the process of dropping out as a result of the ways students of color, language minority students and low income students are silenced in schools. She explores how student and teacher voices were systematically muted by fears of naming and discussing controversies, inequality or critiques at this typical urban high school. For schools to become places where all students can be empowered, she claims that students' experiences and voices need to become a part of education, particularly those voices of students most often pushed to the margins of society.

The Institute for Education in Transformation at the Claremont Graduate School. (1992). *Voices from the Inside: A Report on Schooling from Inside the Classroom.* **Claremont, CA: Claremont Graduate School.**

Noting how school reforms have often left out the voices of parents and those inside schools—students, teachers, principals—these researchers report on what they learned by listening to these voices. They stress that those inside schools should be naming the problems that reforms fail to address, and that real reform must reach the classroom level, shaping the relationships between teachers and students. The authors explore seven issues voiced by those inside schools as key, describe how to listen to these voices and why listening—and the inclusiveness it brings—is so important.

Kreisberg, Seth. (1992). *Transforming Power: Domination, Empowerment and Education.* **Albany, NY: State University of New York Press.**

This book examines power in classrooms, schools and society, and how to create empowering classrooms. Kreisberg presents a theory of power relationships, noting how student-teacher relationships can perpetuate wider patterns of injustice and domination. He argues for an alternate conception of power and authority based on a more equal relationship. In a more equitable environment, students can begin to develop their voices and empower themselves. Through interviews with youth, he explores what a more empowering approach to education could look like: non-dominating student-teacher relationships, greater student voice in decision-making, dialogue and critiques and so on. Student voice, he argues, is linked to changing classroom power dynamics and enabling students to participate in meaningful, democratic dialogue.

Olsen, Laurie and Moore, Melinda. (1984). *Student Views on the Quality of Teaching: A Manual for Student Involvement.* **Oakland, CA: Citizens Policy Center.**

This publication consists of two companion volumes: one, a description of a student-conducted study and its findings about student views of quality teaching; the other, a manual and tool for replicating the approach. The manual was designed to assist middle and high schools in involving their students in identifying issues around the quality of teaching and school-wide efforts to support good teaching. The booklet includes how to identify students for the project, developing and administering the survey and analyzing and reporting findings.

Poplin, Mary and Weeres, Joseph. (1993). Listening at the Learner's Level. *The Executive Educator, 15*(4), 14-19.

This article describes the findings from the Institute for Education in Transformation's study of schools "from the inside" which draws heavily on the voices of parents, teachers and students in the school. It provides a brief and articulate version of *Voices from the Inside*, a classic on data collection that is based upon student voice.

Weis, Lois and Fine, Michelle (Eds.). (1993). *Beyond Silenced Voices: Class, Race and Gender in United States Schools.* **Albany, NY: State University of New York Press.**

In this collection of essays, different authors explore how certain institutional practices and policies silence and discount the voices of students historically marginalized. The authors listen to these voices, bringing them forward to break the code of silence. The editors contend that if we are serious about having truly democratic schools, we need to examine issues of race, class and gender in schooling. Includes essays by Michelle Fine, Jim Cummins, Lisa Delpit, Carol Gilligan, Michelle Foster and others.

STUDENT VOICE RESOURCES

California Association of Peer Programs

This association is the umbrella organization for California's Peer Programs. They are dedicated to the initiation, enhancement and promotion of youth through youth service. Using trainings, curriculum and political education, participants develop their own campaign to create positive change in their schools, peers and community. Youth learn the nuts and bolts of organizing and youth participation: research, outreach and social change strategy and action. California Association of Peer Programs is available to connect schools and other institutions with local Peer Programs, and assist in the development of new programs.

P.O. Box 50725
Pasadena, CA 91115
(626)564-0099

Close Up Program for New Americans

This citizenship education program for immigrant middle and high school students is funded by the Close Up Foundation. The program is divided into three parts: 1) in their own school, students learn about federal, state and local governments; 2) students take a trip to Washington, D.C. and visit national monuments, museums and participate in community service learning activities; and 3) students return to their schools to plan and implement Community Service Learning Projects. Close Up Programs are available in many school districts throughout the United States.

44 Canal Center Plaza
Alexandria, VA 22314-1592
(800)385-1082 ext. 274 or 673
(703)706-0001 fax
E-mail: pna@closeup.org
WWW: www.closeup.org

Community LORE

Community LORE empowers youth by promoting and supporting their participation in evaluation, research and planning. In addition to developing youth leadership, Community LORE works to enhance the capacity of youth-serving organizations to work with youth. They develop this capacity through three methods: 1) coaching youth and adults as they design and run participatory action research and evaluation programs with youth; 2) developing curriculum guides on how to run action research and evaluation programs with youth; and 3) conducting short-term trainings to introduce adult educators and youth leaders to participatory research and evaluation methods.

2017 Mission Street, Suite 302
San Francisco, CA 94110
(415)621-1402 phone and fax
E-mail: comlore@igc.org

Educators for Social Responsibility (ESR)

ESR is dedicated to helping young people develop the convictions and skills to shape a safe, sustainable and just world. Their activities include conflict resolution and violence prevention for teachers, counselors and administrators, and workshops emphasizing creative conflict resolution techniques. They also conduct seminars on promoting a cooperative environment and learning to integrate conflict resolution skills into the existing curriculum. In addition, ESR offers publications encouraging student participation in schools.

23 Garden Street
Cambridge, MA 02138
(617)492-1764
(617)864-5164 fax
WWW: www.benjerry.com/esr

Chapter Six:

CHANGING CLASSROOM PRACTICE TO INCREASE ACHIEVEMENT AND EQUITY

Twenty-five teachers from Robin W. Yardley High School file in for a one-day workshop on how to help second language learners develop their English reading skills. The teachers come from all areas of the curriculum —ESL, sheltered and bilingual content-area teachers; what they have in common is that they all teach English Language Learners. Attending the workshop earns them credit towards the certification required by the state for teaching LEP students. Some already have the certification but want to learn more about helping their students read better; others are still working towards their certificates and need the credits. The Vice Principal of Curriculum and Instruction, Ms. Archuleta, arranged for this workshop partly because the reading scores for Limited English Proficient students were so low. She had heard that these techniques, if instituted widely, could help raise the scores.

The evaluations of the workshop are very positive. The teachers applaud the interactive experience, which allowed them to practice together certain classroom techniques based on the most recent research and theory. Many teachers write that they learned new, useful techniques and some indicate they will try them out in their classes.

Ms. Archuleta, who also attended the workshop, is thrilled to hear the teachers' enthusiastic responses. A few weeks later, she pops in on a few of the teachers' classrooms to see what they are doing differently now. After several observations and chatting with a few of the teachers, she is disappointed to learn that only Mr. Dean, an innovative ESL 4 teacher, has tried any of the reading techniques in his class. And even Mr. Dean isn't sure he will try them again, because he can't tell if they are making a difference for his students or not.

Changing in substantial ways the day-to-day interactions between students and teachers may be the trickiest business of all.

Scenarios like this one are not unusual. The professional development available to help teachers meet the challenges of educating LEP students often does little to make long-term changes in classroom practice. Even the most engaging one-day workshop rarely enables teachers to make deep changes; they need ongoing support and follow-up, help in seeing how effective the changes are. Often staff development is required by the state or district, and teachers see it as complying with mandates or gaining credits needed for certification, not an opportunity to reflect deeply on how to transform their own practice. Even those looking for such opportunities do not often get the ongoing support they need to change their teaching. Rarely does professional development help teachers transform their classrooms, or their schools, into the kinds of engaging, welcoming centers of learning where all students, including English Language Learners, achieve at high levels.

WHAT IT TAKES TO GET DOWN TO THE CLASSROOM LEVEL

Creating classrooms, indeed whole schools, which are joyful hubs of democratic and intellectual inquiry often seems unachievable. Compliance and certification are black and white, touchable, visible, articulated and understood goals. A truly restructured school that embodies all forms of access, including the daily interactions among teachers and students, is much more difficult to envision. Advocates and teachers committed to embarking on the journey that will lead to transformed classrooms often feel isolated. The institutional and human obstacles may appear insurmountable. Lack of working models leaves people in a quandary about where and how to begin.

Changing in substantial ways the day-to-day interactions between students and teachers may be the trickiest business of all in efforts to change schools. As catch phrases, such as "local control" and "site-based," become a reality, the onus for change will rest more and more within schools themselves. Teachers and advocates need a blueprint for how to move beyond whole-school restructuring efforts (e.g., block scheduling or implementation of career academies) to a focus on instruction that will make a difference in terms of equity, access and achievement for their students.

There are several factors that are often overlooked in any effort to craft a professional development program that has the potential to raise the achievement of immigrant students. First, little attention is paid to linking the training to some goal for student achievement—and even less attention is paid to gathering data that is closely connected to what teachers are trying to accomplish in classrooms (Schmoker, 1996).

Secondly, we often forget that teachers learn in much the same way as students do. The best learning is tied to a real problem that needs to be solved, when the learners (teachers) have a chance to question their previous practices and construct new, shared understandings together. Like students, teachers work harder and more effectively when they have identified and defined the problem themselves.

Thirdly, most staff development efforts need to be designed in ways that promote ever deeper explorations into defined achievement goals for particular groups of students. An inquiry-based model, such as the one we describe in this chapter, promotes a cycle of questioning, looking and observing, reading research, trying out some things in classrooms, reviewing data on progress, and listening to students. The inquiry cycle becomes a continual upward spiral as groups of teachers tinker with their practice, in big and small ways, to increase the access and achievement of their students.

USING THIS CHAPTER: WHO AND HOW

This chapter provides a set of strategies that have the potential to reshape what is happening for immigrant students inside classrooms. The strategies are designed to be flexible, used in a variety of ways and in no particular order. The strategies outlined here are best used in the context of an inquiry conducted by a group of staff members interested in finding out how to better serve their English Language Learners, in response to some specific challenge in terms of achievement or equity (see "Constructing an Inquiry," page 147). The strategies include:

❧ Laying the Groundwork for the Use of the Action Strategies: Beginning the Dialogue

❧ Getting Your Inquiry Group Together and Finding the Time

❧ Looking Outward at Other Models and Reading Research

❧ Examining Data

❧ Looking Inward at Your Own Classrooms

❧ Co-Constructing a Coherent Set of Strategies

❧ Observing and Coaching Each Other Based on Evidence.

Your advocacy group may decide that the biggest area of need is indeed restructuring classrooms to address the achievement inequities you see in your school. This chapter can give you a handle on where to begin and how to proceed. On the other hand, you might be the person in charge of staff development for your school or district, and you find yourself discouraged by the many ways in which staff development has failed to reach the students for which it was intended. Again, this chapter provides sequences and sets of activities that will help you and your colleagues examine and change the practices and structures that have blocked your success in the past.

The discussion of each strategy includes a description of it, how to implement it at your school site, and why it works to change the practice of teachers. Throughout the chapter, we include examples of how each strategy played out at one site, Alisal High School in Salinas, California.

The activities used in this chapter have been designed with several purposes:

❧ to allow the reader to reflect on the content of the chapter;

❧ to give ideas to advocates, teachers, inquiry group leaders, and staff developers about how to get their colleagues and staff to engage in the ideas found in the chapter; and

❧ to model some effective teaching techniques that can be used in classrooms.

As you read, you might think about how an individual activity could be used or modified for teachers at your site, or how activities might be changed to work for the students and the content you teach.

STRATEGY 1
LAYING THE GROUNDWORK FOR THE USE OF THE ACTION STRATEGIES: BEGINNING THE DIALOGUE

Before jumping into the strategies, which constitute the actual work of a staff or a group of teachers over the course of time, you might want to take some time with your colleagues to reflect on where you are currently vis-à-vis changing practice inside of classrooms.

First, it helps to get to some common understanding about the challenges teachers face in developing ways to change what they do inside of their classrooms. Bringing these issues to the surface can help in structuring your inquiry. For example, if the main obstacle at your particular site is finding the time to work together, then solving that problem first will facilitate the rest of the work.

It's also very useful to have teachers begin to think about what their classrooms will actually look like when they are well along the road to creating a school that focuses on equity and achievement for immigrant students. Teachers are not often asked, "What would a really great classroom be like at our school, from the beginning of a class period to the end? What would we all want to see happening?" Although the first answers to these questions will often lack specifics or consensus, the discussion allows teachers to begin to see how far and in what directions they may need to go.

Doing this groundwork helps to set up a dialogue and a shared sense of purpose among your colleagues before you begin the strategy work. It is, in fact, one way to begin the professional development. With that in mind, the first three activities below allow staff a view into what it takes to change practice and several ways to envision effective classrooms.

Teachers are not often asked, "What would a really great classroom be like at our school, from the beginning of a class period to the end? What would we all want to see happening?"

ACTIVITY 6.1A
RANKING THE OBSTACLES/RANKING WHAT WORKS

Take a moment and think about your own teaching experiences and those of your friends and colleagues. Think about the factors that make it difficult for you (and others) to change what you're doing in your own classroom on behalf of immigrant students—the obstacles that get in the way of changing what you do day to day, even though you might want to change. You might include ideas such as: fear of changing, not knowing where to begin, and so on.

If you're working with a large group, break into smaller groups of three to four people. Within these groups, make a list of eight to ten of the most important obstacles to changing practice inside of classrooms. Next, rank the obstacles, from the one that you think gets in the way the most, to the one that gets in the way the least. For a more interactive experience, write your rankings on the following "Rank It!" sheet, cut up the individual phrases, spread them out on your table, and allow the members of the group to play with the rankings as you talk. Your group must come to consensus on the ranking. Share with the whole group your top one or two obstacles. As a whole group, you may want to spend some time discussing why each of the most important obstacles rose to the top.

RANK IT!

RANK IT! (continued)

Next, following the same basic procedure, think about and rank the things that you have seen work to overcome the obstacles already ranked and discussed. These might include ideas such as: time for teachers to work together, specialized training, etc. Discuss your rankings with the whole group.

USING AN ANTICIPATION GUIDE: DISCUSSING ASSUMPTIONS, IDEAS, AND FEELINGS ABOUT CHANGING PRACTICE

Another way to begin this dialogue is to discuss what you and your colleagues know or believe to be true about changing the practice of teachers. An anticipation guide, such as Activity 6.1B on the following page, can be very useful in this regard, just as it can be with students. It allows people to come to grips with commonly held assumptions, feelings or opinions that are close to the heart.

Take some time in your group to fill out the following anticipation guide, using the instructions included in the guide. When you finish reading the chapter, you may want to return to the anticipation guide to complete it. Alternately, construct your own anticipation guide, using a series of statements that you feel relate more directly to the situation in your school or district. Include some statements with which people might agree and some statements with which people might disagree. Don't be afraid to include controversial statements—they spark discussion and deeper investigations into how people really feel and think.

ACTIVITY 6.1B
AN ANTICIPATION GUIDE:
CHANGING PRACTICE TO INCREASE EQUITY AND
ACCESS FOR ENGLISH LANGUAGE LEARNERS

Instructions: Silently read the statements below. For each statement, decide if you agree or disagree with the statement, and mark either "Agree" or "Disagree" for each. When you finish reading the chapter, reread the statements to see if you have changed your opinion or not. Say why you did or did not change your mind. Cite some evidence from the reading, other research or your own experience.

Before Reading   **After Reading**

1. _____   1. Teachers know what they need to do to change.   1. _____

2. _____   2. When I go in a classroom, I can tell fairly quickly if the teacher holds high expectations of English Language Learners and scaffolds the instruction for them.   2. _____

3. _____   3. Teachers in my school usually agree on what and how to teach English Language Learners.   3. _____

4. _____   4. I can think of ten research-based strategies that improve achievement for English Language Learners.   4. _____

5. _____   5. Our English Language Learners are doing better than we think; the tests we have to give simply don't show what they can do.   5. _____

6. _____   6. There are effective models out there for educating English Language Learners. All we have to do is go ahead and implement them.   6. _____

7. _____   7. I know what equity and access look like in my own (or a teacher's classroom) and I can give concrete, explicit examples of each.   7. _____

8. _____   8. When I think of English Language Learners, I know what happens in classrooms that either helps or hinders their achievement.   8. _____

ACTIVITY 6.1C
ASSESSING OUR READINESS:
HOW SUPPORTIVE IS OUR SCHOOL CULTURE
IN TERMS OF CHANGING CLASSROOM PRACTICE?

As an individual reflection or group activity, use the following assessment to check how ready your school is to build and sustain the capacity of teachers to change practice inside of their classrooms in order to raise the achievement of immigrant and language minority students. Consider each element in terms of how close or far your school is from having the conditions that will support this goal. Use the center column to describe what you actually see in your school, your evidence for your assessment, and all comments. If you are working as a group, each person should do his or her own assessment first and then compare notes in a general discussion. Based on this assessment, select your highest priority in creating a school that supports sustainable improvements at the classroom level for immigrant students.

Unsupportive School Culture	Comments/Notes	Supportive School Culture
• No policy or enforcement exists to ensure that LEP students are served by teachers who hold proper authorization.		• District policy requires all new hires to possess credentials to teach LEP students or to get training within a specified period of time.
• Authorized teachers are left alone; it is assumed that they are properly trained, and therefore effective deliverers of instruction to LEP students.		• There are ongoing, intensive strategies to maintain the effectiveness of teachers who already have received authorization or training to teach LEP students.
• Professional development is delivered in a one-shot workshop format with no follow-up; priorities are not linked to student need; there is general feeling that "those students are not my problem".		• The school has a defined, planned annual cycle of professional development that centers on priorities drawn from an analysis of student achievement data; the whole faculty takes on the responsibility of becoming skilled in curriculum and instruction for LEP students.
• Administrators and supervisors are ignorant about curriculum and instruction for LEP students; observation and feedback are unrelated to issues of effective pedagogy.		• All administrative leaders and supervisors are knowledgeable about instructional strategies appropriate for LEP students and regularly observe and evaluate teachers in terms of effective pedagogy for bilingual, ESL, and SDAIE classrooms.
• No human resources are allocated to ensure effective classroom implementation of strategies.		• There are on-site resource or mentor teachers (with release time) who regularly and systematically work with groups of teachers on effective classroom strategies, especially scaffolding techniques for second language learners.

Unsupportive School Culture	Comments/Notes	Supportive School Culture
• Teaching is secretive and done behind closed doors.		• All teachers are engaged in observations and peer coaching centered around curriculum and instruction.
• Instruction is erratic, inconsistent, and not based on sound research or theory about instruction for second language learners.		• Instruction is centered around a set of coherent, research-based strategies aimed at increasing literacy and enabling second language learners to access the core content.
• The culture of the school discourages an inquiry-based approach; the staff operates on the assumption that nothing will improve the learning for English Language Learners.		• There are formal structures that encourage and support teachers to engage in small group inquiries (teacher research, collaborative action research, inquiry groups) about the teaching and learning of English Language Learners.
• Any data that are collected on student achievement seem unrelated or distant from the everyday workings of classrooms.		• Student achievement data collected are closely related to what teachers are trying to accomplish in classrooms and the inquiry in which they are engaged.
• No opportunities exist for groups of teachers to improve instruction based on achievement data closely related to classroom practice.		• Teachers have regular, planned opportunities to analyze student achievement data directly related to classroom practice (e.g., performance-based assessments with rubrics) and then plan together for how to improve instruction.
• Teachers assume that what works somewhere else could never work at their school site. No efforts are made to look beyond the school for effective models.		• Teachers seek out, read about, and visit, if possible, schools and models for educating language minority students that have proven success.
• No monetary resources are allocated to support the inquiry process. Inquiry group efforts, if any, are viewed as unconnected to other efforts.		• The work of the inquiry group is supported through allocation of site-based funds. The work is written into the school plan as an integral part of whole-school efforts.
• If an inquiry group exists, no one is aware of their efforts or the potential impacts of their work.		• The "findings" of any inquiry group are cycled into whole-school efforts to improve the achievement of language minority students. The school supports the work of the inquiry group to help the school as a whole.

ACTIVITY 6.1D
ENVISIONING CLASSROOMS

Most of us are somewhat unclear about what classrooms look like when they exemplify access to core content and high expectations for immigrant students. It is helpful, therefore, to have some picture in our heads for what those classrooms might look like. The specifics and some of the major emphases will differ from teacher to teacher, but beginning to get a handle on what might constitute excellence is an important first step.

First, have the group members sit quietly for a few minutes with their eyes closed. Ask them to picture a classroom in their minds, one in which immigrant students are achieving at high levels. It can be any content area and any grade level in a secondary school. As people continue to sit with their eyes closed, ask the following questions:

❧ How does the class begin? How does the class end?

❧ What are the students doing throughout the class period?

❧ What types of interaction are occurring among students and between the teacher and students?

❧ What is the teacher doing?

❧ What do you hear the students saying?

❧ What do you hear the teacher saying?

❧ What do you see on the walls of the classroom? in folders? in portfolios?

Once you have given everyone five minutes or so to visualize this "ideal" classroom, give them a few minutes to jot down what they visualized. You may want to put the prompt questions up for people to see. If the group is small, you might ask everyone to share their visions. Encourage people to use statements such as, "The class begins with. . ." and to get specific; for example, "The class begins with an activity where the teacher is assessing and activating the prior knowledge of the students."

If the group is larger, you may want to put people in pairs or trios to complete the same exercise. When you're finished, take some time to chart the similarities and differences among the groups' visualizations.

To end this activity, you might want to have group members reflect individually on how far or how near they feel the school is, as a whole, to their vision. What are the major areas in which the classrooms at our school come closest to matching the vision? Where are we farthest away from creating classrooms that focus on achievement for immigrant students?

ACTIVITY 6.1E
USING BEFORE/AFTER SCENARIOS:
MAKING IT CONCRETE

You may have found in doing Activity 6.1D that some staff have difficulty in describing in detail what a wonderful classroom looks and sounds like. The following before/after scenarios are written to provide specific, detailed pictures of what one classroom in one content area looks like for one particular group of students (English Language Learners). The before/after format works in the same way as a skillful teacher giving students "examples" and "non-examples" to increase their understanding of an idea or concept. It's just as helpful to know what we don't want to have happening, and what doesn't apply, as it is to know what we do want to see happening.

Step 1: Read Scenario A below. As you read, take notes in the margins. You may want to note:

🖋 What does the teacher do or not do to provide access to the content?

🖋 What are the expectations of the teacher in terms of high achievement for his students?

🖋 This is the students' Literature class. How many of the students are actively engaged in literacy tasks at some point in the lesson? For how many minutes out of the period are students actively engaged?

🖋 What other evidence is there in the scenario that students are engaged in literacy tasks (descriptions of what is in portfolios, on classroom walls, homework, etc.)?

Scenario A

The tardy bell rings, and five or six students shuffle in from the hall to their third-period sheltered Literature class. Of the twenty-seven other students already in the classroom, ten are seated at their desks. The others are milling around, chatting amiably in their primary languages. Several are in line to sharpen their pencils and others are fiddling with their binders or notebooks. Five of the girls are seated in a circle, laughing quietly, obviously engaged in sharing a secret; two of them hold mirrors, lipstick and mascara in their hands, carefully reapplying their makeup.

A quick visual survey of the room reveals a bright, well-lit classroom with 35 desks placed in rows. Colorful posters with motivational slogans line the walls: "You can do it!" etc. A small bookcase under the window holds an assortment of magazines, teacher curriculum guides, and novels. One bulletin board boasts: "Excellent Student Work." Five student essays are tacked up for display. The teacher stands at the front of the class, pulling various stacks of papers out of his briefcase, consulting his roll book, and writing the date and several other items on the blackboard. He talks and jokes pleasantly with Dang, Nelson and Sandra who stand around his desk.

Six minutes into the forty-five-minute period, Mr. Smith calls out genially to the group, "OK, class, it's time to get started. José, sit down now, please. Angelica, would you please pass out the books? Also, everyone please get out a piece of paper for a journal topic." Five more minutes pass as students get seated, shuffle through their binders to find a piece of paper, or ask their neighbor for a piece. "Class, your journal topic is on the board. I want you to write about what you did this weekend." Mr. Smith circulates as the students begin to write. Two students appear to be doing math homework instead of the journal topic. Several students state quietly to Mr. Smith that they don't have paper or a pencil. Ten minutes later, most students have written five to six lines on their papers; some have filled up the page. Some have written nothing.

Twenty-three minutes into the period, Mr. Smith says, "Class, save your papers until Friday. I'll pick them up then. Open your books to page 62. We're going to read a story today and you're going to really enjoy it a lot." Over the course of the next fifteen minutes, the students take turns reading aloud from The Circuit *by Francisco Jimenez. When students stumble over a word, Mr. Smith gently corrects them. Three students refuse to read when called on, and the teacher moves to another student. In the course of the fifteen minutes, eight students get the opportunity to read.*

Domingo and Alice at the back have their eyes closed and are obviously napping. Juan is working diligently on writing a local gang name in old English script. Most of the others appear to be listening to the story, if not actually following along. Mr. Smith stops occasionally to ask a question: "Who is the character? What is he doing? What does that word mean?" With seven minutes left in the period, Mr. Smith tells the students to close their books and to pass them to the front. "For homework tonight, just finish your vocabulary paper you were working on yesterday. If you have it finished, you don't have homework." The students spend the last five minutes of class talking to friends, lining up at the door, and getting money out to buy sodas and chips at the snack bar.

Step 2: After reading Scenario A, discuss with a partner or your group the answers to the questions at the beginning of the activity. You also might want to consider: How unusual is this type of classroom? What do you think students might say about this teacher (e.g., "He's nice.")? What do you think Mr. Smith might say if you were to ask him about his expectations for his students and the amount of actual engagement of his students?

Step 3: Now read Scenario B below. As you read, take notes, considering the same questions you used when reading Scenario A.

Scenario B: Same classroom, same teacher, three years later

The tardy bell rings and Mr. Smith quietly shuts the door. Of the thirty-two students in this Block 3, 98-minute sheltered Literature class, twenty-nine are seated at their desks which are arranged in groups of four. The other three are thumbing through paperback books on a revolving bookcase in the corner of the room. Most of the students have their individual paperbacks open and are already beginning to read. Mr. Smith announces to the class, "The bell has rung and you should be reading now." He then moves to the three students at the bookcase and assists them in picking out new reading material. To one, he suggests, "You've been reading books by Gary Soto. Here is another one you might like." He reminds another student how to peruse the back cover of a book to see if it holds interest. Within about five minutes, the three students have chosen new books to try.

For the next twenty minutes, all students in the class are reading except for Maria and Teresa, who are both fidgeting and seem unable to concentrate. Mr. Smith spends some time talking quietly with each one. After some conversation, Maria begins to read. Teresa is encouraged to try another book—it turns out she thinks the one she began last week is "really boring." Twenty minutes into the period, Mr. Smith rings a small bell and announces, "Please get out your reading logs and work on them for the next few minutes." All students spend the next five minutes recording the number of pages read and fill out the part of the log that asks them to "summarize what happened on the pages you read today."

As students finish their reading logs, Mr. Smith asks individuals in each group to please help in passing out the journals for the group. He turns on the overhead projector to display the journal topic, "Write about a time when you had to move and leave someone or something you loved behind." Nine or ten students have written down the topic already and are beginning to write. Some look like they are stuck, or don't quite understand the prompt. The teacher speaks: "Let's put a few ideas here on the overhead for those of you who can't think of something right away. I'll put the first example. One time when I was eleven, we moved from California to Texas. I had to leave my best friend behind."

He writes "best friend" on the overhead and then asks the class for three or four other examples. "My grandmother," "a pet," "a house you liked," "a school" are subsequently written up for all to see. As the students begin to write, Mr. Smith circulates and quietly assists students who need help with a word or idea, or are just slow getting started.

A look at the classroom this time around shows us a much different environment. Student work covers almost every inch of available wall space. The work appears to be grouped in different categories. Under the sign "Interacting with Text" are examples of dialectical journals, with quotes from The Pearl *on one side, and student responses on the other. Brightly illustrated "Open Minds" dominate one section: the directions above each graphic say: "Show what Kino was thinking and feeling at the end of the book. Use symbols, graphics, and quotes." The side wall closest to the door reveals a collection of student-constructed plot outlines and graphic organizers for three or four pieces of literature. The* printed sign above reads, "Schema-Building—How are these pieces of literature all the same?" Next to the window stand two revolving bookstands stocked with a wide selection of interesting, age-appropriate but readable fiction and nonfiction paperbacks. In boxes labeled "Reading Logs" are class sets of folders—a survey shows that students are engaged in free voluntary reading three times a week, and are responsible for summarizing the stories as they proceed. Manila folders in boxes labeled "Portfolios" contain collections of student- and teacher-selected work, similar to the work displayed on the walls.

Forty minutes into the block, Mr. Smith asks students to finish up their last sentence in their journals, and has one student from their team replace the journals in the appropriate box. He then says, "Remember, I will be reading and commenting on your journals this weekend. You will have your points on Monday. Now please open your books to page 62. We're going to read a story today titled The Circuit. The journal topic you just wrote about is connected to this story in some ways."

Over the course of the next six minutes, Mr. Smith asks the students to predict what the story will be about from the story title, and from the title of the journal topic. He then asks for a student volunteer to come to the front to help him model a strategy, telling the class, "Look at our reciprocal teaching strategy poster on the front wall. Which of the strategies have you learned how to do?" Twenty hands shoot up, and Maria calls out, "We know questioning." "That's right, Maria," Mr. Smith responds. "Today I'm going to model for you, and you are going to practice the next one, summarizing."

Over the course of the next ten minutes, Mr. Smith and Diego, the volunteer, model how to read aloud a paragraph of the text with a partner as one person reads and the other summarizes what has been read. He then tells them that they are going to read the first two pages of the story with their partner, using the summarizing strategy. Students appear to be familiar with pair work; several complain that their partner is absent. Mr. Smith quickly pairs them up. As the students read aloud to each other, the noise level in the room rises considerably. Several pairs pull their desks to the side of the room so they can hear each other better. The teacher circulates to keep students on task, although it seems that they all are reading. Students participate in the reciprocal teaching activity for the next fifteen minutes.

With about 25 minutes left in the period, the teacher passes out a Dialectical Journal form that asks students to summarize in the left-hand column, and to create questions that are "on the surface" and "under the surface" in the right-hand column. He tells the class, "I'm going to model for you how to complete this dialectical journal. You will be practicing summarizing the story, and we will be working hard on how to ask questions that are 'under the surface' of the story, questions that are 'hard' and for which there might or might not be an answer." Mr. Smith reads page 3 of the story aloud, paragraph by paragraph. He calls strategically on students to summarize the different sections, and writes the summaries on the overhead copy of the dialectical journal. He asks students to think of "under the surface" questions for each section, giving them time to think. Twelve different students offer questions to the group—each is recorded in the right-hand column, and all students copy them.

With five minutes left in the period, Mr. Smith says, "OK. Thank you. Nice job. Please put these dialectical journals in your binder. Tomorrow we will continue with the story. You will be reading more of the story in your groups, except you will be summarizing, asking the questions, and recording them without my help. Your homework for tonight is to read again the first two pages, and write down ten good questions, just like you do when you use the questioning strategy with a partner." He models two questions on the overhead, and just as he finishes, the bell rings. The students cram their books in their backpacks, say goodbye, and rush out the door.

Step 4: Take a few minutes and compare the two scenarios. Answer the following questions:

- What vision does Mr. Smith have in each scenario for what his students can accomplish?
- What level of access is there to the core curriculum?
- What are the changes in the level of active engagement of students in literacy? What evidence can you cite for the level of engagement in Scenario B?
- What evidence exists in his instruction or in his classroom that shows pedagogical and content knowledge and an understanding of how to develop the literacy skills of his students?
- What would you guess happened to Mr. Smith in the three years between the two scenarios? What would you guess were the key elements in his transformation?

The following examples show how one group of teachers answered the first four questions above comparing the two scenarios:

1. What vision does Mr. Smith have before and after for what his students can accomplish?

Scenario A: Generally low expectations for students completing work; no sense of "urgency" around assigned tasks; he is probably content with how much his students are learning, although there is little evidence showing what students are able to do; maybe he is pleased that the students seem happy in his class.

Scenario B: A heightened sense of urgency about the class; high expectations for starting class on time, getting busy, completing work; much higher expectations for level of work with text; now he seems to have a real sense for what he wants each student to be able to do.

2. What level of access is there to the core curriculum?

Scenario A: Depends on what is meant by "access." Students are reading the same core text as other students so that's one definition of access; but how many students are really reading? How many are really getting it?

Scenario B: This appears to be truer access; there's some evidence that each student now is really reading, thinking about, and responding to the story.

3. What are the changes in the level of active engagement of students in literacy? What evidence can you cite for the level of engagement in Scenario B?

Scenario A: Little to no active engagement; with the journal topic, some students don't do anything—most have only written 5 or 6 lines; when students take turns reading the story, eight students get the chance to read—even though most of the rest of the class might appear to be attentive (although a couple are napping), we don't know what they're really thinking about; even for the students who are reading, there is no evidence that they are mentally engaged with the story; little evidence on classroom walls or other places of completed literacy tasks.

Scenario B: Major changes in active engagement in literacy; all students doing free voluntary reading, the evidence being the summaries they all complete; teacher has incorporated accountability into the journal writing—he reads and responds, which ups the possibility of active engagement of students; every student is engaged in reciprocal teaching of the story with a partner for fifteen minutes; with the dialectical journal, twelve students offer questions to be posed; others have helped with modeling summarizing and questioning.

4. What evidence exists in his instruction or in his classroom that shows pedagogical and content knowledge and an understanding of how to develop the second language skills of his students?

Scenario A: Evidence that he doesn't know about assessing and activating the prior knowledge of his students—the journal topic does not relate to the story; he wants the students to read and get through the story, but it looks like he doesn't know many ways to do that; he might think that pure exposure to the language in the story, on some level, will increase the students' second language (L2) proficiency, although we don't know for sure what he thinks about that.

<u>Scenario B</u>: Evidence that he wants his students to read widely—books that they choose on their own level; he has built accountability into each step of his practice; the journal topic now has a direct link to the story, showing he understands how assessing and activating prior knowledge can lead to increased comprehension; he models everything, from how to answer the journal topic to how to do the reciprocal teaching; evidence on the classroom walls that he is doing explicit teaching of metacognitive skills, such as the sign that says "Schema-Building— how are these pieces of literature the same?"; evidence of content knowledge— student-constructed plot outlines; multiple kinds of evidence that he knows how to scaffold the instruction for his second language students so they can really access the story.

Alternative Activity:

Think about your own school: What might typify what you don't want to see happening for immigrant students inside of classrooms? What would you like to see instead? Write before/after scenarios that capture your concerns, fears, hopes and dreams. Note that in Scenario A above, there is nothing truly terrible going on. It is simply mediocre. This is often the case in classrooms—and it can be more helpful to paint a picture of the mediocrity than to paint one of dismal failure.

The Mr. Smith we see in Scenario A is representative of legions of well-meaning teachers. Inside of each is the capacity to change, but the conditions rarely exist that enable them to make that change. Many come into teaching with the basic theoretical knowledge necessary to successfully instruct their students. Many have at least a faint inkling of how to fit it all together, as well as the desire to continue teaching their classes. But making the leap from theory or scattered workshops, to actual implementation and true quality instruction, remains problematic for most teachers. So, how can we get ourselves from Scenario A to B? The set of strategies outlined below are one way—a beginning.

Black-and-white X-Acto knife reverse by Gagandeep Kumar, a high school student from India

STRATEGY 2 FORMING AN INQUIRY GROUP AND FINDING THE TIME TO WORK TOGETHER

California Tomorrow's experience in schools has shown us the power of working with a small, voluntary group of teachers committed to an inquiry process. Getting a group together to pursue an inquiry often feels counter to whole-school change efforts at a school. But a group with a mission—and with a way to cycle what they find back to the whole school—can often accomplish what an entire faculty cannot. Depending on the goal of the inquiry, the membership need not be representative of all stakeholders in the school. Rather, the members ought to be those with a heartfelt interest in finding out more about, and responding to, the particular achievement or equity challenge that has been identified.

One key to the success of any sustained, long-term inquiry is requiring the members to make a commitment to the process for a set amount of time. A year at a time is sufficient; in some cases, a semester might be enough to complete the inquiry. If membership falls off, it's useful to find out why, reconfirm the need for consistency and rethink the meeting formats and times, if necessary. Some flux in membership and attendance is inevitable.

Working with the inquiry group to find times to work together upfront is crucial. The best secondary teachers are often committed to a plethora of extracurricular duties: coaching, class advisor, club advisor, department chairperson, tutoring, etc. Some schools have a collaboration time built into the daily or weekly schedule. A well-structured, well-run inquiry group could claim part of that time to conduct some of their work. Using the existing structures, such as department meetings, in new ways is another way to "find" time. There is so much unproductive meeting time in secondary schools that many teachers face the convenings with a mixture of dread and cynicism. Changing the very essence of department meetings so teachers are working on a shared goal to increase student achievement is one way to break through the non-collaborative culture of secondary schools.

Other schools have a culture where afterschool, Saturday, or summer paid time is the norm. Pay is an additional incentive for participation. When an inquiry group is written into the school plan as an integral part of increasing equity and access, site-based monies (such as Title I, EIA-LEP, SB 1882) can rationally fund the effort. Indeed, a well-thought-out inquiry group that leads to changes inside of classrooms is professional development at its best: focused, collaborative, sustained and targeted to increase achievement and access for students.

Alisal High School in Salinas, California worked with California Tomorrow for three years, from 1994 to 1997, as part of a demonstration project funded by the Andrew W. Mellon Foundation. In the first year of the project, Alisal had implemented a new block schedule in response to student needs. With the restructuring of the school day in place, the project shifted from a whole-school effort to an inquiry-based approach. A voluntary core group of teachers and the project site coordinator felt that the new block schedule allowed for a different kind of teaching, but wanted to explore what might work best for immigrant students before restructuring the insides of classrooms. Twenty teachers, representing all content areas and across primary language, sheltered, ESL and mainstream classrooms, were drawn to the idea of an inquiry approach and became the Working Group on Race, Language and Culture.

The group decided to spend a significant amount of time together—a combination of two- to three-hour afterschool meetings and several day-long retreats—throughout the fall and winter of 1995-1996 to launch its investigation. Other time together was scheduled during the following summers—an eight-day institute and two follow-up three-day institutes. Language and language development issues emerged almost immediately as the most pressing, and the group decided to pursue those first. For the next two years, the professional development of the inquiry group involved looking outward at research and other models, examining data on student achievement and progress through school, collaborating to create a plan to improve student literacy, observing and coaching each other, and sharing the findings with the faculty. At times, subgroups of the Working Group pursued different activities and then brought their experiences and knowledge back to the whole group.

A well-thought-out inquiry group that leads to changes inside of classrooms is professional development at its best.

TIPS FOR FORMING AN INQUIRY GROUP

🍂 Spend some time thinking about the composition of your inquiry group. Target teachers whom you know have an interest in working collaboratively around achievement problems for immigrant students. Initially, it is best to have one-on-one conversations with each potential member to create interest and assess how and if he or she might commit to a long-term inquiry. At the same time, you will want to invite everyone to be part of the group, in written form. This helps build inclusiveness. Extend the invitation to join the group during the progression of the process, if it seems that it would be good to either widen the membership or just keep the offer open. If you open it up, however, you can still require a set commitment of time and effort. People who pop in and out will not be able to contribute to the group's effort in a meaningful way.

🍂 Structure time to work together that meets the needs of the group. Compromises will have to be made. Think about a combination of after school, weekends, summers, sub days—whatever will work the best, given the demands of your particular school site. Work hard to get the work of the inquiry group written into your school plan. This legitimizes the work of the group so that site-based funds can be allocated to help carry out the work. Select a teacher-leader or administrator who can help carry the group along and solve problems when issues arise. If attendance starts to fall off, gather everyone together and discuss: What is or is not working about the group? What are the reasons we are not fulfilling our original commitment to attendance? What do we need to do to keep things going?

ACTIVITY 6.2
PLOTTING THE USE OF TIME AT YOUR SCHOOL

One way to help you figure out how to find time together is for your inquiry group to sit down and look at the ways in which your school already uses time for meetings. By looking at how effectively that time is used, you can sometimes find ways to use some of that time for your inquiry group to meet.

Fill out the following chart together and then discuss ways that your school could more efficiently meet the purposes of the time already slated for meetings and, thus, free up some time for your inquiry group to meet.

PLOTTING THE USE OF TIME AT YOUR SCHOOL			
Type of meeting	*Hours (per week, month, or year)*	*What's the purpose of this meeting?*	*How is this time actually used?*	*Could some of this time be used for inquiry group meetings?*
Staff Meetings				
Family/ House/Grade Level Meetings				
Shared Prep Periods				
Department Meetings				
Staff Development				
Minimum Days				
Administrative Team Meetings				
Site Council Meetings				
Curriculum Committee Meetings				
Technology Committee Meetings				
Other:				

(adapted from the High Performance Learning Communities Consortium: RPP International. Collaborators include California Tomorrow and the Bay Area Coalition of Essential Schools.)

STRATEGY 3
READING RESEARCH/LOOKING OUTWARD AT OTHER PERSPECTIVES AND MODELS

Much is already known about effective schooling for immigrant students, and many schools throughout the nation are engaged in cutting-edge development of new models. But busy teachers often do not have the time or energy to follow the latest research in their fields; many do not subscribe to their own professional journals and there are few, if any, forums in schools appropriate for discussions about relevant research. The judicious use of research as part of an inquiry provides teachers with the background—and backup—they need to recommend changes in programs or approaches.

It simply makes no sense for any of us to start at ground zero when good work has already been done. The models out there can serve as springboards for your own work.

It simply makes no sense for any of us to start at ground zero when good work has already been done. The models out there can serve as springboards for your own work. Underachievement and lack of equity issues for immigrant students are so pervasive and pressing that we cannot afford to advocate for teaching strategies that do not have some established research base and track record. This does not mean that there are not new ideas to discover; we are simply suggesting that a re-examination of what has already been done, and its possible application to immigrant students, can reveal rich research-based strategies.

At **Alisal High School**, the inquiry group began its investigation into language with a day-long retreat where two teachers from International High School (IHS) in New York City shared elements of their model for educating immigrant students. This gave the teachers a chance to delve deeply into a structural, curricular and pedagogical model that operated in a different context. IHS uses an interdisciplinary, project-based curriculum for all students; teams of teachers are responsible for a group of students for an extended period of time, and discussions of effective teaching and learning processes occur regularly among teachers as well as students. They also read *Authentic Assessment in Action* (Darling-Hammond, Ancess and Falk, 1995) to broaden their understanding of the IHS model. In addition, they read portions of *The Power of Their Ideas* by Deborah Meier (1995), a moving chronicle of the struggle to establish Central Park East Secondary School in East Harlem. Central Park East uses a curriculum designed around central questions and graduation by portfolio.

This initial exposure to the schools in New York City opened everyone's eyes to other ways of structuring classrooms. In the spring of 1995, ten of the Working Group teachers visited not only International High School and Central Park East, but El Puente Academy for Peace and Justice. El Puente's curriculum is firmly grounded in the development of students' commitment and ability to advocate for human rights and justice.

Upon their return, the teachers shared their experiences with the whole faculty. One important insight surfaced for the group: the schools they saw and read about educate students who are not fundamentally different from students at Alisal High School. They are, by and large, poor and minority. Many of the students speak English as a second language. The teachers saw that a radical restructuring of the teaching and learning process, coupled with faith in students as capable human beings, provides for success on countless levels. In many ways, the trip crystallized the Working Group's ideas. As Physics teacher Paul Quiggle stated:

"New York City was a turning point for all of us who went. It gave us a clear picture of the possibilities. We saw students, very much like our own, engaged in learning at a level that was awe-inspiring. It really turned my thinking around about what I could do in my classroom, not to mention what we eventually could do in the whole school."

The "looking outward" also involved scouting out instructional models much closer to home. The teachers visited multiple classrooms in the two feeder middle schools to Alisal (Harden and El Sausal Middle Schools), observing ESL, sheltered, and Spanish content classrooms in order to view exemplary literacy practices in action at the middle school level. Reading of other writings and digging into other perspectives on schooling language minority students occurred as needed at various times throughout the life of the inquiry group. For example, in the summer institute in which the teachers began to craft a new, articulated set of strategies to use in their classrooms, they read *The Cognitive Academic Language Learning Approach (CALLA) Handbook* (Chamot and O'Malley, 1994); *Reciprocal Teaching in the Classroom* (Palinscar, David and Brown, 1992); *The Power of Reading* (Krashen, 1993); *Sheltered Instruction: Doing It Right* (Walqui, 1991).

TIPS FOR LOOKING OUTWARD

- Read research that is as directly related to the concerns of the inquiry group as possible. The closer the match, the more welcomed it is by overwhelmed and overworked teachers. Make sure there is ample time for discussion and reflection so links can be made from the printed page to real life in the school.

- Read about, hear about and see in person, if possible, models for educating students like your own that are far removed from what teachers are already doing. These have the potential to stretch the imagination, extend the vision of what can be done, force people out of old ways of thinking, and get them to say, "If they can do it, why not us? If their students can do that, why not ours?" You don't have to go far away to accomplish this. Books and copy machines are close at hand. The Alisal teachers were moved to act by merely reading about the New York City schools. Visiting was icing on the cake.

❧ Look at models that exist in your own backyard: your district, your city or someplace you could drive in a few hours. There are often good, and sometimes truly excellent, examples of how to do whole programs or pieces of programs. Look for the results they've gotten in terms of achievement and equity, what they had to do to get there, and what they're doing to sustain their efforts. Pick models to look at that have the potential to address your specific achievement or equity challenges. Structure some significant amount of time after visits to debrief and reflect on what the group saw and heard. Allow time to figure out what the possible applications of the model might be to your school. Don't be afraid to think outside the bounds of what you're doing right now.

❧ Read research about exemplary pedagogical practices that have the potential to address the achievement concerns of immigrant students. If it's been tried out there, if it has a track record of increasing achievement and equity for our students, we are remiss to ignore it. Teachers need a chance to consider effective approaches and practices and think about what they are or are not doing that matches. We have to think strategically about which instructional strategies, approaches and curricular models have the most potential for closing the gap for immigrant students.

ACTIVITY 6.3
USE OF RESEARCH-BASED STRATEGIES IN OUR CLASSROOMS

Give each teacher a copy of this organizer. Give everyone 15 to 20 minutes to fill out the sheet. Teachers can note a multitude of strategies, tasks or activities. It might help to give a few suggestions, such as journal writing, open-ended math questions, anticipatory guides, depending on whether the group is cross-curricular or departmental.

INSTRUCTIONS: Think of three activities/strategies/tasks that you use often in your teaching. Fill out the chart below about each activity you pick. When you are finished, you will share your answers with your colleagues.

Name of the activity/strategy/ task I use often			
Number of minutes per week			
Where I learned about it			
Why I use this activity/strategy/task			
What is the research base? How is this intended to raise achievement?			
What is the evidence I have that this activity/strategy/task raises achievement?			

When the group has finished, discuss your answers, using the prompts below:

☛ What did you discover, in general, about your use of research-based strategies?

☛ Where did we have an easier/more difficult time identifying the research base? How many of the activities do we use because they seem to work, or they're interactive, or fun, etc.?

☛ Are there explicit ties to raising student achievement? Where? Where are the gaps between what we are doing and the links to raising student achievement for immigrant students?

☛ What does this raise for us about what is going on in our classes? Are there assessments we could use, borrow, "steal" from somewhere else? What data could we collect on an ongoing basis that might help us know what is making a difference and what is not?

STRATEGY 4
EXAMINING DATA

Using data to promote the achievement and equity of immigrant students is discussed at length in Chapter Three. In the context of a professional development effort designed as an inquiry, it makes sense to collect data that are closely connected to what the group is trying to accomplish. To hone in on an achievement challenge, you may first need to collect data across the school or across departments. You might want to look at credits accrued, D's and F's given by department, standardized achievement test scores, proficiency test pass rates—disaggregated by race/ethnicity, language status, gender, Free and Reduced Price Lunch, etc. As the focus of the inquiry narrows, the data collected might look more like D's and F's for students in different "tracks," or writing proficiency test scores for 9th graders, or SAT-9 scores in problem-solving for 8th-grade ESL students.

An inquiry group will often take an even more focused look at data collection, over which they have almost total control and which is directly targeted toward increasing the achievement of students. For example, a department could:

🖋 examine the scores on a particular performance assessment, using a rubric;

🖋 analyze where students are having troubles, e.g., form hypotheses;

🖋 work on ways together to explicitly model and teach students how to raise their performance on that one aspect;

❧ re-assess students to look for gains in that particular area;

❧ begin the cycle over again.

A cross-curricular approach to reading would include the same basic steps, but might be conducted around the students' abilities to summarize or question text. The closer the data are to the daily life of teachers, the greater the chance that they will pay attention and be willing to work cooperatively on raising the achievement in a particular area.

Examining data related to student achievement naturally occurs in conjunction with the other strategies. This strategy, however, is often not used effectively. In the worst case scenarios, use of data backfires, setting back progress that has been made.

For **Alisal** teachers, use of data proved crucial to moving the work of the inquiry group forward at one key juncture. A subgroup of the Working Group met for a full-day retreat to look more closely at the newly-arrived immigrant students placed in their bilingual program. In preparation for the meeting, the bilingual clerk for the school assembled key data on all the students in at least one of the classes for each teacher. For example, one Social Studies teacher received data on all the students currently placed in his sheltered World History class.

The teachers examined data, including Language Assessment Scales (LAS) oral and reading/writing scores, current California Test of Basic Skills (CTBS) scores, and Spanish Assessment of Basic Education (SABE) primary language reading and math scores. It was the first opportunity most of the content-area teachers had ever had to see the range of proficiencies present in their classes. The analysis of the data led to some generalized statements about the students' first- and second-language proficiencies, such as, "Even our students at the more advanced levels of ESL are scoring below what we expected in reading and writing."

Later on in the year, the core group of teachers received training in, administered, and scored their students' LAS reading and writing assessments. This gave them hands-on experience with what the scores really meant in terms of student performance. Using data this way provided them with a greater depth of understanding about what the test could and could not tell them about their students.

These experiences with data pushed the inquiry group to consensus on a general goal: accelerating the literacy development of their students was a necessity. They agreed that whatever else happened in the inquiry process, increasing student literacy would sit squarely at the center of their efforts.

STRATEGY 5
LOOKING INWARD

Looking inward at your school, your classrooms and yourself can help frame and ground your next steps. We often rush into doing and trying new things without a good sense of what is actually happening at the moment. The process of looking inward is like holding up a mirror to help you see as clearly as possible your strengths and weaknesses. Teacher's perceptions of what is going on in classrooms throughout the school are often colored by rumor, casual conversations, or spur-of-the-moment exchanges, like, "Try this activity. I got it at the conference last week and it really works." As one teacher commented:

The process of looking inward is like holding up a mirror to help you see as clearly as possible your strengths and weaknesses.

> *"Everyone says I am an excellent ESL teacher, but no one, in my fifteen years of teaching here, has ever seen me teach. Not even for five minutes. How do they know what I really do or if it works?"*

Looking inward can happen at many levels and in many ways, offering insights that other strategies cannot. One group saw and felt the generally passive schooling experience of their students by shadowing a student for a day. Another set of teachers were surprised to discover how vastly different the expectations were from class to class: in some Science classes, the teachers had the students involved in demanding, active tasks from the moment the students walked in the door until the end; in others, they found large chunks of time wasted on administrative tasks and a concentration on seat work. Yet another group happily realized that most teachers were attempting to implement reciprocal teaching, but with varying degrees of success. In every case, looking inward caused the groups to re-evaluate their next step. It grounded their efforts in reality and gave them concrete ideas about what to do next.

The inquiry process requires people to slow down and reflect before leaping into a solution. One middle school involved in an inquiry decided to look closely at classrooms after examining data that showed a continued slide in reading scores. Despite professional development efforts, such as workshops on "Content-Area Reading Strategies," scores had not improved over the course of more than a year. Some teachers argued that they needed more professional development or at least something different. Others began to think that they'd already tried everything they could, and nothing was going to work. They decided to see what was actually happening in their classrooms by looking at the literacy activities or tasks that teachers were employing, the extent to which they were being used, and the number of minutes per class period that students were actively engaged in literacy. Each teacher was released for an entire day in order to observe in classrooms. Armed with the data from the observations, the teachers embarked on a different path than originally planned, which had been more formal professional development. Instead, they began to figure out ways that they could support each other to improve with what they had already learned.

In the case of Alisal, looking inward occurred through three important vehicles: self-reflection and group discussion about the role of English vis-à-vis Spanish at a school like Alisal; expert observation and feedback by the site coordinator to the inquiry group teachers about their classrooms; and self-assessment by group members of their skill in implementation of key instructional strategies.

At Alisal, the process of introspection began early on in the inquiry group's investigation into language. The teachers began with themselves, reflecting on questions such as these:

🍃 What is it like for you being a teacher at Alisal, given your language, culture and background?

🍃 What do you see as your role in showing students you value their home language, yet being sure they gain the English fluency and literacy they need?

🍃 If you are bilingual, how do you think about yourself and your role as a teacher in terms of supporting your students' Spanish development?

🍃 What is the actual language use in your classes?

Teachers began to make honest yet painful assessments. One young Latina teacher, a graduate of Alisal herself and a member of the community where the school is located, said:

> "I am a role model for my students. I understand them and where they come from, and I am here to help them get somewhere. There is a constant tension, for me, around language use in my sheltered classes. When and how much should I clarify in Spanish? When and how do I insist on English? What is the right balance?"

The second route to looking inward involved work done by the site coordinator of the project, Ann Jaramillo, inside of teachers' classrooms. In conjunction with the afterschool meetings and retreats, she began observing in the inquiry group's classrooms. After each observation, Ann provided the teachers with private, written feedback that incorporated extensive questioning in areas of mutual concern and the emerging focus on accelerating literacy. The written feedback was followed by a time when the teacher and the site coordinator sat down and talked about the questions.

The types of questions included:

🖢 What do you hold to be the primary role of Spanish content courses—the development of content ideas or primary language, or both?

🖢 Could the same strategies that you learned for sheltered content courses be applied to primary language instruction, especially when you take our underschooled students into consideration? (Underschooled students at Alisal are newly-arrived immigrant students who read below Grade 4 level in their primary language and have significant gaps in schooling in their home country.)

🖢 What do you think the relationship should be between your class and other classes your students have, in terms of literacy demands?

In discussing these questions and observations, Ann and the teachers explored the issues, brought intuitions and unspoken thoughts to the surface and made tentative conclusions. By asking questions about literacy and the purpose of primary language, teachers clarified their own views. As one teacher realized:

> *"I think I do have a responsibility to increase the literacy of my students, even though I'm not an English teacher—maybe we could work together on that, even though I'm not sure what we would do."*

Another teacher noted:

> *"It helped to have Ann say to me straight out, 'you aren't using everything you've learned,' and I'd have to say, 'yes, that's true.' I knew I had to try."*

The third major "look inward" involved the teachers' self-assessments of their implementation of SDAIE (Specially Designed Academic Instruction in English) strategies. Most of the teachers acknowledged a strong understanding of second language learning and had had intensive training in SDAIE strategies. The site coordinator for the project created a self-assessment rubric based on a SDAIE framework (Walqui, 1991) to help the teachers ground their past training in practice (this activity is detailed on page 378, "Using a Self-Assessment Rubric"). The teachers' self-reflection on competence was revealing. Their honest, and often painful, assessments—"I thought I knew these things!" "This was brutal—looking at myself like that—but good at the same time"—fueled the teachers' desire to really begin to use and understand strategies that could truly accelerate the literacy of their students.

Tips for Looking Inward

🕊 Think of ways to cycle "looks inward" throughout your efforts to increase achievement and equity. The following questions can help you to structure the kinds of activities that would be most helpful in your inquiry:

☛ Have we asked ourselves the hard questions that need to be asked? Have we talked together about the issues most closely related to the inquiry in real and honest ways?

☛ Do we know what is going on inside of our classrooms? If we're not sure, how will we find out?

☛ How do we assess where we are in terms of implementation of strategies, programs or approaches? Do we have a picture of where each of us is and where we would like to be?

🕊 Think of looking inward processes as reality checks. The best checks have the potential to pull you up short, even knock the wind out of you momentarily. You want to try to provide as many people as possible with experiences that allow them to get to "Wow!" "Ouch!" "So this is what is really happening" or "Now I understand what we need to do and how far we have to go." Looking inward can identify patterns of failure and underachievement that might have shown up in the data, but experiencing them firsthand often brings up anger and sadness at just how far the group has to go to make a difference. So, you want to ensure that there is a positive place to go from any sort of painful realizations made by the group, that there is a step-by-step plan to move forward in addressing the issues.

🕊 If you structure some observation of classrooms done by an "expert" coach (as was done at Alisal), be clear that the observations are non-evaluative and that the specific feedback given is private and confidential. The coach can provide general observations across classrooms, on the order of, "One area of strength I saw among most teachers was assessing and activating prior knowledge. . ." As much as possible, your expert coach should already have established trust with your teachers and obviously ought to have the depth of content and pedagogical knowledge necessary to provide the teachers with feedback they would not be able to give each other.

ACTIVITY 6.5A
REFLECTING ON THE POWER
OF OBSERVATION BY A COACH

Read the following memo written by an expert coach to one of her inquiry group teachers after an observation. Imagine for a moment that the memo is coming to you, that you've been looking forward to the observation, and that the observation is one of a series that are being conducted in order to get a handle on what is going on in the classrooms in your school. Imagine also that you and the coach are well-acquainted and that there is a significant level of trust between you.

Memo to a Teacher:

I am so glad I finally had the time to observe you teaching a Science class instead of Math. Thank you so much for letting me come, unannounced, and sit through the whole class. It was really fascinating for me because a number of the students in your class are also students in the ESL 2 class that I have been co-teaching. It is instructive to see them operating in different contexts and in different languages. I can't tell you how much I appreciate your genuine concern and affection for your students. It is obviously mutual, as they accord you much esteem and respect.

Since this particular class period centered primarily on reading the text, I have a whole series of questions for you related to literacy, primary language instruction, content knowledge and sheltered instruction. You might wonder why I would even mention sheltered instruction, since this is a Spanish language Science class, but some things have occurred to me in the past couple of days that I think we might like to talk about together. Since we are friends, I feel comfortable taking a more direct approach with you than I might with someone else. We have enjoyed a fruitful professional relationship, so I know that my comments will spark some interesting dialogue between us. Anyway, I'm curious as to why you did not employ any of the scaffolding activities for reading text that you learned about in your SDAIE training. I know from observing some of your students in ESL that they do not possess "on grade level" reading in Spanish. It seems to me that sheltering is appropriate for them, even though they are studying in Spanish, not English. Do you hold a different view of that?

Here are some other questions to consider—when we get together we can decide which ones are the most interesting or vital for both of us. If you have any questions you want us to talk about in response to the observation or the memo, jot them down.

— What do you hold to be the primary role of Spanish content courses—the development of content ideas or primary language literacy, or both?

— What did you do to assess students' prior knowledge of the topic (in this instance, earthquakes)?

— Had you done anything in particular to get a view of their possible scientific mis-conceptions on the topic? I'm thinking here of an Anticipation Guide, or something like that to assess.

— With text reading, have you tried reciprocal teaching with this group? This seems like a good text to use it with. It's not too terribly difficult and it would be a way to get the students through the text and increase their reading comprehension at the same time.

— What other literacy strategies have you tried? Do you want to experiment with some to see what the possible effects might be on comprehension?

I'm not sure what some of the answers are to at least some of those questions. It will be fun to get into exploring what we think. It also seems like it might be time to try out some ideas together in your class. It would be a little scary for both of us but it might be reward-ing as well. Plus, if we're really going to try to structure something different for our ESL stu-dents, I think we ought to step out instructionally as well. Thanks again for letting me come. I'll be gone Friday, but I'll come by Monday during your prep to chat, as planned. Take care.

After reading the memo, take a few minutes to think about the answers to the follow-ing questions. Share your ideas with a partner, or with the whole group.

- What basic conditions need to be in place to allow for the kind of frankness found in this memo?

- When would this particular strategy work best? When would it not work well?

- Given the fact that this particular coach and teacher have a solid, mutually respectful rela-tionship, what are some of the possible outcomes of the conversation they will have together as a result of the observation and the memo?

- Do you think this kind of feedback might move a teacher to change his or her practice? Why? Why not?

- What might be the result of many members of an inquiry group having this same oppor-tunity? What do you think would surface for the group, in response to individual ques-tioning and dialogue with the coach?

- Imagine that an inquiry group at your school has the opportunity to be observed and receive feedback in a similar kind of way. What would you want to have happen as a result? How would you structure the process for maximum results and progress?

ACTIVITY 6.5B
USING A SELF-ASSESSMENT RUBRIC

Look carefully at the following self-assessment rubric. Take a few minutes and assess yourself in one or two of the categories that you are familiar with. Share with a partner what you found out about yourself. Were you surprised at where you placed yourself? What did you find out about how you view yourself and your competence?

Now think about your school site. Is there a program, an approach, or a set of instructional strategies that teachers of your group of students have been trained in? Do you have a picture in your own mind for what the level of implementation might be in various classrooms—and how the teachers in those classrooms would rate their own levels of implementation?

Talk with your group about how a self-assessment similar to this one, but perhaps with entirely different categories, might assist individual teachers to reflect on their own practice. How could an assessment like this be used with teachers over time? What is the value to this particular process of "looking inward"?

SDAIE (Specially Designed Academic Instruction in English) SCAFFOLDING INSTRUCTION SELF-ASSESSMENT RUBRIC

Instructions: Take a few minutes to reflect on your current level of competence as a SDAIE instructor. For each scaffolding category or strategy, place yourself on the scale as accurately as possible. Use the following descriptors of each number to rate yourself.

0 = I have **no understanding** of this scaffolding strategy.
1 = I have only a **vague understanding** of this scaffold. I have heard of it.
2 = I **can name** the scaffold, say how it supports students' building of understanding, and **give several examples** of it.
3 = I **can name** the scaffold, say how it supports students' building of understanding, and I use it **occasionally in class.**
4 = I have **incorporated** this scaffold in my repertoire, use it almost daily, and there is **evidence** of it on my classroom walls, in portfolios, or in observations of my teaching.
5 = I know this scaffolding category well enough to teach other teachers about it and assist them with implementation.

Modeling and Contextualization

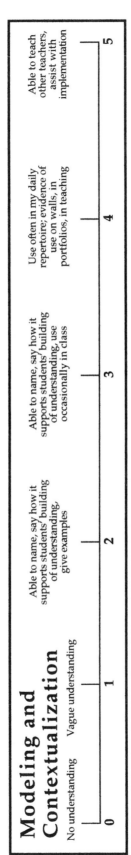

No understanding	Vague understanding	Able to name, say how it supports students' building of understanding, give examples	Able to name, say how it supports students' building of understanding, use occasionally in class	Use often in my daily repertoire; evidence of use on walls, in portfolios, in teaching	Able to teach other teachers, assist with implementation
0	1	2	3	4	5

If you rate yourself a "2" or above, write here how this scaffolding supports students and give two to three examples of strategies for classroom use:

Bridging: Assessing and Activating Prior Knowledge

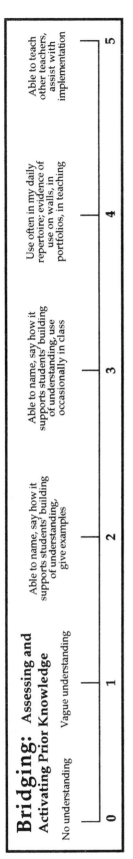

No understanding	Vague understanding	Able to name, say how it supports students' building of understanding, give examples	Able to name, say how it supports students' building of understanding, use occasionally in class	Use often in my daily repertoire; evidence of use on walls, in portfolios, in teaching	Able to teach other teachers, assist with implementation
0	1	2	3	4	5

If you rate yourself a "2" or above, write here how this scaffolding supports students and give two to three examples of strategies for classroom use:

A. Jaramillo (from A. Walqui, 1991).

Schema Building and Re-Building

0	1	2	3	4	5
No understanding	Vague understanding	Able to name, say how it supports students' building of understanding, give examples	Able to name, say how it supports students' building of understanding, use occasionally in class	Use often in my daily repertoire; evidence of use on walls, in portfolios, in teaching	Able to teach other teachers, assist with implementation

If you rate yourself a "2" or above, write here how this scaffolding supports students and give two to three examples of strategies for classroom use:

Metacognitive Development and Reading Process

0	1	2	3	4	5
No understanding	Vague understanding	Able to name, say how it supports students' building of understanding, give examples	Able to name, say how it supports students' building of understanding, use occasionally in class	Use often in my daily repertoire; evidence of use on walls, in portfolios, in teaching	Able to teach other teachers, assist with implementation

If you rate yourself a "2" or above, write here how this scaffolding supports students and give two to three examples of strategies for classroom use:

Text Representation

0	1	2	3	4	5
No understanding	Vague understanding	Able to name, say how it supports students' building of understanding, give examples	Able to name, say how it supports students' building of understanding, use occasionally in class	Use often in my daily repertoire; evidence of use on walls, in portfolios, in teaching	Able to teach other teachers, assist with implementation

If you rate yourself a "2" or above, write here how this scaffolding supports students and give two to three examples of strategies for classroom use:

Authentic Assessment

0	1	2	3	4	5
No understanding	Vague understanding	Able to name, say how it supports students' building of understanding, give examples	Able to name, say how it supports students' building of understanding, use occasionally in class	Use often in my daily repertoire; evidence of use on walls, in portfolios, in teaching	Able to teach other teachers, assist with implementation

If you rate yourself a "2" or above, write here how this scaffolding supports students and give two to three examples of strategies for classroom use:

A. Jaramillo (from A. Walqui, 1991).

STRATEGY 6
AGREEING ON WHAT TO
WORK ON

When teachers are given the gift of time to sit down and decide together how they will instruct their students, wonderful things can happen. Mental and emotional doors open up; old barriers of tradition, safety and insecurity come down. This work might be as small as a group of teachers figuring out how to get their students to provide evidence more effectively in their

essays. Or it might be as big as constructing a coherent set of strategies to be used across the curriculum. Whatever the focus, when the work is firmly rooted in a long-term inquiry designed to increase the achievement of students, what arises will surely be promising practices worth trying out.

Tempera paint by Joyce Singh, a high school student from Fiji

The value of working together in this way cannot be overstated. It takes teachers out of the "solo practice" mode and into the group collaboration that focuses on what we are going to do together and how we are going to do it. Rarely can teachers change classroom practices alone.

As the second year of the project ended at **Alisal High School**—a year where the inquiry group was deeply involved in looking outward, looking inward and examining data—a core group of ten teachers and the site coordinator sat down for eight days in the summer to define the teaching framework from which the group would agree to operate in the coming year. The eight days were designed so the teachers could jointly construct strategies that could accelerate literacy. The core group teachers represented all main content areas—science, social studies, math, ESL, Spanish for Native Speakers—and taught a range of classes in different modes, from Spanish content to sheltered content to mainstream.

The teachers began the hard business of forging an approach that would work across the curriculum, content areas, and all levels of language proficiency in Spanish and English to accelerate the literacy of their students. Despite the work they had already done together, unspoken doubts and fears hung in the air: Can we agree on what an accelerated literacy approach looks like? Do we, or I, know enough to even do it? Will these eight days be worthwhile? Can we put aside our old, tried-and-true ways of doing things and risk experimenting with strategies that may or may not work?

Over the course of the eight days, the group read research, such as: Chamot and O'Malley (1994) on learning strategies; Palinscar, David and Brown (1992) on reciprocal teaching; and Krashen (1993) on free voluntary reading. They discussed how to apply the research in classes at Alisal. They developed a preliminary list of tasks that could exemplify the classroom application of SDAIE categories from the self-assessment rubric. This led to sorting out where a task might best fit. This negotiation of the placement of activities in categories forced a new level of understanding of strategies the teachers had used, seen or heard about. It prompted more reflection on the huge repertoire of strategies required to teach their students successfully.

And central to each discussion was a newfound sense of purpose on the part of the teachers. They not only forged a set of agreed-upon strategies that they would all use the next year, but also a new, shared responsibility toward each other and their students. Each teacher felt the promise this beginning held for a new way of doing things. Chas Frode, one of the ESL teachers, remarked:

> *"At the end of those memorable two weeks, ten teachers emerged hopeful and confident that we would improve student literacy and, thus, student success at Alisal. We had appropriated and gathered the best research-based teaching and learning strategies for reading, writing, cognitive development and pedagogical effectiveness. We had worked together as teachers, and in doing so had the good fortune to be able to build a strong and purposeful team."*

Tips for Agreeing About What to Work On

🍃 This strategy requires significant amounts of time. It also requires gathering a group of people who are willing to work together, to compromise, and to reach consensus on what to try. These ways of operating run counter to the cultures of most secondary schools, where the norm more often runs toward individual expressions of teaching "freedom"—closing the classroom door, not wanting anyone to tell them how they ought to be doing their jobs, with little or no accountability to colleagues and no sense of shared purpose.

🍃 Whatever coherent set of strategies you put together, they should have a sound research base and evidence that they really work to raise student achievement (e.g., reciprocal teaching or metacognitive learning strategies). Fewer strategies are better than more, especially if much of what the teachers are going to attempt is new. Part of the goal may also be to "renew" forgotten or unused, but effective, strategies. Teachers often have a repertoire of "old" strategies that have somehow acquired "new" names in recent literature (e.g., "old" = assessing and activating prior knowledge; "new" = bridging). Dusting off tried-and-true techniques and showing the links between new and old give teachers confidence that they don't have to build their teaching framework from the ground up.

💐 It helps to develop broad categories in which to fit various strategies, tasks and activities that might exemplify the category. A group of Math teachers, for example, might use some of the same categories as in the SDAIE framework (Schema-Building, for example) but also might want to add a category for Problem-Solving.

💐 Realize that getting teachers to agree on a set of strategies that they all will use in their classrooms is only the first step. Implementation must follow, keeping the banner of "This is what we all said we would do" waving in front of everyone constantly.

ACTIVITY 6.6
TAKING STOCK

Take some time with your group to complete the following sentences related to efforts to reach some common understandings about the instruction going on in classrooms at your school.

💐 The things that most of the teachers do in common at our school are...

💐 If we had a conversation about commonly used strategies or the value of coming to agreements about what to do, the direction the conversation would take...because...

💐 The main reason we would not be able to reach agreement is...

💐 The main value in coming to some agreements would be...

💐 One place to start this conversation in a wider arena would be...

STRATEGY 7
OBSERVING FOR EVIDENCE
OF IMPLEMENTATION

Most efforts at improving instruction with a goal of increasing student achievement do not incorporate accountability once implementation has begun. Teachers are rarely required to formally evaluate if they are doing what the training says to do. But there are two ways to map the effectiveness of changed classroom instruction: peer observations and examination of student work.

Peer observations are uncommon in schools, certainly anything beyond "pop-in" visits lasting more than five or ten minutes. Targeted, focused observations geared at gathering evidence on programmatic implementation happen even less frequently. A school or inquiry group can reap rich rewards when they take the bold step of making sure that teachers see each other teach, and they have a common tool and language to talk about what they see.

A redefined model of peer coaching proposed by Joyce and Showers (1996) streamlines the process so that coaching can occur more easily within the complexities of a secondary school schedule. It eliminates the pre- and post-observation discussions and turns the tables so that the teacher who is teaching is the *coach* and the teacher who is observing is the *coached*. Here, observing means learning from each other and getting a sense for what is happening throughout the classrooms of the teachers working jointly on improving curriculum and instruction. The emphasis is on programmatic improvement rather than individual enhancement of skills.

Another underused barometer of instructional efficacy is the examination of student work. Gathering teachers to look at student work on a regular basis provides opportunities for them to chart where their students are successful and where they still need help. English teachers might be working on improving their students' autobiographical essays. A look at a cross-section of student work across all classes might reveal that most of the students do not know how to use dialogue effectively in their writing, and a rubric used for scoring shows where the problems lie. Math teachers working on improving scores on "problems of the week" might discover that most of their students are struggling with using appropriate mathematical language in their explanations. Teachers can then begin to plan to improve their teaching around the use of mathematical lexicon.

In the case of Alisal, when school opened for the third year of the project, the inquiry group teachers were eager to try out their new accelerated literacy approach. Evidence of the eight-day summer work appeared in all classes—bright yellow reciprocal teaching posters and revolving bookcases full of paperbacks for free voluntary reading were in all classrooms. It was not long, however, before the site coordinator realized that the group needed an observation tool to chart the implementation of literacy strategies on an individual and programmatic level.

Based on an evidence check model developed by Kelly Smith and Cindy Lenners of the Salinas Union High School District, the group constructed the following observation log, which could be used in different ways, by different people, for various purposes.

OBSERVATION LOG

Name_____Date_____Block_____Teacher observed_____Class name_____

Accelerated Literacy/Scaffolding Criteria	Evidence Observed
Modeling/Contextualization/Other Teacher Behaviors: Evidence that the teacher shows students step-by-step how to accomplish a task, providing concrete examples of finished product. Evidence that the teacher models how to think about and complete processes such as reciprocal teaching. Evidence that the teacher actively engages students during teacher instruction time. Might include: • teacher models a process (how to ask "good" questions) • use of wait time (5-7 seconds) • equitable distribution of questions • use of higher-order questions • use of comprehension checks, active participation • in ESL, SDAIE use of paraphrasing, rephrasing, repetition	(e.g., in teacher instruction, on classroom walls, in student interactions, in portfolios)
Bridging: Assessing and Activating Prior Knowledge and Relating the Content to the Personal Lives and Experience of Students: Evidence of students engaging in tasks that provide a personal connection between them and the content to be learned; evidence of students engaging in tasks that tap into their prior knowledge. Might include: • journal writing • brainstorming, clustering • novel ideas only • values ranking • anticipatory guides • think-pair-share • three-step interview • KWL guides (Know—Want to Know—Learned) • tea party • voting with your feet	
Schema-Building (Related to literacy): Evidence of students engaging in tasks that help them establish the connections that exist among concepts, to see where ideas fit in a larger scheme. Might include: • advance/graphic organizers • concept maps • double/triple Venn diagrams • compare/contrast matrix • story maps, character logs • fishbone or leaf notes • graphic outlines of text • cause/effect chart • problem/solution outline • jigsaw projects	
Metacognitive Development and Reading Process: Evidence of students engaging in tasks that help them internalize what good readers do and tasks that foster student autonomy; evidence of students interacting with text, both self-selected and teacher-selected, and developing understanding through multiple interactions. Might include: • reciprocal teaching (summarizing, predicting, questioning, clarifying) • double-entry journals • learning logs • graphic logs • character report cards • budget tour • key questions • open minds • lecture/response logs • think alouds • reading logs • character logs • semantic feature analysis • journey map • colorful conversations • classroom libraries	
Text Representation: Evidence of students extending their understanding of text and applying it to novel formats. Might include: • open minds • bio-poems, "I am" poems • collaborative posters • postcards • hot seat • dioramas	
Authentic Assessment: Evidence of student portfolios that include teacher- and student-selected artifacts that show progress over time; evidence of teacher- and student-constructed rubrics to measure levels of performance. Might include: • class sets of "working portfolios" • class sets of "show portfolios" • student self-evaluation/learning logs • performance assessment tasks with rubrics • collaborative projects with rubrics	

A. Jaramillo, 1996 (adapted from A. Walqui, 1991).

In constructing the log, the teachers once again realized that many tasks could fit into several categories and that the assignment of some activities to one category or another is somewhat arbitrary. Nevertheless, they attempted to fit tasks into the category that seemed most appropriate.

Making the log useful revived the idea that the teachers needed to see for themselves what was going on in each other's classrooms and gave them answers to such questions as:

- How can we be encouraged to try what we said we wanted to try?
- How can we get a picture of what is happening across the program?
- What would constitute evidence of an accelerated literacy approach in individual classrooms?
- How can we be assured that the strategies are being used across the curriculum?

With the observation log in hand, the teachers began to observe each other's classes, believing that these observations would solidify and extend their shared understandings. They sat in their colleagues' classrooms and, using the log, collected evidence of strategy use. The teachers observed for an entire day, sitting in three of their colleagues' classrooms for the full 98-minute block periods so they could get a sense of the students' experience in a whole day of school.

After everyone had a chance to observe, the teachers got together to gauge their implementation of strategies across the program. They found, for example, much evidence of students engaged in tasks to assess and activate their prior knowledge. They found few examples, on the other hand, of students engaged in tasks designed to help them build their schema. They also began to get a picture not just of program implementation, but of their own implementation. As Angelica López-Simons, teacher of Spanish for Native Speakers, said:

> "When I'm being observed, I find myself focusing on the various literacy strategies I'm using and thinking at the same time about why I'm using them. I also see my weaknesses. My senses are sharpened, and that allows me to analyze my errors after the visitor has gone. The observations really serve as tools to motivate self-analysis and critical awareness."

Tips for Observing for Evidence of Implementation

❧ Creating some sort of tool for observations is well worth the effort. You can double or triple the power of the observations with an observation log. The use of an observation log for peer coaching provides teachers with a shared understanding of excellence, a way of noting what is present or absent in instruction or student engagement, and a solid sense that "we are all in this together for the students."

❧ Making sure that the observations happen is not easy. But it's worth it to hang in there and cajole people into doing it. On a practical level, it's best to have one teacher a day observing, two maximum if you have a large staff, plenty of substitutes available, and many teachers ready to be observed. Insist that teachers observe for an entire day, from the very beginning to the very end of each period. Aside from making sure that teachers get a total instructional picture, it gives them a fresh perspective on what students go through in a day. Several of the teachers at Alisal commented on the "passive" nature of the schooling experience of many students.

❧ Before the observations happen, take some time with the group to do a run-through with the observation log. For this to work, it is not necessary to do it during a class period. In fact, to learn how to use the log and come to some agreements about what and how to note evidence, it's better to use one of the teacher's classrooms after school. The classroom used to practice should have plenty of evidence to look at: many different kinds of student work on the walls, in portfolios, in journals. Give teachers copies of the log and let them roam through the room, noting evidence of student engagement in the different categories of the log. There are wonderful opportunities for dialogue among the teachers as they negotiate whether a sample of student work exemplifies, for example, "Schema-Building" or "Developing Metacognition." Although the teachers will not have a chance to see actual teaching, they will still have a chance to sharpen their understandings of what constitutes evidence and why.

❧ After a cycle of observations, when everyone has had a chance for a full-day look into classrooms, schedule a two- to three-hour block of time when everyone can get together and debrief the observations. Frame the discussion around, "How are we doing? What did we see that we're doing well? As a group, where do we need to put in some effort?" It is crucial to make sure that there is a set of ground rules that lay out the parameters of the discussion, including confidentiality of what was seen in each other's classrooms. Everyone feels more secure when they know that what's observed in their own classroom will be held in private, except for the generalizations about implementation that can be shared with everyone.

❦ Even multiple observations may not provide clear evidence of improved student achievement. Here is where gathering some data through the examination of student work is essential. This can answer the nagging questions, like, "OK, we're all trying all of this, but how do we know it is making a difference?"

ACTIVITY 6.7
LOOKING BACK AT THE SET OF STRATEGIES FOR CHANGING PRACTICE INSIDE OF CLASSROOMS

Look back at the strategies discussed in this chapter. With a partner, or with your group, design a few simple first steps that you could take to get started along this path of changing practice inside of classrooms. Use the following prompts to guide you.

❦ What might be the best way "in" for your school? Data? The opportunity to work together as a team?

❦ What do you think the major obstacles are now? Have your ideas changed about what the obstacles are and how you might get around them?

❦ Who are your allies in this process? Who is most interested in this? How can you get together and get going?

❦ What concrete first steps can you take?

❦ Where would you like to be in this process in 6 months' time? In a year?

❦ What will your classrooms look like then?

CONCLUSION

Each minute is precious in a teacher's day. The combined duties of attendance, grades, district and site level committee meetings, department and faculty meetings, parent phone calls and conferences, club and class sponsorship, coaching—all tend to take up every available moment of a teacher's time. Any time set aside for staff development has, in many schools, seemed disjointed and unconnected to the daily practice in classrooms, leaving teachers feeling frustrated, dissatisfied, and unwilling to put in the extra effort required to carry out a thoughtful program aimed at changing practice inside of classrooms to increase achievement and equity.

Yet, the need has never been greater to use our time wisely. The achievement and equity gaps for immigrant students continue to grow. Efforts that are not aimed at eventually getting down to the classroom level have limited potential to change what is happening for our students long-term. And efforts that do not engage teachers themselves directly in the inquiry about what needs to be changed are also doomed to stay at a superficial level. California Tomorrow's work has shown that when teachers are given the tools and the time to work on improving the daily instruction of their students, real change can happen.

As this chapter illustrates, the following elements must become essential parts of any inquiry-based staff development effort aimed at changing practice inside of classrooms:

1) multiple opportunities to study student achievement data closely related to their classroom practice;

2) open discussions about what obstacles exist to changing practice and how to overcome them;

3) time to work with like-minded teachers in a long-term cyclical inquiry process;

4) timely opportunities to read research and look beyond the school to other perspectives and other effective models of educating students;

5) ways for teachers to thoughtfully examine their current practice through self-analysis and peer observations;

6) facilitated meetings where teachers can explore and agree on the real meat of what needs to be changed and how they plan to go about it; and

7) the time to tinker with and change practice based on student achievement data closely related to daily practice.

A continuing cycle of inquiry into improving instruction can become a vital part of a school's culture. The school then becomes a place where teachers' curiosities and love for their students are given productive ways to thrive and where achievement and equity sit at the heart of the work.

REFERENCES

Chamot, A. U. and O'Malley, J. M. (1994). *The CALLA Handbook: Implementing the Cognitive Academic Language Learning Approach.* New York, NY: Addison-Wesley.

Darling-Hammond, L., Ancess, J., and Falk, B. (1995). *Authentic Assessment in Action: Studies of Schools and Students at Work.* New York, NY: Teachers College Press.

Joyce, B. and Showers, B. (1996). The Evolution of Peer Coaching. *Educational Leadership* 53(6), 12-16.

Meier, D. (1995). *The Power of Their Ideas: Lessons for America from a Small School in Harlem.* Boston, MA: Beacon Press.

Palinscar, A. S., David, Y. and Brown, A.L. (1992). *Using Reciprocal Teaching in the Classroom.* Berkeley, CA: Brown/Campione Research Group.

Schmoker, M. J. (1996). *Results: The Key to Continuous School Improvement.* Alexandria, VA: Association for Supervision and Curriculum Development.

Walqui, A. (1991). *Sheltered Instruction: Doing It Right.* Unpublished manuscript.

CHANGING CLASSROOM PRACTICE
ANNOTATED BIBLIOGRAPHY

Boles, Katherine and Troen, Vivian. (1992). How Teachers Make Restructuring Happen. *Educational Leadership, 49*(5), 53-56.

A brief case study of two classroom teachers and their efforts to restructure the profession. Dissatisfied with the lack of career advancement in the teaching profession, high numbers of good teachers leaving the field, and the poor quality of entering teachers, the authors initiated a quest to redefine the profession. In collaboration with a local college and their district superintendent, "Learning/Teaching Collaborative Teams" were organized at various sites to support student-teacher learning and provide experienced teachers with "Alternative Professional Teaching" and time to develop themselves as researchers, writers, and/or trainers.

Darling-Hammond, Linda, Ancess, Jacqueline and Falk, Beverly. (1995). *Authentic Assessment in Action: Studies of Schools and Students at Work.* **New York, NY: Teachers College Press.**

This book is a must for teachers who are interested in seeing what authentic assessment looks like in some very different contexts. Of particular interest to secondary educators are the chapters that describe the process of graduation by portfolio at Central Park East Secondary School and collaborative learning and assessment at International High School, both in New York City. How these schools use authentic assessment as a way of ensuring success for students of color and second language students is inspiring. The book is rich with examples of student work, as well as teacher dialogue and reflection about what it takes to put authentic assessment at the heart of the schooling experience.

Echevarria, Jana and Graves, Anne. (1998). *Sheltered Content Instruction: Teaching English Language Learners with Diverse Abilities.* **Washington, D.C.: Center for Applied Linguistics.**

This book defines and describes what sheltered instruction and SDAIE looks like in classrooms through stories, case studies and sample scenarios. The authors provide strategies for implementation of sheltered instruction, and practical ways for improving content-area instruction. The book also provides effective ways to work with a wide range of English language abilities in the same classroom.

González, Josué M. and Darling-Hammond, Linda. (1997). *New Concepts for New Challenges: Professional Development for Teachers of Immigrant Youth.* **Washington, D.C.: Center for Applied Linguistics.**

This volume looks at new structures and strategies for professional development. The authors pay special attention to professional development that develops "community, collegiality and collaboration." Several successful preservice and inservice programs are highlighted and described.

Jaramillo, Ann. (1998). Professional Development from the Inside Out. *TESOL Journal,* **Autumn, 12-18.**

This article tells the story of a teacher-driven, teacher-defined professional development effort that grew from a multi-year project aimed at creating immigrant-responsive secondary schools. This professional development effort included inquiry, looking at other models, self-assessment, examining data, and creating and implementing an accelerated literacy approach.

Minicucci, C. et al. (1995). School Reform and Student Diversity. *Phi Delta Kappan,* **77(1), 77-80.**

This article explores case studies of eight exemplary schools which demonstrate that language minority students can learn the same academic curriculum as native English speakers and pursue English literacy at the same time. Teachers and other educators can learn much from the characteristics of these exemplary schools, such as: having a schoolwide vision of excellence, creating a community of learners engaged in active discovery, and implementing well-designed, carefully executed language development programs.

Sahakian, Pauline and Stockton, John. (1996). Opening Doors: Teacher-Guided Observations. *Educational Leadership,* **53(6), 50-53.**

This engaging article focuses on a teacher-generated observation and collaboration model. In the example cited, six teacher triads observed one another in classrooms, then gathered to reflect in a post-observation conference. Teachers collaboratively established issues they found relevant, such as self-determination and professional development, designed a process that promoted improved relationships among staff and created more opportunities for student academic development. The process stressed professional growth, not evaluation. The collaboration utilized six basic tenets as a guide: evolving a instructional and curricular development program; treating teachers as professionals; providing growth opportunities in a safe environment; giving teachers responsibility for curriculum and analysis; helping them to feel comfortable with change; and providing opportunity for camaraderie and trust-building.

Schmoker, Mike. (1996). *Results: The Key to Continuous School Improvement.* **Alexandria, VA: Association for Supervision and Curriculum Development.**

Schmoker's small but powerful book outlines practical ways for schools to insert teamwork, goal-setting, and the use of performance data into the every-day lives of teachers. Multiple examples exhibit the ways in which a focus on results can lead to improved student achievement at a district, school or department level. The book gives many immediately useable ideas for how to make data on student performance part of every school's ongoing business, including ways to make the time and structure you have a place where work can get done. Schmoker clearly and eloquently articulates the need to close the achievement gap—and then provides the research and stories from schools where it has been done.

Showers, Beverly and Joyce, Bruce. (1996). The Evolution of Peer Coaching. *Educational Leadership,* **53(6), 12-16.**

An informative, historical look at the evolution of "peer coaching" in the last twenty-five years which emphasizes on its role in providing ongoing assistance to teachers mastering new teaching strategies. The model uses a traditional design of pre-conference, observation and post-conference. The process adheres to four key principles: all participants must have agreed to be members of peer coaching study teams; omission of verbal feedback as a coaching component; when working in pairs, the person teaching is the coach, while the person observing is being coached; the collaborative work of peer coaching involves not only observations and conferences but planning instruction, developing support materials, and working with students as well.

Walqui, Aída. (1998). *Access and Engagement: Effective Program Design and Instructional Approach for Immigrant Students at the Secondary Level.* **Washington, D.C.: Center for Applied Linguistics.**

This paper looks at current practices in immigrant education in secondary schools. It contains a literature review on current classroom strategies and program design and presents promising new programs which represent a variety of bilingual and multilingual classrooms. Walqui also provides policy recommendations and strategies for pedagogical practice and professional development.

CHANGING CLASSROOM PRACTICE RESOURCES

Association for Supervision and Curriculum Development (ASCD)

ASCD is an international, nonprofit, nonpartisan education organization committed to the success of all learners. Its nearly 200,000 members include school superintendents, principals and other administrative staff, teachers, parents and students who share the belief that all students can succeed in a challenging, well-planned educational program. ASCD celebrates diversity as a means to enrich the academic achievement of all students. The organization holds numerous conferences each year focusing on different educational issues, as well as producing its own publications.

1703 N. Beauregard Street
Alexandria, VA 22311-1714
(800)933-ASCD
(703)575-5400 fax
WWW: www.ascd.org

California Association for Bilingual Education (CABE)

CABE offers professional development to educators and advocates through their annual conference, seminars and workshops. For a complete listing of services, contact their main headquarters or check out their website. CABE's local chapters offer an extensive network of bilingual educators and teachers of English language development.

660 S. Figueroa, Suite 1040
Los Angeles, CA 90017
(213)532-3850
(213)532-3860 fax
WWW: www.cabe.org

California Association of Teachers of English to Speakers of Other Languages (CATESOL)

CATESOL is a nonprofit organization, founded in 1969, open to anyone concerned with teaching English as a second or foreign language, teaching standard English as a second dialect, or bilingual education. Members come from all school levels and include administrators, university students and teacher educators in California and Nevada. CATESOL holds an annual state conference in the spring and publishes a newsletter five times a year, as well as a scholarly journal. They also publish position statements.

> 1146 N. Central Avenue #195
> Glendale, CA 91202
> (916)663-4885
> (916)663-4885 fax
> E-mail: catesol@catesol.org
> WWW: www.catesol.org

Center for Applied Linguistics (CAL)

CAL provides a variety of language-related services to both public and private institutions, including curriculum development, dissemination, evaluation and needs assessment. CAL also provides professional development for language teachers ranging from K-12 to college, university and adult education. Their nationwide projects are documented in numerous publications which can be requested by phone, mail or E-mail. Their website offers education and policy links by topic area.

> 1118 22nd Street, NW
> Washington, D.C. 20037-1214
> (202)429-9292
> (202)659-5641 fax
> E-mail: info@cal.org
> WWW: www.cal.org

Center for Language Minority and Education Research (CLMER)

This center provides professional development and technical assistance. Areas of focus include: literacy strategies, multicultural curriculum, math/science SDAIE, and two-way immersion education. CLMER's Regional Technology Center offers computer-related professional development, such as webpage development, Internet resources and services and downloadable interactive tools for educators. Their website offers instructions on how to create a website and K-12 Teacher Pages.

> California State University, Long Beach
> College of Education
> 1250 Bellflower Boulevard
> Long Beach, CA 90840
> (562)985-5806
> (562)985-4528 fax
> E-mail: clmer@csulb.edu
> WWW: www.clmer.csulb.edu

Center for Research on Education, Diversity and Excellence (CREDE)

CREDE provides technical assistance, professional development training and portfolio and evaluation assessment. They also conduct research to identify and develop effective educational practices for linguistic and cultural minority students. CREDE produces publications and a seasonal newsletter.

University of California, Santa Cruz
College Eight, Room 201
1156 High Street
Santa Cruz, CA 95064
(202)429-9292
E-mail: crede@cats.ucsc.edu
WWW: www.crede.ucsc.edu

ERIC Clearinghouse on Languages and Linguistics

Operated by the Center for Applied Linguistics, ERIC Clearinghouse on Languages and Linguistics offers a powerful research resource. Services are offered via phone and Internet on publications, newsletters, digests, bibliographies and educational products. This website also offers links to other language-related websites and clearinghouses.

1118 22nd Street, NW
Washington, D.C. 20037
(800)276-9834
E-mail: eric@cal.org
WWW: www.cal.org/ericcll

National Association for Asian and Pacific American Education (NAAPAE)

NAAPAE works to increase public awareness of Asian and Pacific American educational issues and needs, and advocates for including Asian and Pacific American history in the school curriculum. Membership provides access to a resource-sharing network of educators and community people as well as a subscription to the NAAPAE newsletter.

c/o ARC Associates
1212 Broadway, Suite 400
Oakland, CA 94612
(415)749-3430

National Association for Multicultural Education (NAME)

NAME works to promote the development of culturally responsible and responsive curricula and to achieve social, political, economic and educational equity. NAME supports professional development primarily through its quarterly magazine. This publication offers articles, reviews and promising practices on issues and activities in the field of multicultural education.

2101-A North Rolfe Street
Arlington, VA 22209-1007
(703)243-4525

National Clearinghouse for Bilingual Education (NCBE)

Based at George Washington University, NCBE is a clearinghouse service for bilingual educators and trainers. NCBE also produces its own publications and offers an extensive index of articles, research reports, resource lists and bibliographies. This organization houses the U.S. Department of Education's Technical Assistance Network of national and regional service providers. Anyone needing resource information on subject areas such as curriculum and instruction, education research, parent and community involvement, language and culture, etc., can phone or E-mail NCBE's office.

(800)321-NCBE
E-mail: askncbe@ncbe.gwu.edu
WWW: www.ncbe.gwu.edu

School Counseling in Today's Real World

This project seeks to increase access for ethnic and language minority public school students to appropriate guidance and counseling services. Their focus is on training school counselors to deliver quality services to minority students and their families in a cross-cultural manner. School Counseling in Today's Real World is a project of the National Coalition of Advocates for Students (NCAS).

Jan Buettner
100 Boylston Street, Suite 737
Boston, MA 02116
(617)357-8507
(617)357-4703
E-mail: ncasmfe@aol.com
WWW: www.ncas1.org

The Strategic Literacy Initiative

The Strategic Literacy Initiative's mission is to promote reading performance for middle and high school students from all academic and language backgrounds. The project supports interdisciplinary teams of teachers, administrators and superintendents with practical strategies for their content-area classes. Beginning in the fall of 1999 services will be available to most areas in California.

c/o WestEd
730 Harrison Street
San Francisco, CA 94107
(415)565-3000

Teachers of English to Speakers of Other Languages (TESOL)

TESOL's mission is to develop the expertise of its members and others involved in teaching English to speakers of other languages, to help them foster effective communication in diverse settings while respecting individual language rights. TESOL offers standards for professional preparation and employment, continuing education and student programs, a worldwide resource bank of language specialists, and publications that promote advocacy for English Language Learners.

1600 Cameron Street, Suite 300
Alexandria, VA 22314-2751
(703)836-0774
(703)836-7864 fax
E-mail: tesol@tesol.edu
WWW: www.tesol.edu

Chapter Seven:
CONCLUSION

Working together strategically, collecting data, pursuing inquiries, creating forums for student voice, designing and implementing new programs and ways of teaching—these are the essential building blocks advocates use to create truly accessible, inclusive schools. Together, it can add up to a very full plate for educators already balancing a full load.

But there are three more activities that are well worth your time as you proceed on your journey. We encourage you to pause every now and then to document and tell your stories, to let others know about the successes of your programs, the pain you witness when children are excluded, and what it takes to bring about change. We also hope you will take the time to connect to those beyond your school who work on the same issues as you. Their support, ideas and perspectives can be a crucial lifeline. Finally, we encourage you to take the time to celebrate whenever you manage to create changes—big or small—that make our schools that much more welcoming and effective for all our students.

DOCUMENT AND TELL YOUR STORIES

In the course of everyday life in a school, "doing" seems enough. But in the larger task of changing schools, you also have to document and tell the stories of what you do to make change. You need to tell your stories to people in your school who don't see the problems or understand what you do, and to the public, which needs to understand the challenges—and solutions—in our public schools.

We reach people best when we speak to their hearts through human stories. Stories can help people see the pain, as well as the possibilities. People will not change unless they feel an urgency that makes maintaining the status quo too uncomfortable. And they will not change without the hope that their efforts can make a difference. Stories can both build the urgency and the hope needed for change.

Stories can help people see the pain, as well as the possibilities.

Stories are essential to the survival of your work and its impact. Without knowing what is and isn't working for immigrant students, people in your school and in the larger community can be tragically misinformed.

Such was the case in California, when Proposition 227, which sought to dismantle bilingual education, swept to victory in a public election. Educators who understood the crucial role of primary language instruction could not respond effectively to widespread public misinformation about bilingual education, because we didn't have effective stories or data ready. We hadn't been regularly feeding the public imagination with information about what we do and its positive impacts on children.

The campaign behind Proposition 227, however, powerfully used one story, one set of statistics, and two images to fuel their campaign. The single story was of a parent boycott at a bilingual school—told again and again until it was known throughout the state and became larger than life. The single statistic was a low redesignation rate placed in a distorted context. The two images were of children trapped in Spanish-speaking classrooms, unable to get out, and bilingual educators making money by holding those children back.

There is nothing new about political campaigns that use such imagery and stories to sway the public. But the lesson here is how willing the public was to believe those stories, because we had not told our own stories or put forth our data to show how effective bilingual education can be.

Unfortunately, documenting and writing down our stories often fall to the wayside—it doesn't come naturally for people busy teaching and running schools and it takes precious time. But if we don't find the time to write it down, to document both the harm done to children blocked from access and the beneficial effects of support programs, then we face both a public and a school community that does not have the information needed to support our programs.

But we need to document and tell our stories for other reasons as well. We have to hold in our hearts and minds the very human stories that drive our advocacy. These are the stories that we need to tell each other, to remind ourselves why we continue working against the tide. Stories keep the focus on kids. Stories touch the heart. Stories motivate change.

ACTIVITY 7.1
DEVELOP THE STORIES THAT CAN MOVE PEOPLE

Think of an LEP student you have known (it could be yourself at a younger age, a sibling, a student of yours, a friend) who suffered because the school was not aware, willing or able to provide the support needed to participate and learn fully. Perhaps it's a story about being ashamed of the home language, being frustrated in trying to learn, being discouraged and giving up, or not having the information needed to benefit from the school. Take a few notes about key parts of that story. Tell that story to a partner, trying to make this child real. After swapping stories, talk about how each other's stories impacted you. Did the story move you? What parts were the most moving? What would you have needed to know more about? What imagery worked and what didn't?

Each of you should then either tape-record (and then transcribe) or simply write these stories down. Put them together in a collection, organized by the types of barriers or hurts these students faced, or by the type of school responses that were lacking. This collection becomes a source to use in making speeches, talking with colleagues and reminding yourselves about the human needs that motivate your advocacy.

Repeat this activity, thinking of an LEP student you have known for whom doors were opened, lights went on, learning was engaged because of something the school had done or is doing. Describe what worked. Tell (if you know) what happened to that student down the road. As before, tell the story to a partner, write it down and then compile these success stories in a collection. Organize these stories around the kinds of opportunities and supports students encountered that helped them on the road to their dreams.

CONFIDENTIALITY: PROTECTING STUDENTS WHEN TELLING THEIR STORIES

Students are very vulnerable in their schools. Teachers have real power over their lives there and some aspects of the student experience are very personal. For both these reasons, it is essential that any sharing of students' stories be done respectfully and with confidentiality. Change the names of students when you write or tell their stories. If there are particular details related to their experiences with another teacher or administrator in the school, do not name that educator directly. Be sure that any details that would lead to clear identification of the student are omitted. If you are planning on publishing or handing out written versions of a student's story with the name changed, you might want to let the student see what you've written. Students are often happy to have us tell their stories, especially if doing so will help end inequities and make the school better for other students, but we need to do so with respect.

FIND RESOURCES AND SUPPORT BEYOND THE SCHOOL

Telling your stories, indeed advocating for immigrant students in any of the ways discussed in this book, can be hard work. But it's easier when you know you are not alone in seeking to shape schools that meet the needs of LEP students. It's important to find ways to tap into resources and support that exist beyond your school and help others in your school tap into those resources as well.

There are many people who view going to conferences as part of their ongoing professional development. But attending conferences isn't just a chance to get new ideas; it is also a visceral way to experience being part of a larger movement, to realize that those in your school attempting to bring about change aren't the only ones. While there, you can find out about materials, groups, other schools and strategies that may be helpful to your efforts at your school.

Keeping yourself current with the research and the experiences of people in other schools is also essential. There is an exciting, growing knowledge base about what works for LEP students, how they learn and how to structure schools to serve them. The more you can keep current with that knowledge base, the more you can educate others at your school and help them find avenues to learn.

One way to stay current, besides attending conferences yourself, is to get on the mailing lists of major organizations that produce materials and research. You might want to get subscriptions or memberships in these groups and set up a professional library in your school of the latest research and materials related to the access and achievement of LEP students.

The following list of organizations is a good starting place for getting in touch with resources outside your school. Contact information for these organizations is given on the pages listed in the chart.

Organization	Contact info page	Membership	Conferences	Publications/ newsletters	Research clearinghouse
Association for Supervision and Curriculum Development	396	X	X	X	
California Association for Bilingual Education	98, 396	X	X	X	
California Association of Teachers of English to Speakers of Other Languages	396	X	X	X	
California Tomorrow	176			X	
Center for Applied Linguistics	397			X	
Center for Language Minority and Education and Research	397				X
Center for Research on Education, Diversity and Excellence	398			X	X
ERIC Clearinghouse on Languages and Linguistics	398			X	X
National Association for Asian and Pacific American Education	398	X	X	X	
National Association for Bilingual Education	99	X	X	X	
National Association for Multicultural Education	399		X	X	X
National Clearinghouse for Bilingual Education	399			X	X
National Coalition of Advocates for Students	99			X	X
National Coalition of Education Activists	100	X	X	X	
National Council of La Raza	100	X	X	X	
Rethinking Schools	101			X	
Teachers of English to Speakers of Other Languages	400	X	X	X	X

TAKE THE TIME TO CELEBRATE

Our last advice for you is that you take the time to celebrate your successes. Creating schools that provide full access and result in high achievement for our LEP students is a mighty task with a long history and a long road ahead. Sometimes it is clear that a major step forward has been taken, but mostly change is made up of small steps that add up: you manage to get one more teacher to sign up for a workshop on second language acquisition; you arrange for the student handbook to be produced in six different languages; a bilingual math class is added; a policy that would have barred ESL students from enrolling in a career academy gets dropped.

These small steps add up, in the end, to creating schools that serve all children. But it often feels like the little victories are swallowed up in the wake of your vision of all that still has to happen. *Make yourselves take the time to celebrate the small steps.* Take pride in yourself and each other. And take the time to enjoy, honor and celebrate the work you do together as you take your steps. Do whatever feels right to honor and celebrate your work—provide yourselves with special treats at a meeting, throw small parties at victorious moments, go out to dinner together after a significant meeting or send appreciative notes to those who have been part of making progress.

Together, we can turn the tides.

Remember, it is our collective strength, wisdom and hard work that will write a new and proud chapter in the history of the public schools of this nation. We are privileged to travel this road with you, forging the paths of a just and democratic multicultural society. Together we *can* turn the tides.